MW01091984

Psychosocial Assessment and Treatment of Bariatric Surgery Patients

Psychosocial Assessment and Treatment of Bariatric Surgery Patients

James E. Mitchell and Martina de Zwaan

EDITORS

Routledge
Taylor & Francis Group
New York   London

Routledge
Taylor & Francis Group
711 Third Avenue
New York, NY 10017

Routledge
Taylor & Francis Group
27 Church Road
Hove, East Sussex BN3 2FA

© 2012 by Taylor & Francis Group, LLC
Routledge is an imprint of Taylor & Francis Group, an Informa business

Printed in the United States of America on acid-free paper
Version Date: 20110603

International Standard Book Number: 978-0-415-89219-3 (Hardback)

For permission to photocopy or use material electronically from this work, please access www.copyright.com (http://www.copyright.com/) or contact the Copyright Clearance Center, Inc. (CCC), 222 Rosewood Drive, Danvers, MA 01923, 978-750-8400. CCC is a not-for-profit organization that provides licenses and registration for a variety of users. For organizations that have been granted a photocopy license by the CCC, a separate system of payment has been arranged.

Trademark Notice: Product or corporate names may be trademarks or registered trademarks, and are used only for identification and explanation without intent to infringe.

Library of Congress Cataloging-in-Publication Data

Psychosocial assessment and treatment of bariatric surgery patients / edited by
James Mitchell, Martina de Zwaan.
    p. ; cm.
    Includes bibliographical references and index.
    ISBN 978-0-415-89219-3 (hardback : alk. paper)
    1. Obesity--Surgery--Psychological aspects. 2.
Obesity--Surgery--Patients--Mental health. I. Mitchell, James E. (James Edward),
1947- II. De Zwaan, Martina.
    [DNLM: 1. Bariatric Surgery--psychology. 2. Adolescent. 3. Bariatric
Surgery--methods. 4. Obesity, Morbid--psychology. 5. Obesity, Morbid--therapy.
WI 900]

    RD540.P92 2012
    617.4'3--dc23   2011015033

Visit the Taylor & Francis Web site at
http://www.taylorandfrancis.com

and the Routledge Web site at
http://www.routledgementalhealth.com

Contents

Editors

James E. Mitchell, MD, is the NRI/Lee A. Christoferson, MD Professor and chairman of the Department of Clinical Neuroscience at the University of North Dakota School of Medicine and Health Sciences. He is also the Chester Fritz Distinguished University Professor at the University of North Dakota and the president and scientific director of the Neuropsychiatric Research Institute. Dr. Mitchell's research has focused on eating disorders, obesity, and bariatric surgery. He is a past president of the Academy for Eating Disorders and the Eating Disorders Research Society. He has received the Award for Research from the Academy for Eating Disorders, the National Eating Disorders Coalition Award for Research Leadership, and the Eating Disorders Research Society Award for Visionary Research. He has served as principal investigator on 12 grants from the National Institutes of Health and is on the editorial boards of the *International Journal of Eating Disorders* and *Obesity Reviews*. He has been an author of over 430 scientific articles and has authored, coauthored, or edited 18 books.

Martina de Zwaan, MD, is a professor and the head of the Department of Psychosomatic Medicine and Psychotherapy at Hannover Medical School of Hannover, Germany. Dr. de Zwaan went to medical school in Vienna and did her residency in psychiatry at the Department of Psychiatry in Vienna. She is a trained behavior therapist. She began studying binge eating disorder during her time as a postdoctoral fellow at the Eating Disorders Research Program of the Department of Psychiatry, University of Minnesota. In 2001 she returned to the United States as a visiting scientist at the Neuropsychiatric Research Institute in Fargo, North Dakota, for a period of two years to work with Dr. Mitchell, again in the field of eating disorders and obesity. She is the author of numerous scientific and clinical papers on the subjects of eating disorders, mainly bulimia nervosa, binge eating disorder, and obesity.

Contributors

Kelly C. Berg, PhD
Department of Psychiatry
University of Minnesota
Minneapolis, Minnesota

Eva Conceição, PhD
Escola de Psicologia
Universidade do Minho
Braga, Portugal

Sue Cummings, MS, RD
MGH Weight Center
Massachusetts General Hospital
Boston, Massachusetts

Michael J. Devlin, MD
Columbia Center for Eating
    Disorders
New York State Psychiatric Institute
New York, New York

Martina de Zwaan, MD
Department of Psychosomatic
    Medicine and Psychotherapy
Hannover Medical School
Hannover, Germany

Scott G. Engel, PhD
Neuropsychiatric Research
    Institute
Fargo, North Dakota

Margaret Furtado, MS, RD
Johns Hopkins Center for Bariatric
    Surgery
Johns Hopkins Bayview Medical
    Center
Baltimore, Maryland

Luis Garcia, MD, FACS, MBA
Weight Loss Surgery Program
and
Sanford Health System and
    Department of Surgery
University of North Dakota
Fargo, North Dakota

John Gunstad, PhD
Department of Psychology
Kent State University
Kent, Ohio

Bernhard Hain, MD
Department of General Internal
 Medicine and Psychosomatics
University Hospital Heidelberg
Heidelberg, Germany

Stephan Herpertz, MD
Clinic for Psychosomatic Medicine
 and Psychotherapy
LWL—University Hospital
 Bochum
Ruhr, Germany

Wolfgang Herzog, MD
Department of General
 Internal Medicine and
 Psychosomatics
University Hospital Heidelberg
Heidelberg, Germany

Thomas Horbach, MD
Department of Surgery
Obesity Control Center
Municipal Hospital Schwabach
Schawabach, Germany

Melissa A. Kalarchian, PhD
Western Psychiatric Institute
 and Clinic
University of Pittsburgh
 Medical Center
Pittsburgh, Pennsylvania

Trisha M. Karr, PhD
Neuropsychiatric Research
 Institute
Fargo, North Dakota

Wendy King, PhD
Department of Epidemiology
University of Pittsburgh
Pittsburgh, Pennsylvania

Johann F. Kinzl, MD
Department of Psychiatry and
 Psychotherapy
Innsbruck University
Innsbruck, Austria

Kim T. LaHaise, PhD
Sanford Eating Disorders Institute
Fargo, North Dakota

Tanja Legenbauer, PhD
Research Department
LWL—University Hospital
 Bochum
Ruhr, Germany

Paulo Machado, PhD
Escola de Psicologia
Universidade do Minho
Braga, Portugal

Marsha D. Marcus, PhD
Behavioral Medicine and Eating
 Disorders
WPIC Psychology Internship
 Program
University of Pittsburgh
 School of Medicine
Pittsburgh, Pennsylvania

James E. Mitchell, MD
Department of Clinical
 Neuroscience
University of North Dakota
Fargo, North Dakota

Astrid Mueller, MD, PhD
Department of Psychosomatic
 Medicine and Psychotherapy
University of Erlangen–Nuremberg
Erlangen, Germany

Carol B. Peterson, PhD
Department of Psychiatry
University of Minnesota
Minneapolis, Minnesota

Nicole Rieber, PsyD
Department of Psychosomatic
    Medicine and Psychotherapy
University Hospital Tuebingen
Tuebingen, Germany

James L. Roerig, PharmD, BCPP
Neuropsychiatry Research Institute
Fargo, North Dakota

and

Department of Neuroscience
University of North Dakota
Grand Forks, North Dakota

Ronna Saunders, LCSW
Center for Behavioral Change
Richmond, Virginia

Stephanie Sogg, PhD
Massachusetts General Hospital
    Weight Center
Boston, Massachusetts

Mary Beth Spitznagel, PhD
Department of Psychology
Kent State University
Kent, Ohio

Kelly Stanek, PhD
Department of Psychology
Kent State University
Kent, Ohio

Kristine J. Steffen
Neuropsychiatric Research
    Institute
Fargo, North Dakota

Robyn Sysko, PhD
Columbia Center for Eating
    Disorders
New York State Psychiatric
    Institute
and
Columbia University College of
    Physicians and Surgeons
New York, New York

Martin Teufel, MD
Department of Psychosomatic
    Medicine and Psychotherapy
University Hospital Tuebingen
Tuebingen, Germany

Beate Wild, PhD
Department of General
    Internal Medicine and
    Psychosomatics
University Hospital Heidelberg
Heidelberg, Germany

Stephan Zipfel, MD
Department of Psychosomatic
    Medicine and Psychotherapy
University Hospital Tuebingen
Tuebingen, Germany

Christie Zunker, PhD, CPH, CHES
Neuropsychiatric Research
    Institute
University of North Dakota
Fargo, North Dakota

CHAPTER 1

Overview of Bariatric Surgery Procedures

JAMES E. MITCHELL, LUIS GARCIA,
MARTINA DE ZWAAN, and THOMAS HORBACH

As is now widely known, there is an obesity epidemic threatening the population of the United States and much of the world. Two-thirds of adults in the United States now are overweight (BMI = 25–29.9 kg/m²) or obese (BMI > 30 kg/m²). Also of particular concern, rates of obesity are rising rapidly among children and adolescents. This is particularly an issue for minority Americans, such as African Americans and Hispanics (Ogden, Carroll, & Flegal, 2003).

Accompanying this growing increase in rates of overweight and obesity have been the growing documentation that most treatments for obesity result in modest and frequently short-term benefits and the growing documentation that obesity is associated with a variety of untoward health consequences (Bray, 2003; Sowers, 2003). These include elevated lipids, increased rates of cardiovascular disease including coronary artery disease and heart failure, obstructive sleep apnea, asthma, severe liver dysfunction that can result in nonalcoholic steatohepatitis, osteoarthritis, a variety of malignancies, and infertility (Coviello & Nystrom, 2003; Bray, 2003; Gami, Caples, & Somers, 2003; Shah & Ginsburg, 2010). Given these factors it is not surprising that bariatric surgery is playing an increasingly important role in treatment of obesity in the United States and elsewhere (Balsiger, Murr, Poggio, & Sarr, 2000; Herron, 2004; Mattison & Jensen, 2004; Colquitt, Clegg, Sidhu, & Royle, 2003).

While in general guidelines have favored bariatric surgery for those with a BMI of >40 kg/m², increasingly such procedures are being used for individuals with a BMI at a minimum of 35 kg/m² with comorbidities (such as hypertension, diabetes, sleep apnea, and hypercholesterolemia), and many of these individuals have such complications (Pories, Dohm, & Manfield, 2010; Klein, Ghosh, Cremieux, Eapen, & McGavock, 2010; Mingrone & Castagneto-Gissey, 2009). There also has been recent interest in performing bariatric surgery as a treatment for Type II diabetes in individuals with a BMI of <35 kg/m² (Dandona, Aljada, & Bandyopadhyay, 2004; Renard, 2009; Scheen, De Flines, De Roover, & Paquot, 2009; Mingrone & Castagneto-Gissey, 2009), although the development of this latter approach has resulted in some controversy (Laville & Disse, 2009).

A pivotal study in demonstrating that mortality was decreased after bariatric surgery was the Swedish Obesity Study (Sjöström et al., 2004, 2007). More recently gastric bypass and gastric banding appear to be cost-effective methods of reducing the mortality and morbidity in adults with diabetes and severe obesity (Hoerger et al., 2010). Bariatric surgery has also been shown to be associated with reductions in the use of medications as well as overall health costs in patients with Type II diabetes (Makary et al., 2010). Preliminary data also suggest the effectiveness of surgical treatment for diabetes in patients who do not meet criteria for morbid obesity (DeMaria et al., 2010). Also, bariatric surgery is increasingly being considered an option for severely obese adolescents (Garcia, Langford, & Inge, 2003).

In this initial chapter we will briefly review the history of bariatric surgery procedures and then we will focus on those procedures that are currently being widely used, which include Roux-en-Y gastric bypass, laparoscopic adjustable banding, biliopancreatic diversion, and most recently sleeve gastrectomy.

The first types of procedures that were widely employed, now approximately 50 years ago, were known as jejunoileal bypass (JIB) procedures (Balsiger et al., 2000). Depending on how the proximal intestine was connected to the distal ileum there were two types of JIB, one using an end-to-end anastomosis (Scott procedure shown in Figure 1.1) and one using an end-to-side anastomosis (the Payne procedure).

The JIB procedure resulted in significant weight loss, but this result was achieved through extreme malabsorption, which caused problems with chronic diarrhea and multiple deficiencies including bile salt loss; protein calorie malnutrition; loss of vitamin B¹², vitamin K, and vitamin A; magnesium; and the development of hypocalcemia and osteoporosis (Balsiger, et al., 2000; Latifi, Kellum, DeMaria, & Sugerman, 2003; Våge, Sohlhaug, Berstad, Svanes, & Viste, 2002). Because of these complications, many of these procedures were surgically reversed, and this approach to bariatric surgery has been abandoned.

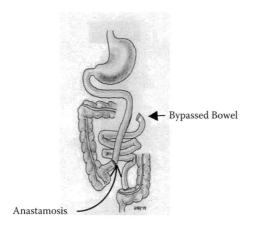

Bypassed Bowel

Anastamosis

Figure 1.1 Jejunoileal bypass.

The next generation of approach was represented by gastroplasties, which accomplished gastric restriction rather than malabsorption (Goldberg, Rivers, Smith, & Homan, 2000). These included horizontal gastroplasty, where a horizontal suture line was created with an open area (stoma) to allow for the passage of food (Figure 1.2), and a vertical banded gastroplasty (illustrated in Figure 1.3) (Våge et al., 2002).

However, the amount of weight loss with these procedures was less than desired, and not uncommonly the patients would regain a great deal of weight following staple line failures after the procedures (Sugerman, 2001; Goldberg et al., 2000).

The next generation of procedures, first introduced in 1969 by Mason and Ito, was the gastric bypass, which combined creation of a gastric pouch and a bypass of the first portion of the small intestine, resulting in both restriction and more limited malabsorption (Figure 1.4).

Subsequently this procedure was refined in several ways. First, it was found that the size of the proximal gastric pouch needed to be quite small (and now is approximately 15–20 ml), and that a Roux-en-Y type of anastomosis for the draining of the proximal gastric pouch was necessary to avoid bile reflux. Also, to avoid staple line failure, transection of the staple line was introduced. This modified form is now usually referred to as the Roux-en-Y gastric bypass (Figure 1.5). It is the most commonly utilized form of surgery in the United States and is becoming increasingly popular in many other countries as well.

There has been considerable debate about the optimal length for the gastric bypass limbs. Of interest, in a recent review, no significant impact of alimentary limb length on weight loss for patients with a BMI less than 50 was found, while longer Roux limb lengths (at least 150 cm) were associated with a modest weight loss advantage in the short-term period. It has been

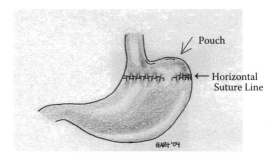

Figure 1.2 Horizontal gastroplasty.

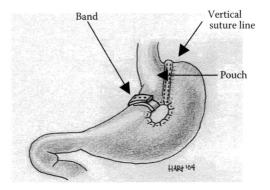

Figure 1.3 Vertical banded gastroplasty.

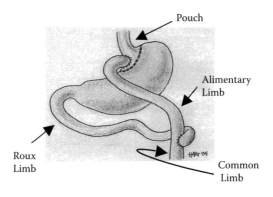

Figure 1.4 Gastric bypass.

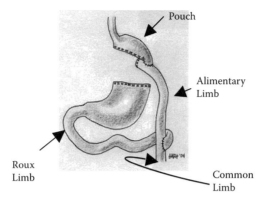

Pouch

Alimentary
Limb

Roux
Limb

Common
Limb

Figure 1.5 Roux-en-Y gastric bypass.

recommended that bariatric surgeons focus on the length of the common channel rather than the alimentary or biliopancreatic limbs since this may be more important in generating weight loss; when the length of the common channel approaches 100 cm, there appears to be an important positive impact on the amount of weight loss (Stefanidis, Kuwada, & Gersin, 2011).

Most recently the most common surgical approach is laparoscopic, which results in less pain, earlier discharge from the hospital, and fewer problems with infection (Courcoulas, Perry, Buenaventura, & Luketich, 2003).

The next generation of bariatric surgery to be introduced was gastric banding, which results in a restrictive procedure (Figure 1.6) (Favretti et al., 2002).

A band is placed around the upper stomach creating a small pouch. Initially the band was nonadjustable, but Kuzmak introduced an adjustable banding procedure (Kuzmak, 1991). This device includes a reservoir that is placed under the skin through which fluid can be injected to adjust the band size (Figure 1.7) (Schneider et al., 2003).

This procedure requires frequent follow-up visits so that the band can be adjusted to achieve an optimal weight loss effect (Favretti et al., 2002; Busetto et al., 2002). This device was originally quite popular in many parts of the world, and following its introduction in the United States became widely used as well (O'Brien et al., 2002). In general the experience has been that the amount of weight loss after laparoscopic adjustable banding is significantly less than that achieved following laparoscopioc Roux-en-Y gastric bypass (Boza et al., 2010), and in some instances results can be disappointing (DeMaria et al., 2010). Advantages of this procedure include that it does not cause the malabsorption problems as seen with other procedures but does require that the patients follow really strict dietary guidelines. Some complications associated to this procedure include erosion of the band (Busetto et al., 2002), band slippage, and port and balloon

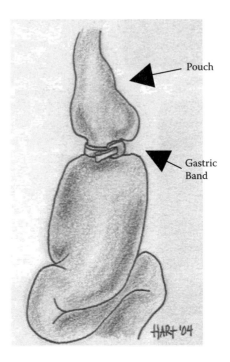

Figure 1.6 Gastric band.

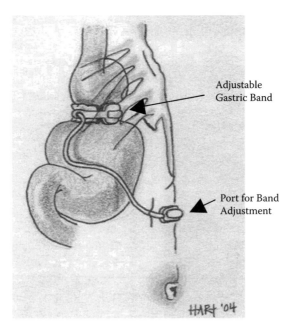

Figure 1.7 Adjustable gastric band.

dysfunction. Overall, the rate of failure with the laparoscopically adjustable band is significant and the need for reoperation is not uncommon (Boza et al., 2010). Of interest, there is a high correlation between erosion following banding and band slippage if a paragastric technique of insertion is used (Singhal et al., 2010). The pars flaccida technique has reduced band slippage significantly.

Another form of surgery to be introduced was biliopancreatic diversion (BPD) (Baltasar et al., 2002; Paiva, Bernardes, & Suretti, 2000; Scorpinaro, Marinari, & Camerini, 2002). This procedure includes a very long limb with a Roux-en-Y anastomosis, which results in significant problems with malabsorption. Because of this, this procedure is reserved for the most obese patients, where a higher degree of malabsorption is desirable. Others have argued that a BPD with duodenal switch can be efficient in terms of weight loss to patients' satisfaction in non-super-obese individuals (Biertho et al., 2010). However, this procedure results in a number of problems similar to those that were seen with JIB including vitamin and mineral deficiencies, anemia, and the development of protein-calorie malnutrition in a subgroup of patients. The procedure was subsequently modified to include a duodenal switch that results in the first portion of the intestine remaining in the food stream, thus reducing the rate of ulceration and dumping (Figure 1.8). However, the short-term complication rate with this procedure remains substantial, with significant complications occurring in 4–12% of patients (Gagner, Steffen, Biertho, & Horber, 2003).

The most recent procedure to gain in popularity is the gastric sleeve (Figure 1.9) (Abu-Jaish & Rosenthal, 2010; Karmali, Schauer, Birch, Sharma, & Sherman, 2010). This is a procedure that was originally developed for severely obese patients where it was important to minimize surgery and anesthesia time. The procedure was originally envisioned as a two-stage one wherein the patient would receive the gastric sleeve, the surgeon would then wait a period of months while the patient lost weight, and then sometime

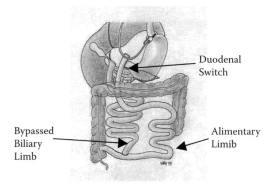

Figure 1.8 Biliopancreatic diversion with duodenal switch.

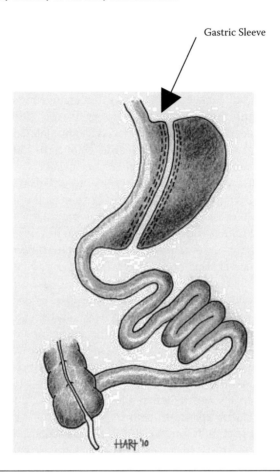

Figure 1.9 Gastric sleeve.

in the future would reoperate to do a more extensive procedure. However, the results have shown that some patients will have an adequate weight loss with this procedure alone. Future directions in bariatric surgery include endoluminal surgery and natural orifice endoscopic surgery (Tsesmeli & Coumaros, 2010; Ibrahim, Blero, & Deviere, 2010).

Risks Versus Benefits

As has been mentioned previously, many medical comorbidities that characterize obesity can be reversed or more easily controlled after the weight loss engendered by bariatric surgery including improved cardiac functioning, a decrease in rates of hypertension, elimination or improvement on sleep apnea, elimination or improvement in diabetes mellitus, and a lowering of pro-inflammatory cytokines that may mediate a variety of untoward outcomes (Deitel, 2002; Gami et al., 2003). Also, as has been demonstrated recently in the Longitudinal Assessment of Bariatric Surgery (LABS) study, short-term morbidity and mortality are quite low, and risk factors for untoward outcomes have been identified (LABS et al., 2009).

One area that has received increased attention in the literature is the impact of bariatric surgery on sexual functioning and reproduction. Female sexual dysfunction has been shown to resolve in a very high proportion of women after bariatric surgery (Bond et al., 2011). Because of this pregnancy is not an unlikely outcome following bariatric surgery. Relative to a normal BMI control group, patients' status post Roux-en-Y gastric bypass have been shown to have somewhat reduced birth weight, in infants, suggesting a possible role of nutritional growth restriction in pregnancy (Santulli et al., 2010). Clearly these patients require special attention on the part of obstetricians (Kominiarek, 2010). However, overall, pregnancy after bariatric surgery appears to be safe and to have fewer complications than pregnancy in morbidly obese women (Bebber et al., 2010). There also have been some concerns that there may be a change in the effectiveness in contraceptives after bariatric surgery; this remains an open question (Paulen, Zapata, Cansino, Curtis, & Jamieson, 2010).

As mentioned earlier, bariatric procedures are not without complications. Many of the complications noted are specific to certain kinds of procedures depending on whether they are malabsorptive or restrictive, and the degree to which they are malabsorptive. Complications can occur during the intraoperative period: complications of anesthesia, bleeding, and trauma to other internal organs (Byrne, 2001; Elliot, 2003). Complications that occur during the short term include the possibility of intestinal leaks between the connections linking the stomach to the intestine, bowel obstruction, and pulmonary embolus, as well as infection and persistent nausea and vomiting (Latifi et al., 2002). Late complications usually include gallbladder disease; internal hernias; vitamin mineral deficiencies such as B_{12}, magnesium, and calcium; iron deficiency anemia (Latifi et al., 2002; Byrne, 2001; Elliot, 2003; Ziegler, Sirveaux, Brunaud, Reibel, & Quilliot, 2009; Koch & Finelli, 2010); dumping syndrome; and reactive hyploglycemia. Of interest, anemia after bariatric surgery may not be explained solely by iron deficiency, anemia and other mechanisms may be involved (Von Drygalski et al., 2011). Zinc deficiency also occurs and may be an underrecognized complication (Sallé et al., 2010). The presence of dumping syndrome, advanced age, and greater change in BMI may help identify patients with an increased risk for nutritional deficiencies (Naghshineh et al., 2010). Fortunately for many patients who are severely obese, the benefits outweigh the risks, although all patients clearly need to be carefully informed about issues in both categories.

References

Abu-Jaish, W., & Rosenthal, R.J. (2010). Sleeve gastrectomy: A new surgical approach for morbid obesity. *Expert Review of Gastroenterology and Hepatology, 4,* 101–119.

Balsiger, B.M., Murr, M.M., Poggio, J.L., & Sarr, M.G. (2000). Surgery for weight control in patients with morbid obesity. *Medical Clinics of North America, 84,* 477–489.

Baltasar, A., Bou, R., Miró, J., Bengochea, M., Serra, C., & Pérez, N. (2002). Laparoscopic biliopancreatic diversion with duodenal switch: Technique and initial experience. *Obesity Surgery, 12,* 245–248.

Bebber, F.E., Rizzolli, J., Casagrande, D.S., Rodrigues, M.T., Padoin, A.V., Mottin, C.C. et al. (2010). Pregnancy after bariatric surgery: 39 pregnancies follow-up in a multidisciplinary team. *Obesity Surgery,* ahead of print.

Biertho, L., Biron, S., Hould, F.S., Lebel, S., Marceau, S., & Marceau, P. (2010). Is biliopancreatic diversion with duodenal switch indicated for patients with body mass index <50 kg/m^2? *Surgery for Obesity and Related Diseases, 6,* 508–514.

Bond, D.S., Wing, R.R., Vithiananthan, S., Sax, H.C., Roye, G.D., Ryder, B.A. et al. (2011). Significant resolution of female sexual dysfunction after bariatric surgery. *Surgery for Obesity and Related Diseases, 7,* 1–7.

Boza, C., Gamboa, C., Awruch, D., Perez, G., Escalona, A., & Ibañez, L. (2010). Laparoscopic Roux-en-Y gastric bypass versus laparoscopic adjustable gastric banding: Five years of follow-up. *Surgery for Obesity and Related Diseases, 6,* 570–575.

Bray, G.A. (2003). Risks of obesity. *Endocrinology and Metabolism Clinics of North America, 32,* 787–804.

Busetto, L., Segato, G., DeMarchi, F., Foletto, M., De Luca, M., Caniato, D. et al. (2002). Outcome predictors in morbidly obese recipients of an adjustable gastric band. *Obesity Surgery, 12,* 83–92.

Byrne, T.K. (2001). Complications of surgery for obesity. *Surgical Clinics of North America, 81,* 1181–1193.

Colquitt, J., Clegg, A., Sidhu, M., & Royle, P. (2003). Surgery for morbid obesity. *Cochrane Database System Review,* 2003.

Courcoulas, A., Perry, Y., Buenaventura, P., & Luketich, J. (2003). Comparing the outcomes after laparoscopic versus open gastric bypass: A matched paired analysis. *Obesity Surgery, 13,* 341–346.

Coviello, J.S., & Nystrom, K.V. (2003). Obesity and heart failure. *Journal of Cardiovascular Nursing, 18,* 360–366.

Dandona, P., Aljada, A., & Bandyopadhyay, A. (2004). Inflammation: The link between insulin resistance, obesity, and diabetes. *Trends in Immunology, 25,* 4–7.

Deitel, M. (2002). The early effect of the bariatric operations on diabetes. *Obesity Surgery, 12,* 349.

DeMaria, E.J., Winegar, D.A., Pate, V.W., Hutcher, N.E., Ponce, J., & Pories, W.J. (2010). Early postoperative outcomes of metabolic surgery to treat diabetes from sites participating in the ASMBS bariatric surgery center of excellence program as reported in the Bariatric Outcomes Longitudinal Database. *Annals of Surgery, 252,* 559–566.

Elliot, K. (2003). Nutritional considerations after bariatric surgery. *Critical Care Nursing Quarterly, 26*, 133–138.

Favretti, F., Cadiére, G.B., Segeto, G., Himpens, J., DeLuca, M., Busetto, L. et al. (2002). Laparoscopic banding: Selection and technique in 830 patients. *Obesity Surgery, 12*, 385–390.

Gagner, M., Steffen, R., Biertho, L., & Horber, F. (2003). Modern surgery: Technical innovation. Laparoscopic adjustable gastric banding with duodenal switch for morbid obesity: Technique and preliminary results. *Obesity Surgery, 13*, 444–449.

Gami, A.S., Caples, S.M., & Somers, V.K. (2003). Obesity and obstructive sleep apnea. *Endocrinology and Metabolism Clinics of North America, 32*, 869–894.

Garcia, V.F., Langford, L., & Inge, T.H. (2003). Application of laparoscopy for bariatric surgery in adolescents. *Current Opinion in Pediatrics, 15*, 248–255.

Goldberg, S., Rivers, P., Smith, K., & Homan, W. (2000). Vertical banded gastroplasty: A treatment for morbid obesity. *AORN Journal, 72*, 988–1003.

Herron, D.M. (2004). The surgical management of severe obesity. *The Mount Sinai Journal of Medicine, 71*, 63–71.

Hoerger, T.J., Zhang, P., Segel, J.E., Kahn, H.S., Barker, L.E., & Couper, S. (2010). Cost-effectiveness of bariatric surgery for severely obese adults with diabetes. *Diabetes Care, 33*, 1933–1939.

Ibrahim, M., Blero, D., & Deviere, J. (2010). Endoscopic options for the treatment of obesity. *Gastroenterology, 138*, 2228–2232.

Karmali, S., Schauer, P., Birch, D., Sharma, A.M., & Sherman, V. (2010). Laparoscopic sleeve gastrectomy: An innovative new tool in the battle against the obesity epidemic in Canada. *Canadian Journal of Surgery, 53*, 126–132.

Klein, S., Ghosh, A., Cremieux, P.Y., Eapen, S., & McGavock, T.J. (2010). Economic impact of the clinical benefits of bariatric surgery in diabetes patients with BMI ≥ 35 kg/m². *Obesity (Silver Spring), 19*, 581–587.

Koch, T.R., & Finelli, F.C. (2010). Postoperative metabolic and nutritional complications of bariatric surgery. *Gastroenterology Clinics of North America, 39*, 109–124.

Kominiarek, M.A. (2010). Pregnancy after bariatric surgery. *Obstetrics and Gynecology Clinics of North America, 37*, 305–320.

Kuzmak, L.I. (1991). A review of seven years' experience with silicone gastric banding. *Obesity Surgery, 1*, 403–408.

Latifi, R., Kellum, J.M., DeMaria, E.J., & Sugerman, H.J. (2002). Surgical treatment of obesity. In T. Wadden & A.J. Stunkard (Eds.), *Handbook of obesity treatment* (pp. 339–356). New York: Guilford Press.

Laville, M., & Disse, E. (2009). Bariatric surgery for diabetes treatment: Why should we go rapidly to surgery. *Diabetes and Metabolism, 35*, 562–563.

Longitudinal Assessment of Bariatric Surgery (LABS) Consortium, Flum, D.R., Belle, S.H., King, W.C., Wahed, A.S., Berk, P., Chapman, W. et al. (2009). Perioperative safety in the Longitudinal Assessment of Bariatric Surgery. *New England Journal of Medicine, 361*, 445–454.

Makary, M.A., Clarke, J.M., Shore, A.D., Magnuson, T.H., Richards, T., Bass, E.B. et al. (2010). Medication utilization and annual health care costs in patients with type 2 diabetes mellitus before and after bariatric surgery. *Archives of Surgery, 145*, 726–731.

Mason, E.E., & Ito, C. (1969). Gastric bypass. *Annals of Surgery, 170*, 329–339.

Mattison, R., & Jensen, M.D. (2004). Bariatric surgery: For the right patient, procedure can be effective. *Postgraduate Medicine, 115,* 49–58.

Mingrone, G., & Castagneto-Gissey, L. (2009). Mechanisms of early improvement/resolution of type 2 diabetes after bariatric surgery. *Diabetes and Metabolism, 35,* 518–523.

Naghshineh, N., O'Brien Coon, D., McTigue, K., Courcoulas, A.P., Fernstrom, M., & Rubin, J.P. (2010). Nutritional assessment of bariatric surgery patients presenting for plastic surgery: A prospective analysis. *Plastic and Reconstructive Surgery, 126,* 602–610.

O'Brien, P.E., Dixon, J.B., Brown, W., Schachter, L.M., Chapman, L., Burn, A.J. et al. (2002). The laparoscopic adjustable gastric band (Lap-Band®): A prospective study of medium-term effects on weight, health and quality of life. *Obesity Surgery, 12,* 652–660.

Ogden, C.L., Carroll, M.D., & Flegal, K.M. (2003). Epidemiologic trends in overweight and obesity. *Endocrinology and Metabolism Clinics of North America, 32,* 741–760.

Paiva, D., Bernardes, L., & Suretti, L. (2002). Laparoscopic biliopancreatic diversion: Technique and initial results. *Obesity Surgery, 12,* 358–361.

Paulen, M.E., Zapata, L.B., Cansino, C., Curtis, K.M., & Jamieson, D.J. (2010). Contraceptive use among women with a history of bariatric surgery: A systematic review. *Contraception, 82,* 86–94.

Pories, W.J., Dohm, L.G., & Manfield, C.J. (2010). Beyond the BMI: The search for better guidelines for bariatric surgery. *Obesity, 18,* 865–871.

Renard, E. (2009). Bariatric surgery in patients with late-stage type 2 diabetes: Expected beneficial effects on risk ratio and outcomes. *Diabetes and Metabolism, 35,* 564–568.

Sallé, A., Demarsy, D., Poirier, A.L., Lelièvre, B., Topart, P., Guilloteau, G., et al. (2010). Zinc deficiency: A frequent and underestimated complication after bariatric surgery. *Obesity Surgery, 20,* 1660–1670.

Santulli, P., Mandelbrot, L., Facchiano, E., Dussaux, C., Ceccaldi, P.F., Ledoux, S. et al. (2010). Obstetrical and neonatal outcomes of pregnancies following gastric bypass surgery: A retrospective cohort study in a French referral centre. *Obesity Surgery, 20,* 1501–1508.

Scheen, A.J., De Flines, J., De Roover, A., & Pacquot, N. (2009). Bariatric surgery in patients with type 2 diabetes: Benefits, risks, indications and perspectives. *Diabetes and Metabolism, 35,* 537–543.

Schneider, B.E., Villegas, L., Blackburn, G.L., Mun, E.C., Critchlow, J.F., & Jones, D.B. (2003). Laparoscopic gastric bypass surgery: Outcomes. *Journal of Laparoendoscopic Advanced Surgery Techniques, 13,* 247–255.

Scopinaro, N., Marinari, G.M., & Camerini, G. (2002). Laparoscopic standard biliopandreatic diversion: Technique and preliminary results. *Obesity Surgery, 12,* 362–365.

Shah, D.K., & Ginsburg, E.S. (2010). Bariatric surgery and fertility. *Current Opinion in Obstetrics and Gynecology, 22,* 248–254.

Singhal, R., Bryant, C., Kitchen, M., Khan, K.S., Deeks, J., Guo, B., et al. (2010). Band slippage and erosion after laparoscopic gastric banding: A meta-analysis. *Surgery Endoscopically, 12,* 2980–2986.

Sjöström, L., Lindroos, A.K., Peltonen, M., Torgerson, J., Bouchard, C., Carlsson, B. et al., for the Swedish Obese Subjects Study Scientific Group. (2004). Lifestyle, diabetes, and cardiovascular risk factors 10 years after bariatric surgery. *New England Journal of Medicine, 351*, 2683–2693.

Sjöström, L., Narbro, K., Sjöström, C.D., Karason, K., Larsson, B., Wedel H. et al., for the Swedish Obese Subjects Study. (2007). Effects of bariatric surgery on mortality in Swedish obese subjects. *New England Journal of Medicine, 357*, 741–752.

Sowers, J.R. (2003). Obesity as a cardiovascular risk factor. *American Journal of Medicine, 115*, 37–41.

Stefanidis, D., Kuwada, T.S., & Gersin, K.S. (2011). The importance of the length of the limbs for gastric bypass patients—An evidence-based review. *Obesity Surgery, 21*, 119–124.

Sugerman, H.J. (2001). Bariatric surgery for severe obesity. *Journal of the Associations for Academic Minority Physicians, 12*, 129–136.

Tsesmeli, N., & Coumaros, D. (2010). The future of bariatrics: Endoscopy, endoluminal surgery, and natural orifice transluminal endoscopic surgery. *Endoscopy, 42*, 155–162.

Våge, V., Solhaug, J., Berstad, A., Svanes, K., & Viste, A. (2002). Jejunoileal bypass in the treatment of morbid obesity: A 25-year follow-up study of 36 patients. *Obesity Surgery, 12*, 312–318.

Von Drygalski, A., Andris, D.A., Nuttleman, P.R., Jackson, S., Klein, J., & Wallace, J.R. (2011). Anemia after bariatric surgery cannot be explained by iron deficiency alone: Results of a large cohort study. *Surgery for Obesity and Related Diseases, 7*, 151–156

Ziegler, O., Sirveaux, M.A., Brunaud, L., Reibel, N., & Quilliot, D. (2009). Medical follow up after bariatric surgery: Nutritional and drug issues. General recommendations for the prevention and treatment of nutritional deficiencies. *Diabetes and Metabolism, 35*, 544–557.

CHAPTER 2

Assessment of Bariatric Surgery Candidates
The Clinical Interview

STEPHANIE SOGG

Introduction

Few medical treatments are as inherently intertwined with psychosocial factors as weight loss surgery (WLS). By its very nature, WLS engenders rapid and significant weight loss, which is likely to result in major changes not only in the patient's body image, but also in the patient's medical status, overall physical and emotional well-being, day-to-day functioning, and social relationships and interactions (Bocchieri, Meana, & Fisher, 2002). Conversely, just as WLS has the potential to affect many aspects of patients' psychosocial functioning, patients' psychosocial functioning may affect preparation for and adjustment after surgery in many ways. Thus, psychosocial evaluation of patients seeking WLS is widely considered to be strongly indicated. Psychosocial evaluation for WLS is currently required by the majority of third-party payers in the United States, and by over 80% of WLS programs in the United States (Bauchowitz et al., 2005; Kalarchian et al., 2007). In addition, when conducted skillfully, the pre-WLS psychosocial evaluation can serve as a clinical intervention in its own right, providing opportunities for education and preparation even as evaluation is taking place (Sogg & Mori, 2009).

A recent survey found that 98.5% of clinicians evaluating patients for WLS include a clinical interview in their assessment protocol (Fabricatore, Crerand, Wadden, Sarwer, & Krasucki, 2006). This chapter begins with a review of the aims of the presurgical clinical interview, as well as a number of issues specific to WLS evaluation. Next, specific information about evaluation content will be presented, followed by a discussion of how best to synthesize the information gathered during the interview to formulate appropriate and comprehensive treatment recommendations.

The Purpose of the Pre-WLS Clinical Interview

Although it is common for third-party payers to require a psychosocial evaluation as a condition of approval for WLS, and for surgical practices to require a psychosocial evaluation to determine whether a patient is a candidate for surgery, when done well, the psychosocial evaluation for WLS goes well beyond a gatekeeping function (Bauchowitz, Azarbad, Day, & Gonder-Frederick, 2007; Friedman, Applegate, & Grant, 2007; Sogg & Mori, 2008, 2009). The psychosocial evaluation for WLS serves a very different purpose, and thus should cover different content areas than a general psychodiagnostic assessment (Greenberg, Sogg, & Perna, 2009; Huberman, 2008; Sogg & Mori, 2008). The goal of a good pre-WLS evaluation is not to uncover factors that contraindicate surgery. Rather, given that WLS is the only effective, long-term treatment for obesity (Wadden, Butryn, & Byrne, 2004; Wing & Phelan, 2005), the evaluator should begin with the premise that the patient has a medical need for surgery. The focus should be on the goal of developing a set of recommendations designed to facilitate the safe and effective outcome of WLS, in terms of medical and weight loss outcomes, as well as psychosocial adjustment. Information gathered during the pre-WLS psychosocial evaluation should enable the clinician to formulate an individualized treatment plan, with recommendations that capitalize on the patient's strengths and address potential challenges to optimal adjustment after surgery (Sogg & Mori, 2008, 2009).

The Evaluating Clinician

Few recommendations exist in the empirical or clinical literature regarding optimal educational or experiential background for clinicians conducting pre-WLS psychosocial evaluations. However, it is strongly recommended that they possess the appropriate background knowledge to be able to meaningfully synthesize the information gathered during the assessment process (Huberman, 2008; Walfish, Vance, & Fabricatore, 2007).

The pre-WLS evaluation must include assessment of a number of factors specific to the WLS process, so specialized background knowledge is necessary. Though no formal guidelines exist, a recent study (West-Smith & Sogg, 2010) found that the vast majority of a sample of American Society for Metabolic and Bariatric Surgery (ASMBS) members felt that behavioral health professionals who work within this field should have extensive and specific background knowledge and experience in a number of WLS-related areas, such as obesity in general, weight loss surgery, and nonsurgical treatments for obesity. In addition, the majority of respondents felt it was important for evaluating clinicians to have some experience working with patients with obesity, and particularly with those who have already undergone WLS. Clinicians equipped with a thorough knowledge of the empirical and clinical literatures regarding obesity and the spectrum of obesity treatments, and who have firsthand clinical experience with patients who have undergone WLS, will be better prepared to conduct pre-WLS evaluations (Bauchowitz et al., 2005, 2007; Greenberg et al., 2009; Sogg & Mori, 2009; Wadden & Sarwer, 2006; Wadden et al., 2007; Walfish et al., 2007).

Standards of Practice in Psychosocial Evaluation for WLS

Currently, there is no single, widely agreed upon model of psychosocial evaluation for WLS. Clinicians performing these evaluations use varying tools and collect information in varying domains (Bauchowitz et al., 2005; Fabricatore et al., 2006; Greenberg et al., 2009; Wadden & Sarwer, 2006). Some guidelines do exist regarding evaluation of WLS patients (Greenberg et al., 2009; LeMont, Moorehead, Parish, Reto, & Ritz, 2004), but they tend to be fairly general. One factor that may contribute to the lack of standardization in WLS assessment is that, to date, very few empirical studies have successfully identified specific psychosocial factors that consistently predict any domain of WLS outcome (Bauchowitz, Gonder-Frederick, Olbrisch, Azarbad, Ryee, Woodson et al. 2005; Fabricatore, Crerand, Wadden, Sarwer, & Krasucki, 2006; Herpertz et al., 2004; Sarwer, Wadden, & Fabricatore, 2005; van Hout, Verschure, & van Heck, 2005; Wadden & Sarwer, 2006).

However, a few comprehensive, standardized assessment protocols do exist in the literature. Each has its own distinctive features, advantages, and drawbacks. The first such instrument to be published is the Weight and Lifestyle Inventory (WALI) (Wadden & Foster, 2006). The WALI was constructed as a self-report questionnaire about obesity in general, rather than focusing specifically on WLS, but serves as an excellent framework for conducting the WLS evaluation interview, covering domains including weight history, eating habits and pathology, physical activity, outcome expectations, and medical history, in addition to general psychological domains. One advantage of the WALI is its incorporation of several existing validated measures of eating pathology, such as the Questionnaire on Eating and Weight Patterns–Revised (QEWP-R) (Yanovski, 1993), which assesses the symptoms of binge eating disorder.

The Boston Interview for Bariatric Surgery (BIBS) (Sogg & Mori, 2004, 2008, 2009), a semistructured interview protocol, was specifically designed for use in the pre-WLS assessment process, is based on the empirical literature regarding obesity and WLS, and covers a variety of domains specific to WLS, as well as a general assessment of psychosocial history and functioning.

In contrast to these two instruments, the Cleveland Clinic Behavioral Rating System (CCBRS) (Heinberg, Ashton, & Windover, 2010) is not an interview protocol, but an algorithm to facilitate decision making based on data that the clinician gathers in whatever format he or she chooses, comprising nine domains specific to WLS, as well as an "overall impression" score.

Areas for Assessment in Psychosocial Evaluation for WLS

Despite the absence of formal standards for WLS evaluation, there appears to be some consensus that certain domains are important to evaluate. Below, suggested areas for evaluation are discussed in detail. In multidisciplinary settings, clinicians from other disciplines may assess certain areas of these domains, whereas clinicians working alone will need to evaluate all areas themselves.

Weight and Diet History

One useful way to begin the interview is to ask the patient to outline the trajectory of his or her weight over time. This allows the interviewer to get a sense of the impact that the patient's weight has had over his or her lifetime and, conversely, of how various life events and circumstances have affected the patient's weight (Kushner & Roth, 2005). Identifying past triggers for weight gain will help the interviewer and the patient to better foresee potential postsurgical challenges to adherence to the postoperative behavioral regimen, and suggests potential supports or strategies that might enhance the patient's long-term success.

It is particularly informative to examine the various weight loss methods that the patient has previously tried, as well as factors that have either promoted or impeded these efforts, which is valuable in formulating plans for the pre- and postsurgery strategies or interventions. In addition, it is important to document previous weight loss attempts, as NIH guidelines (and most third-party payers) specify that WLS is an appropriate treatment option only when nonsurgical weight loss methods have proven ineffective (NIH Consensus Panel, 1991).

General Eating Behaviors and Patterns

It is important to get a basic sense of the typical eating patterns and behaviors in which the patient is currently engaging. Information about factors such as food preferences, a tendency to rely on convenience foods, and the nature of the barriers to consuming healthy foods will be relevant to the patient's ability to adhere to the postsurgical regimen. Information should also be gathered regarding typical portion sizes and meal patterns, as meal skipping or overly frequent snacking may be detrimental to WLS outcome. After WLS, the patient will need to establish a habit of eating planned and structured meals and snacks at regular intervals throughout the day; some patients may benefit from a period of instruction and practice around these skills. Learning about the patient's typical meal choices and patterns also yields information about the patient's organizational and self-care skills, as well as logistical or other factors that may pose barriers to long-term adherence to the post-WLS regimen. For instance, a patient who reports eating fast food or takeout meals several times per week may be doing so due to being overwhelmed by work or family responsibilities, or this may be due to poor planning or organizational skills; such factors are important to consider when formulating individualized treatment recommendations.

Eating Pathology

Eating pathology is widely considered a standard part of any pre-WLS evaluation (Bauchowitz et al., 2005; Fabricatore et al., 2006). When assessing for past and current eating disorders, it is recommended that the clinician be familiar with the formal criteria for each disorder. These criteria can be obtained from the *Diagnostic and Statistical Manual, Fourth Edition, Text Revision* (*DSM-IV-TR*) (American Psychiatric Association, 2000), or from the planned *DSM-5* revisions (www.DSM5. org). Alternatively, the clinician may use one of several standardized, structured questionnaires or interviews that have been developed to assess these disorders.

Binge Eating   The eating disorder most likely to be encountered in the pre-WLS evaluation is binge eating disorder (BED). This disorder involves episodes in which objectively large amounts of food are consumed, with an experience of loss of control over eating, in the absence of compensatory behaviors. BED is included in the *DSM-IV-TR* as a provisional diagnosis warranting further study, but is currently widely used in clinical and research settings and likely will be added to *DSM-5*. BED is generally recognized to be fairly prevalent in the population of patients seeking weight loss treatment, including WLS (Allison et al., 2006; Colles, Dixon, & O'Brien, 2008b; Delinsky, Latner, & Wilson,

2006). To meet diagnostic criteria for BED, the patient must engage in binge eating at least twice per week (although this criteria is likely to be lowered to once a week in *DSM-5*), and binge eating episodes must involve at least three of five clinical features (e.g., rapid intake, eating beyond satiety, etc.).

Arguably, the most salient aspect of assessment of binge eating within the WLS evaluation is to examine the factors that trigger these episodes. Research has established important clinical differences between individuals whose binge eating is triggered by dietary patterns, such as meal skipping, and those with affective disturbances (Grilo, Masheb, & Wilson, 2001). For some patients, binge eating episodes are triggered solely by excessive hunger (Grilo et al., 2001; Stice, Agras, Telch, Halmi, Mitchell, & Willson, 2001), and in fact research has found that behavioral weight loss treatment is equally effective as psychotherapy targeting the eating binges specifically (Munsch et al., 2007). For other patients, however, binge eating episodes are triggered by negative emotions, such as stress or depression. The subset of BED patients with accompanying affective symptoms has been found to have a higher level of eating pathology and overall disturbance, and to respond less well to treatment (Grilo et al., 2001; Stice et al., 2001; Wilson, Wilfley, Agras, & Bryson 2010). It is of particular concern when binge eating serves as the patient's main means of coping with negative affect, even if the eating binges occur with subclinical frequency or do not involve objectively large amounts of food. Concerns here are twofold: First, early after WLS, most patients are disinclined and physically unable to consume large amounts of food in one sitting. While this may temporarily preclude binge eating completely, the patient is still left without one of his or her main strategies for coping with negative emotions. Second, as time goes on after WLS, many patients find that their desire and ability to eat for emotional reasons does return, and if alternative coping skills have not been developed, binge eating, or some other form of pathological eating, may recur. Several studies have demonstrated fairly prevalent eating pathology in long-term follow-up after WLS (Colles, Dixon, & O' Brien, 2008b; de Zwaan, Hilbert, Swan-Kremeier, Simonich, Lancaster, Howell et al., 2010; Niego, Kofman, Weiss, & Geliebter, 2007).

Much research has examined the relationship between BED and WLS outcome, and although findings are somewhat mixed, the overall conclusion would appear to be that there is insufficient evidence that BED predicts poorer psychological or weight loss outcomes in the short term, and BED does not seem to represent a clear contraindication to WLS (Niego et al., 2007; Wadden & Sarwer, 2006). However, longer-term studies have shown that presurgical BED does increase the risk of pathological eating behaviors after surgery, and that those who do experience such postsurgical eating pathology have poorer weight loss outcomes (de Zwaan et al., 2010; Mitchell, Lancaster, Burgard, Howell, Krahn, Crosby et al., 2001; Niego et al., 2007). However, it is also worth noting that even in those studies in which patients with baseline binge eating were found to have poorer weight loss outcomes, their outcomes were still significantly better than those typically seen with nonsurgical treatments for obesity (de Zwaan et al., 2010; Niego et al., 2007), a convincing argument against withholding WLS for patients with binge eating (Wadden & Sarwer, 2006). Rather, these findings suggest the importance of educating patients about the risk of recurrence of eating pathology after surgery, as well as pre- or postsurgical interventions designed to reduce that risk (de Zwaan et al., 2010; Niego et al., 2007; Sogg & Mori, 2008, 2009).

Compensatory Behaviors Some authors have suggested that purging represents a serious contraindication to surgery (Clark et al., 2003; Friedman et al., 2007). Few studies have examined the prevalence of compensatory behaviors before or after WLS, or the relationship between compensatory behaviors and surgery outcome. One recent study (Chen et al., 2009) found that 8.5% of patients being evaluated for WLS reported current compensatory behaviors; however, presurgical compensatory behaviors had no significant relationship to one-year weight loss outcome. In another, long-term study (de Zwaan et al., 2010), the majority of participants reported some trouble with vomiting after surgery, and 12% reporting vomiting as a means of controlling weight. The authors hypothesized that the involuntary vomiting often experienced after Roux-en-Y gastric bypass (RYGB) might evolve into a deliberate means of enhancing or maintaining weight loss. In general it has been posited that compensatory behavior serves as a marker for a greater degree of eating pathology and general psychological disturbance (O'Kearney, Gertler, Conti, & Duff, 1998), which should be taken into account in the overall synthesis of evaluation data.

Anorexia Nervosa Although, by definition, patients with obesity seeking WLS would not be expected to present with anorexia nervosa, some patients presenting for WLS may have experienced symptoms of anorexia nervosa in the past. There is no published work examining the prevalence of anorexia nervosa either before or after WLS. However, a history of experiencing such symptoms in the past may be an indicator that the patient is likely to hold a rigid, all-or-nothing or overly restrictive attitude toward eating and weight that may be reinforced and exacerbated in the postoperative period.

Night Eating Syndrome In night eating syndrome (NES), food intake is shifted to occur disproportionately late in the day, or upon waking in the night (Allison et al., 2010). This syndrome is not currently recognized as an eating disorder in the DSM-IV-TR, but this form of eating pathology has been widely described and studied over the past few decades (O'Reardon, Peshek, & Allison, 2005; Stunkard & Allison, 2003). Although the study of NES has been hampered by lack of uniformity in different researchers' definitions of the syndrome, there is now a formalized set of proposed criteria that will aid the clinician in evaluating this type of behavior (Allison et al., 2010). NES can contribute significantly to an individual's weight (O'Reardon et al., 2005), as well as disrupting his or her sleep patterns and general well-being, and thus is an area for pre-WLS assessment. However, in and of itself, NES does not appear to represent a clear contraindication for WLS (Colles & Dixon, 2006; Morrow, Gluck, Lorence, Flancbaum, & Geliebter, 2008).

Sleep-Related Eating Disorder   Sleep-related eating disorder (SRED) is a parasomnia in which an individual eats while asleep. SRED is a relatively rare phenomenon, but it is thought to be more prevalent among individuals with obesity, and in some cases may be a significant contributor to obesity (Winkelman, Herzog, & Fava, 1999). Although SRED, by definition, involves pathological eating behavior, it is currently thought to be most appropriately characterized as a sleep disorder rather than an eating disorder (Winkelman et al., 1999). When identified, it is advisable that attempts be made to treat this behavior, either before or after surgery; treatment for SRED typically involves withdrawal of medications that may induce it, such as certain sleep medications, or using psychotropic medication such as topiramate (Winkelman, 2003).

Problematic Eating Patterns—Emotionally Triggered Eating and Grazing   In addition to formal eating disorders, there are other problematic eating behaviors that are relevant to WLS, and a complete evaluation will assess both types of eating problems. One example of such a behavior is emotionally triggered eating. No standardized definition of emotionally triggered eating exists, but it can be generally defined as a tendency to eat in response to—and as a means of coping with—negative emotions (Canetti, Berry, & Elizur, 2009). While there is no empirical basis for considering emotionally triggered eating to be a clear contraindication for WLS, it may be beneficial for the patient to prepare for surgery by working to develop alternative, healthier ways to cope with negative emotions (Sogg & Mori, 2008, 2009). However, as yet there is no empirical data suggesting that this must take place before surgery, and given that most patients experience a sharply reduced desire to eat for at least the first several months after surgery, it may be appropriate to address this problem by educating the patient about the challenges that may arise postsurgically, and provide a list of resources for help with this pattern if it does recur after surgery (Greenberg, Sogg, & Perna, 2009; Sogg & Mori, 2008, 2009).

Another eating pattern that may affect WLS outcome is grazing. Although WLS limits the amount that an individual can eat at any one time, weight loss outcomes may be compromised if the patient consumes small amounts of food continuously over time. In fact, one recent study found that individuals who engaged in grazing before surgery were more likely to engage in unhealthy eating after surgery, and those who continued to engage in grazing after surgery achieved poorer weight loss outcomes (Colles et al., 2008b). Patients who engage in grazing behavior may benefit from interventions designed to promote regular intake of planned, structured meals and snacks throughout the day, which is a foundation of the post-WLS eating regimen (Sogg & Mori, 2008, 2009).

Physical Activity Patterns

It is widely documented that individuals with obesity tend to spend less time in moderate to vigorous physical activity than their lean counterparts, and more time in sedentary activities (Bond, Jakicic, Vithianathan, Thomas, Leahy, Sax et al., 2010; Davis, Hodges, & Gillham, 2006; Ekkekakis, Lind, & Vazou, 2010). Physical activity level may be explored by starting with a neutral, open-ended question, such as "tell me about your current physical activity patterns." Not only does this minimize defensiveness, but it also broadens the scope of what is considered to be physical activity beyond the realm of planned, structured "exercise."

In addition to evaluating current type, quantity, and frequency of physical activity, the evaluator should also explore current and past barriers to physical activity. There are many factors that may make it difficult for the patient to be active. For instance, patients with obesity often have comorbid conditions, such as osteoarthritis or asthma, which make vigorous activity painful or contraindicated. Even in the absence of such conditions, research suggests that exercise is significantly more aversive for people with obesity (Brock et al., 2010; Ekkekakis et al., 2010). Together, these and other similar findings suggest that the current recommended activity guidelines may be difficult to meet for people who have obesity (Bond et al., 2010).

However, although there are many factors that may create legitimate barriers to exercise for patients seeking WLS, it is clear that regular physical activity is an important part of the post-WLS regimen. Physical activity levels have been found to be related to weight loss outcomes after WLS (Colles et al., 2008a; Silver, Wesolowski, Piepul, Kuhn, Romanelli, & Garb, 2006; Welch, Torquati, Jensen, & Richards, 2008). It is important to educate patients about the necessity of maintaining consistent exercise after surgery, and exploring the barriers to activity forms a foundation for creating realistic strategies to facilitate exercise after surgery.

Psychosocial History and Functioning

In the psychosocial evaluation for WLS, the goal is not to arrive at specific diagnoses per se, but to evaluate all psychosocial factors that may affect the outcome surgery, with the purpose of formulating recommendations for strategies or interventions that will ensure the best possible outcome. Although assessment of current and past psychopathology is not the main focus of the pre-WLS evaluation, it is important to get a sense of how the patient is currently functioning, and what his or her history has been.

Psychopathology Evaluation of psychiatric symptoms should be a standard part of the pre-WLS evaluation; these symptoms should be evaluated from the viewpoint of determining how they may affect the WLS process. Studies have shown that patients with obesity, especially women, and those with more severe obesity (Wadden et al., 2006) or seeking weight loss treatment have elevated rates of many Axis I disorders, including major depression and dysthymia, and mania or hypomania, as well as generalized anxiety disorder, panic, and specific phobias (Kalarchian et al., 2007; Petry, Barry, Pietrzak, & Wagner, 2008). What is important to consider is not the diagnosis in and of itself, but whether psychiatric symptoms are well managed and the extent to which these symptoms may create challenges in adjustment and adherence to self-care after WLS. For instance, although many patients seeking WLS present with active depression symptoms, these symptoms in and of themselves are not necessarily a contraindication for WLS. In fact, some studies have found that a higher baseline level of depression was actually correlated with greater weight loss after surgery (Averbukh et al., 2003), and many studies have found that depression symptoms improve significantly in the short term after surgery (Schowalter et al., 2008; Thonney, Pataky, Badel, Bobbioni-Harsch, & Coley, 2010; Wadden et al., 2001). However, if a patient reports depression or anxiety symptoms so severe that they interfere with basic self-care such as healthy eating, physical activity, and adhering to medical appointments and treatment, the evaluator might recommend that WLS be deferred until the patient's symptoms are better controlled.

Clinicians may be hesitant about recommending WLS for patients who have more severe psychopathology, such as bipolar or psychotic disorders. There is currently very little research describing WLS outcomes for patients with these disorders, perhaps because they are less likely to be referred or accepted for surgery. However, as with less severe forms of psychiatric illness, the main consideration in such cases is whether the symptoms are currently well controlled and adequately treated, how stable the patient has been over time, and the degree to which the symptoms may interfere with adherence and adjustment after WLS (Greenberg et al., 2009; Sogg & Mori, 2008, 2009).

It should be noted that it is always important for the evaluator to bear in mind what the costs may be to the patient when delaying or denying surgery. While there may be concerns about the impact of a patient's psychiatric symptoms on surgery outcome, it is important to remember that as yet, no other treatment for obesity has been found to be nearly as effective or durable, and potential challenges must be weighed against the medical and functional benefits of surgery. It is notable that in previous studies, it has been found that when a delay has been recommended on psychological grounds, a significant proportion of patients become lost to follow-up and may not get the surgical care that they need (Friedman et al., 2007; Marcus, Kalarchian, & Courcoulas, 2009; Pawlow et al., 2005).

Substance Abuse Though, in general, people with obesity are typically found to have a lower prevalence of current substance misuse problems than in the general population (Kalarchian et al., 2007), some studies have found a higher prevalence of lifetime history of such problems among people with obesity (Kalarchian et al., 2007; Petry et al., 2008). Few studies have examined the relationship between substance abuse and WLS, but the existing research suggests that a remote history of substance abuse does not seem to be related to poorer weight loss or psychosocial adjustment after WLS (Clark et al., 2003; Heinberg & Ashton, 2010). However, active substance misuse is commonly considered to be a contraindication for surgery (Fabricatore et al., 2006; Greenberg et al., 2009). In light of the finding that some individuals exhibit problem drinking after WLS (Buffington, 2006; 2007; Ertelt et al., 2008), it is recommended that evaluation for WLS include a screening for past and current substance use disorders, and that patients be educated about the risks of such problems after surgery (Sogg, 2007). For patients who are actively abusing drugs or alcohol at the time of evaluation, it is commonly recommended that surgery be delayed until the patient can achieve some period of abstinence (e.g., 6–12 months) before undergoing surgery (Clark, Balsiger, Sletten, Dahiman, Ames, Williams et al., 2003).

Trauma History It is also advisable to assess patients' history of trauma, particularly sexual trauma. A history of trauma, or even active symptoms of posttraumatic stress disorder (PTSD), does not necessarily contraindicate surgery; most research has found that neither a history of trauma in general nor a history of sexual trauma is related to poorer weight loss after surgery (Clark et al., 2007; Larsen & Geenen, 2005; Oppong, Nickels, & Sax, 2006). However, as patients lose weight after surgery, they may feel more vulnerable because of their smaller size, or experience increased sexual attention or romantic advances, which may be anxiety provoking

(Bocchieri et al., 2002; Kalarchian et al., 2007). When there is a trauma history, and particularly when there are current, active trauma symptoms, it is recommended that the evaluator encourage the patient to think about whether losing weight may result in experiences that he or she would find anxiety provoking, and to consider what strategies he or she might use to cope with such experiences. In some cases referral to outside treatment may be warranted to help the patient to prepare for and cope with these experiences.

Mental Health Treatment　The evaluator should obtain a brief overview of the patient's current and past mental health treatment, if any. If the patient has had mental health treatment in the past, it is helpful to examine how adherent the patient was to this treatment, and whether or not this treatment was helpful. When the patient is already engaged in mental health treatment, it is informative to contact these treatment providers to obtain their input (with appropriate consent), and to discuss any impressions the evaluator may have about various psychosocial interventions that might be beneficial to the patient in preparing for or adjusting after WLS.

Stressors and Coping Skills　In addition to evaluating current and previous psychopathology, the patient's current stressors should also be examined. These may include ongoing and chronic stressors, such as marital conflict or chronic health conditions in the patient or family members, as well as acute stressors, such as recent deaths in the family or starting a demanding new job. As with psychiatric symptoms, the main relevance of current stressors is not the stressors themselves, but how they are affecting the patient, and the adequacy of the patient's skills and resources for coping with them. It is recommended that the evaluation include a brief assessment of the patient's functioning in a variety of domains, including occupational, social, and activities of daily living. For patients whose current stressors are unusually numerous or severe, it may be appropriate to recommend supportive psychotherapy, or even delaying surgery.

Social Support

Interpersonal relationships play an important role in general psychosocial functioning. Given the many challenges involved in preparing for and adjusting after WLS, the evaluator should assess the nature and availability of the patient's social supports. Assessment of available supports need not be time consuming; the evaluator might ask about the general nature and quality of relationships with romantic partners, family, friends, coworkers, and, when applicable, organizations within the patient's community, such as civic groups, religious affiliations, and so forth. Patients with suboptimal interpersonal support may benefit from psychoeducation about the value of building and enlisting a social support network, suggestions about how he or she might begin to do so, or, in some cases, a referral to a mental health provider to ensure some external support.

Just as interpersonal relationships affect adjustment after surgery, these relationships, in turn, may also be affected as the patient undergoes WLS (Bocchieri et al., 2002; Sogg & Gorman, 2008). Patients typically report numerous positive changes in their interpersonal functioning after WLS. For instance, patients often report that improved health and mobility enable them to do more activities with their partners and friends, enhancing those relationships. They report that improvements in mood and self-confidence lead to increased participation in, and enjoyment of, social activities. They often note that people respond very positively to the changes in their appearance, and that even strangers treat them with more courtesy and respect after they have lost weight. However, even positive changes can give rise to challenges, and these challenges differ depending on the type of relationship in question. For instance, WLS patients sometimes report that their newfound health, mobility, and self-confidence disrupt an entrenched dependency dynamic in romantic partnerships or close friendships, and the friend or partner may feel threatened by a sense that the patient no longer depends as much on him or her. Some partners of WLS patients may feel worry that after losing weight, their partners will be more attractive to others, giving rise to insecurity. Patients often find that after WLS, they are able to be more assertive and more focused on meeting their own needs, which may not be a welcome change for the other people in their lives. In addition, patients may find that friends, relatives, and colleagues are jealous of their weight loss. During the WLS evaluation, it is helpful to encourage the patient to think about what the reactions of their significant others may be, and how they will manage potential interpersonal challenges.

Knowledge About WLS

The 1991 NIH Consensus Statement regarding WLS specifies that WLS is appropriate only for patients who are well informed about surgery (NIH Consensus Panel, 1991). By definition, a patient cannot give truly informed consent for treatment if he or she lacks information about the treatment itself, risks and benefits, and outcomes. Thus, any pre-WLS psychosocial evaluation should include assessment of the patient's knowledge about WLS. In addition to the importance to informed consent, evaluating the patient's knowledge about WLS may yield information about his or her motivational level, judgment, and potential for postsurgical adherence to medical follow-up and behavioral changes (Sogg & Mori, 2009).

It should be determined how much the patient knows about what is actually done in the WLS procedure of choice. Although it may not be critical to the surgery's outcome that the patient understand the anatomical details of the procedure, a patient who presents for surgery without knowing anything about the surgical procedure may be someone who is typically disengaged from or passive about his or her medical care. Alternatively, he or she may be so focused on the surgery as the solution to all of his or her problems that he or she is not interested in or is overlooking the details about how surgery works and its risks and complications.

Similarly, the post-WLS regimen involves a comprehensive set of behavioral guidelines, and it is helpful to assess the patient's knowledge about postsurgical behavioral changes. Here is an instance in which assessment also serves the functions of education and preparation. Reviewing and supplementing what the patient knows about the required postsurgical behavior changes creates a more concrete and detailed picture for the patient and allows him or her to begin to anticipate or even practice these changes proactively (Sogg & Mori, 2009).

Finally, examining knowledge about WLS also provides the evaluator with an overview of general intellectual functioning. When deficits are identified, recommendations should be made as to how to address these— for instance, the evaluator may recommend that information be presented at a very basic level of complexity, or that a friend or family member accompany the patient to educational sessions (Sogg & Mori, 2009).

Outcome Expectations

It is important to assess patients' expectations about various domains of outcome, including magnitude and trajectory of weight loss, physiological changes, and psychosocial changes that may result from surgery and significant weight loss.

The amount and rapidity of weight loss resulting from WLS varies by procedure; the evaluator should familiarize himself or herself generally with information available about weight loss outcomes in the WLS literature. It is well documented that, in general, patients seeking weight loss treatment hold unrealistic outcome expectations (Fabricatore et al., 2007; Foster & Kendall, 1994; Wee, Jones, Davis, Bourland, & Hamel, 2006), and that these beliefs are fairly resistant to change (Fabricatore et al., 2007; Wadden et al., 2003). However, informed consent would not be complete without discussion of realistic weight loss outcomes, and thus this topic should be included in the pre-WLS evaluation (Sogg & Mori, 2009). It is particularly helpful to get a sense of the patient's expectations about how much effort will be required for a successful long-term outcome. That is, does the patient understand that, although surgery is the most effective weight loss treatment that currently exists, it is not a "magic bullet"? Though many patients will experience dramatic weight loss in the short term, optimal weight loss outcomes in the long term are highly dependent upon the degree of effort the patient devotes to behavioral change (Sarwer et al., 2008; van Hout et al., 2006; Welch et al., 2008). Patients who are unaware of (or inclined to dismiss) the importance of lasting behavior change may be unprepared to enact these changes, and as a result may experience suboptimal outcomes.

Of course, weight loss, in and of itself, is not the only type of outcome that results from WLS, and the empirical literature indicates that patients seek WLS for a variety of reasons. Though the most frequently cited motivation is improved health (Libeton et al., 2004; Wee et al., 2006), other motivating factors include improved appearance, mobility, fitness, and job prospects or occupational functioning (Dixon et al., 2009; Libeton et al., 2004; Ogden, Clementi, & Aylwin, 2006). A thorough presurgical assessment should include an examination of the entire spectrum of changes the patient expects to see as a result of undergoing surgery. Unrealistic expectations may be cause for concern, as they may be related to poorer postsurgical satisfaction and, consequently, poorer adherence, low mood, and poor overall adjustment.

Formulating Treatment Recommendations

Gathering detailed information with a comprehensive interview is only the first step in the pre-WLS evaluation. As noted above, ideally, the purpose of the evaluation is to enable the formulation of recommendations for interventions that will enhance the safety and effectiveness of WLS and facilitate optimal surgery outcome. The individualized treatment plan that results from the evaluation is the evaluator's main contribution both to the patient and to the rest of the surgical treatment team.

Good treatment recommendations include ways to capitalize on existing strengths that the patient already possesses. This is why the evaluation process should include assessment of what types of supports or other factors have been helpful to the patient in the past. This can yield information about strengths that the patient has demonstrated in other areas (e.g., good problem-solving skills, a robust support network, strong religious faith) that could be enlisted during the WLS process to improve adjustment and outcome.

Of course, the psychosocial evaluation may also uncover factors that could represent challenges to adjustment and outcome after surgery. It is important that the evaluation report does not simply identify these challenges, but also includes recommendations for ways to address them to enhance outcome.

Conclusion

The psychosocial evaluation for WLS serves a highly specialized purpose that goes well beyond determining whether a patient should be "cleared" for surgery or merely to diagnose psychopathology. It provides an opportunity to gather comprehensive information in a wide array of domains that will allow the evaluator to formulate an individualized set of treatment recommendations designed to capitalize on patient strengths and address factors that pose potential challenges for the surgery process, to help the patient achieve the best possible outcome—medically, behaviorally, and psychosocially.

References

Allison, K.C., Lundgren, J.D., O'Reardon, J.P., Geliebter, A., Gluck, M.E., Vinai, P. et al. (2010). Proposed diagnostic criteria for night eating syndrome. *International Journal of Eating Disorders, 43,* 241–247.

Allison, K.C., Wadden, T.A., Sarwer, D.B., Fabricatore, A.N., Crerand, C.E., Gibbons, L.M. et al. (2006). Night eating syndrome and binge eating disorder among persons seeking bariatric surgery: Prevalence and related features. *Obesity (Silver Spring), 14,* 77S–82S.

American Psychiatric Association. (2000). *Diagnostic and statistical manual of mental disorders* (4th ed., text rev.). Washington, DC: Author.

Averbukh, Y., Heshka, S., El-Shoreya, H., Flancbaum, L., Geliebter, A., Kamel, S. et al. (2003). Depression score predicts weight loss following Roux-en-Y gastric bypass. *Obesity Surgery, 13,* 833–836.

Bauchowitz, A., Azarbad, L., Day, K., & Gonder-Frederick, L. (2007). Evaluation of expectations and knowledge in bariatric surgery patients. *Surgery for Obesity and Related Disorders, 3,* 554–558.

Bauchowitz, A.U., Gonder-Frederick, L.A., Olbrisch, M.E., Azarbad, L., Ryee, M.Y., Woodson, M. et al. (2005). Psychosocial evaluation of bariatric surgery candidates: A survey of present practices. *Psychosomatic Medicine, 67,* 825–832.

Bocchieri, L.E., Meana, M., & Fisher, B.L. (2002). Perceived psychosocial outcomes of gastric bypass surgery: A qualitative study. *Obesity Surgery, 12,* 781–788.

Bond, D., Jakicic, J., Vithiananthan, S., Thomas, J.G., Leahey, T.M., Sax, H.C. et al. (2010). Objective quantification of physical activity in bariatric surgery candidates and normal-weight controls. *Surgery for Obesity and Related Diseases, 6,* 72–78.

Brock, D.W., Chandler-Laney, P.C., Alvarez, J.A., Gower, B.A., Gaesser, G.A. & Hunter, G.R. (2010). Perception of exercise difficulty predicts weight regain in formerly overweight women. *Obesity, 18,* 982–986.

Buffington, C.K. (2006). Alcohol and the gastric bypass patient. *Bariatric Times, 3,* 1–10.

Buffington, C.K. (2007). Alcohol use and health risks: Survey results. *Bariatric Times, 4,* 21–23.

Canetti, L., Berry, E., & Elizur, Y. (2009). Psychosocial predictors of weight loss and psychological adjustment following bariatric surgery and a weight-loss program: The mediating role of emotional eating. *International Journal of Eating Disorders, 42*, 109–117.

Chen, E., Roehrig, M., Herbozo, S., McCloskey, M.S., Roehrig, J., Cummings, H. et al. (2009). Compensatory eating disorder behaviors and gastric bypass surgery outcome. *International Journal of Eating Disorders, 42*, 363–366.

Clark, M., Hanna, B., Mai, J.L., Graszer, K.M., Krochta, J.G., McAlpine, D.E. et al. (2007). Sexual abuse survivors and psychiatric hospitalization after bariatric surgery. *Obesity Surgery, 17*, 465–469.

Clark, M.M., Balsiger, B.M., Sletten C.D., Dahlman, K.L., Ames, G., Williams, D.E., Abu-Lebdeh, H.D., & Sarr, M.G. (2003). Psychosocial factors and 2-year outcome following bariatric surgery for weight loss. *Obesity Surgery, 13*, 739–745.

Colles, S.L., & Dixon, J.B. (2006). Night eating syndrome: Impact on bariatric surgery. *Obesity Surgery, 16*, 811–820.

Colles, S., Dixon, J., & O'Brien, P. (2008a). Hunger control and regular physical activity facilitate weight loss after laparoscopic adjustable gastric banding. *Obesity Surgery, 18*, 833–840.

Colles, S.L., Dixon, J.B., & O'Brien, P.E. (2008b). Grazing and loss of control related to eating: Two high-risk factors following bariatric surgery. *Obesity, 16*, 615–622.

Davis, J.N., Hodges, V.A., & Gillham, M.B. (2006). Physical activity compliance: Differences between overweight/obese and normal-weight adults. *Obesity, 14*, 2259–2265.

Delinsky, S.S., Latner, J.D., & Wilson, G.T. (2006). Binge eating and weight loss in a self-help behavior modification program. *Obesity (Silver Spring), 14*, 1244–1249.

de Zwaan, M., Hilbert, A., Swan-Kremeier, L., Simonich, H., Lancaster, K., Howell, L.M. et al. (2010). Comprehensive interview assessment of eating behavior 18–35 months after gastric bypass surgery for morbid obesity. *Surgery for Obesity and Related Diseases, 6*, 79–85.

Dixon, J.B., Laurie, C.P., Anderson, M.L., Hayden, M.J., Dixon, M.E., & O'Brien, P.E. (2009). Motivation, readiness to change, and weight loss following adjustable gastric band surgery. *Obesity, 17*, 698–705.

Ekkekakis, P., Lind, E., & Vazou, S. (2010). Affective responses to increasing levels of exercise intensity in normal-weight, overweight, and obese middle-aged women. *Obesity, 18*, 79–85.

Ertelt, T.W., Mitchell, J.E., Lancaster, K., Crosby, R.D., Steffen, K.J., & Marino, J.M. (2008). Alcohol abuse and dependence before and after bariatric surgery: A review of the literature and report of a new data set. *Surgery for Obesity and Related Diseases, 4*, 647–650.

Fabricatore, A.N., Crerand, C.E., Wadden, T.A., Sarwer, D.B., & Krasucki, J.L. (2006). How do mental health professionals evaluate candidates for bariatric surgery? Survey results. *Obesity Surgery, 16*, 567–573.

Fabricatore, A.N., Wadden, T.A., Womble, L.G., Sarwer, D.B., Berkowitz, R.I., Foster, G.D. et al. (2007). The role of patients' expectations and goals in the behavioral and pharmacological treatment of obesity. *International Journal of Obesity, 31*, 1739–1745.

Foster, G.D., & Kendall, P.C. (1994). The realistic treatment of obesity: Changing the scales of success. *Clinical Psychology Review, 14*, 701–736.

Friedman, K.E., Applegate, K.L., & Grant, J. (2007). Who is adherent with preoperative psychological treatment recommendations among weight loss surgery candidates? *Surgery for Obesity and Related Diseases, 3*, 376–382.

Greenberg, I., Sogg, S., & Perna, F. (2009). Behavioral and psychological care in weight loss surgery: Best practice update. *Obesity, 17*, 880–884.

Grilo, C.M., Masheb, R.M., & Wilson, G.T. (2001). Subtyping binge eating disorder. *Journal of Consulting Clinical Psychology, 69*, 1066–1072.

Heinberg, L., & Ashton, K. (2010). History of substance abuse relates to improved postbariatric body mass index outcomes. *Surgery for Obesity and Related Diseases, 6*, 417–421.

Heinberg, L., Ashton, K., & Windover, A. (2010). Moving beyond dichotomous psychological evaluation: The Cleveland Clinic behavioral rating system for weight loss surgery. *Surgery for Obesity and Related Diseases, 6*, 185–190.

Herpertz, S., Kielmann, R., Wolf, A.M., Hebebrand, J., & Senf, W. (2004). Do psychosocial variables predict weight loss or mental health after obesity surgery? A systematic review. *Obesity Research, 12*, 1554–1569.

Huberman, W. (2008). One psychologist's 7-year experience in working with surgical weight loss: The role of the mental health professional. *Primary Psychiatry, 15*, 42–47.

Kalarchian, M.A., Marcus, M.D., Levine, M.D., Courcoulas, A.P., Pilkonis, P.A., Ringham, R.M. et al. (2007). Psychiatric disorders among bariatric surgery candidates: Relationship to obesity and functional health status. *American Journal of Psychiatry, 164*, 328–334.

Kushner, R.F., & Roth, J.L. (2005). Medical evaluation of the obese individual. *Psychiatric Clinics of North America, 28*, 89–103.

Larsen, J.K., & Geenen, R. (2005). Childhood sexual abuse is not associated with a poor outcome after gastric banding for severe obesity. *Obesity Surgery, 15*, 534–537.

LeMont, D., Moorehead, M., Parish, M.S., Reto, C.S. & Ritz, S.J. (2004). *Suggestions for the pre-surgical psychological assessment of bariatric surgery candidates*. Accessed November 17, 2010, from http://www.asbs.org/html/pdf/PsychPreSurgicalAssessment.pdf

Libeton, M., Dixon, J.B., Laurie C., & O'Brien, P.E. (2004). Patient motivation for bariatric surgery: Characteristics and impact on outcomes. *Obesity Surgery, 14*, 392–398.

Marcus, M.D., Kalarchian, M.A., & Courcoulas, A.P. (2009). Psychiatric evaluation and follow-up of bariatric surgery patients. *American Journal of Psychiatry, 166*, 285–291.

Mitchell, J.E., Lancaster, K.L., Burgard, M.A., Howell, L.M., Krahn, D.D., Crosby, R.D. et al. (2001). Long-term follow-up of patients' status after gastric bypass. *Obesity Surgery, 11*, 464–468.

Morrow, J., Gluck, M., Lorence, M., Flancbaum, L., & Geliebter, A. (2008). Night eating status and influence on body weight, body image, hunger, and cortisol pre- and post- Roux-en-Y gastric bypass (RYGB) surgery. *Eating and Weight Disorders, 13*, e96–e99.

Munsch, S., Biedert, E., Meyer, A., Michael, T., Schlup, B., Tuch, A., & Magraf, J. (2007). A randomized comparison of cognitive behavioral therapy and behavioral weight loss treatment for overweight individuals with binge eating disorder. *International Journal of Eating Disorders, 40*, 102–113.

Niego, S.H., Kofman, M.D., Weiss, J.J., & Geliebter, A. (2007). Binge eating in the bariatric surgery population: A review of the literature. *International Journal of Eating Disorders, 40*, 349–359.

NIH Consensus Panel. (1991). Gastrointestinal surgery for severe obesity. Consensus development conference panel. *Annals of Internal Medicine, 115*, 956–961.

Ogden, J., Clementi, C., & Aylwin, S. (2006). The impact of obesity surgery and the paradox of control: A qualitative study. *Psychological Health, 21*, 273–293.

O'Kearney, R., Gertler, R., Conti, J., & Duff, M. (1998). A comparison of purging and nonpurging eating-disordered outpatients: Mediating effects of weight and general psychopathology. *International Journal of Eating Disorders, 23*, 261–266.

Oppong, B.A., Nickels, M.W., & Sax, H.C. (2006). The impact of a history of sexual abuse on weight loss in gastric bypass patients. *Psychosomatics, 47*, 108–111.

O'Reardon, J.P., Peshek, A., & Allison, K.C. (2005). Night eating syndrome: Diagnosis, epidemiology and management. *CNS Drugs, 19*, 997–1008.

Pawlow, L.A., O'Neil, P.M., White, M.A., & Byrne, T.K. (2005). Findings and outcomes of psychological evaluations of gastric bypass applicants. *Surgery for Obesity and Related Diseases, 1*, 523–527; discussion, 528–529.

Petry, N.M., Barry, D., Pietrzak, R.H., & Wagner, J.A. (2008). Overweight and obesity are associated with psychiatric disorders: Results from the National Epidemiologic Survey on Alcohol and Related Conditions. *Psychosomatic Medicine, 70*, 288–297.

Sarwer, D.B., Wadden, T.A., & Fabricatore, A.N. (2005). Psychosocial and behavioral aspects of bariatric surgery. *Obesity Research, 13*, 639–648.

Sarwer, D.B., Wadden, T.A., Moore, R.H., Baker, A.W., Gibbons. L.M., Raper, S.E. et al. (2008). Preoperative eating behavior, postoperative dietary adherence, and weight loss after gastric bypass surgery. *Surgery for Obesity and Related Diseases, 4*, 640–646.

Schowalter, M., Benecke, A., Lager, C., Heimbucher, J., Bueter, M., Thalheimer, A. et al. (2008). Changes in depression following gastric banding: A 5- to 7-year prospective study. *Obesity Surgery, 18*, 314–320.

Silver, H.J., Torquati, A., Jensen, G.L., & Richards, W.O. (2006). Weight, dietary and physical activity behaviors two years after gastric bypass. *Obesity Surgery, 16*, 859–864.

Sogg, S. (2007). Alcohol misuse after bariatric surgery: Epiphenomenon or "Oprah" phenomenon? *Surgery for Obesity and Related Diseases, 3*, 366–368.

Sogg, S., & Gorman, M. (2008). Interpersonal changes and challenges after weight-loss surgery. *Primary Psychiatry, 15*, 61–66.

Sogg, S., & Mori, D.L. (2004). The Boston interview for gastric bypass: Determining the psychological suitability of surgical candidates. *Obesity Surgery, 14*, 370–380.

Sogg, S., & Mori, D.L. (2008). Revising the Boston interview: Incorporating new knowledge and experience. *Surgery for Obesity and Related Diseases, 4*, 455–463.

Sogg, S., & Mori, D.L. (2009). Psychosocial evaluation for bariatric surgery: The Boston interview and opportunities for intervention. *Obesity Surgery, 19,* 369–377.

Stice, E., Agras, W.S., Telch, C.F., Halmi, K.A., Mitchell, J.E., & Wilson, T. (2001). Subtyping binge eating-disordered women along dieting and negative affect dimensions. *International Journal of Eating Disorders, 30,* 11–27.

Stunkard, A.J., & Allison, K.C. (2003). Two forms of disordered eating in obesity: Binge eating and night eating. *International Journal of Obesity and Related Metabolic Disorders, 27,* 1–12.

Thonney, B., Pataky, Z., Badel, S., Bobbioni-Harsch, E., & Golay, A. (2010). The relationship between weight loss and psychosocial functioning among bariatric surgery patients. *American Journal of Surgery, 199,* 183–188.

Van Hout, G.C., Boekestein, P., Fortuin, F.A., Pelle, A.J., & van Heck, G.L. (2006). Psychosocial functioning following bariatric surgery. *Obesity Surgery, 16,* 787–794.

Van Hout, G.C., Verschure, S.K., & Van Heck, G.L. (2005). Psychosocial predictors of success following bariatric surgery. *Obesity Surgery, 15,* 552–560.

Wadden, T.A., Butryn, M.L., & Byrne, K.J. (2004). Efficacy of lifestyle modification for long-term weight control. *Obesity Research, 12* (Suppl.), 151S–162S.

Wadden, T.A., Butryn, M.L., Sarwer, D.B., Fabricatore, A.N., Crerand, C.E., Lipschutz, P.E. et al. (2006). Comparison of psychosocial status in treatment-seeking women with class III vs. class I-II obesity. *Obesity, 14,* 90S–98S.

Wadden, T.A., & Foster, G.D. (2006). Weight and lifestyle inventory (WALI). *Obesity (Silver Spring), 14* (Suppl. 2), 99S–118S.

Wadden, T.A., & Sarwer, D.B. (2006). Behavioral assessment of candidates for bariatric surgery: A patient-oriented approach. *Obesity, 14* (Suppl. 2), 53S–62S.

Wadden, T.A., Sarwer, D.B., Fabricatore, A.N., Jones, L., Stack, R., & Williams, N.S. (2007). Psychosocial and behavioral status of patients undergoing bariatric surgery: What to expect before and after surgery. *Medical Clinics of North America, 91,* 451–469.

Wadden, T.A., Sarwer, D.B., Womble, L.G., Foster, G.D., McGuckin, B.G., & Schimmel, A. (2001). Psychosocial aspects of obesity and obesity surgery. *Surgical Clinics of North America, 81,* 1001–1024.

Wadden, T.A., Womble, L.G., Sarwer, D.B., Berkowitz, R.I., Clark, V.L., & Foster, G.D. (2003). Great expectations: "I'm losing 25% of my weight no matter what you say." *Journal of Consulting and Clinical Psychology, 71,* 1084–1089.

Walfish, S., Vance, D., & Fabricatore, A. (2007). Psychological evaluation of bariatric surgery applicants: Procedures and reasons for delay or denial of surgery. *Obesity Surgery, 17,* 1578–1583.

Wee, C.C., Jones, D.B., Davis, R.B., Bourland, A.C., & Hamel, M.B. (2006). Understanding patients' value of weight loss and expectations for bariatric surgery. *Obesity Surgery, 16,* 496–500.

Welch, G., Wesolowski, C., Piepul, B., Kuhn, J., Romanelli, J., & Garb, J. (2008). Physical activity predicts weight loss following gastric bypass surgery: Findings from a support group survey. *Obesity Surgery, 18,* 517–524.

West-Smith, L., & Sogg, S. (2010). Creating a credential for bariatric behavioral health professionals: Potential benefits, pitfalls, and provider opinion. *Surgery for Obesity and Related Diseases, 6*, 695–701.

Wilson, G., Wilfley, D., Agras, W.S., & Bryson, S.W. (2010). Psychological treatments of binge eating disorder. *Archives of General Psychiatry, 67,* 94–101.

Wing, R.R., & Phelan, S. (2005). Long-term weight loss maintenance. *American Journal of Clinical Nutrition, 82,* 222S–225S.

Winkelman, J. (2003). Treatment of nocturnal eating syndrome and sleep-related eating disorder with topiramate. *Sleep Medicine, 4,* 243–246.

Winkelman, J.W., Herzog, D.B., & Fava, M. (1999). The prevalence of sleep-related eating disorder in psychiatric and non-psychiatric populations. *Psychological Medicine, 29,* 1461–1466.

Yanovski, S.Z. (1993). Binge eating disorder: Current knowledge and future directions. *Obesity Research, 1,* 306–324.

CHAPTER 3

Assessment of Bariatric Surgery Candidates

Structured Interviews and Self-Report Measures

CAROL B. PETERSON, KELLY C. BERG,
and JAMES E. MITCHELL

Accurate assessment of psychosocial variables serves as a foundation for effective bariatric surgery. Although the collection of assessment data can be time-consuming, the immediate and longer-term benefits of multidimensional psychosocial measurement are numerous. Through the use of structured interviews and questionnaires as adjunct measures to unstructured clinical interviews, the clinician can conduct comprehensive assessments that can be used in multiple contexts in bariatric surgery including screening, treatment planning, and prognostic assessment (Blackstone, Cortes, Messer, & Engstrom, 2010; Wadden & Sarwer, 2006). When used in conjunction with unstructured interviewing, structured assessment instruments can improve the reliability and scope of self-reported data as well as provide an opportunity for collaborative treatment planning (Peterson, 2005). Structured interviews and questionnaires have the additional benefits of improving communication among treatment centers through the use of common instruments, and providing data for multidimensional outcome assessment for each patient as well as data aggregated by the center.

Structured interviews and self-report questionnaires can be used as assessment tools at several points during the assessment and follow-up of bariatric surgery patients. One of the most common uses of these measures has been to screen potential candidates for the appropriateness of surgery (Fabricatore, Crerand, Wadden, Sarwer, & Krasucki, 2006; Pull, 2010). Psychopathology measures of substance use disorders, eating disorders, and mood disorders have been used to identify individuals for whom surgery may be ineffective or even dangerous (Fabricatore et al., 2006; Krukowski, Friedman, & Applegate, 2010; Wadden & Sarwer, 2006). Although response biases, particularly minimization of symptoms, can limit the accuracy of self-reported data (Schacter, 1999), patients may be more likely to be honest in structured (compared to unstructured) assessment formats, and particularly when questionnaires or interviews are administered anonymously (Keel, Crow, Davis, & Mitchell, 2002; Lavender & Anderson, 2009). Comprehensive structured assessment instruments also minimize the likelihood of omissions and missing information.

Psychological assessment can also be conducted to determine the need for additional support or services among candidates who are eligible for surgery but show areas of impairment (e.g., psychiatric symptoms, lack of social support) (Blackstone et al., 2010). Presurgery assessment facilitates treatment planning for all stages of the bariatric surgery process and reduces the likelihood of noncompliance when these issues can be addressed prior to and following surgery. In addition, assessment facilitates the identification of problematic behaviors including binge eating that can be targeted prior to or following surgery (Kalarchian, Marcus, & Courcoulas, 2010). These variables can also be measured to help determine likely short-term and long-term prognosis postsurgery.

An additional benefit of comprehensive assessment is the clinical relationship. When administered, scored, and discussed with the patient effectively, structured assessment instruments can enhance clinical rapport and collaboration (Peterson, 2005; Wadden & Sarwer, 2006). The use of comprehensive interviews and questionnaires with items that the patient views as relevant to his or her own experience conveys both expertise and empathy on behalf of the clinician administering these measures. Providing thoughtful feedback to patients using assessment data can improve the patient's confidence in the clinician, elevate the patient's engagement in the surgery process, and potentially enhance longer-term outcomes by eliciting compliance. Because a primary risk to the quality of data and rapport is assessment burden, the clinician should balance the needs for a comprehensive assessment and the need to build rapport with the needs of the patient in terms of time and efficiency (Peterson, 2010). Cost of assessment instruments and staff training, time burden on staff for administering and scoring instruments, and the psychometric support of instruments based on reliability and validity data are other considerations in determining assessment procedures.

Typically, bariatric surgery assessment relies on a combination of structured interviews, self-report questionnaires, and unstructured clinical interviews (Fabricatore et al., 2006). Structured interviews including the Eating Disorder Examination (EDE) (Fairburn, Cooper, O' Connor, 2008; see below) and the Structured Clinical Interview for DSM-IV (SCID) (First et al., 2001) can be used as comprehensive measures of a range of behaviors, symptoms, and other variables. These instruments typically require advanced clinical knowledge and training of the interviewer in order to administer, score, and interpret them reliably. The advantage of these types of interviews is that the clinician can score a patient's response based on specific criteria, thereby reducing error and response bias (e.g., underestimating/overestimating) on the part of the patient, and increasing the interrater reliability on the part of the clinician (Wilson, 1993). The EDE, for example, requires the patient to provide concrete examples of binge eating episodes that the clinical interviewer must rate according to designated criteria in order to be considered DSM-IV episodes of binge eating. Although structured interviews are time intensive for administration and required training procedures, these instruments can be extremely useful in the context of multidimensional assessment, particularly to measure complicated variables that could be prone to misinterpretation when described in the questionnaire.

Self-administered questionnaires are a commonly used assessment method. These instruments typically require patients to answer questions using paper-and-pencil or computer-based formats. Questionnaires administered by computer generally yield comparable data to paper-and-pencil methods, although there is some suggestion that respondents provide more honest self-report data when using computer-administered compared to paper-and-pencil questionnaires (e.g., Bonevski, Campbell, & Sanson-Fisher, 2010). Compared to structured interviews, questionnaires typically take less time to administer and provide less assessment burden on patients.

The following sections include descriptions of specific assessment interviews and questionnaires that can be used in the context of bariatric surgery assessment.

Eating Behavior, Physical Activity, and Eating Disorders

Dietary Intake

Assessing dietary intake accurately is difficult, and self-reported data of amount of food intake are generally underreported, which may be due to social desirability bias (e.g., Stice, Fisher, & Lowe, 2004). Daily self-monitoring of food intake is a widely used measure. However, daily self-monitoring may be reactive as dietary patterns appear to change after the onset of self-monitoring; for this reason, although self-monitoring of food intake is potentially useful clinically, the fact that it is both reactive and potentially inaccurate makes it a less than ideal measure (Wilson, 1993). In contrast to daily self-monitoring, asking individuals to recall their dietary intake, particularly using telephone interviews, can provide a more accurate measure of food intake (Casey, Goolsby, Lensing, Perloff, & Bogle, 1999). Dietary recall procedures in which the interviewer is guided by a computer-administered database and specific queries can be especially helpful in eliciting accurate self-reported dietary intake (e.g., Nutritional Data Systems for Research; Feskanich et al., 1988). Food frequency questionnaires, in which patients report the frequency of food types consumed (e.g., Feskanich et al., 1993; Block et al., 1986), can also be used to assess type and frequency of food consumption. Although questionnaires provide less assessment burden on patients and staff, dietary intake data may be less accurate than data elicited by comprehensive dietary recall interviews.

Physical Activity

Similar to self-reported food intake, reports of physical activity may be biased by social desirability. Nonetheless, questionnaires can provide useful data for bariatric surgery assessment, including the Godin method (Godin & Shephard, 1985), which has psychometric data to support its use (Gionet & Godin, 1989; Godin, Jobin, & Boullon, 1986). Although accelerometers and doubly labeled water provide more accurate information about energy expenditure and physical activity in bariatric surgery patients (e.g., Bond et al., 2010), these approaches are usually impractical in clinical settings because of logistics and the expense involved.

Binge Eating and Eating Disorders

Eating Disorder Examination The Eating Disorder Examination (EDE) (Fairburn & Cooper, 1993; Fairburn et al., 2008) is a semi-structured interview that is widely considered the preeminent assessment of the cognitive and behavioral symptoms of eating disorders (Wilson, 1993). The EDE can be used as either a dimensional assessment of symptom severity or a diagnostic tool. Eating disorder cognitions (e.g., intent to restrict dietary intake, fear of weight gain) during the past 28 days are assessed using a 7-point Likert scale, with higher scores indicating more severe pathology. These scores can be averaged to create four subscale scores (i.e., Restraint, Eating Concern, Shape Concern, and Weight Concern) that can be compared to normative data from community samples. The EDE also measures the frequency of binge eating and compensatory behaviors during the past three months. The psychometric properties of the EDE have been evaluated extensively (Berg, Peterson, Frazier, & Crow, in press): EDE subscale scores have demonstrated test-retest reliability (.50–.88), internal consistency (as = .44–.85), and interrater reliability (.65–.99). Behavioral frequency scores have also demonstrated test-retest reliability (.70–.97) and interrater reliability (.98–1.0). Research also supports the validity of the EDE when used to distinguish between overweight women with and without binge eating disorder (BED) (Wilfley, Schwartz, Spurrell, & Fairburn, 2000).

The EDE has been adapted for use with pre- and postoperative bariatric surgery patients (EDE-BSV) (unpublished manuscript available from de Zwaan and Swan-Kremeier by request; de Zwaan et al., 2010). In the EDE-BSV, several items from the original EDE have been modified to account for postoperative changes in eating patterns and to differentiate between dietary restriction and compensatory behaviors due to shape/weight and those resulting from bariatric surgery. Additionally, the EDE-BSV includes several items that assess physical complications of bariatric surgery associated with eating (e.g., plugging, dumping).

Eating Disorder Examination–Questionnaire The Eating Disorder Examination–Questionnaire (EDE-Q) (Fairburn & Beglin, 1994, 2008) is a self-report questionnaire based on the EDE (described above). Although the EDE is considered the most accurate and comprehensive eating disorder assessment instrument, it requires significant amounts of time and assessor training to administer. The EDE-Q was developed in response to these limitations and assesses the same cognitive and behavioral symptoms as the EDE using nearly identical item content, phrasing, and scoring. A recent review of the psychometric properties of the EDE-Q supports the test-retest reliability (.66–.94) and internal consistency (αs = .70–.93) of the EDE-Q subscales as well as the test-retest reliability of the items measuring binge eating and compensatory behaviors (.54–.92) (Berg et al., in press). Research on the convergence of the EDE and EDE-Q has found strong positive correlations between subscale scores on the two instruments. For bariatric surgery candidates specifically, correlations between EDE and EDE-Q subscale scores have ranged from .58 to .78. Although there is a strong relationship between the interview and questionnaire versions of the EDE, it is notable that in published studies, bariatric surgery candidates have scored approximately one standard deviation higher on the questionnaire than the interview (Berg, Peterson, Frazier, & Crow, 2011). Whether this discrepancy represents overreporting of symptoms on the questionnaire or underreporting during the interview version is unclear.

Eating Disorder Questionnaire The Eating Disorder Questionnaire (EDQ) (Mitchell, Hatsukami, Eckert, & Pyle, 1985; Mitchell, 2005) is a self-report questionnaire that was designed to gather comprehensive data about patients that can be used to supplement information garnered from a clinical interview. The EDQ includes questions on current and lifetime disordered eating symptoms (e.g., dieting, binge eating, use of compensatory behaviors, body image) and the respondent's psychosocial, medical, and psychiatric history. Also relevant to bariatric surgery candidates is a section on respondents' weight histories. EDQ scores can be used to assign eating disorder diagnoses; however, research has shown only moderate diagnostic agreement between the EDQ and a structured clinical interview (κ = .64) (Keel et al., 2002). There is no published research on the psychometric properties of the EDQ in bariatric surgery candidates.

Eating Disorder Diagnostic Scale   The Eating Disorder Diagnostic Scale (EDDS) (Stice, Telch, & Rizvi, 2000) is a 22-item self-report questionnaire based on the DSM-IV-TR criteria for anorexia nervosa, bulimia nervosa (BN), and BED. Scores from the EDDS can be used to derive either eating disorder diagnoses (algorithms are included in Stice et al., 2000) or as a dimensional measure of symptom severity (αs = .86–.91) (Stice et al., 2000; Stice, Fisher, & Martinez, 2004). Psychometric data on the EDDS support the one-week test-retest reliability of both EDDS diagnoses (κs = .71–.95) and EDDS composite scores (.87) (Stice et al., 2000). Individuals diagnosed with an eating disorder by the EDDS tend to score significantly higher on other measures of eating pathology, and the EDDS has demonstrated both sensitivity (.77–.93) and specificity (.96–1.00) when compared to a structured interview (Stice et al., 2000; Stice, Fisher, & Martinez, 2004). Lastly, EDDS composite scores correlate with measures of similar constructs (range = .36–.82) (Stice et al., 2000; Stice, Fisher, & Martinez, 2004). Further research is needed on the psychometric properties of the EDDS when used with bariatric surgery candidates.

Questionnaire on Eating and Weight Patterns–Revised   The Questionnaire on Eating and Weight Patterns–Revised (QEWP-R) (Spitzer et al., 1992, 1993) is a self-report questionnaire that can be used to derive diagnoses of BN and BED. The instrument also includes questions on respondents' dieting and weight histories. The QEWP-R has demonstrated criterion-related validity as individuals diagnosed with BED by the QEWP-R score higher on other measures of binge eating and depression, have higher rates of psychopathology, and have earlier onsets of overweight and dieting (Gladis, Wadden, Foster, Vogt, & Wingate, 1998; Spitzer et al., 1993). Diagnostic agreement between the QEWP-R and other structured interviews and questionnaires is moderate (κs = .45–.57) (de Zwaan et al., 1993; Gladis et al., 1998) and is similar to the stability of diagnoses obtained by the QEWP-R three weeks apart (κ = .57) (Nangle, Johnson, Carr-Nangle, & Engler, 1994). Among bariatric surgery patients (Elder et al., 2006), there is low diagnostic agreement between the QEWP-R and the EDE-Q for both weekly binge eaters (κ = .26) and twice-weekly binge eaters (κ = .05).

Binge Eating Scale The Binge Eating Scale (BES) (Gormally, Black, Daston, & Rardin, 1982) is a 16-item self-report questionnaire used to measure the presence and severity of binge eating symptoms. Each item includes four statements describing either cognitive or behavioral symptoms associated with binge eating, and respondents are instructed to indicate which statement best describes themselves. Possible scores range from 0 to 47, with scores of 17 or below indicating no binge eating and scores of 27 or higher indicating severe binge eating. BES scores correlate with measures of similar constructs (Timmerman, 1999) and have demonstrated internal consistency (Freitas, Lopes, Appolinario, & Coutinho, 2006; Gormally et al., 1982) and test-retest reliability (Freitas et al., 2006; Timmerman, 1999). When compared to structured interviews for identifying individuals with BED, the sensitivities and specificities of the BES have varied substantially, ranging from .20 to .97 (Celio, Wilfley, Crow, Mitchell, & Walsh, 2004; Freitas et al., 2006; Gladis et al., 1998; Greeno, Marcus, & Wing, 1995). However, most studies have found that the BES demonstrates relatively higher sensitivity than specificity, suggesting that the BES overidentifies respondents as having BED. This characteristic of the BES may make it a useful screening instrument for BED in bariatric surgery candidates, provided that a diagnosis of BED is confirmed in a follow-up assessment.

Three-Factor Eating Questionnaire The Three-Factor Eating Questionnaire (TFEQ) (Stunkard & Messick, 1985), also known as the Eating Inventory (EI), is a 51-item self-report questionnaire originally designed to measure three constructs associated with eating behavior: Restraint, Disinhibition, and Hunger. Although subsequent factor analyses have failed to replicate the original three factors (Ganley, 1988; Hyland, Irvine, Thacker, Dann, & Dennis, 1989; Karlsson, Persson, Sjostrom, & Sullivan, 2000; Mazzeo, Aggen, Anderson, Tozzi, & Bulik, 2003), researchers have found factors approximating "restraint" and "emotional eating" in several studies (Ganley, 1988; Hyland et al., 1989; Karlsson et al., 2000; Mazzeo et al., 2003). Research on the original three subscales supports the internal consistency coefficients (αs = .70–.93) (Bardone-Cone & Boyd, 2007; Karlsson et al., 2000; Laessle, Tuschl, Kotthaus, & Pirke, 1989; Shearin, Russ, Hull, Clarkin, & Smith, 1994; Stunkard & Messick, 1985), test-retest reliability (.80–.93) (Allison, Kalinsky, & Gorman, 1992; Stunkard & Messick, 1985), and temporal stability (63–.82) of the BES (Bardone-Cone & Boyd, 2007). There are also data suggesting that the original three subscales correlate with self-report measures of similar constructs (Allison et al., 1992; Bardone-Cone & Boyd, 2007; Shearin et al., 1994); however, there is mixed support for the relationship between scores on the restraint subscale and behavioral restriction (e.g., caloric intake) (French, Jeffrey, &

Wing, 1994; Laessle et al., 1989; Stice, Fisher, & Lowe, 2004; Williamson et al., 2006). Although the TFEQ is used frequently in bariatric surgery clinics, there is little psychometric data on the TFEQ in preoperative surgical patients and none in postoperative patients. Only one study has examined the validity of the TFEQ for use with bariatric surgery candidates, finding that respondents endorsing regular binge eating score significantly higher on the disinhibition and hunger subscales than non-binge eaters (Kalarchian, Wilson, Brolin, & Bradley, 1998).

Dutch Eating Behavior Questionnaire The Dutch Eating Behavior Questionnaire (DEBQ) (van Strien, Frijters, Bergers, & Defares, 1986) is a 33-item self-report questionnaire designed to measure three patterns of eating: restraint, emotional eating, and external eating. Respondents are asked to rate the frequency with which they engage or have a desire to engage in specific eating behaviors on a 5-point Likert scale, ranging from 1 (never) to 5 (very often). The three factors of the DEBQ have been replicated by an independent researcher (Wardle, 1987), the subscales demonstrate internal consistency ($\alpha s = .80–.95$) (Allison et al., 1992; Laessle et al., 1989; van Strien et al., 1986), and the subscale scores predict expected group differences between AN, BN, overweight control, and normal weight control women (Wardle, 1987). However, as has been found with the restraint subscale of the TFEQ, there is evidence that DEBQ restraint subscale scores correlate with scores on other self-reported measures of restraint (Allison et al., 1992; Laessle et al., 1989), but not necessarily with behavioral measures of dietary restriction (Allison et al., 1992; Laessle et al., 1989; Williamson et al., 2007). There is no published data on the psychometric properties of the DEBQ in bariatric surgery candidates.

Night Eating Syndrome

The Night Eating Questionnaire (NEQ) (Allison et al., 2008) is a self-report questionnaire that measures the severity of symptoms associated with night eating syndrome (NES). Because the criteria for NES have been revised several times since it was first described in 1955 (Stunkard, Grace, & Wolff, 1955), the NEQ has also been modified. The most recent version of the NEQ includes 14 items that are scored using a 5-point Likert scale as well as psychometric properties and scoring instructions (Allison et al., 2008). Because one item (#13) is used solely to rule out sleep-related eating disorder, total scores range from 0 to 52. A factor analysis of NEQ scores identified four factors (i.e., nocturnal ingestion, evening hyperphagia, morning anorexia, and mood/sleep) whose covariation was explained by a single higher-order factor, supporting the use of the NEQ total score. Total scores on the NEQ have demonstrated both internal consistency ($\alpha = .70$) and convergent validity. The NEQ has been validated in bariatric surgery patients; specifically, bariatric surgery candidates diagnosed with NES were found to score higher on the NEQ than bariatric surgery candidates without NES. The authors of the instrument do not recommend using the NEQ to diagnose individuals with NES; rather, they suggest using the NEQ as a screening instrument with a score of 30 as the cutoff in bariatric surgery candidates. The Night Eating Syndrome History and Inventory (NESHI) (unpublished interview available from Allison by request) is a structured interview that includes items from the NEQ as well as items to assess distress, impairment in functioning, course of NES, and the relationship between NES and dieting/weight history. The psychometric properties of the NESHI have not been evaluated with bariatric surgery candidates.

Body Image

Body image is a multidimensional construct that incorporates various aspects of cognitive, emotional, and behavioral components (Thompson, 2004). For example, body image assessment can examine the subjective appraisal of overall weight and shape or specific body parts, the accuracy of visual perception of body size and shape, the frequency of body checking or body avoidance behaviors, and the extent to which weight and shape dominate the individual's self-evaluation (see comprehensive review by Thompson, Roehrig, Cafri, & Heinberg, 2005).

The Body Shape Questionnaire (BSQ) (Cooper et al., 1987) is a 34-item measure of body dissatisfaction and distress that is easy to administer and score and provides an overall subjective measure. In addition, several studies have provided support for the reliability and validity of the BSQ (e.g., Rosen, Jones, Ramirez, & Waxman, 1996). The Multidimensional Body–Self Relations Questionnaire (MBSRQ) (Brown, Cash, & Mikulka, 1990) is a comprehensive body image measure with 69 items that assesses subjective appraisal and degree of importance of health, illness, appearance, and physical fitness. The Weight Concern and Shape Concern subscales of the EDE and EDE-Q are widely used measures that incorporate attitudinal and behavioral components, although they have not been utilized frequently with bariatric surgery patients.

Psychopathology

Comprehensive Assessment

The Structured Clinical Interview for DSM-IV (SCID-I) (First et al., 2001) is a semistructured interview that assesses DSM-IV Axis I disorders (a separate version of the SCID assesses Axis II psychopathology). Widely used to assess psychopathology including mood, anxiety, substance use, and eating disorders, the SCID has been administered to bariatric surgery patients in several studies that demonstrated high rates of co-occurring psychiatric diagnoses (Muhlhans, Horbach, & de Zwaan, 2009; Kalarchian et al., 2007; Rosenberger, Henderson, & Grilo, 2006). The SCID is a diagnostic measure that allows the interviewer to determine whether the patient has ever met criteria for a disorder (i.e., lifetime diagnosis) and whether the patient has the diagnosis at the present time (i.e., current diagnosis). A number of studies have found evidence to support the reliability and validity of the SCID (e.g., Zanarini et al., 2000).

Two studies have examined the congruence between the SCID and unstructured clinical interviews in presurgical bariatric patients (Mitchell et al., 2010; Schlick et al., 2010). These studies found considerable variability between these two interview techniques. Specifically, the SCID-I yielded more Axis I diagnoses than the unstructured interview (Schlick et al., 2010). In general, better agreement was observed for lifetime than current diagnoses (e.g., kappa for lifetime mood disorder = .45) (Mitchell et al., 2010) with poor agreement between measures in both studies for anxiety and eating disorders. These studies provide preliminary support for the utility of the SCID over unstructured interviews in determining psychiatric diagnoses in presurgical bariatric patients.

Depression

Several studies have observed elevated rates of depression and mood disorders in bariatric surgery samples (Muhlhans et al., 2009; Kalarchian et al., 2007; Rosenberger et al., 2006; Wadden et al., 2007), and untreated depression might be a reason for denial of surgery (Walfish, Vance, & Fabricatore, 2007). A number of interviews and questionnaires can be used to assess depressive symptoms in terms of severity as well as determine whether a patient meets diagnostic criteria for a mood disorder. In addition to the SCID-I (described above), the Hamilton Depression Rating Scale (HDRS) (Hamilton, 1960) is a structured interview that has been used to assess depression in bariatric surgery patients (Mauri et al., 2008). Although its use in bariatric surgery samples has been limited, the Montgomery-Asberg Rating Scale for Depression (MADRS) (Montgomery & Asberg, 1979) is another interview-based measure that can be used to assess severity of depression. Among questionnaires, the most frequently used measure of depressive symptoms severity is the Beck Depression Inventory (BDI) (Beck, Ward, Mendelson, Mock, & Erbaugh, 1961), a 21-item instrument that includes items about mood, suicidal ideation, cognition, and physical symptoms. One of the most widely used instruments in the psychiatric field, the BDI has extensive reliability and validity data (Beck, Steer, & Garbin, 1988). Krukowski et al. (2010) recently found that the BDI was an effective screening measure for bariatric surgery candidates, including those reporting chronic pain. The Inventory of Depressive Symptomatology–Self Report (IDS-SR) (Rush et al., 1986) is a 30-item measure of psychological and physical symptoms of depression. Although it has only been used in a limited number of studies with bariatric surgery samples (e.g., de Zwaan et al., 2003), the IDS-SR has extensive psychometric data supporting its use (e.g., Rush et al., 1986, 1996). Similarly, the Zung Self-Rating Depression Scale (Zung, 1965), a frequency and severity measure of depression, and the Inventory to Diagnose Depression (Zimmerman & Coryell, 1987), a diagnostic and severity measure, are supported by reliability and validity data but have not been widely used in bariatric surgery assessment. The primary limitation of using these measures of depression in obesity samples in general and bariatric surgery populations in particular is the risk of inflated scores due to high rates of somatic symptoms. As described below, the Hospital Anxiety and Depression Scale (HADS) (Zigmond & Snaith, 1983) can be used as an alternative measure of depression to reduce the risk of false positive depression scores due to physical complaints.

Anxiety

There are many instruments available for assessing anxiety, some of which focus on symptoms of specific anxiety disorders (e.g., social phobia), whereas others are broader in scope and ask about anxiety in general. Two of the most commonly used instruments can be used to measure the severity of global anxiety symptoms. The Hamilton Anxiety Rating Scale (HAM-A) (Hamilton, 1959, 1969) contains 14 items that measure affective (e.g., fears), cognitive (e.g., difficulty concentrating), somatic (e.g., gastrointestinal problems), and behavioral (e.g., psychomotor agitation) symptoms of anxiety. Items are rated by an interviewer on a 5-point Likert scale ranging from 0 to 4, with higher scores indicating more severe symptoms. Though the original version of the HAM-A did not include standardized interview questions, several structured interviews have been developed to enhance the interrater reliability of the measure (Bruss, Gruenberg, Goldstein, & Barber, 1994; Shear et al., 2001). The Beck Anxiety Inventory (BAI) (Beck, Epstein, Brown, & Steer, 1988) is a self-report questionnaire that measures the extent to which respondents have been bothered by 21 symptoms of anxiety. Respondents rate each symptom on a 4-point Likert scale from 0 to 3, with higher scores indicating more severe pathology. It is worth noting that several items on the HAM-A and BAI assess somatic symptoms of anxiety that may be confounded by the physical complications of obesity and bariatric surgery (e.g., gastrointestinal discomfort, insomnia, excessive sweating). Thus, clinicians working with bariatric surgery patients may choose to use the HADS (Zigmond & Snaith, 1983) as an alternative to the HAM-A and BAI because it focuses on the cognitive and affective symptoms of anxiety and depression. The HADS, a self-report questionnaire, includes 14 items that ask respondents to rate symptoms of anxiety and depression on a 4-point Likert scale from 0 to 3. Half the items assess anxiety symptoms and half assess depressive symptoms; thus, the HADS can be used to assess either anxiety or depression, or both. Although the HAM-A, BAI, and HADS are useful as dimensional assessments of symptom severity, a clinical interview should be used to diagnose anxiety disorders because these instruments are not intended for diagnostic purposes.

Substance Use

Several screening instruments exist to identify individuals with substance use disorders, and although a comprehensive review of these instruments is beyond the scope of this chapter, this review is limited to a brief description of three commonly used screening tools. The CAGE Questionnaire (Ewing, 1984; Mayfield, McLeod, & Hall, 1974) is a screening test comprised of four questions related to the pathology of alcohol dependence: attempts at *cutting down*, feeling *annoyed* by criticism about drinking, feeling *guilty* about drinking, and using alcohol as an *eye-opener*. Each symptom is rated as present or absent, and the more symptoms endorsed, the greater the likelihood that the respondent suffers from alcohol dependence. The Michigan Alcohol Screening Test (MAST) (Selzer, 1971) and the Drug Abuse Screening Test (DAST) (Skinner, 1982) are screening tools for alcohol and drug dependence, respectively. The MAST and the DAST contain 25 and 28 true-false questions that assess common symptoms and associated features of alcohol dependence (e.g., "Do you ever drink before noon?" "Have you ever been told you have liver trouble?") and drug dependence (e.g., "Have you abused prescription drugs?" "Have you ever lost a job because of drug abuse?"), respectively. Like the CAGE questionnaire, higher scores on the MAST and the DAST indicate a higher probability of alcohol and drug dependence. It is important to note that none of these assessments are designed to diagnose substance use disorders, and positive screening results should be followed by a comprehensive unstructured clinical interview or the substance use disorder section of the SCID.

Personality and Personality Disorders

Minnesota Multiphasic Personality Inventory-2 The Minnesota Multiphasic Personality Inventory-2 (MMPI-2) (Butcher, Dahlstrom, Graham, Tellegen, & Kaemmer, 1989) is a 567-item self-report questionnaire used to assess dimensions of personality and symptoms of psychopathology. The MMPI-2 is one of the most researched psychological assessment tools; however, it requires approximately one to two hours to administer, extensive training to interpret, and because it is copyrighted, clinicians must pay to use the instrument. When used with bariatric surgery candidates, the restructured clinical scales of the MMPI-2 have demonstrated better internal consistency, convergent validity, and discriminatory validity than the clinical scales (Wygant et al., 2007). However, research also illustrates that the validity scales, clinical scales, and content scales can identify bariatric surgery candidates who may be challenging to manage (Bannen et al., 2008) and those who are likely to lose more than 50% of their excess weight (Tsushima, Bridenstine, & Balfour, 2004).

Millon Clinical Multiaxial Inventory-3   The Millon Clinical Multiaxial Inventory-3 (MCMI-3) (Millon, 1994; Millon, Davis, & Millon, 1997) is a self-report questionnaire with 175 true–false items. The MCMI-3 includes 24 subscales (14 personality disorders, 10 clinical syndromes) and can be used to differentiate between personality style and more severe pathology. In addition, the MCMI-3 can be used both dimensionally and diagnostically and has empirical support of its reliability (Millon et al., 1997). When used in bariatric surgery samples, several of the MCMI-3 subscales (e.g., schizoid, schizotypical, compulsive) have been associated with poorer prognosis and binge eating (Belanger, Wechsler, Nademin, & Virden, 2010; Macias & Leal, 2003).

Impulsivity and Attention Deficit/Hyperactivity Disorder   Given that impulsivity and attention deficit/hyperactivity disorder (ADHD) have been associated with overweight and obesity (Fuemmeler, Ostbye, Yang, McClernon, & Kollins, 2010; Pagoto et al., 2009; Terracciano et al., 2009), clinicians may choose to assess for impulsivity, hyperactivity, and attentional problems among bariatric surgery patients. The 11th version of the Barratt Impulsiveness Scale (BIS-11) (Patton, Stanford, & Barratt, 1995) is a 30-item self-report questionnaire that measures global impulsivity as well as three subtraits of impulsivity: attentional impulsiveness, motor impulsiveness, and nonplanning impulsiveness. Items are scored on a 4-point Likert scale with higher scores indicating higher levels of impulsivity. ADHD can also be assessed using measures including the Adult ADHD Clinical Diagnostic Scale (Adler & Cohen, 2004; Adler & Spencer, 2004) and the ADHD Rating Scale (DuPaul, Power, Anastopoulous, & Reid, 1998). Although these measures may be useful clinically, their psychometric properties have not been examined in bariatric surgery samples.

Psychosocial Variables

Quality of Life

Impact of Weight on Quality of Life–Lite   The Impact of Weight on Quality of Life–Lite (IWQOL-Lite) (Kolotkin, Crosby, Kosloski, & Williams, 2001) is a 31-item self-report questionnaire that measures the extent to which obesity impairs five areas of psychosocial functioning: physical function, self-esteem, sexual life, public distress, and work. Respondents are asked to rate the accuracy of 31 statements on a 5-point Likert scale from "never true" to "always true." Scores on the IWQOL-Lite have demonstrated internal consistency and test-retest reliability, and research supports the construct validity of the measure (Kolotkin et al., 2001; Kolotkin & Crosby, 2002). Bariatric surgery candidates with comorbid BED report significantly more impairment in self-esteem, sexual life, and work functioning on the IWQOL-Lite than bariatric surgery candidates without comorbid BED (de Zwaan et al., 2003).

36-Item Short Form Health Survey   The 36-Item Short Form Health Survey (SF-36) (Ware & Sherbourne, 1992) is a self-report questionnaire that measures functioning across eight areas of physical and emotional health: physical functioning, social functioning, general physical health, general mental health, pain, vitality (i.e., energy, fatigue), role limitations related to physical problems, and role limitations related to emotional problems. Each item is rated on a 10-point Likert scale. The psychometric properties of the SF-36 have been evaluated in psychiatric populations but not in bariatric surgery candidates (McHorney, Ware, & Raczek, 1993; McHorney, Ware, Lu, & Sherbourne, 1994). However, bariatric surgery candidates with comorbid psychopathology report more severe impairments across all eight areas of functioning on the SF-36 than controls (Kalarchian et al., 2007).

Social Adjustment Scale–Self-Report   The Social Adjustment Scale–Self-Report (SAS-SR) (Weissman & Bothwell, 1976) is a 42-item self-report questionnaire that measures impairment in six areas of social functioning: work, social and leisure, extended family, marital, parental, and family unit. Items are scored on a 5-point Likert scale with higher scores indicating more severe impairment. Research on the psychometric properties of the SAS-SR support the reliability of SAS-SR scores as well as the validity of the instrument to measure social adjustment (Weissman & Bothwell, 1976; Weissman, Prusoff, Thompson, Harding, & Myers, 1978; Weissman, Olfson, Gameroff, Feder, & Fuentes, 2001). The psychometric properties of the SAS-SR have not been evaluated in a sample of bariatric surgery candidates, and because the instrument was developed for use with patients in their childbearing years, it may not be appropriate for older or younger patients (Weissman et al., 1978).

Bariatric Analysis and Reporting Outcome System   The Bariatric Analysis and Reporting Outcome System (BAROS) (Oria & Moorehead, 1998, 2009) is an instrument designed to measure the outcome of bariatric surgery in three domains: percentage of excess weight lost, changes in medical comorbidities, and quality of life. Percentage of excess weight lost and changes in medical complications are physician rated. Quality of life is measured using the Moorehead-Ardelt Quality of Life Questionnaire-II (Oria & Moorehead, 2009), a six-item questionnaire that assesses functioning in the following domains: self-esteem, physical, social, labor, sexual, and eating behavior. An overall outcome score for the BAROS is calculated by summing the ratings from the three domains and assigning the total score to one of five outcome categories, ranging from "failure" to "excellent."

Self-Esteem

Rosenberg Self-Esteem Scale   The Rosenberg Self-Esteem Scale (RSE) (Rosenberg, 1965) is a self-report questionnaire of general self-esteem. Participants are asked to indicate the extent to which 10 statements are true on a 4-point Likert scale ranging from "strongly agree" to "strongly disagree." Negatively valenced items are reverse scored. Research supports the test-retest reliability and the internal consistency of the RSE scores (Blascovich & Tomaka, 1993; Rosenberg, 1965). There are no published psychometric data on the RSE in bariatric surgery candidates; however, the measure has been used with this population. No differences in RSE scores were found between bariatric surgery candidates with and without comorbid BED (de Zwaan et al., 2003).

Motivation

University of Rhode Island Change Assessment   The University of Rhode Island Change Assessment (URICA) (DiClemente & Hughes, 1990) is a 32-item self-report questionnaire used to measure the extent to which an individual is ready to make changes in his or her life. Respondents are asked to rate the extent to which they agree with statements about problems they may be facing and their motivation to change (e.g., "I've been thinking that I might want to change something about myself"). Each statement is rated on a 5-point Likert scale ranging from "strongly disagree" to "strongly agree." The measure is theoretically based on Prochaska and DiClemente's stages of change model (Prochaska & DiClemente, 1983) and includes four subscales: Precontemplation, Contemplation, Action, and Maintenance. The psychometric properties of the URICA have been evaluated in community and psychiatric populations (e.g., DiClemente & Hughes, 1990; Dozois, Westra, Collins, Fung, & Garry, 2004); however, there is no published research on the reliability of the instrument in bariatric surgery candidates. In a study of bariatric surgery patients, baseline URICA scores did not predict either weight loss at 2-year follow up or the number of follow-up visits attended (Dixon et al., 2009).

Conclusion

Structured assessment methods including semi-structured interviews and questionnaires are valuable tools for bariatric surgery screening, evaluation, and prognosis. Used in the context of multidimensional assessment, these instruments provide empirically based and comprehensive data prior to and following surgery. Although a substantial amount of research supports the use of these measures in individuals with weight disorders, eating disorders, and psychiatric disorders, further investigations are needed to establish the reliability and validity of these instruments in bariatric surgery samples. To date, many of the studies using these measures in bariatric surgery samples are often preliminary in nature and inadequately powered. Perhaps one of the most problematic deficits is the limited use of psychosocial assessments in postoperative samples. Although there are exceptions (e.g., de Zwaan et al., 2010), the vast majority of psychosocial assessment studies have utilized preoperative surgery participants. The need for longitudinal psychosocial assessment, as well as the identification of reliable and valid measures for this type of research, is particularly notable. More research is also needed to increase self-report accuracy and minimize the impact of social desirability and symptom minimization in the bariatric surgery screening process (Fabricatore, Sarwer, Wadden, Combs, & Krasucki, 2007). In addition, future investigations are needed to identify ways that these measures can provide optimal utility (e.g., for screening, prognosis, and need for interventions) for clinicians working with bariatric surgery patients prior to and following surgery.

References

Adler, L., & Cohen, J. (2004). Diagnosis and evaluation of adults with attention deficit/hyperactivity disorder. *Psychiatric Clinics of North America, 27,* 187–201.

Adler, L., & Spencer, T. (2004). *The adult ADHD clinical diagnostic scale* (ACDS, version 1.2). New York: University School of Medicine.

Allison, D.B., Kalinsky, L.B., & Gorman, B.S. (1992). A comparison of the psychometric properties of three measures of dietary restraint. *Psychological Assessment, 4,* 391–398.

Allison, K.C., Lundgren, J.D., O'Reardon, J.P., Martino, N.S., Sarwer, D.B., Wadden, T.A. et al. (2008). The Night Eating Questionnaire (NEQ): Psychometric properties of a measure of severity of the night eating syndrome. *Eating Behaviors, 9,* 62–72.

Bannen, M.A., Lambert, P.J., Gustafson, H.L., Mathiason, M.A., Larson, C.J., & Kothari, S.N. (2008). Use of the Minnesota Multiphasic Personality Inventory-2 to identify challenging-to-manage bariatric patients: Efforts to promote success in all patients. *Bariatric Nursing and Surgical Patient Care, 3,* 211–216.

Bardone-Cone, A.M., & Boyd, C. A. (2007). Psychometric properties of eating disorder instruments in black and white young women: Internal consistency, temporal stability, and validity. *Psychological Assessment, 19*, 356–362.

Beck, A.T., Epstein, N., Brown, G., & Steer, R.A. (1988). An inventory for measuring clinical anxiety: Psychometric properties. *Journal of Consulting and Clinical Psychology, 56*, 893–897.

Beck, A.T., Steer, R.A., & Garbin, M.G. (1988). Psychometric properties of the Beck Depression Inventory: Twenty-five years of evaluation. *Clinical Psychology Review, 8*, 77–100.

Beck, A.T., Ward, C.H., Mendelson, M., Mock, J., & Erbaugh, J. (1961). An inventory for measuring depression. *Archives of General Psychiatry, 4*, 561–571.

Belanger, S.B., Wechsler, F.S., Nademin, M.E., & Virden, T.B. (2010). Predicting outcome of gastric bypass surgery utilizing personality scale elevations, psychosocial factors, and diagnostic group membership. *Obesity Surgery, 20*, 1361–1371.

Berg, K.C., Peterson, C.B., Frazier, P., & Crow, S.C. in press. Psychometric evaluation of the Eating Disorder Examination and Eating Disorder Examination-Questionnaire: A systematic review of the literature. *International Journal of Eating Disorders*.

Berg, K.C., Peterson, C.B., Frazier, P., & Crow, S.J. (2011) Convergence of scores on the interview and questionnaire versions of the Eating Disorder Examination: A meta-analytic review. *Psychological Assessment,* advance online puplication. doi: 10.105420023246.

Blackstone, R.P., Cortes, M.C., Messer, L.B., & Engstrom, D. (2010). Psychological classification as a communication and management tool in obese patients undergoing bariatric surgery. *Surgery for Obesity and Related Diseases, 6*, 274–281.

Blascovich, J., & Tomaka, J. (1993). Measures of self-esteem. In J.P. Robinson, P.R. Shaver, & L.S. Wrightsman (Eds.), *Measures of personality and social psychological attitudes* (3rd ed., pp. 115–160). Ann Arbor, MI: Institute for Social Research.

Block, G., Hartman, A.M., Dresser, C.M., Carroll, M.D., Gannon, J., & Gardner, L. (1986). A data-based approach to diet questionnaire design and testing. *American Journal of Epidemiology, 124*, 453–469.

Bond, D.S., Jackicic, J.M., Unick, J.L., Vithiananthan S., Pohl, D., Roye, G.D., (2010). Pre- to postoperative physical activity changes in bariatric surgery patients: Self report vs. objective measures. *Obesity, 18*, 2395–2397.

Bonevski, B., Campbell, E., & Sanson-Fisher, R.W. (2010). The validity and reliability of an interactive computer tobacco and alcohol use survey in general practice. *Addictive Behaviors, 35*, 492–498.

Brown, T.A., Cash, T.F., & Mikulka, P.J. (1990). Attitudinal body-image assessment: Factor analysis of the Body–Self Relations Questionnaire. *Journal of Personality Assessment, 55*, 135–144.

Bruss, G.S., Gruenberg, A.M., Goldstein, R.D., & Barber, J.P. (1994). Hamilton anxiety rating scale interview guide: Joint interview and test-retest methods for interrater reliability. *Psychiatric Research, 53*, 191–202.

Butcher, J.N., Dahlstrom, W.G., Graham, J.R., Tellegen, A., & Kaemmer, B. (1989). The Minnesota Multiphasic Personality Inventory-2 (MMPI-2): Manual for administration and scoring. Minneapolis: University of Minnesota Press.

Casey, P.H., Goolsby, S.L., Lensing, S.Y., Perloff, B.P., & Bogle, M.L. (1999). The use of telephone interview methodology to obtain 24-hour dietary recalls. *Journal of the American Dietetic Association, 99*, 1406–1411.

Celio, A.A., Wilfley, D.E., Crow, S.J., Mitchell, J., & Walsh, B.T. (2004). A comparison of the Binge Eating Scale, Questionnaire for Eating and Weight Patterns-Revised, and Eating Disorder Examination Questionnaire with instructions with the Eating Disorder Examination in the assessment of binge eating disorder and its symptoms. *International Journal of Eating Disorders, 36*, 434–444.

Cooper, P.J., Taylor, M.J., Cooper, Z., & Fairburn, C.G. (1987). The development and validation of the Body Shape Questionnaire. *International Journal of Eating Disorders, 6*, 485–494.

de Zwaan, M., Hilbert, A., Swan Kremeier, L., Simonich, H., Lancaster, K., Howell, L.M. et al. (2010). Comprehensive interview assessment of eating behavior 18–35 months after gastric bypass surgery for morbid obesity. *Surgery for Obesity and Related Diseases, 6*, 79–85.

de Zwaan, M., Mitchell, J.E., Howell, L. M., Monson, N., Swan-Kremeier, L., Crosby, R.D. et al. (2003). Characteristics of morbidly obese patients before gastric bypass surgery. *Comprehensive Psychiatry, 44*, 428–434.

de Zwaan, M., Mitchell, J.E., Specker, S.M., Pyle, R.L., Mussell, M.P., & Seim, H.C. (1993). Diagnosing binge eating disorder: Level of agreement between self-report and expert-rating. *International Journal of Eating Disorders, 14*, 289–295.

DiClemente, C.C., & Hughes, S.O. (1990). Stages of change profiles in outpatient alcoholism treatment. *Journal of Substance Abuse, 2*, 217–235.

Dixon, J.B., Laurie, C.P., Anderson, M.L., Hayden, M.J., Dixon, M.E., & O'Brien, P.E. (2009). Motivation, readiness to change, and weight loss following adjustable gastric band surgery. *Obesity, 17*, 698–705.

Dozois, D.J.A., Westra, H.A., Collins, K.A., Fung, T.S., & Garry, J.K.F. (2004). Stages of change in anxiety: Psychometric properties of the University of Rhode Island Change Assessment (URICA) scale. *Behavior Research and Therapy, 42*, 711–729.

DuPaul, G.J., Power, T.J., Anastopoulous, A.D., & Reid, R. (1998). *ADHD Rating Scale-IV: Checklists, norms, and clinical interpretations.* New York: Guilford.

Elder, K.A., Grilo, C.M., Masheb, R.M., Rothschild, B.S., Burke-Martindale, C.H., & Brody, M.L. (2006). Comparison of two self-report instruments for assessing binge eating in bariatric surgery candidates. *Behaviour Research and Therapy, 44*, 545–560.

Ewing, J.A. (1984). Detecting alcoholism: The CAGE questionnaire. *Journal of the American Medical Association, 252*, 1905–1907.

Fabricatore, A.N., Crerand, C.E., Wadden, T.A., Sarwer, D.B., & Krasucki, J.L. (2006). How do mental health professionals evaluate candidates for bariatric surgery? Survey results. *Obesity Surgery, 16*, 567–573.

Fabricatore, A.N., Sarwer, D.B., Wadden, T.A., Combs, C.J., & Krasucki, J.L. (2007). Impression management or real change? Reports of depressive symptoms before and after the preoperative psychological evaluation for bariatric surgery. *Obesity Surgery, 17*, 1213–1219.

Fairburn, C.G., & Beglin, S.J. (1994). Assessment of eating disorders: Interview or self-report questionnaire? *International Journal of Eating Disorders, 16,* 363–370.

Fairburn, C.G., & Beglin, S. (2008). Eating disorder examination questionnaire. In C.G. Fairburn (Ed.), *Cognitive behavior therapy and eating disorders* (pp. 309–314). New York: Guilford Press.

Fairburn, C.G., & Cooper, Z. (1993). The Eating Disorder Examination (12th edition). In C.G. Fairburn & G.T. Wilson (Eds.), *Binge eating: Nature, assessment, and treatment* (pp. 317–360). New York: Guilford Press.

Fairburn, C.G., Cooper, Z., & O'Connor, M. (2008). Eating disorder examination, edition 16.0D. In C.G. Fairburn (Ed.), *Cognitive behavior therapy and eating disorders* (pp. 265–308). New York: Guilford Press.

Feskanich, D., Buzzard, I., Welch, B., Asp, E.H., Dielman, L.S., Chong, K.R. et al. (1988). Comparison of a computerized and manual method of food coding for nutrient intake studies. *Journal of the American Dietetic Association, 88,* 1263–1267.

Feskanich, D., Rimm, E.B., Giovannucci, E.L, Colditz, G.A., Stampfer, M.J., Litin, L.B. et al. (1993). Reproducibility and validity of food intake measurements from a semiquantitative food frequency questionnaire. *Journal of the American Dietetic Association, 93,* 790–796.

First, M.B., Spitzer, R.L., Gibbon, M., & Williams, J.B.W. (2001). *Structured Clinical Interview for DSM-IV-TR Axis I Disorders-Patient Edition (SCID-I/P).* New York: Biometrics Research, New York State Psychiatric Institute.

Freitas, S.R., Lopes, C.S., Appolinario, J.C., & Coutinho, W. (2006). The assessment of binge eating disorder in obese women: A comparison of the binge eating scale with the structured clinical interview for the DSM-IV. *Eating Behaviors, 7,* 282–289.

French, S.A., Jeffrey, R.W., & Wing, R.R. (1994). Food intake and physical activity: A comparison of three measures of dieting. *Addictive Behaviors, 19,* 401–409.

Fuemmeler, B.F., Ostbye, T., Yang, C., McClernon, F.J., & Kollins, S.H. (2010). Association between attention deficit/hyperactivity disorder symptoms and obesity and hypertension in early adulthood: A population-based study. *International Journal of Obesity, 35,* 852–862.

Ganley, R.M. (1988). Emotional eating and how it relates to dietary restraint, disinhibition, and perceived hunger. *International Journal of Eating Disorders, 7,* 635–647.

Gionet, N.J., & Godin, G. (1989). Self-reported exercise behavior of employees: A validity study. *Journal of Occupational Medicine, 31,* 969–973.

Gladis, M.M., Wadden, T.A., Foster, G.D., Vogt, R.A., & Wingate, B.J. (1998). A comparison of two approaches to the assessment of binge eating in obesity. *International Journal of Eating Disorders, 23,* 17–26.

Godin, G., Jobin, J., & Boullon, J. (1986). Assessment of leisure exercise behavior by self-report: A concurrent validity study. *Canadian Journal of Public Health, 77,* 359–362.

Godin, G., & Shephard, R.A. (1985). A simple method to assess exercise behavior in the community. *Canadian Journal of Applied Sport Science, 10,* 141–146.

Gormally, J., Black, S., Daston, S., & Rardin, D. (1982). The assessment of binge eating severity among obese persons. *Addictive Behaviors, 7,* 47–55.

Greeno, C.G., Marcus, M.D., & Wing, R.R. (1995). Diagnosis of binge eating disorder: Discrepancies between a questionnaire and clinical interview. *International Journal of Eating Disorders, 17*, 153–160.

Hamilton, M. (1959). The assessment of anxiety states by rating. *British Journal of Medical Psychology, 32*, 50–55.

Hamilton, M. (1960). A rating scale for depression. *Journal of Neurology, Neurosurgery, and Psychiatry, 23*, 56–62.

Hamilton, M. (1969). Diagnosis and rating of anxiety. *British Journal of Psychiatry Special Publication, 3*, 76–79.

Hyland, M.E., Irvine, S.H., Thacker, C., Dann, P.L., & Dennis, I. (1989). Psychometric analysis of the Stunkard-Messick Eating Questionnaire (SMEQ) and comparison with the Dutch Eating Behavior Questionnaire (DEBQ). *Current Psychology: Research and Reviews, 8*, 228–233.

Kalarchian, M.A., Marcus, M.D., & Courcoulas, A.P. (2010). Eating problems and bariatric surgery. In C.M. Grilo & J.E. Mitchell (Eds.), *The treatment of eating disorders: A clinical handbook* (pp. 437–446). New York: Guilford.

Kalarchian, M.A., Marcus, M.D., Levine, M.D., Courcoulas, A.P., Pilkonis, P.A., Ringham, R.M. et al. (2007). Psychiatric disorders among bariatric surgery candidates: Relationship to obesity and functional health status. *American Journal of Psychiatry, 164*, 328–334.

Kalarchian, M.A., Wilson, G.T., Brolin, R.E., & Bradley, L. (1998). Binge eating in bariatric surgery patients. *International Journal of Eating Disorders, 23*, 89–92.

Karlsson, J., Persson, L.O., Sjostrom, L., & Sullivan, M. (2000). Psychometric properties and factor structure of the Three-Factor Eating Questionnaire (TFEQ) in obese men and women. Results from the Swedish Obese Subjects (SOS) study. *International Journal of Obesity, 24*, 1715–1725.

Keel, P.K., Crow, S.J., Davis, T.L., & Mitchell, J.E. (2002). Assessment of eating disorders: Comparison of interview and questionnaire data from a long-term follow-up study of bulimia nervosa. *Journal of Psychosomatic Research, 53*, 1043–1047.

Kolotkin, R.L., & Crosby, R.D. (2002). Psychometric evaluation of the Impact of Weight on Quality of Life–Lite questionnaire (IWQOL-Lite) in a community sample. *Quality of Life Research, 11*, 157–171.

Kolotkin, R.L., Crosby, R.D., Kosloski, K.D., & Williams, G.R. (2001). Development of a brief measure to assess quality of life in obesity. *Obesity Research, 9*, 102–111.

Krukowski, R.A., Friedman, K.E., & Applegate, K.L. (2010). The utility of the Beck Depression Inventory in a bariatric surgery population. *Obesity Surgery, 20*, 426–431.

Laessle, R.G., Tuschl, R.J., Kotthaus, B.C., & Pirke, K.M. (1989). A comparison of the validity of three scales for the assessment of dietary restraint. *Journal of Abnormal Psychology, 98*, 504–507.

Lavender, J.M., & Anderson, D.A. (2009). Effect of perceived anonymity in assessments of eating disordered behaviors and attitudes. *International Journal of Eating Disorders, 42*, 546–551.

Macias, J.A.G., & Leal, F.J.V. (2003). Psychopathological differences between morbidly obese binge eaters and non-binge eaters after bariatric surgery. *Eating and Weight Disorders, 8*, 315–318.

Mauri, M., Rucci, P., Calderone, A., Santini, F., Oppo, A., Romano, A. et al. (2008). Axis I and II disorders and quality of life in bariatric surgery candidates. *Journal of Clinical Psychiatry*, *69*, 295–301.

Mayfield, D., McLeod, G., & Hall, P. (1974). The CAGE questionnaire: Validation of a new alcoholism screening instrument. *American Journal of Psychiatry*, *131*, 1121–1123.

Mazzeo, S.E., Aggen, S.H., Anderson, C., Tozzi, F., & Bulik, C.M. (2003). Investigating the structure of the eating inventory (Three-Factor Eating Questionnaire): A confirmatory approach. *International Journal of Eating Disorders*, *34*, 255–264.

McHorney, C.A., Ware, J.E., Lu, J.F.R., & Sherbourne, C.D. (1994). The MOS 36-Item Short-Form Health Survey (SF-36). III. Tests of data quality, scaling assumptions, and reliability across diverse patient groups. *Medical Care*, *32*, 40–66.

McHorney, C.A., Ware, J.E., & Raczek, A.E. (1993). The MOS 36-Item Short-Form Health Survey (SF-36). II. Psychometric and clinical tests of validity in measuring physical and mental health constructs. *Medical Care*, *31*, 247–263.

Millon, T. (1994). *Millon Clinical Multiaxial Inventory-III*. Minneapolis: National Computer Systems.

Millon, T., Davis, R., & Millon, C. (1997). *MCMI-III Manual* (2nd ed.). Minneapolis: National Computer Systems.

Mitchell, J.E. (2005). A standardized database. In J.E. Mitchell & C.B. Peterson (Eds.), *Assessment of eating disorders* (pp. 59–78). New York: Guilford Press.

Mitchell, J.E., Hatsukami, D., Eckert, E.D., & Pyle, R.L. (1985). The Eating Disorders Questionnaire. *Psychopharmacology Bulletin*, *21*, 1025–1043.

Mitchell, J.E., Steffen, K.J., de Zwaan, M., Ertelt, T.W., Marino, J.M., & Mueller, A. (2010). Congruence between clinical and research-based psychiatric assessment in bariatric surgical candidates. *Surgery for Obesity and Related Disorders*, *6*, 628–634.

Montgomery, S.A., & Asberg, M.C. (1979). A new depression scale designed to be sensitive to change. *British Journal of Psychiatry*, *134*, 382–389.

Muhlhans, B., Horbach, T., & de Zwaan, M. (2009). Psychiatric disorders in bariatric surgery candidates: A review of the literature and results of a German prebariatric surgery sample. *General Hospital Psychiatry*, *31*, 414–421.

Nangle, D.W., Johnson, W.G., Carr-Nangle, R.E., & Engler, L.B. (1994). Binge eating disorder and the proposed DSM-IV criteria: Psychometric analysis of the questionnaire of eating and weight patterns. *International Journal of Eating Disorders*, *16*, 147–157.

Oria, H.E., & Moorehead, M.K. (1998). Bariatric analysis and reporting outcome system (BAROS). *Obesity Surgery*, *8*, 487–499.

Oria, H.E., & Moorehead, M.K. (2009). Updated bariatric analysis and reporting outcome system (BAROS). *Surgery of Obesity and Related Diseases*, *5*, 60–66.

Pagoto, S. L, Curtin, C., Lemon, S.C., Bandini, L.G., Schneider, K.L., Bodenlos, J.S. et al. (2009). Association between adult attention deficit/hyperactivity disorder and obesity in the U.S. population. *Obesity*, *17*, 539–544.

Patton, J.H., Stanford, M.S., & Barratt, E.S. (1995). Factor structure of the Barratt Impulsiveness Scale. *Journal of Clinical Psychology*, *51*, 768–774.

Peterson, C.B. (2005). Conducting the diagnostic interview. In J.E. Mitchell & C.B. Peterson (Eds.), *Assessment of eating disorders* (pp. 32–58). New York: Guilford.

Peterson, C.B. (2010). Assessment of eating disorder treatment efficacy. In C.M. Grilo & J.E. Mitchell (Eds.), *The treatment of eating disorders: A clinical handbook* (pp. 524–534). New York: Guilford.

Prochaska, J.O., & DiClemente, C.C. (1983). Stages and processes of self-change of smoking: Toward an integrative model of change. *Journal of Consulting and Clinical Psychology, 51*, 390–395.

Pull, C.B. (2010). Current psychological assessment practices in obesity surgery programs: What to assess and why. *Current Opinions in Psychiatry, 23*, 30–36.

Rosen, J.C., Jones, A., Ramirez, E., & Waxman, S. (1996). Body Shape Questionnaire: Studies of validity and reliability. *International Journal of Eating Disorders, 20*, 315–319.

Rosenberg, M. (1965). *Society and the adolescent self-image.* Princeton, NJ: Princeton University Press.

Rosenberger, P.H., Henderson, K.E., & Grilo, C.M. (2006). Psychiatric disorder comorbidity and association with eating disorders in bariatric surgery patients: A cross-sectional study using structured interview-based diagnosis. *Journal of Clinical Psychiatry, 67*, 1080–1085.

Rush, A.J., Giles, D.E., Schlesser, M.A., Fulton, C.L., Weissenburger, J., & Burns, C. (1986). The Inventory for Depressive Symptomatology (IDS): Preliminary findings. *Psychiatry Research, 18*, 65–87.

Rush, A.J., Guillion, C.M., Basco, M.R., Jarrett, R.B., & Trivedi, M.H. (1996). The Inventory of Depressive Symptomatology (IDS): Psychometric properties. *Psychological Medicine, 26*, 477–486.

Schacter, D.L. (1999). The seven sins of memory: Insights from psychology and cognitive neuroscience. *American Psychologist, 54*, 182–203.

Schlick, A., Wagner, S.A., Muhlhans, B., Horbach, T., Muller, A., Mitchell, J.E. et al. (2010). Agreement between clinical evaluation and structured clinical interviews (SCID for DSM-IV) in morbidly obese pre-bariatric surgery patients. *Psychotherapy and Psychosomatics Medical Psychology, 60*, 469–473.

Selzer, M.L. (1971). The Michigan Alcoholism Screening Test: The quest for a new diagnostic instrument. *American Journal of Psychiatry, 127*, 1653–1658.

Shear, M.K., Vander Bilt, J., Rucci, P., Endicott, J., Lydiard, B., Otto, M.W. et al. (2001). Reliability and validity of a structured interview guide for the Hamilton Anxiety Rating Scale. *Depression and Anxiety, 13*, 166–178.

Shearin, E.N., Russ, M.J., Hull, J.W., Clarkin, J.F., & Smith, G.P. (1994). Construct validity of the Three-Factor Eating Questionnaire: Flexible and rigid control subscales. *International Journal of Eating Disorders, 16*, 187–198.

Skinner, H.A. (1982). The drug abuse screening test. *Addictive Behaviors, 7*, 363–371.

Spitzer, R.L., Devlin, M., Walsh, B.T., Hasin, D., Wing, R., Marcus, M. et al. (1992). Binge eating disorder: A multisite field trial of the diagnostic criteria. *International Journal of Eating Disorders, 11*, 191–203.

Spitzer, R.L., Yanovski, S., Wadden, T., Wing, R., Marcus, M.D., Stunkard, A. et al. (1993). Binge eating disorder: Its further validation in a multisite study. *International Journal of Eating Disorders, 13*, 137–153.

Stice, E., Fisher, M., & Lowe, M.R. (2004). Are dietary restraint scales valid measures of acute dietary restriction? Unobtrusive observational data suggest not. *Psychological Assessment, 16*, 51–59.

Stice, E., Fisher, M., & Martinez, E. (2004). Eating disorder diagnostic scale: Additional evidence of reliability and validity. *Psychological Assessment, 16,* 60–71.

Stice, E., Telch, C.F., & Rizvi, S.L. (2000). Development and validation of the eating disorder diagnostic scale: A brief self-report measure of anorexia, bulimia, and binge-eating disorder. *Psychological Assessment, 12*, 123–131.

Stunkard, A.J., Grace, W.J., & Wolff, H.G. (1955). The night-eating syndrome: A pattern of food intake among certain obese patients. *American Journal of Medicine, 19,* 78–86.

Stunkard, A.J., & Messick, S. (1985). The Three-Factor Eating Questionnaire to measure dietary restraint, disinhibition, and hunger. *Journal of Psychosomatic Research, 29,* 71–83.

Terracciano, A., Sutin, A.R., McCrae, R.R., Deiana, B., Ferrucci, L., Schlessinger, D. et al. (2009). Facets of personality linked to underweight and overweight. *Psychosomatic Medicine, 71*, 682–689.

Thompson, J.K. (2004). The (mis)measurement of body image: Ten strategies to improve assessment for applied and research purposes. *Body Image, 1*, 7–14.

Thompson, J.K., Roehrig, M., Cafri, G., & Heinberg, L.J. (2005). Assessment of body image disturbance. In J.E. Mitchell & C.B. Peterson (Eds.), *Assessment of eating disorders* (pp. 175–202). New York: Guilford.

Timmerman, G.M. (1999). Binge eating scale: Further assessment of validity and reliability. *Journal of Applied Biobehavioral Research, 4*, 1–12.

Tsushima, W., Bridenstine, M., & Balfour, J. (2004). MMPI-2 scores in the outcome prediction of gastric bypass surgery. *Obesity Surgery, 14*, 528–532.

van Strien, T., Frijters, J.E.R., Bergers, G.P.A., & Defares, P.B. (1986). The Dutch Eating Behavior Questionnaire (DEBQ) for assessment of restrained, emotional, and external eating behavior. *International Journal of Eating Disorders, 5*, 295–315.

Wadden, T.A., & Sarwer, D.B. (2006). Behavioral assessment of candidates for bariatric surgery: A patient-oriented approach. *Obesity, 14*, 53S-62S.

Wadden, T.A., Sarwer, D.B., Fabricatore, A.N., Jones, L., Stack, R., & Williams, N.S. (2007). Psychosocial and behavioral status of patients undergoing bariatric surgery: What to expect before and after surgery. *Medical Clinics of North America, 91*, 451–469.

Walfish, S., Vance, D., & Fabricatore, A.N. (2007). Psychological evaluation of bariatric surgery applicants: Procedures and reasons for delay or denial of surgery. *Obesity Surgery, 17*, 1587–1583.

Wardle, J. (1987). Eating style: A validation study of the Dutch Eating Behaviour Questionnaire in normal subjects and women with eating disorders. *Journal of Psychosomatic Research, 31*, 161–169.

Ware, J.E., & Sherbourne, C.D. (1992). The MOS 36-Item Short-Form Health Survey (SF-36). I. Conceptual framework and item selection. *Medical Care, 30*, 473–483.

Weissman, M.M., & Bothwell, S. (1976). Assessment of social adjustment by patient self-report. *Archives of General Psychiatry, 33*, 1111–1115.

Weissman, M.M., Olfson, M., Gameroff, M.J., Feder, A., & Fuentes, M. (2001). A comparison of three scales for assessing social functioning in primary care. *American Journal of Psychiatry, 158*, 460–466.

Weissman, M.M., Prusoff, B.A., Thompson, W.D., Harding, P.S., & Myers, J.K. (1978). Social adjustment by self-report in a community sample and in psychiatric outpatients. *Journal of Nervous and Mental Disease, 166*, 317–326.

Wilfley, D.E., Schwartz, M.B., Spurrell, E.B., & Fairburn, C.G. (2000). Using the eating disorder examination to identify the specific psychopathology of binge eating disorder. *International Journal of Eating Disorders, 27*, 259–269.

Williamson, D.A., Martin, C.K., York-Crowe, E., Anton, S.D., Redman, L.M., Han, H. et al. (2007). Measurement of dietary restraint: Validity tests of four questionnaires. *Appetite, 48*, 183–192.

Wilson, G.T. (1993). Assessment of binge eating. In C.G. Fairburn & G.T. Wilson (Eds.), *Binge eating: Nature, assessment, and treatment* (pp. 227–249). New York: Guilford Press.

Wygant, D.B., Boutacoff, L.I., Arbisi, P.A., Ben-Porath, Y.S., Kelly, P.H., & Rupp, W.M. (2007). Examination of the MMPI-2 restructured clinical (RC) scales in a sample of bariatric surgery candidates. *Journal of Clinical Psychology in Medical Settings, 14*, 197–205.

Zanarini, M.C., Skodol, A.E., Bender, D., Dolan, R., Sanislow, C., Schaefer, E., et al. (2000). The Collaborative Longitudinal Personality Disorders Study: Reliability of Axis I and II diagnoses. *Journal of Personality Disorders, 14*, 291–299.

Zigmond, A.S., & Snaith, R.P. (1983). The Hospital Anxiety and Depression Scale. *Acta Psychiatrica Scandinavica, 67*, 361–370.

Zimmerman, M., & Coryell, W. (1987). The Inventory to Diagnose Depression (IDD): A self-report scale to diagnose major depressive disorder. *Journal of Consulting and Clinical Psychology, 55*, 55–59.

Zung, W.W.K. (1965). A self-rating depression scale. *Archives of General Psychiatry, 12*, 63–70.

CHAPTER 4

Psychosocial Problems and Psychiatric Disorders Pre- and Postbariatric Surgery

TANJA LEGENBAUER, STEPHAN HERPERTZ, and MARTINA DE ZWAAN

As there are hardly any other effective weight control options for persons with extreme obesity (Sarwer, Wadden, & Fabricatore, 2005), bariatric surgery has become the treatment of choice for individuals with extreme obesity (defined as a BMI > 40 kg/m²) or those with less severe obesity accompanied by significant somatic comorbidities (Monteforte & Turkelson, 2000; National Task Force, 2000). With surgery, large weight losses can be achieved and maintained compared to modest and transient weight losses after dietary and behavioral treatment programs (Sarwer et al., 2005; Wadden et al., 2007). Besides the considerable weight loss and improvement of somatic comorbidities (Christou et al., 2004), there is general agreement that obesity surgery also helps to improve mental health, quality of life, and psychosocial functioning (Dixon, Dixon, & O'Brien, 2001, 2003; Herpertz et al., 2003; Karlsson, Sjöström, & Sullivan, 1998; de Zwaan, Lancaster, et al., 2002).

Nevertheless, there is a wide variability in weight loss after surgery (Kral, 1998; Legenbauer, Petrak, de Zwaan, & Herpertz, 2011; Sugerman et al., 1989; Wadden et al., 2007), and there is evidence that not only somatic and surgical factors predict the amount of weight loss, but also psychosocial and behavioral factors contribute to postoperative outcomes (Greenberg, Perna, Kaplan, & Sullivan, 2005; Hsu et al., 1998; Sarwer et al., 2005). Consequently, a better understanding of how psychosocial factors are

61

related to weight loss and other parameters of success following bariatric surgery is needed to improve outcome (Devlin, Goldfein, Flancbaum, Bessler, & Eisenstadt, 2004; Walfish, 2004).

In this chapter, psychosocial problems as well as the presence and course of psychiatric disorders in obese patients seeking bariatric surgery are described. Furthermore, the predictive value of psychosocial and psychological variables for weight loss following surgery and implications for presurgery evaluation and postsurgery support are discussed.

Psychosocial Problems

There are many reports on psychosocial functioning pre- and postbariatric surgery (Burgmer et al., 2007; Choban, Onyejekwe, Burge, & Flancbaum, 1999; de Zwaan, Lancaster et al., 2002; Dixon et al., 2001; Karlsson et al., 1998; Kolotkin et al., 2003; Schok et al., 2000) including meta-analyses (e.g., van Nunen, Wouters, Vingerhoets, Hox, & Geenen, 2007) and several reviews (e.g., Bocchieri, Meana, & Fisher, 2002; Herpertz et al., 2003; Herpertz, Kielmann, Wolf, Hebebrand, & Senf, 2004). It is generally agreed that obesity grade 3 (BMI > 40kg/m^2) is associated with social discrimination, lower educational achievement, lower income, and higher rates of unemployment (Willett, Dietz, & Colditz, 1999). The severely obese also experience stigmatization (Hayden, Dixon, Dixon, Playfair, & O'Brien, 2010), and report impaired health-related quality of life (Kolotkin et al., 2003; van Nunen et al., 2007).

Health-Related Quality of Life (HRQOL)

HRQOL encompasses physical activity and its limitations, physical functioning, pain, vitality, social life, mental health, and limitations due to a person's psychological state (Fontaine & Barofsky, 2001; Guyatt, Feeny, & Patrick, 1993; Wan, Counte, & Cella, 1997). HRQOL is determined not only by the patient's health status but also by the emotional response to these problems (Kamphuis et al., 2002). Hence, HRQOL refers to the effects of medical condition on physical, mental, and social functioning and well-being as subjectively evaluated and reported by the patient (de Zwaan, Mitchell et al., 2002).

HRQOL can be assessed with scales that measure HRQOL in a general way. These scales are widely used instruments. They are applicable to any population, and because population norms can be obtained, the relative burden of different conditions can be evaluated, and the longitudinal course can be assessed (de Zwaan, Mitchell et al., 2002; Fontaine, Cheskin, & Barofsky, 1996; Dixon et al., 2001). An example for such a scale is the Medical Outcomes Study Short-Form Health Survey (SF-36) (Ware, 1994, 1997). The SF-36 assesses various domains of physical and social functioning. Two aggregate summary measures reflect physical and mental/emotional well-being. Other common generic assessment tools are the Nottingham Health Profile (Hunt, McKenna, McEwen, Williams, & Papp, 1981) and the Sickness Impact Profile (Bergner, Bobbitt, Carter, & Gilson, 1981). However, generic HRQOL assessments may not be adequately sensitive to measure important changes following surgery (de Zwaan, Mitchell et al., 2002; Kolotkin et al., 2009). Therefore, disease-specific HRQOL instruments such as the Impact of Weight on Quality of Life Questionnaire (IWQOL) (Kolotkin, Head, Hamilton, & Tse, 1995; Kolotkin, Head, & Brookhart, 1997) or its shorter version, the IWQOL–Lite (Kolotkin, Crosby, Kosloski, & Williams, 2001; Kolotkin & Crosby, 2002; Kolotkin, Crosby, & Williams, 2002), were developed to assess clinically relevant obesity-specific aspects in various areas of functioning, for example, physical function, self-esteem, sexual life, public distress, and work. Other validated obesity-specific instruments are the Obesity Specific Quality of Life scale (OSQOL) (Le Pen, Levy, Loos, Banzet, & Basdevant, 1998), the Health Related Quality of Life scale (HRQL) (Mathias, Fifer, & Patrick, 1994; Mathias et al., 1997), the Obesity Related Well-Being scale (Orwell, 1997; Mannucci et al., 1999), and the Obesity Adjustment Survey (Butler et al., 1999). Surgeons often use the Bariatric Analysis and Reporting Outcome System (BAROS), which combines a surgery outcome measure with a short five-item non-validated QOL questionnaire (Oria & Moorehead, 1998).

Presurgery Status

Most studies investigating HRQOL in prebariatric surgery patients demonstrated HRQOL levels significantly lower than the corresponding national norms (Anandacoomarasamy et al., 2009; Choban et al., 1999; Dixon et al., 2001; Schok et al., 2000; Sullivan et al., 1993; van Nunen et al., 2007). There appears to be a negative association between HRQOL and level of obesity (Yancy, Olsen, Westman, Bosworth, & Edelman, 2002), with bariatric surgery patients exhibiting the most impaired HRQOL (Kolotkin et al., 2003). This trend was found for both generic (SF-36) and obesity-specific instruments (IWQOL) of HRQOL (de Zwaan, Mitchell et al., 2002; Kolotkin et al., 2009; van Nunen et al., 2007).

Using generic assessment tools (in particular the SF-36), various studies show that the impact of obesity is more pronounced on the physical domains of functioning and less on emotional domains (Dixon et al., 2001). De Zwaan and colleagues (2009) conducted a cross-sectional study with 640 men and women clustered into four BMI classes. Results showed an overall dose-response association between BMI and degree of physical

HRQOL impairment assessed with the SF-36; that is, the higher the BMI, the poorer the physical HRQOL. Moreover, a higher number of comorbid, chronic somatic illnesses was associated with higher impairment of physical HRQOL (de Zwaan et al., 2009).

Despite the fact that the emotional subscales of the SF-36 showed less impairment compared with the physical subscales (de Zwaan et al., 2002b; Dixon et al., 2001), there is also evidence that the mental component of HRQOL is significantly impaired (Kolotkin et al., 1995; Mathias et al., 1997; Roberts, Deleger, Strawbridge, & Kaplan, 2003), particularly in morbidly obese individuals (Onyike, Crum, Lee, Lyketsos, & Eaton, 2003). However, results are inconsistent. Several studies report lower mental HRQOL in extremely obese patients prior to surgery compared with U.S. norms, but there are also epidemiological and clinical studies describing mental HRQOL to be comparable in overweight and normal weight individuals (Doll, Petersen, & Stewart-Brown, 2000; Fontaine, Cheskin, & Barofsky, 1997; Friedman & Brownell, 1995). Because of these inconsistencies, several authors tried to identify variables that may moderate the relationship between mental HRQOL and obesity. One assumption was that other medical or mental comorbidities may moderate the impairment of mental HRQOL in obese individuals. One study demonstrated that the number of current mental and somatic disorders correlated significantly with the impairment of mental HRQOL, and a regression analysis including physical and mental health, age, and gender revealed that both mental and physical illness are independent negative predictors of mental HRQL (de Zwaan et al., 2009).

In relation to obesity-specific instruments, the IWQOL is most frequently used. In their meta-analysis, van Nunen and colleagues (2007) reported differences on the IWQOL between presurgery patients and other populations, such as obese conservative treatment-seeking samples, obese non-treatment-seeking samples, and the general population, with the presurgery population demonstrating the highest impairment in HRQOL. This is in line with other studies that consistently report significantly stronger impairment on IWQOL scales for presurgery patients than for non-treatment-seeking obese individuals or the general population (de Zwaan, Mitchell et al., 2002; Dymek, Le Grange, Neven, & Alverdy, 2002; Kolotkin et al., 2003).

In sum, the vast majority of studies report generic as well as obesity-specific impairments of HRQOL in various domains for morbidly obese patients representing for bariatric surgery.

Postsurgery Status

Many studies have demonstrated improvements in HRQOL after surgery (e.g., Andersen et al., 2010; Bocchieri et al., 2002; Burgmer et al., 2007;

Herpertz et al., 2003; Karlssoon et al., 1998; Nickel, Loew, & Bachler, 2007; van Nunen et al., 2007). There is evidence that significant changes in mental and physical HRQOL occur even before larger changes in BMI take place, and despite the fact that most individuals report surgery-related pain, fatigue, and functional limitations immediately following surgery. One explanation for this rapid improvement in HRQOL might be that surgery-related impairment is not disturbing enough to override the more positive overall health appraisal (Dymek, le Grange, Neven, & Alverdy, 2001). However, HRQOL continues to improve and remains stable long term (Andersen et al., 2010; Brancatisano, Wahlroos, & Brancatisano, 2008; Dixon et al., 2001; Dymek et al., 2001; Nguyen, Slone, Nguyen, Hartman, & Hoyt, 2009; Nickel et al., 2007). There is even evidence that the scores of some HRQOL subscales (e.g., social functioning, role activities, bodily pain, and vitality) exceed the normal population scores (Choban et al., 1999). Folope and colleagues showed that HRQOL gradually improved during the first 5 years and worsened thereafter; however, it remained better than before surgery (Folope et al., 2008). Improvements in HRQOL seem to be positively associated with the percentage of weight loss after surgery. Similar results were found in the Swedish Obese Subjects (SOS) Study: The authors reported improvements in HRQOL 10 years following surgery. These improvements were more pronounced than in a conventional treatment group (Karlsson, Taft, Rydén, Sjöström, & Sullivan, 2007). Improvements in HRQOL were associated with the magnitude of weight loss and weight regain was associated with a gradual decrease of HRQOL. A sustained improvement in HRQOL was particularly found in patients who maintained a weight loss of 10% over 10 years (Karlsson et al., 2007).

Improvements in HRQOL could be shown for both generic (SF-36) and obesity-specific instruments (IWQOL) (Kolotkin et al., 2009); however, greater improvements were found for the obesity-specific scale (IWQOL). Moreover, a closer association between the amount of weight loss and the IWQOL than the SF-36 was reported (Kolotkin et al., 2009). This is most likely due to the higher sensitivity for change of the IWQOL than for the SF-36 (Dymek et al., 2002).

In sum, successful weight reduction after bariatric surgery is associated with a long-lasting improvement of HRQOL in the majority of patients. Nevertheless, difficulties of some surgical patients to control and maintain the weight loss over time may result in decreased HRQOL after initial improvements.

Self-Esteem

It is broadly assumed that obesity has a negative impact on self-esteem (van Hout, Fortuin, Pelle, & van Heck, 2008). However, the relationship between obesity and self-esteem is not necessarily unidirectional. Weight-based stigmatization might contribute to lower self-esteem (Hayden et al., 2010; Myers & Rosen, 1999). However, it is also possible that poor self-esteem might contribute to obesity; for example, as a response to feelings of inadequacy, disturbed eating behaviors may evolve (van Hout, Fortuin, Pelle, Blokland-Koomen, & van Heck, 2009).

One of the most frequently used assessment tools for measuring self-esteem is the Rosenberg Self-Esteem Scale (RSES) (Rosenberg, 1965). The RSES was originally developed to measure global feelings of self-worth or self-acceptance, and is considered the standard against which other measures of self-esteem are compared. It includes 10 items that are aggregated into two subscales depicting a positive and a negative dimension (Blascovich & Tomaka, 1991). Similar psychological constructs such as self-confidence, self-image, self-consciousness about appearance, liking oneself, and self-(dis)satisfaction have been investigated by various authors (Chandarana, Conlon, Holliday, Deslippe, & Field, 1990; Hawke et al., 1990; Kinzl et al., 2001; Larsen & Torgersen, 1989; van Gemert, Severeijns, Greve, Groenman, & Soeters, 1998).

Presurgery Status

There are several studies showing low levels of self-esteem in extremely obese patients (Osei-Assibey, Kyrou, Kumar, Saravanan, & Matyka, 2010; van Hout et al., 2008) compared to less obese individuals (Wadden et al., 2006). This association is particularly strong in women (Kinzl et al., 2007; Wadden et al., 2006).

Postsurgery Assessment

Burgmer and colleagues (2007) investigated 149 patients 1 and 2 years postsurgery. The authors report a considerable improvement in self-esteem during the first year after surgery, but no further significant changes during the second year. This is in line with other studies that report short-term improvements in self-esteem (Dymek et al., 2001, 2002; Guisado et al., 2002). A study by Larsen and colleagues (Larsen et al., 2004) concluded that greater weight loss was positively correlated with increased self-esteem. There are only a few studies providing evidence about long-term effects of weight loss on changes in self-esteem. For example, a longitudinal prospective study with a small sample of 50 obesity surgery patients showed improvements in perceived attractiveness as well as self-worth during the first year and the following four years despite tapering weight loss. In subjects who achieved and maintained a BMI below 30 kg/m^2 5 years after surgery, scores even improved to values of normal weight individuals (Mathus-Vliegen & de Wit, 2007). It is assumed that improvement in self-esteem may be related to the amount of weight loss and the growing satisfaction of the patients (Frigg, Peterli, Peters, Ackermann, & Tondelli, 2004; Guisado et al., 2002).

However, there is also evidence that improvements in self-esteem might wane over time (van Hout et al., 2008). Some studies suggest that despite substantial decreases in psychopathology, personality pathology is largely unchanged (Larsen et al., 2003), and no significant changes are found in self-esteem (Gentry, Halverson, & Heisler, 1984). Findings of Legenbauer and Herpertz (unpublished data) support this finding. In a sample of 151 obese patients who underwent bariatric surgery with adjustable gastric banding or vertical gastroplasty, intention to treat analyses showed that a significant increase in self-esteem 1 year after surgery; however, this improvement was not evident 4 years after surgery.

In sum, research widely supports impaired self-esteem in extremely obese patients prior to surgery and positive changes in self-esteem following surgery within the first year. Results regarding the long-term changes in self-esteem are conflicting, and decreases in self-esteem may be associated with weight regain or dissatisfaction with surgery outcome.

Partnership and Sexuality

Despite the assumed influence of weight loss on sexuality and marital satisfaction, studies specifically investigating these topics are rare (Bocchieri et al., 2002). Most studies use single-item instruments to assess marital adjustment and sexual activities (e.g., Chandarana et al., 1990; Dubovsy, Haddenhorst, Murphy, Liechty, & Coyle, 1985; Hafner, Rogers, & Watts, 1990; Issacson, Frederiksen, Nilsson, & Hedenbro, 1997). Overall, results are limited due to small samples and lack of control groups (Sarwer et al., 2005) as well as failure to use valid and reliable measures of marital satisfaction, and sexual functioning such as the Dyadic Adjustment Scale or the Female Sexual Function Index.

Presurgery Status

Surgery patients frequently report unsatisfactory marital relationships and difficulties with sexual functioning (Camps, Zervos, Goode, & Rosemurgy, 1996; Hafner et al., 1990; Rand, Kuldau, & Robbins, 1982). However, there is also evidence that many morbidly obese individuals are satisfied with their relationships before surgery (Chandarana et al., 1990; Hawke et al., 1990; Larsen, 1990).

Postsurgery Status

Studies assessing changes in marital satisfaction and sexual functioning following surgery mostly show improvements in both areas (Bocchieri et al., 2002; Goble, Rand, & Kuldau, 1986; Herpertz et al., 2003; Rand,

Kowalske, & Kuldau, 1984; Sarwer et al., 2005). For example, Chandarana et al. (1990) found that 77% of their sample reported improved sexual activity following surgery. Isacsson, Frederiksen, Nilsson, and Hedenbro (1997) reported overall postoperative improvements concerning the quality of sexual activities and partnership. However, in terms of marital quality, results are mixed: Andersen et al. (2010) found a higher number of obese individuals after duodenal switch living in a partnership 6 years following surgery compared to their marital status prior to surgery. Hafner et al. (1990) assessed marital quality with the Marital Attitudes Questionnaire (MATE) and found only one significant postoperative change indicating a decrease in the Affection Feeling/Behavior Scale of the measure. The authors interpret this to suggest that husbands may have problems adapting to their wives' new self-confidence after surgery. The wives rated themselves as significantly more attractive and sociable, whereas their husbands were judged as being less sociable and interesting, than before surgery. One study even reported higher divorce rates after surgery (Rand et al., 1982), which was most likely due to dysfunction present in the marriages prior to surgery (Stunkard, Stinnett, & Smoller, 1986).

In summary, it is difficult to come to conclusions in terms of the relation between marital adjustment and changes following bariatric surgery, as evidence is conflicting and shows methodological limitations.

Employment, Sick Leave, and Disability Pension

As morbid obesity is associated with physical impairment and sometimes with serious medical illnesses such as diabetes and cardiovascular diseases (Brancatisano et al., 2008; Rydén & Torgerson, 2006), individuals suffering from obesity grade 3 are frequently impaired in their occupational functioning. Moreover, discrimination and weight-related stigmatization is associated with more difficulties at the workplace or with regard to job opportunities (Hayden et al., 2010). Consequently, employment and occupational functioning are important psychosocial variables that need to be considered when outcome after weight loss treatment is evaluated.

Presurgery Status

Cross-sectional analyses of obese individuals seeking surgery showed that sick leave during a period of one year was 1.5 to 1.9 times higher than that of the general population (Karlsson et al., 1998), independent of age and gender (Narbro et al., 1996, 1999). Moreover, the number of obese persons receiving disability pension was about twice as frequent as in the general Swedish population (Karlsson et al., 1998; Narbro et al., 1996, 1999). However, there were no significant differences in terms of sick leave and disability pension between patients seeking surgery compared to obese individuals seeking nonsurgical weight loss treatment (Narbro et al., 1999).

Postsurgery Status

In almost all longitudinal studies investigating occupational issues, improvement in terms of days lost to sick leave and employment status are reported (Herpertz et al., 2003; Mathus-Vliegen, de Weerd, & de Wit, 2004; Näslund & Ågren, 1991; Narbro et al., 1996). For example, the results of the SOS study showed that obese individuals undergoing surgery reported 35% more days of sickness during the first year after surgery than obese individuals seeking nonsurgical treatment, whereas the number of days decreased markedly during years 2 to 3. By then, patients of the surgery group reported 10–14% fewer days of sick leave than obese controls (Narbro et al., 1999). Comparable results were obtained in a study by Mathus-Vliegen and colleagues (2004), who investigated 50 obese individuals before and 1 year after surgery. They found that the proportion of patients reporting sick leave within the first year was comparable to the year before inclusion in the study; however, the number of days of sick leave decreased markedly from on average 12 to 6 days (Mathus-Vliegen et al., 2004). Another longitudinal study followed 79 patients after gastric restrictive surgery and a similar group of 54 nonoperated patients over 5 years and showed that bariatric surgery was significantly associated with fewer days of sick leave and less sickness-related retirement than nonsurgical controls. Moreover, the surgery group revealed a higher employment rate, more working hours, and a higher income than controls (Näslund & Ågren, 1991). A study by Peace, Dyne, Russell, and Stewart (1989) indicates that more than a third of obese individuals who had undergone bariatric surgery had better occupational functioning than before surgery, whereas only one-fifth of patients reported worsening of their occupational functioning following surgery. Other authors also report that educational or occupational status improved in about one-third of their sample within the first postoperative year (Valley & Grace, 1987).

In sum, there is evidence that in the majority of individuals undergoing bariatric surgery, occupational functioning stayed the same or improved even over longer periods of time. However, there are a minority of surgery patients that do not profit in terms of employment or occupational functioning.

Psychiatric Symptoms and Disorders

It is assumed that weight-related stigmatization and discrimination as well as physical impairment and poor medical conditions contribute to higher rates of psychopathology among extremely obese individuals (Wadden et al., 2007). However, there are also biological pathways such as inflammation, HPA axis dysregulation, and biological changes in relation to diabetes that are considered important biological mediators for the association between obesity and depression (Luppino et al., 2010). Overall, most studies point to a higher level of psychopathology among bariatric surgery candidates. Several studies reported elevated levels of anxiety and depressive symptoms assessed with self-report measures (Burgmer et al., 2007; Sullivan et al., 1993; Wadden et al., 2001b, 2006) and higher prevalence rates of mental disorders among obese individuals than among normal-weight individuals in the general population (Herpertz et al., 2006; Petry, Barry, Pietrzak, & Wagner, 2008; Scott et al., 2008). Even higher rates of mental disorders are found in subsamples of obese persons seeking bariatric surgery (Herpertz et al., 2006; Kalarchian et al., 2007; Mühlhans, Horbach, & de Zwaan, 2009; Rosenberger, Henderson, & Grilo, 2006).

Symptoms of Depression and Anxiety

The most commonly used instruments to assess levels of depression and anxiety are the Hospital Anxiety and Depression Scale (HADS) (Zigmond & Snaith, 1983) and the Beck Depression Inventory (BDI) (Beck, Ward, Mock, Erbaugh, & Mendelson, 1961).

Presurgery Status

In general, studies assessing depressive symptoms using self-report measures indicate elevated levels of depressive symptoms in surgery candidates. For example, baseline data from the SOS study demonstrated that depression scores are unequivocally above the average in both the obese patients who received surgery and in obese control cases (Rydén & Torgerson, 2006). Of the total baseline sample of obese individuals (n = 800 men and n = 943 women), 8.6% of the males and 11% of the females reported scores indicative of depression (HADS > 10; Sullivan et al., 1993). When considering the various treatment groups, 24% of surgery candidates and 16% of individuals in conventional treatment were classified as having probable depression before treatment compared to 6% in a nonobese control population (Karlsson et al., 1998). Another study in 149 bariatric surgery candidates (Burgmer et al., 2007) reported elevated depression scores in 40% (HADS > 8) at baseline. In a cross-sectional study (Wadden et al., 2006) women with grade 3 obesity presenting for bariatric surgery reported significantly more symptoms of depression as assessed with the BDI, as compared with women with grades 1 and 2 obesity seeking behavioral treatment; 25% of the morbidly obese women showed a significant mood disorder. Schowalter and colleagues (2008) found that 35% of all preoperatively assessed patients (n = 248) suffered from clinically relevant depressive symptoms (BDI score ≥ 18), whereas Dymek et al. (2002) reported that 75% of surgery candidates were classified as depressed (BDI score > 10).

There is evidence that among bariatric surgery candidates depressive symptoms are significantly associated with younger age, female gender, poorer body image, and impairments in health-related quality of life (Dixon et al., 2003).

With regard to anxiety the literature is sparse. Again, the SOS study provides valuable information. About 17% of the men and 18% of the women, respectively, reported elevated anxiety scale scores (HADS between 8 and 10) (Sullivan et al., 1993). In addition, one-fifth of the men (19.9%) and more than one-fourth of the women (27.7%) reported HADS anxiety scores of above 10. Again, surgery candidates (34%) and individuals receiving conventional weight loss treatment (30%) reported significantly higher HADS anxiety scale scores (HADS > 10) than the nonobese reference population (17%) (Karlsson et al., 1998). A similar number (34%) of bariatric surgery candidates reporting clinically relevant anxiety scores were described by Burgmer et al. (2007).

In summary, there is strong evidence that morbidly obese individuals exhibit clinically relevant symptoms of depression and anxiety when self-report measures are applied. However, the number of patients with clinically relevant scores shows great variability among studies, which might be due to differences in sample characteristics such as age and gender distribution or prevalence of other psychosocial impairment.

Postsurgery Status

Studies investigating depressive and anxiety symptoms over time could demonstrate significant decreases in the severity of symptoms after surgery. Van Hout and colleagues (2008) reported lower scores of depressive symptoms assessed with the BDI 6 months and 1 year after surgery compared to presurgery levels; however, this difference was not present 2 years after surgery. Similarly Dymek et al. (2002) reported no additional decreases 6 months to 1 year following surgery. Nevertheless, the level was still considerable below the presurgery status (Dymek et al., 2002). Such an effect was also shown by Burgmer et al. (2007); the authors reported that the number of patients with clinically relevant depressive symptoms had decreased by more than 50% (from 40% to almost 17%) 1 year following surgery. After 2 years, there was no additional reduction of the HADS mean score, and the number of patients reporting HADS scores of >8 (about 16%) were comparable to the 1-year follow-up assessment. Schowalter and colleagues (2008) reported that even 5 years after surgery the mean score of the BDI was significantly below a control group of obese patients who did not receive surgery. Moreover, they reported a positive association between reductions in depression scores and the amount of weight loss. The SOS study (Karlsson et al., 1998; Rydén & Torgerson, 2006) reported sustained reductions of depressive and anxiety symptoms even 10 years after surgery compared to presurgical levels. Again, a significant association was found between the amount of weight loss and the magnitude of change of depressive and anxiety symptoms (Karlsson et al., 1998; Rydén & Torgerson, 2006). The number of bariatric surgery patients with probable depression (HADS depression scale score > 10) decreased from 24% at baseline to 15% at the 10-year follow-up assessment (Karlsson et al., 1998); however, the authors reported significant differences between patients who had lost at least 25% of their initial weight and those with less weight loss. The number of individuals reporting HADS depression scale scores of > 10 was 10% in patients with a weight loss of 25% or more, compared to 14% in patients with less weight loss at the 10-year follow-up (Rydén & Torgerson, 2006).

In summary, these results are encouraging. They imply that improvements of symptoms of depression and anxiety are most pronounced during the initial phase after surgery and appear to be associated with the amount of weight loss in the long term. However, many studies suffer from methodological limitations including small sample sizes, short-term follow-ups, lack of inclusion of a control or matched comparison group, and inconsistencies in the definition of clinically relevant depressive symptoms. These limitations make it difficult to draw firm conclusions from the research.

Prevalence of Psychiatric Disorders

Most population-based studies (Heo, Pietrobelli, Fontaine, Sirey, & Faith, 2006; Simon et al., 2006) as well as studies investigating obese treatment-seeking individuals (Black, Goldstein, & Mason, 1992; Fitzgibbon, Stolley, & Kirschenbaum, 1993; Herpertz et al., 2006; Mühlhans et al., 2009) reveal higher lifetime prevalence rates of eating disorders, anxiety, and affective disorders in obese individuals than in normal-weight individuals. This is even more pronounced in morbidly obese subjects (Herpertz et al., 2006; Mühlhans et al., 2009; Wadden et al., 2001a, 2006). For example, Onyike et al. (2003) found in a population-based study that morbidly obese individuals had a fivefold increase in the risk of depression compared with persons of average weight. Moreover, the risk of depression seems to be higher for obese women than for obese men (Herpertz et al., 2006; Mühlhans et al., 2009).

A recent meta-analysis (Luppino et al., 2010) found a bidirectional association between depression and obesity. Obese persons have a 55%

increased risk of developing depression over time (OR 1.55) and depressed persons have a 58% increased risk of becoming obese (OR 1.58). This is true for women and for men. The association is still significant but weaker between depression and overweight.

Presurgery Status

There are only five studies available that applied structured clinical interviews on the basis of DSM-IV criteria in bariatric surgery candidates (Kalarchian et al., 2007; Herpertz et al., 2006; Mauri et al., 2008; Mühlhans et al., 2009; Rosenberger et al., 2006). The lifetime history of any Axis I disorder was reported to be as high as 70%. Mood disorders, such as major depressive disorder and dysthymia, were the most commonly diagnosed disorders with a prevalence rate for lifetime major depression of up to 50% and of 8.2% for dysthymia. Anxiety disorders, including generalized anxiety disorder and social phobia, were diagnosed in up to 37.5% of the patients. Sizable minorities were diagnosed with substance use disorders (between 1 and 15%); Kalarchian et al. (2007) even reported a lifetime diagnosis of substance use/dependence in 32% of their patients.

In sum, in bariatric surgery candidates, prevalence rates of both affective and anxiety disorders have been found to be above the rates found in the general population. However, as can be seen in Table 4.1, there is some variability in the prevalence rates found in different samples and in

Table 4.1 Lifetime Psychiatric Comorbidity in Obese Patients Seeking Bariatric Surgery Assessed With Structured Clinical Interviews (SCID)

Psychiatric Comorbidity	Mühlhans et al., 2009 (N = 146)	Herpertz et al., 2006 (N = 153)	Kalarchian et al., 2007 (N = 288)	Rosenberger et al., 2008 (N = 174)	Mauri[a] et al., 2008 (N = 255)
Number of diagnoses ≥ 1	72.6%	53.6%	66.3%	36.8%	38.0%
Affective disorders	54.8%	28.1%	45.5%	22.4%	22.0%
Anxiety disorders	21.2%	24.2%	37.5%	15.5%	18.0%
Substance use disorders	15.1%	10.5%	32.6%	5.2%	1.2%
Somatoform disorders	3.4%	22.9%	—[b]	0%	—[b]

Note: Modified from Muhlhans, B., & de Zwaan, M. Mentel comorbidity in obese patients, *Adipositas*, 23, 148–154, 2008.

[a] Patients with a BMI of ≥35 kg/m^2; patients with a BMI below were excluded.

[b] Not assessed.

different countries (Mühlhans et al., 2009): This might be due to differences in demographic variables (age, gender, and weight) and differences in the categorization of the disorders (e.g., different kinds of disorders summarized under the category anxiety disorders). Moreover, the link between obesity and depression still needs further research. New evidence shows that the link between both disorders is bidirectional; however, further knowledge about possible moderators of this reciprocal interaction is needed (Luppino et al., 2010).

Postsurgery Psychiatric Status

There are hardly any studies prospectively assessing psychiatric disorders with structured clinical interviews after surgery. However, of the few studies available, there are reports of both reduction and increases in the number of psychiatric disorders following surgery. For example, Larsen (1990) reported that the prevalence of Axis I disorders based on a clinical interview almost halved 3 years following surgery (from 41% to 22%). Others reported a reduction to one-third of the presurgical rate (Gertler & Ramsay-Stewart, 1986) or even no diagnosable psychiatric disorder at all following surgery (Gentry et al., 1984). Mitchell and colleagues (2001) reported that the percentage of patients with a depression or a phobia had almost doubled 13 to 15 years after surgery. Scholtz and colleagues (2007) even showed that half of their sample of obese patients developed a psychiatric disorder within 5 years following gastric banding.

In summary, there is evidence that the prevalence of DSM-IV psychiatric disorders is elevated in bariatric surgery candidates; however, there is some variability between studies, most likely attributable to methodological issues and differences in sample characteristics. However, as there are hardly any studies providing information about the prevalence of psychiatric disorders following surgery, it remains unclear whether surgery-induced weight loss has a positive influence on the long-term course of psychiatric disorders.

Suicide After Bariatric Surgery

Adams et al. (2007) reported that even though long-term mortality from any cause decreased by 40% seven years after bariatric surgery, death not caused by disease, such as accidents and suicide, was 58% higher in postbariatric surgery patients than in a control group.

Recently, Tindle et al. (2010) reported 31 suicides over 10 years in 16,683 postbariatric surgery patients in Pennsylvania. Hence, the overall suicide rate was 13.7 per 10,000 person-years among men and 5.2 per 10,000 among women. These rates are much higher than age- and sex-matched U.S. rates (2.4/10,000 among men and 0.7/10,000 among women). Seventy percent of the suicides occurred within 3 years after surgery. Suicides are not necessarily attributed to the bariatric surgery, but may be related to many factors.

Predictive Value of Psychosocial Factors

It is not fully understood why some patients improve considerably and others do not after bariatric surgery. For example, some patients regain their weight, need psychological or psychiatric treatment, or report a reduction of their quality of life (Papageorgiou, Papakonstantinou, Mamplekou, Terzis, & Melissas, 2002). A recent nationwide survey in the United States showed that successful bariatric surgery patients are younger than 40 years, report a BMI of <50 kg/m^2 prior to surgery, are willing to change their eating habits, and increase their physical activity after surgery (Chevallier et al., 2007). Hence, psychological and psychosocial factors that might interfere with these characteristics, such as motivation, depression, self-esteem, or the presence of psychiatric disorders, have been considered as possible predictors of postoperative weight loss (Herpertz et al., 2004; Wadden et al., 2007). Unfortunately, there is a lack of systematic studies on the influence of psychosocial factors on bariatric surgery outcomes, and the studies conducted are inconclusive or even contradictory (Bocchieri et al., 2002; Herpertz et al., 2003). For example, only two studies found a positive association between self-esteem and weight loss after surgery; individuals with higher self-esteem at baseline lost more weight than those with lower self-esteem (Delin, Watts, & Bassett, 1995; van Gemert et al., 1998). Another study found a positive influence of marital satisfaction on weight loss following surgery (Hafner et al., 1990). More studies examined the possible influence of psychiatric disorders, in particular depression on postsurgery weight loss. However, a consistent influence of depression or other mental disorders at baseline on weight loss after surgery has not been shown (Wadden et al., 2007); there is evidence for both greater weight loss of those with depression (Averbukh et al., 2003; van Hout, Jakimowicz, Fortuin, Pelle, & van Heck, 2007) and less BMI reduction in patients that report mental disorders at baseline than for those without any mental disorder (Kinzl et al., 2006). A recent study assessed the influence of both lifetime and current diagnoses at baseline with structured clinical interviews (Kalarchian et al., 2008). The authors reported that patients who ever had an Axis I mental disorder, especially mood or anxiety disorder, exhibited a poorer weight outcome 6 months after gastric bypass than those who never had an Axis I disorder. Another study by Legenbauer, Petrak, de Zwaan, and Herpertz (2011) revealed that lifetime and current depressive disorders assessed at baseline were of negative predictive value for the percentage of BMI lost 4 years following restrictive surgery, but not for short-term weight loss (1 year after surgery). The authors hypothesized that the association between depressive disorders and weight loss might emerge especially in the long term when improvements due to the surgical procedure have waned. An additional study reported less weight loss at 1-year follow-up in patients with mood disorders; however, this effect disappeared when patients suffering from bipolar disorders were excluded from the analyses (Semanscin-Doerr, Windover, Ashton, & Heinberg, 2010).

There are three reviews on possible psychosocial predictors on the course of weight following surgery (Bocchieri et al., 2002; Herpertz et al., 2003, 2004). They all concluded that the evidence for a predictive value of psychiatric disorders at baseline for weight loss following surgery is rather meager, and due to methodological limitations, no ultimate conclusions can be drawn. Herpertz et al. (2004) further suggested that in addition to the presence of psychiatric disorders, the severity of the psychiatric disorder and the reoccurrence after surgery might influence weight loss and its maintenance and therefore should be investigated.

Conclusion

There is considerable evidence that bariatric surgery candidates have high levels of psychosocial impairment and high prevalence rates of psychiatric disorders. After surgery, psychosocial impairment usually improves significantly and psychiatric disorders decrease in most patients. There appears to be a positive association between the amount of weight loss and the reduction of psychiatric symptoms. However, a significant number of patients regain some of the weight and redevelop psychosocial impairments following surgery. Subsequently, it has been suggested that postsurgical factors such as the reoccurrence of psychiatric symptoms and their severity might be associated with weight loss following surgery.

However, for the time being, a presurgery evaluation is needed due to the high comorbidity in obese individuals seeking surgery. Patients with severe comorbid disorders should be identified and admitted to surgery only after careful consideration and therapy. Moreover, after surgery patients should be accompanied, and if necessary, psychological counseling should be offered in order to handle problems arising from the reoccurrence of psychological problems and to further enhance treatment outcome.

References

Adams, T.D., Gress, R.E., Smith, S.C., Halverson, R.C., Simper, S.C., Rosamond, W.D. et al. (2007). Long-term mortality after gastric bypass surgery. *New England Journal of Medicine, 357*, 753–761.

Anandacoomarasamy, A., Caterson, I.D., Leibman, S., Smith, G.S., Sambrook, P.N., Fransen, M. et al. (2009). Influence of BMI on health-related quality of life: Comparison between an obese adult cohort and age-matched population norms. *Obesity, 17,* 2114–2118.

Andersen, J.R., Aasprang, A., Bergsholm, P., Sletteskog, N., Våge, V., & Natvig, G.K. (2010). Anxiety and depression in association with morbid obesity: Changes with improved physical health after duodenal switch. *Health and Quality of Life Outcomes, 8,* 52.

Averbukh, Y., Heshka, S., El-Shoreya, H., Flancbaum, L., Geliebter, A., Kamel, S. et al. (2003). Depression score predicts weight loss following Roux-en-Y gastric bypass. *Obesity Surgery, 13,* 833–836.

Beck, A.T., Ward, C., Mendelson, M., Mock, J., & Erbaugh, J. (1961). An inventory for measuring depression. *Archives of General Psychiatry, 4,* 561–571.

Bergner, M., Bobbitt, R.A., Carter, W.B., & Gilson, B.S. (1981). The Sickness Impact Profile: Development and final revision of a health status measure. *Medical Care, 19,* 787–805.

Black, D.W., Goldstein, R.B., & Mason, E.E. (1992). Prevalence of mental disorder in 88 morbidly obese bariatric clinic patients. *American Journal of Psychiatry, 149,* 227–234.

Blascovich, J., & Tomaka, J. (1991). Measures of self-esteem. In J.P. Robinson, P.R. Shaver, & L.E. Wrightsman (Eds.), *Measures of personality and social psychological attitudes* (pp. 115–160). San Diego, CA: Academic Press.

Bocchieri, L.E., Meana, M., & Fisher, B.L. (2002). A review of psychosocial surgery for morbid obesity. *Journal of Psychosomatic Research, 52,* 155–165.

Brancatisano, A., Wahlroos, S., & Brancatisano, R. (2008). Improvement in comorbid illness after placement of the Swedish adjustable gastric band. *Surgery for Obesity and Related Diseases, 4,* S39–S46.

Burgmer, R., Petersen, I., Burgmer, M., de Zwaan, M., Wolf, A.M., & Herpertz, S. (2007). Psychological outcome two years after restrictive bariatric surgery. *Obesity Surgery, 17,* 785–791.

Butler, G.S., Vallis, T.M., Perey, B., Veldhuyzen van Zanten, S.J., MacDonald, A.S., & Konok, G. (1999). The Obesity Adjustment Survey: Development of a scale to assess psychological adjustment to morbid obesity. *International Journal for Obesity and Related Metabolic Disorders, 23,* 505–511.

Camps, M.A., Zervos, E., Goode, S., & Rosemurgy, A.S. (1996). Impact of bariatric surgery on body image perception and sexuality in morbidly obese patients and their partners. *Obesity Surgery, 6,* 356–360.

Chandarana, P.C., Conlon, P., Holliday, R.L., Deslippe, T., & Field, V.A. (1990). A prospective study of psychosocial aspects of gastric stapling surgery. *Psychiatric Journal of the University of Ottawa, 15,* 32–35.

Chevallier, J.M., Paita, M., Rodde-Dunet, M.H., Marty, M., Nogues, F., Slim, K. et al. (2007). Predictive factors of outcome after gastric banding: A nationwide survey on the role of center activity and patients' behavior. *Annals of Surgery, 246,* 1034–1039.

Choban, P.S., Onyejekwe, J., Burge, J.C., & Flancbaum, L. (1999). A health status assessment of the impact of weight loss following Roux-en-Y gastric bypass for clinically severe obesity. *Journal of the American College of Surgeons, 188,* 491–497.

Christou, N.V., Sampalis, J.S., Liberman, M., Look, D., Auger, S., McLean, A.P. et al. (2004). Surgery decreases long-term mortality, morbidity, and health care use in morbidly obese patients. *Annals of Surgery, 240,* 416–423.

Delin, C.R., Watts, J.M., & Bassett, D.L. (1995). An exploration of the outcomes of gastric bypass surgery for morbid obesity: Patient characteristics and indices of success. *Obesity Surgery, 5,* 159–170.

Devlin, M.J., Goldfein, J.A., Flancbaum, L., Bessler, M., & Eisenstadt, R. (2004). Surgical management of obese patients with eating disorders: A survey of current practice. *Obesity Surgery, 14,* 1252–1257.

de Zwaan, M., Lancaster, K.L., Mitchell, J.E., Howell, L.M., Monson, N., Roerig, J.L. et al. (2002). Health-related quality of life in morbidly obese patients: Effect of gastric bypass surgery. *Obesity Surgery, 12,* 773–780.

de Zwaan, M., Mitchell, J.E., Howell, L.M., Monson, N., Swan-Kremeier, L., Roerig, J.L. et al. (2002). Two measures of health-related quality of life in morbid obesity. *Obesity Research, 10,* 1143–1151.

de Zwaan, M., Petersen, I., Kaerber, M., Burgmer, R., Nolting, B., Legenbauer, T. et al. (2009). Obesity and quality of life: A controlled study of normal-weight and obese individuals. *Psychosomatics, 50,* 474–482.

Dixon, J.B., Dixon, M.E., & O'Brien, P.E. (2001). Quality of life after lap-band placement: Influence of time, weight loss, and comorbidities. *Obesity Research, 9,* 713–721.

Dixon, J.B., Dixon, M.E., & O'Brien, P.E. (2003). Depression in association with severe obesity: Changes with weight loss. *Archives of Internal Medicine, 163,* 2058–2065.

Doll, H.A., Petersen, S.E.K., & Stewart-Brown, S.L. (2000). Obesity and physical and emotional well-being: Associations between body mass index, chronic illness, and the physical and mental components of the SF–36 Questionnaire. *Obesity Research, 8,* 160–170.

Dubovsky, S.L., Haddenhorst, A., Murphy, J., Liechty, R.D., & Coyle, D.A. (1985). A preliminary study of the relationship between preoperative depression and weight loss following surgery for morbid obesity. *International Journal of Psychiatry in Medicine, 15,* 185–196.

Dymek, M.P., Le Grange, D., Neven, K., & Alverdy, J. (2001). Quality of life and psychosocial adjustment in patients after Roux-en-Y gastric bypass: A brief report. *Obesity Surgery, 11,* 32–39.

Dymek, M.P., Le Grange, D., Neven, K., & Alverdy, J. (2002). Quality of life after gastric bypass surgery: A cross-sectional study. *Obesity Research, 10,* 1135–1142.

Fitzgibbon, M.L., Stolley, M.R., & Kirschenbaum, D.S. (1993). Obese people who seek treatment have different characteristics than those who do not seek treatment. *Health Psychology, 12,* 342–345.

Folope, V., Hellot, M.F., Kuhn, J.M., Ténière, P., Scotté, M., & Déchelotte, P. (2008). Weight loss and quality of life after bariatric surgery: A study of 200 patients after vertical gastroplasty or adjustable gastric banding. *European Journal of Clinical Nutrition, 62,* 1022–1030.

Fontaine, K.R., & Barofsky, I. (2001). Obesity and health-related quality of life. *Obesity Review, 2,* 173–182.

Fontaine, K.R., Cheskin, L.J., & Barofsky, I. (1996). Health-related quality of life in obese persons seeking treatment. *Journal of Family Practice, 43,* 265–270.

Fontaine, K.R., Cheskin, L.J., & Barofsky, I. (1997). Predictors of quality of life for obese persons. *Journal of Nervous and Mental Disease, 185,* 120–122.

Friedman, M.A., & Brownell, K.D. (1995). Psychological correlates of obesity: Moving to the next research generation. *Psychological Bulletin, 117,* 3–20.

Frigg, A., Peterli, R., Peters, T., Ackermann, C., & Tondelli, P. (2004). Reduction in comorbidities 4 years after laparoscopic adjustable gastric banding. *Obesity Surgery, 14,* 216–223.

Gentry, K., Halverson, J.D., & Heisler, S. (1984). Psychological assessment of morbidly obese patients undergoing gastric bypass: A comparison of preoperative and postoperative adjustments. *Surgery, 95,* 215–220.

Gertler, R., & Ramsey-Stewart, G. (1986). Pre-operative psychiatric assessment of patients presenting for gastric bariatric surgery (surgical control of morbid obesity). *Australian and New Zealand Journal of Surgery, 56,* 157–161.

Goble, L.K., Rand, C.S., & Kuldau, J.M. (1986). Understanding marital relationships following obesity surgery. *Family Therapy, 8,* 196–202.

Greenberg, I., Perna, F., Kaplan, M., & Sullivan, M.A. (2005). Behavioral and psychological factors in the assessment and treatment of obesity surgery patients. *Obesity Research, 13,* 244–249.

Guisado, J.A., Vaz, F.J., Alarcón, J., López-Ibor, J.J. Jr, Rubio, M.A., & Gaite, L. (2002). Psychopathological status and interpersonal functioning following weight loss in morbidly obese patients undergoing bariatric surgery. *Obesity Surgery, 12,* 835–840.

Guyatt, G.H., Feeny, D.H., & Patrick, D.L. (1993). Measuring health-related quality of life. *Annals of Internal Medicine, 118,* 622–629.

Hafner, R.J., Rogers, J., & Watts, J.M. (1990). Psychological status before and after gastric restriction as predictors of weight loss in the morbidly obese. *Journal of Psychosomatic Research, 34,* 295–302.

Hawke, A., O'Brien, P., Watts, J.M., Hall, J., Dunstan, R.E., Walsh, J.F. et al. (1990). Psychosocial and physical activity changes after gastric restrictive procedures for morbid obesity. *Australian and New Zealand Journal of Surgery, 60,* 755–758.

Hayden, M.J., Dixon, M.E., Dixon, J.B., Playfair, J., & O'Brien, P.E. (2010). Perceived discrimination and stigmatisation against severely obese women: Age and weight loss make a difference. *Obesity Facts, 3,* 7–14.

Heo, M., Pietrobelli, A., Fontaine, K.R., Sirey, J.A., & Faith, M.S. (2006). Depressive mood and obesity in US adults: Comparison and moderation by sex, age, and race. *International Journal of Obesity, 30,* 513–519.

Herpertz, S., Burgmer, R., Stang, A., de Zwaan, M., Wolf, A.M., Chen-Stute, A. et al. (2006). Prevalence of mental disorders in normal-weight and obese individuals with and without weight loss treatment in a German urban population. *Journal of Psychosomatic Research, 61,* 95–103.

Herpertz, S., Kielmann, R., Wolf, A.M., Hebebrand, J., & Senf, W. (2004). Do psychosocial variables predict weight loss or mental health after obesity surgery? A systematic review. *Obesity Research, 12,* 1554–1569.

Herpertz, S., Kielmann, R., Wolf, A.M., Langkafel, M., Senf, W., & Hebebrand, J. (2003). Does obesity surgery improve psychosocial functioning? A systematic review. *International Journal of Obesity and Related Metabolic Disorders, 27,* 1300–1314.

Hsu, L.K.G., Benotti, P.N., Dwyer, J., Roberts, S.B., Saltzman, E., Shikora, S. et al. (1998). Nonsurgical factors that influence the outcome of bariatric surgery: A review. *Psychosomatic Medicine, 60,* 338–346.

Hunt, S.M., McKenna, S.P., McEwen, J., Williams, J., & Papp, E. (1981). The Nottingham Health Profile: Subjective health status and medical consultations. *Social Science and Medicine. Part A, Medical Sociology, 15,* 221–229.

Isacsson, A., Frederiksen, S.G., Nilsson, P., & Hedenbro, J.L. (1997). Quality of life after gastroplasty is normal: A controlled study. *European Journal of Surgery, 163,* 181–186.

Kalarchian, M.A., Marcus, M.D., Levine, M.D., Courcoulas, A.P., Pilkonis, P.A., Ringham, R.M. et al. (2007). Psychiatric disorders among bariatric surgery candidates: Relationship to obesity and functional health status. *American Journal of Psychiatry, 164,* 328–334.

Kalarchian, M.A., Marcus, M.D., Levine, M.D., Soulakova, J.N., Courcoulas, A.P., & Wisinski, M.S. (2008). Relationship of psychiatric disorders to 6-month outcomes after gastric bypass. *Surgery for Obesity and Related Diseases, 4,* 544–549.

Kamphuis, M., Ottenkamp, J., Vliegen, H.W., Vogels, T., Zwinderman, K.H., Kamphuis, R.P. et al. (2002). Health related quality of life and health status in adult survivors with previously operated complex congenital heart disease. *Heart, 87,* 356–362.

Karlsson, J., Sjostrom, L., & Sullivan, M. (1998). Swedish obese subjects (SOS)—An intervention study of obesity. Two-year follow-up of health-related quality of life (HRQL) and eating behavior after gastric surgery for severe obesity. *International Journal of Obesity and Related Metabolic Disorders, 22,* 113–126.

Karlsson, J., Taft, C., Rydén, A., Sjöström, L., & Sullivan, M. (2007). Ten-year trends in health-related quality of life after surgical and conventional treatment for severe obesity: The SOS intervention study. *International Journal of Obesity, 31,* 1248–1261.

Kinzl, J.F., Schrattenecker, M., Traweger, C., Aigner, F., Fiala, M., & Biebl, W. (2007). Quality of life in morbidly obese patients after surgical weight loss. *Obesity Surgery, 17,* 229–235.

Kinzl, J.F., Schrattenecker, M., Traweger, C., Mattesich, M., Fiala, M., & Biebl, W. (2006). Psychosocial predictors of weight loss after bariatric surgery. *Obesity Surgery, 16,* 1609–1614.

Kinzl, J.F., Trefalt, E., Fiala, M., Hotter, A., Biebl, W., & Aigner, F. (2001). Partnership, sexuality, and sexual disorders in morbidly obese women: Consequences of weight loss after gastric banding. *Obesity Surgery, 11,* 455–458.

Kolotkin, R.L., & Crosby, R.D. (2002). Psychometric evaluation of the Impact of Weight on Quality of Life questionnaire (IWQOL-Lite) in a community sample. *Quality of Life Research, 11,* 157–171.

Kolotkin, R.L., Crosby, R.D., Kosloski, K.D., & Williams, G.R. (2001). Development of a brief measure to assess quality of life in obesity. *Obesity Research*, *9*, 102–111.

Kolotkin, R.L., Crosby, R.D., Pendleton, R., Strong, M., Gress, R.E., & Adams, T. (2003). Health-related quality of life in patients seeking gastric bypass surgery vs. non-treatment-seeking controls. *Obesity Surgery*, *13*, 371–377.

Kolotkin, R.L., Crosby, R.D., & Williams, G.R. (2002). Health-related quality of life varies among obese subgroups. *Obesity Research*, *10*, 748–756.

Kolotkin, R.L., Head, S., & Brookhart, A. (1997). Construct validity of the Impact of Weight on Quality of Life questionnaire. *Obesity Research*, *5*, 434–441.

Kolotkin, R.L., Head, S., Hamilton, M., & Tse, C.K. (1995). Assessing impact of weight on quality of life. *Obesity Research*, *3*, 49–56.

Kolotkin, R.L., Norquist, J.M., Crosby, R.D., Suryawanshi, S., Teixeira, P.J., Heymsfield, S.B. et al. (2009). One-year health-related quality of life outcomes in weight loss trial participants: Comparison of three measures. *Health and Quality of Life Outcomes*, *7*, 53.

Kral, J.G. (1998). Surgical treatment of obesity. *The Medical Clinics of North America*, *73*, 251–264.

Larsen, F. (1990). Psychosocial function before and after gastric banding surgery for morbid obesity. *Acta Psychiatrica Scandinavia*, *359*, 1–57.

Larsen, J.K., Geenen, R., Maas, C., De Wit, P., Van Antwerpen, T., Brand, N. et al. (2004). Personality as a predictor of weight loss maintenance after surgery for morbid obesity. *Obesity Research*, *12*, 1828–1834.

Larsen, J.K., Geenen, R., Van Ramshorst, B., Brand, N., De Wit, P., Stroebe, W. et al. (2003). Psychosocial functioning before and after laparoscopic adjustable gastric banding for morbid obesity: A cross-sectional study. *Obesity Surgery*, *13*, 629–636.

Larsen, F., & Torgersen, S. (1989). Personality changes after gastric banding surgery for morbid obesity. A prospective study. *Journal of Psychosomatic Research*, *33*, 323–334.

Legenbauer, T., Petrak, F., de Zwaan, M., & Herpertz, S. (2011). Influence of depressive and eating disorders on short- and long-term course of weight after surgical and nonsurgical weight loss treatment. *Comprehensive Psychiatry*, *52*, 301–311.

Le Pen, C., Levy, E., Loos, F., Banzet, M.N., & Basdevant, A. (1998). "Specific" scale compared with "generic" scale: A double measurement of the quality of life in a French community sample of obese subjects. *Journal of Epidemiology and Community Health*, *52*, 445–450.

Luppino, F.S., de Wit, L.M., Bouvy, P.F., Stijnen, T., Cuijpers, P., Penninx, B.W. et al. (2010). Overweight, obesity, and depression: A systematic review and meta-analysis of longitudinal studies. *Archives of General Psychiatry*, *67*, 220–229.

Mannucci, E., Ricca, V., Barciulli, E., Di Bernardo, M., Travaglini, R., Cabras, P.L. et al. (1999). Quality of life and overweight: The obesity related well-being (Orwell 97) questionnaire. *Addictive Behavior*, *24*, 345–357.

Mathias, S.D., Fifer, S.K., & Patrick, D.L. (1994). Rapid translation of quality of life measures for international clinical trials: Avoiding errors in the minimalist approach. *Quality of Life Research*, *3*, 403–412.

Mathias, S.D., Williamson, C.L., Colwell, H.H., Cisternas, M.G., Pasta, D.J., Stolshek, B.S. et al. (1997). Assessing health-related quality-of-life and health-state preference in persons with obesity: A validation study. *Quality of Life Research*, *6*, 311–322.

Mathus-Vliegen, E.M., de Weerd, S., & de Wit, L.T. (2004). Health-related quality-of-life in patients with morbid obesity after gastric banding for surgically induced weight loss. *Surgery, 135*, 489–497.

Mathus-Vliegen, E.M., & de Wit, L.T. (2007). Health-related quality of life after gastric banding. *British Journal of Surgery, 94*, 457–465.

Mauri, M., Rucci, P., Calderone, A., Santini, F., Oppo, A., Romano, A. et al. (2008). Axis I and II disorders and quality of life in bariatric surgery candidates. *Journal of Clinical Psychiatry, 69*, 295–301.

Mitchell, J.E., Lancaster, K.L., Burgard, M.A., Howell, L.M., Krahn, D.D., Crosby, R.D. et al. (2001). Long-term follow-up of patients' status after gastric bypass. *Obesity Surgery, 11*, 464–468.

Monteforte, M.J., & Turkelson, C.M. (2000). Bariatric surgery for morbid obesity. *Obesity Surgery, 10*, 391–401.

Mühlhans, B., Horbach, T., & de Zwaan, M. (2009). Psychiatric disorders in bariatric surgery candidates: A review of the literature and results of a German prebariatric surgery sample. *General Hospital Psychiatry, 31*, 414–421.

Myers, A., & Rosen, J.C. (1999). Obesity stigmatization and coping: Relation to mental health symptoms, body image, and self-esteem. *International Journal of Obesity and Related Metabolic Disorders, 23*, 221–230.

Narbro, K., Agren, G., Jonsson, E., Larsson, B., Näslund, I., Wedel, H. et al. (1999). Sick leave and disability pension before and after treatment for obesity: A report from the Swedish Obese Subjects (SOS) study. *International Journal of Obesity and Related Metabolic Disorders, 23*, 619–624.

Narbro, K., Jonsson, E., Larsson, B., Waaler, H., Wedel, H., & Sjöström, L. (1996). Economic consequences of sick-leave and early retirement in obese Swedish women. *International Journal of Obesity and Related Metabolic Disorders, 20*, 895–903.

Näslund, I. I., & Ågren, G. (1991). Social and economic effects of bariatric surgery. *Obesity Surgery, 1*, 137–140.

National Task Force on the Prevention and Treatment of Obesity. (2000). Overweight, obesity, and health risk. *Archives of Internal Medicine, 160*, 898–904.

Neill, J.R., Marshall, J.R., & Yale, C.E. (1978). Marital changes after intestinal bypass surgery. *Journal of the American Medical Association, 240*, 447–450.

Nguyen, N.T., Slone, J.A., Nguyen, X.M.T., Hartman, J.S., & Hoyt, D.B. (2009). A prospective randomized trial of laparoscopic gastric bypass versus laparoscopic adjustable gastric banding for the treatment of morbid obesity: Outcomes, quality of life, and costs. *Annals of Surgery, 250*, 631–641.

Nickel, M.K., Loew, T.H., & Bachler E. (2007). Change in mental symptoms in extreme obesity patients after gastric banding. Part II: Six-year follow up. *International Journal of Psychiatry in Medicine, 37*, 69–79.

Onyike, C.U., Crum, R.M., Lee, H.B., Lyketsos, C.G., & Eaton, W.W. (2003). Is obesity associated with major depression? Results from the Third National Health and Nutrition Examination Survey. *American Journal of Epidemiology, 158*, 1139–1147.

Oria, H.E., & Moorehead, M.K. (1998). Bariatric Analysis and Reporting Outcome System (BAROS). *Obesity Surgery, 8*, 487–499.

Osei-Assibey, G., Kyrou, I., Kumar, S., Saravanan, P., & Matyka, K.A. (2010). Self-reported psychosocial health in obese patients before and after weight loss. *Journal of Obesity, pii,* 372463. Epub 2010 Apr 29.

Papageorgiou, G.M., Papakonstantinou, A., Mamplekou, E., Terzis, I., & Melissas, J. (2002). Pre- and postoperative psychological characteristics in morbidly obese patients. *Obesity Surgery, 12,* 534–539.

Peace, K., Dyne, J., Russell, G., & Stewart, R. (1989). Psychobiological effects of gastric restriction surgery for morbid obesity. *New Zealand Medical Journal, 102,* 76–78.

Petry, N.M., Barry, D., Pietrzak, R.H., & Wagner, J.A. (2008). Overweight and obesity are associated with psychiatric disorders: Results from the National Epidemiologic Survey on Alcohol and Related Conditions. *Psychosomatic Medicine, 70,* 288–297.

Rand, C.S., Kowalske, K., & Kuldau, J.M. (1984). Characteristics of marital improvement following obesity surgery. *Psychosomatics, 25,* 221–226.

Rand, C.S., Kuldau, J.M., & Robbins, L. (1982). Surgery for obesity and marriage quality. *JAMA: Journal of the American Medical Association, 247,* 1419–1422.

Roberts, R.E., Deleger, S., Strawbridge, W.J., & Kaplan, G.A. (2003). Prospective association between obesity and depression: Evidence from the Alameda County Study. *International Journal of Obesity, 27,* 514–521.

Rosenberg, M. (1965). *Society and the adolescent self-image.* Princeton, NJ: Princeton University Press.

Rosenberger, P.H., Henderson, K.E., & Grilo, C.M. (2006). Psychiatric disorder comorbidity and association with eating disorders in bariatric surgery patients: A cross-sectional study using structured interview-based diagnosis. *Journal of Clinical Psychiatry, 67,* 1080–1085.

Rydén, A., & Torgerson, J.S. (2006). The Swedish Obese Subjects Study—What has been accomplished to date? *Surgery for Obesity and Related Diseases, 2,* 549–560.

Sarwer, D.B., Wadden, T.A., & Fabricatore, A.N. (2005). Psychosocial and behavioral aspects of bariatric surgery. *Obesity Research, 13,* 639–648.

Schok, M., Geenen, R., van Antwerpen, T., de Wit, P., Brand, N., & van Ramshorst, B. (2000). Quality of life after laparoscopic adjustable gastric banding for severe obesity: Postoperative and retrospective preoperative evaluations. *Obesity Surgery, 10,* 502–508.

Scholtz, S., Bidlake, L., Morgan, J., Fiennes, A., El-Etar, A., Lacey, J.H. et al. (2007). Long-term outcomes following laparoscopic adjustable gastric banding: Postoperative psychological sequelae predict outcome at 5-year follow-up. *Obesity Surgery, 17,* 1220–1225.

Schowalter, M., Benecke, A., Lager, C., Heimbucher, J., Bueter, M., Thalheimer, A. et al. (2008). Changes in depression following gastric banding: A 5- to 7-year prospective study. *Obesity Surgery, 18,* 314–320.

Scott, K.M., Bruffaerts, R., Simon, G.E., Alonso, J., Angermeyer, M., de Girolamo, G. et al. (2008). Obesity and mental disorders in the general population: Results from the world mental health surveys. *International Journal of Obesity, 32,* 192–200.

Semanscin-Doerr, D.A., Windover, A., Ashton, K., & Heinberg, L.J. (2010). Mood disorders in laparoscopic sleeve gastrectomy patients: Does it affect early weight loss? *Surgery for Obesity and Related Diseases, 6*, 191–196.

Simon, G.E., Von Korff, M., Saunders, K., Miglioretti, D.L., Crane, P.K., van Belle, G. et al. (2006). Association between obesity and psychiatric disorders in the US adult population. *Archives of General Psychiatry, 63*, 824–830.

Stunkard, A.J., Stinnett, J.L., & Smoller, J.W. (1986). Psychological and social aspects of the surgical treatment of obesity. *American Journal of Psychiatry, 143*, 417–429.

Sugerman, H.J., Londrey, G.L., Kellum, J.M., Wolf, L., Liszka, T., Engle, K.M. et al. (1989). Weight loss with vertical banded gastroplasty and Roux-Y gastric bypass for morbid obesity with selective versus random assignment. *American Journal of Surgery, 157*, 93–102.

Sullivan, M., Karlsson, J., Sjöström, L., Backman, L., Bengtsson, C., Bouchard, C. et al. (1993). Swedish obese subjects (SOS)—An intervention study of obesity. Baseline evaluation of health and psychosocial functioning in the first 1743 subjects examined. *International Journal of Obesity and Related Metabolic Disorders, 17*, 503–512.

Tindle, H.A., Omalu, B., Courcoulas, A., Marcus, M., Hammers, J., & Kuller, L.H. (2010). Risk of suicide after long-term follow-up from bariatric surgery. *American Journal of Medicine, 123*, 1036–1042.

Valley, V., & Grace, D.M. (1987). Psychosocial risk factors in gastric surgery for obesity: Identifying guidelines for screening. *International Journal of Obesity, 11*, 105–113.

van Gemert, W.G., Severeijns, R.M., Greve, J.W., Groenman, N., & Soeters, P.B. (1998). Psychological functioning of morbidly obese patients after surgical treatment. *International Journal of Obesity, 22*, 393–398.

van Hout, G.C.M, Fortuin, F.A.M., Pelle, A.J.M., Blokland-Koomen, M.E., & van Heck, G.L. (2009). Health-related quality of life following vertical banded gastroplasty. *Surgical Endoscopy, 23*, 550–556.

van Hout, G.C.M, Fortuin, F.A.M., Pelle, A.J.M., & van Heck G.L. (2008). Psychosocial functioning, personality, and body image following vertical banded gastroplasty. *Obesity Surgery, 18*, 115–120.

van Hout, G.C., Jakimowicz, J.J., Fortuin, F.A., Pelle, A.J., & van Heck, G.L. (2007). Weight loss and eating behavior following vertical banded gastroplasty. *Obesity Surgery, 17*, 1226–1234.

van Nunen, A.M., Wouters, E.J., Vingerhoets, A.J., Hox, J.J., & Geenen, R. (2007). The health-related quality of life of obese persons seeking or not seeking surgical or non-surgical treatment: A meta-analysis. *Obesity Surgery, 17*, 1357–1366.

Wadden, T.A., Butryn, M.L., Sarwer, D.B., Fabricatore, A.N., Crerand, C.E., Lipschutz, P.E. et al. (2006). Comparison of psychosocial status in treatment-seeking women with class III vs. class I-II obesity. *Surgery for Obesity and Related Disorders, 2*, 138–145.

Wadden, T.A., Sarwer, D.B., Fabricatore, A.N., Jones, L., Stack, R., & Williams, N.S. (2007). Psychosocial and behavioral status of patients undergoing bariatric surgery: What to expect before and after surgery. *The Medical Clinics of North America, 91*, 451–469.

Wadden, T.A., Sarwer, D.B., Womble, L.G., Foster, G.D., McGuckin, B.G., & Schimmel, A. (2001b). Psychosocial aspects of obesity and obesity surgery. *Obesity Surgery, 81*, 1001–1024.

Wadden, T.A., Sarwer, D.B., Womble, L.G. Foster, G.D., McGuckin, B.G., & Schimmel, A. (2001a). Psychosocial aspects of obesity and obesity surgery. *The Surgical Clinics of North America, 81*, 1001–1024.

Walfish, S. (2004). Self-assessed emotional factors contributing to increased weight gain in pre-surgical bariatric patients. *Obesity Surgery, 14*, 1402–1405.

Wan, G.J., Counte, M.A., & Cella, D.F. (1997). A framework for organizing health-related quality of life research. *Journal of Rehabilitation and Outcomes Measures, 1*, 31–37.

Ware, J. (1994). *SF-36 Physical and Mental Health Summary Scales: A user's manual.* Boston, MA: The Health Institute, New England Medical Center.

Ware, J. (1997). *SF-36 Health Survey: Manual and interpretation guide.* Boston, MA: The Health institute, New England Medical Center.

Willett, W.C., Dietz, W.H., & Colditz, G.A. (1999). Guidelines for healthy weight. *New England Journal of Medicine, 341*, 427–434.

Yancy, W.S., Olsen, M.K., Westman, E.C., Bosworth, H.B., & Edelman, D. (2002). Relationship between obesity and health related quality of life in men. *Obesity Research, 10*, 1057–1064.

Zigmond, A.S., & Snaith, R.P. (1983). The Hospital Anxiety and Depression Scale. *Acta Psychiatrica Scandinavica, 67*, 361–370.

CHAPTER **5**

Eating Disorders and Eating Problems Pre- and Postbariatric Surgery

SCOTT G. ENGEL, JAMES E. MITCHELL,
MARTINA DE ZWAAN, and KRISTINE J. STEFFEN

Introduction

It is widely known that bariatric surgery generally results in improved physical and psychological functioning. Not all patients, however, see such improvements. After surgery a significant minority of patients experience a range of problems associated with their weight: insufficient weight loss, eventual weight regain, or at times excessive weight loss. The current literature suggests that obese patients seeking bariatric surgery are likely to exhibit eating disordered behavior such as binge eating and are likely to meet criteria for binge eating disorder (BED). Additionally, some research has suggested that a small, but significant, number of bariatric surgery patients develop eating disorders following surgery. Finally, behaviors associated with eating disorders (e.g., binge eating and purging) have been implicated as predictors of outcome. Although some behaviors have been studied (binge eating), other behaviors have not received much research attention.

For the past three decades research has examined bariatric surgery patients and sought to determine the prevalence of eating pathology and eating-related problems, both before and after surgery. Considerable research has examined binge eating and BED in bariatric surgery patients. Additionally, a small number of papers (primarily case studies) have examined the emergence of eating disorders, such as anorexia nervosa and bulimia nervosa, following surgery. This chapter will attempt to describe and discuss eating disorders and eating problems in both pre- and post-bariatric surgery patients.

Presurgery

Eating Disorders and Associated Behaviors

Binge Eating and BED   A binge eating episode is frequently defined as an eating episode in which an individual consumes an objectively large amount of food, in a discrete period of time, while experiencing a loss of control over eating (Fairburn & Cooper, 1993). Binge eating disorder is included in the *Diagnostic and Statistical Manual of Mental Disorders*, 4th Edition, Text Revision (DSM-IV) (American Psychiatric Association, 2000) as an example of an eating disorder not otherwise specified (EDNOS), and listed in the appendices as a possible new disorder. BED is characterized in the DSM-IV by binge eating and is not accompanied by compensatory behaviors, such as those seen in bulimia nervosa.

It is widely known that binge eating and BED are common among obese patients seeking bariatric surgery (de Zwaan, 2005). In reviewing 22 studies published from 1995 to 2008, examining the reported frequency of binge eating in presurgery bariatric patients across these studies, binge eating frequency ranged from as low as 6% (Allison et al., 2006; Sansone, Schumacher, Widererman, & Routston-Weichers, 2008) to as high as 69% (Adami, Gandolfo, Bauer, & Scopinaro, 1995). The average percentage of patients who reported binge eating was approximately 36%. The large range in frequency of binge eating behavior is attributable to different assessment methods and variability in the definition of binge eating. In the 17 studies that reported rates of BED in individuals seeking bariatric surgery, prevalence rates ranged from as low as 1% (Herpertz & Saller, 2001) to as high as 49% (Mitchell et al., 2001). Again, the assessment methods in these studies varied greatly, and not all definitions of BED were identical across studies. The average rate of BED in these studies was approximately 25%.

An important research question is whether presurgery binge eating or BED predicts outcome after bariatric surgery. The findings have not been perfectly consistent, but they generally suggest that there is no relationship, or at least a relatively weak one, between presurgery binge eating or BED status and amount of weight loss or weight regain (see Table 5.1). While four studies have found significant predictive power (Hsu, Sullivan, & Benotti, 1997; Dymek, le Grange, Neven, & Alverdy, 2001; Green et al., 2004; Sallet, Sallet, & Dixon, 2007), most studies have not found this relationship (Busetto et al., 1996; Hsu, Betancourt, & Sullivan, 1996; Powers,

Table 5.1 Is Preoperative Binge Eating (Disorder) Predictive of Postoperative Weight Loss?

Authors	Method	N	Follow-up Duration	Is BE(D) Predictive?
Busetto et al., 1996	Roux-en-Y	80	12 mos	No
Hsu et al., 1996	Gastroplasty	24	3.5 yrs	No
Hsu et al., 1997	Roux-en-Y	27	21 mo	Yes
Powers et al., 1999	Restrictive	72	5.5 yrs	No
Dymek et al., 2001	Roux-en-Y	32	6 mos	Yes
Busetto et al., 2002	Banding	260	3 yrs	No
Sabbioni et al., 2002	Gastroplasty	82	2 yrs	No
Boan et al., 2004	Roux-en-Y	40	6 mos	No
Green et al., 2004	Roux-en-Y	65	6 mos	Yes
Burgmer et al., 2005	Banding	118	>12 mos	No
Busetto et al., 2005	Banding	379	5 yrs	No
Malone & Alger-Mayer, 2005	Roux-en-Y	109	12 mos	No
Bocchieri-Ricciardi et al., 2006	Roux-en-Y	72	18 mos	No
Sallet et al., 2007	Roux-en-Y	216	2 yrs	Yes
Kalarchian et al., 2008	Roux-en-Y	207	6 mos	No
White et al., 2009	Roux-en-Y	361	1 and 2 yrs	No
de Zwaan et al., 2010	Roux-en-Y	59	2 yrs	No

Perez, Boyd, & Rosemurgy, 1999; Busetto et al., 2002; Sabbioni et al., 2002; Boan, Kolotkin, Westman, McMahon, & Grant, 2004; Burgmer et al., 2005). Importantly, two of the four studies that did find a relationship between presurgery binge eating/BED and weight regain were relatively small, with Hsu and colleagues (1997) studying 27 participants and Dymek and colleagues (2001) investigating 32 participants. In total, the data currently suggest that if there is any relationship between presurgery binge eating or BED and postsurgery weight regain, it is modest.

Other Eating Disordered Behavior Besides binge eating and BED, very few data are available examining the prevalence rates of BN and other eating disordered behavior in patients before bariatric surgery. One probable reason for this might be considerable underreporting of these behaviors before surgery. Patients are often highly guarded about the eating-related information they are willing to share during assessment prior to surgery. This is typically caused by the fact that they are fearful that the information they provide may exclude them from being eligible for surgery. de Zwaan and colleagues (2010) reported that two of their 59 participants in their study met criteria for bulimia nervosa prior to surgery. Interestingly, both of these patients had a poor outcome.

Night Eating Night eating behavior has been reported in the literature since the 1950s (Stunkard, Grace, & Wolf, 1955). Although the criteria for meeting night eating syndrome (NES) has changed a number of times, according to Allison et al. (2010) NES is defined by a set of core symptoms that include: (1) consumption of at least 25% of intake after the evening meal, and (2) nocturnal awakenings during which the individual ingests food at least twice per week. These core symptoms must be accompanied by an awareness of the behaviors such that the patient is not amnestic for the event, and there must also be some impairment associated with the behavior.

A number of studies have reported NES rates in bariatric surgery patients. Adami, Meneghelli, and Scopinaro (1999) reported that 8% of a bariatric surgery–seeking group met criteria for NES. Powers et al. (1999) found that approximately 10% of a bariatric surgery group reported presurgery NES. Rand and Kuldau (1993) reported that 65 of 255 (15%) patients seeking surgery met criteria for NES. Although not necessarily meeting full criteria for NES, 36 of 65 (55%) presurgery patients reported nocturnal ingestions occurring at least twice per week (Latner, Wetzler, Goodman, & Glinski, 2004). Finally, Allison et al. (2006) found that among patients seeking bariatric surgery, 1.9% met strict criteria for NES and 8.9% met any definition of NES.

Grazing The term *grazing* has been used to describe eating smaller amounts of food continuously throughout the day or eating large amounts of food over a long period of time (Saunders, 2001). Although some have considered grazing to be a demeaning term, it has been used commonly in the literature. In fact, some patients report "liking the term" (Saunders, 2010). Grazing behavior is not well studied, and few data are available in bariatric surgery samples. In a sample of 125 patients seeking bariatric surgery, Saunders (1999) found that 59.8% of patients reported engaging in grazing behavior. Of the patients who reported grazing, over two-thirds reported grazing "2–3 days a week" or more frequently. The only other data on grazing in presurgery patients that is available comes from Colles, Dixon, and O'Brien (2008). They found that 26.4% of prebariatric surgery patients report grazing behavior. Relative to nongrazing participants, individuals who reported grazing had lower levels of dietary restraint, higher dietary disinhibition, and hunger. Twelve months after surgery individuals who reported grazing at baseline had significantly higher depression symptoms and had lost less weight than those who did not report grazing at baseline.

High Caloric Fluid Intake Two studies have reported a small percentage of bariatric surgery patients drinking excessive quantities of fluids before surgery. Hsu et al. (1996) reported that 8 of the 24 patients they interviewed reported excessive fluid intake prior to surgery. Similarly, Hsu et al. (1997)

also reported excessive fluid intake in a sample of bariatric surgery patients. Eleven of their 27 patients recalled excessive fluid intake prior.

Sweet Eating   Another behavior of clinical and research interest has been the eating of sweets by bariatric surgery patients. A number of studies have investigated the extent to which patients' presurgery eating of sweets predicts weight loss. Although Sugerman and colleagues (1987) found that increased sweet eating predicted less weight loss, six more recent studies have found that presurgery sweet eating does not predict postsurgery outcome (Lindroos, Lissner, & Sjostrom, 1996; Busetto et al., 2002; Hudson, Dixon, & O'Brien, 2002; Burgmer et al., 2005; Korenkov, Kneist, Heintz, & Junginger, 2004; Kim et al., 2006).

Postsurgery

Studying pathological eating behavior following bariatric surgery is a difficult task. Although a growing literature has investigated this topic, this has occurred in a very heterogeneous group of patients following a variety of weight loss surgery procedures. While some data are available on the outcome of different ethnic/racial groups, little is still known about how descriptive and demographic variances may impact the likelihood of eating pathology following bariatric surgery. Further, the different bariatric surgery procedures currently available may have considerable and differential effects on eating pathology. Lastly, little is known about actual eating behavior in patients who have undergone bariatric surgery. What constitutes "typical" or "normal" eating behavior after bariatric surgery is unclear. Medical complications and specialized diets may mimic eating disordered behaviors or symptoms. Other common symptoms following surgery, such as "plugging," "dumping," constipation, or dysphagia, may result in patients engaging in restrictive or compensatory behaviors in an effort to deal with the difficulties they encounter with food consumption. Lastly, patients are at times instructed to engage in eating behaviors that may look, at least at first blush, to be pathological in nature. For example, patients are instructed to eat very small meals frequently, to chew food extensively, and to only eat certain types of food. Some surgeons have recommended patients "chew and spit" food out, or engage in self-induced vomiting if they are uncomfortable after a meal. In considering whether or not these behaviors are pathological, one must consider the motivation behind them and understand if they are driven by body and shape-related concerns or if they are merely a way of accommodating the considerable changes in the digestive tract that result from the surgery.

Interestingly, some of the key constructs of interest are necessarily different in presurgery versus postsurgery patients. For example, the most commonly used definition of binge eating in presurgery patients typically involves both an objectively large amount of food and a sense of loss of control over eating this food. However, after surgery, some research considers binge eating to have occurred when the patient has eaten a much smaller amount of food, but has experienced a loss of control while consuming this food (e.g., Hsu et al., 1996). The logic behind this difference is, of course, because the changes in the digestive tract in postsurgery patients do not allow for as large an amount of food to be eaten. The end result, however, is that one term (binge eating) has multiple definitions depending upon the temporal relationship to the surgical procedure, and this makes interpretation of research findings difficult.

Eating Disorders and Associated Behaviors

Binge Eating and BED   Not surprisingly, rates of binge eating and BED are generally lower after surgery than they are prior to surgery. Rates of binge eating range from 0% (e.g., Boan et al., 2004) to as high as 71% (Lang, Hauser, Buddeberg, & Klaghofer, 2002). The large range appears to be at least partially due to the definition of binge eating used. Rates of BED following surgery are also generally lower after surgery and range from 0% (Dymek et al., 2001) to 21% (Hsu et al., 1996).

Regarding the predictive power of postoperative binge eating on outcome in bariatric surgery, a recent review addressed this issue. According to Marino and colleagues (in press), the available data suggest that individuals who engage in loss of control eating after surgery are more likely to lose less weight or regain more weight. It appears that, compared to eating behavior prior to surgery, eating behavior after surgery has greater predictive power. See Table 5.2 for a review of this literature.

Other Eating Disordered Behavior   A number of case reports have discussed the development of bulimia nervosa and anorexia nervosa following bariatric surgery (e.g., Mitchell, 1985; Taylor & Sharma, 2006; Atchison, Wade, Higgins, & Slavotinke, 1998; Deitel, 2002). Additionally, Guisado and colleagues (2002) describe the behavior of a vertical band gastroplasty patient as "anorectic-like." Segal and colleagues (2004) also describe the behavior of a bariatric surgery patient as pathologically avoiding eating.

One study that attempted to assess eating behavior after gastric bypass surgery was conducted by de Zwaan and colleagues (2010). They studied 59 Roux-en-Y gastric bypass patients by interviewing them about a wide range of eating and eating-related behaviors, and found that in the 6 months prior to surgery, approximately 25% of their sample reported eating with a loss of control. Additionally, although 63% of their sample reported vomiting (planned or unplanned), only 12% of them reported this to be self-induced vomiting that was motivated by weight loss or fear of weight

Table 5.2 Is Postoperative Binge Eating/Loss of Control Eating Predictive of Weight Loss?

Authors	Method	N	Follow-up Duration	Is BE(D)/LOC Predictive?
Rowston et al., 1992	BPD*	16	2 yrs	Yes
Pekkarinen et al., 1994	Gastroplasty	27	5.4 yrs	Yes
Hsu et al., 1996	Gastroplasty	24	3.5 yrs	Yes
Mitchell et al., 2001	Roux-en-Y	78	14 yrs	Yes
Kalarchian et al., 2002	Roux-en-Y	99	2–7 yrs	Yes
Guisado & Vaz, 2003	Gastroplasty	140	18 mos	Yes
Larsen et al., 2004, 2006	Banding	157	>2 yrs	Yes
White et al., 2009	Roux-en-Y	361	1 and 2 yrs	Yes
de Zwaan et al., 2010	Roux-en-Y	59	2 yrs	Yes

*Biliopancreatic Diversion

regain. Thirty and one-half percent of the sample reported putting food into their mouths and spitting it out without swallowing it. This study suggests that what might otherwise be considered pathological eating behaviors may be relatively common in bariatric surgery patients, and are not necessarily indicative of a full-blown eating disorder.

Night Eating   Hsu et al. (1996) reported that of the 24 postsurgery patients who they interviewed, only 2 continued to report night eating behavior 12 and 18 months after surgery. After surgery, night eating was observed less frequently than before surgery, and both participants who engaged in this behavior after surgery reported eating smaller amounts of food during night eating episodes. Similarly, Hsu et al. (1997) reported that 3 of 27 postsurgery patients reported engaging in night eating behavior. Finally, de Zwaan et al. (2010) reported that, out of a sample of 59 post-Roux-en-Y patients, 7 reported night eating behavior.

Grazing   Similar to before surgery, few data are available on postsurgery patients regarding grazing behavior. Colles et al. (2008) reported on 129 patients who underwent bariatric surgery. Twelve months after surgery they found that 38.0% of patients reported grazing behavior while 26.4% reported grazing before surgery. Although not necessarily the same construct as grazing, Faria, Kelly, Faria, and Ito (2009) reported that frequent snacking, a construct conceptually similar to grazing, predicted less weight loss in a sample of postsurgery Roux-en-Y patients.

High Caloric Fluid Intake   Similar to before surgery, there are few data available to indicate the frequency of excessive fluid intake in bariatric surgery patients after surgery. The same two studies that reported presurgery rates also reported a very small percentage of bariatric surgery patients drinking excessive quantities of high calorie fluids after surgery. Hsu et al. (1996) reported that 4 of their 24 postsurgery patients resumed consuming a large amount of fluids, and Hsu et al. (1997) reported that 2 of 27 patients reported drinking an excessive amount of fluids after surgery.

Sweet Eating   A small amount of research has investigated whether eating sweets after surgery is predictive of weight loss. The findings in this area have been mixed, with one study (Burgmer et al., 2005) showing that sweet eaters lost less weight, one study (Hudson et al., 2002) showing no relationship, and one study (Lindroos, Lissner, & Sjostrom, 1996) showing that postoperative sweet eaters lost more weight.

Plugging and Dumping   The term *dumping* has been used since the 1920s (Wyllys, Andrews, & Mix, 1920) and initially described the radiographic observation of rapid gastric emptying of contrast material in some patients after gastrectomy. Recently, the more commonly preferred term appears to be dumping syndrome. After Roux-en-Y gastric bypass surgery, approximately 50–70% of patients experience dumping syndrome in the early postoperative period (Mallory, Macgregor, & Rand, 1996). The symptoms of dumping syndrome tend to subside after approximately 15–18 months after surgery (Ukleja, 2006).

Two forms of dumping syndrome have been delineated in the literature: early and late dumping. Symptoms of early dumping typically occur less than 30 minutes after food consumption. By contrast, late dumping occurs between 1 and 3 hours after a meal. Early dumping symptoms result from accelerated gastric emptying into the small bowel, while late dumping symptoms are a consequence of hypoglycemia resulting from an exaggerated release of insulin (Holst, 1994). Symptoms of early dumping constitute approximately 75% of dumping syndrome cases, while late dumping comprises only about 25% of these cases (Ukleja, 2006). In a recent survey of Roux-en-Y patients 18–35 months after surgery, 50% of patients reported problems with dumping (either early or late dumping; de Zwaan et al., 2010).

Another eating-related problem that is common following bariatric surgery occurs when food gets stuck in the small outlet from the pouch. This phenomenon is frequently referred to as plugging. Plugging is commonly discussed clinically, but has received very little research attention. This is interesting, particularly given that it appears to be very common in postbariatric surgery patients. When examining 59 patients who were 18–35 months after their surgery, de Zwaan and colleagues (2010) found that 76.3% reported having problems with plugging.

Conclusion

Despite increasing awareness about the potential emergence of problematic eating behavior following bariatric surgery, there are few data addressing this issue. To try to prevent the manifestation of eating disorder pathology after bariatric surgery, research will be needed to identify predictors of poor outcome among bariatric surgery patients. This would allow clinicians to target such behaviors prior to surgery and to increase patient education and monitoring of those deemed to be at risk. The emergence of anorexia nervosa or bulimia nervosa is of particular concern. Currently, evidence to guide the treatment of individuals who develop these disorders is lacking. It is not clear whether eating disorder diagnostic and treatment algorithms can be appropriately extrapolated to patients with eating disorder sequelae following bariatric surgery. Therefore, it may be necessary to develop new sets of guidelines for these patients, informed by research addressing the typical presentation, prognosis, and treatment response observed. Clinicians are encouraged to monitor patients for eating disorder symptoms and atypical presentations that may be associated with excessive weight loss. Services of specialized eating disorder treatment facilities may be required for some of these patients. These facilities are in a unique position to contribute to the literature regarding the treatment of these patients.

References

Adami, G.F., Gandolfo, P., Bauer, B., & Scopinaro, N. (1995). Binge eating in massively obese patients undergoing bariatric surgery. *International Journal of Eating Disorders, 17*, 45–50.

Adami, G.F., Meneghelli, A., & Scopinaro, N. (1999). Night eating and binge eating disorder in obese patients. *International Journal of Eating Disorders, 25*, 335–338.

Allison, K.C., Lundgren, J.D., O'Reardon, J.P., Geliebter, A., Gluck, M.E., Vinai, P. et al. (2010). Proposed diagnostic criteria for night eating syndrome. *International Journal of Eating Disorders, 43*, 241–247.

Allison, K.C., Wadden, T.A., Sarwer, D.B., Fabricatore, A.N., Crerand, C.E., Gibbons, L.M. et al. (2006). Night eating syndrome and binge eating disorder among persons seeking bariatric surgery: Prevalence and related features. *Surgery for Obesity and Related Diseases, 2*, 153–158.

American Psychiatric Association. (2000). *Diagnostic and statistical manual of mental disorders* (4th ed., text rev.). Washington, DC: Author.

Atchison, M., Wade, T., Higgins, B., & Slavotinke, T. (1998). Anorexia nervosa following gastric reduction surgery for morbid obesity. *International Journal of Eating Disorders, 23*, 111–116.

Boan, J., Kolotkin, R.L., Westman, E.C., McMahon, R.L., & Grant, J.P. (2004). Binge eating, quality of life and physical activity improve after Roux-en-Y gastric bypass for morbid obesity. *Obesity Surgery, 14*, 341–348.

Burgmer, R., Grigutsch, K., Zipfel, S., Wolf, A.M., de Zwaan, M., Husemann, B. et al. (2005). The influence of eating behavior and eating pathology on weight loss after gastric restriction operations. *Obesity Surgery*, *15*, 684–691.

Busetto, L., Segato, G., de Marchi, F., Foletto, M., De Luca, M., Caniato, D. et al. (2002). Outcome predictors of morbidly obese recipients of an adjustable gastric band. *Obesity Surgery*, *12*, 83–92.

Busetto, L., Valente, P., Pisent, C., Segato, G., de Marchi, F., Favretti, F. et al. (1996). Eating pattern in the first year following adjustable silicone gastric banding (ASGB) for morbid obesity. *International Journal of Obesity*, *20*, 539–546.

Colles, S.L., Dixon, J.B., & O'Brien, P.E. (2008). Loss of control is central to psychological disturbance associated with binge eating disorder. *Obesity*, *16*, 608–614.

Deitel, M. (2002). Anorexia nervosa following bariatric surgery (Editorial). *Obesity Surgery*, *12*, 729–730.

de Zwaan, M. (2005). Weight and eating changes after bariatric surgery. In J.E. Mitchell & M. de Zwaan (Eds.), *Bariatric surgery: A guide for mental health professionals* (pp. 77–100). New York: Routledge.

de Zwaan, M., Hilbert, A., Swan-Kremeier, L., Simonich, H., Lancaster, K., Howell, L.M. et al. (2010). Comprehensive interview assessment of eating behavior 18–35 months after gastric bypass surgery for morbid obesity. *Surgery for Obesity and Related Diseases*, *6*, 79–85.

Dymek, M.P., le Grange, D., Neven, K., & Alverdy, J. (2001). Quality of life and psychosocial adjustment in patients after Roux-en-Y gastric bypass: A brief report. *Obesity Surgery*, *11*, 32–39.

Fairburn, D., & Cooper, Z. (1993). The eating disorder examination. In C.G. Fairburn & G.T. Wilson (Eds.), *Binge eating: Nature, assessment and treatment* (pp. 317–360). New York: Guilford.

Faria, S.L., Kelly, E.D.O., Faria, O.P., & Ito, M.K. (2009). Snack-eating patients experience lesser weight loss after Roux-en-Y gastric bypass surgery. *Obesity Surgery*, *19*, 1293–1296.

Green, A., Dymek-Valentine, M., leGrange, D., Pyluk, S., & Alverdy, J. (2004). Psychosocial outcome of gastric bypass surgery for patients with and without binge eating. *Obesity Surgery*, *14*, 975–986.

Guisado, J.A., Vaz, F.J., Lopez-Ibor, J.J., Lopez-Ibor, M.I., del Rio, J., & Rubio, M.A. (2002). Gastric surgery and restraint from food as triggering factors of eating disorders in morbid obesity. *International Journal of Eating Disorders*, *31*, 97–100.

Herpertz, S., & Saller, B. (2001). Psychosomatic aspects of obesity. *Psychotherapy Psychosomatic Medicine Psychology*, *51*, 336–349.

Holst, J.J. (1994). Glucagon-like peptide 1: A newly discovered gastrointestinal hormone. *Gastroenterology*, *107*, 1848–1855.

Hsu, L., Betancourt, S., & Sullivan, S. (1996). Eating disturbances before and after vertical banded gastroplasty: A pilot study. *International Journal of Eating Disorders*, *19*, 23–34.

Hsu, L.K., Sullivan, S.P., & Benotti, P.N. (1997). Eating disturbances and outcome of gastric bypass surgery: A pilot study. *International Journal of Eating Disorders*, *21*, 385–390.

Hudson, S.M., Dixon, J.B., & O'Brien, P.E. (2002). Sweet eating is not a predictor of outcome following Lap-Band placement. Can we finally bury the myth? *Obesity Surgery, 12,* 789–794.

Kim, T.H., Daud, A., Ude, A.O., DiGiorgi, M., Olivero-Rivera, L., Schrope, B. et al. (2006). Early U.S. outcomes of laparoscopic gastric bypass versus laparoscopic adjustable silicone gastric banding for morbid obesity. *Surgical Endoscopy, 20,* 202–209.

Korenkov, M., Kneist, W., Heintz, A., & Junginger, T. (2004). Laparoscopic gastric banding as a universal method for the treatment of patients with morbid obesity. *Obesity Surgery, 14,* 1123–1127.

Lang, T., Hauser, R., Buddeberg, C., & Klaghofer, R. (2002). Impact of gastric banding on eating behavior and weight. *Obesity Surgery, 12,* 100–107.

Latner, J.D., Wetzler, S., Goodman, E.R., & Glinski, J. (2004). Gastric bypass in a low-income, inner-city population: Eating disturbances and weight loss. *Obesity Research, 12,* 956–961.

Lindroos, A.K., Lissner, L., & Sjostrom, L. (1996). Weight change in relation to intake of sugar and sweet foods before and after weight reducing gastric surgery. *International Journal of Obesity and Related Metabolic Disorders. 20,* 634–643.

Mallory, G.N., Macgregor, A.M., & Rand, C.S. (1996). The influence of dumping on weight loss after gastric restrictive surgery for morbid obesity. *Obesity Surgery, 6,* 474–478.

Marino, J.M., Ertelt, T.W., Lancaster, K., Steffen, K., Peterson, L., de Zwaan, M. et al. (In press). The emergence of eating pathology after bariatric surgery: A rare outcome with important clinical implications. *International Journal of Eating Disorders.*

Mitchell, J.E. (1985). Bulimia with self-induced vomiting after gastric stapling. *American Journal of Psychiatry, 142,* 656.

Mitchell, J.E., Lancaster, K.L., Burgard, M.A., Howell, L.M., Krahn, D.D., Crosby, R.D. et al. (2001). Long-term follow-up of patients' status after gastric bypass. *Obesity Surgery, 11,* 464–468.

Powers, P.S., Perez, A., Boyd, F., & Rosemurgy, A. (1999). Eating pathology before and after bariatric surgery: A prospective study. *International Journal of Eating Disorders, 25,* 293–300.

Rand, C.S.W., & Kuldau, J.M. (1993). Morbid obesity: A comparison between a general population and obesity surgery patients. *International Journal of Obesity, 17,* 657–661.

Sabbioni, M.E.E., Dickson, M.H., Eychmuller, S., Francke, D., Goetz, S., Hurny, C. et al. (2002). Intermediate results of health related quality of life after vertical banded gastroplasty. *International Journal of Obesity, 26,* 277–280.

Sallet, P.C., Sallet, J.A., & Dixon, J.B. (2007). Eating behavior as a prognostic factor for weight loss after gastric bypass. *Obesity Surgery, 17,* 445–451.

Sansone, R.A., Schumacher, D., Wiederman, M.W., & Routson-Weichers, L. (2008). The prevalence of binge eating disorder and borderline personality symptomatology among gastric surgery patients. *Eating Behavior, 9,* 197–202.

Saunders, R. (1999). Binge eating in gastric bypass patients before surgery. *Obesity Surgery, 9,* 72–76.

Saunders, R. (2001). Compulsive eating and gastric bypass surgery: What does hunger have to do with it? *Obesity Surgery, 11,* 757–761.

Saunders, R. (2010, September). Personal communication.

Segal, A., Kinoshita Kussunoki, D., & Larino, M. A. (2004). Post-surgical refusal to eat: Anorexia nervosa, bulimia nervosa, or a new eating disorder? A case series. *Obesity Surgery, 14*, 353–360.

Stunkard, A.J., Grace, W.J., & Wolf, H.G. (1955). The night-eating syndrome: A pattern of food intake among certain obese patients. *American Journal of Medicine, 19*, 78–86.

Sugerman, H.J., Starkey, J.V., & Birkenhauer, R. (1987). A randomized prospective trial of gastric bypass versus vertical banded gastroplasty for morbid obesity and their effects on sweets versus non-sweets eaters. *Annals of Surgery, 205*, 613–624.

Taylor, V.H., & Sharma, A.M. (2006). A patient with personal control of the adjustable gastric band and bulimia: A psychiatric complication. *Obesity Surgery, 16*, 1386–1387.

Ukleja, A. (2006). Dumping syndrome. *Practical Gastroenterology, 29*, 32–46.

Wyllys, E., Andrews, E., & Mix, C.L. (1920). "Dumping stomach" and other results of gastrojejunostomy: Operative cure by disconnecting old stoma. *Surgery Clinic Chicago, 4*, 879–892.

CHAPTER 6

Cognitive Dysfunction in Obesity
Implications for Bariatric Surgery Patients

JOHN GUNSTAD, ASTRID MUELLER, KELLY
STANEK, and MARY BETH SPITZNAGEL

More than 700 million adults worldwide will be obese by 2015. As reviewed elsewhere in this book, obesity is linked to greater morbidity and mortality (Adams et al., 2006; Ogden, Yanovski, Carroll, & Flegal, 2007), as well as multiple medical and mental health problems (O'Brien, Dixon, & Brown, 2004). Rapidly growing evidence demonstrates that obesity is also associated with poor neurocognitive outcomes. These adverse effects of obesity have been detected across the life span, using a broad range of methodologies (e.g., cognitive testing, neuroimaging, neuropathology), and from countries around the globe. Due to their significant excess weight and many medical comorbidities, bariatric surgery candidates appear to at very high risk for these adverse cognitive consequences.

The current chapter will briefly review the existing literature on the neurocognitive effects of obesity and highlight the findings most important for health care providers working with bariatric surgery patients. To do so, the chapter is divided into four sections:

- Patterns of cognitive impairment in obese persons
- Mechanisms for cognitive impairment in obesity
- Cognitive effects of bariatric surgery
- Neuropsychological assessment of bariatric surgery candidates

Information will also be provided to identify those areas most in need of further empirical studies, with the ultimate goal of optimizing surgical outcomes in this population.

Patterns of Cognitive Impairment in Obese Persons

Though findings vary somewhat across studies, higher rates of memory and frontal/subcortical dysfunction are generally found in overweight and obese adults. This section will introduce a subset of the studies in this area. Particular emphasis will be placed on those studies that have examined impulsivity, a construct closely linked to weight status in multiple samples.

Memory

There is evidence that obesity is associated with memory deficits. In an early study, Elias, Elias, Sullivan, Wolf, and D'Agostino (2003) examined the influence of obesity and hypertension on cognitive performance in middle-aged and older participants in the Framingham Heart Study. Body mass index (BMI) and blood pressure were assessed 4 to 6 years prior to cognitive testing. The authors found independent and cumulative adverse effects of hypertension and obesity on learning and memory for males, but not for females.

Kuo et al. (2006) explored cognitive function in 2,684 elderly people aged 64 to 94 years. They found a nonlinear relationship between cognitive performance and BMI in normal weight, overweight, and obese older people. In this study, overweight participants exhibited better performance on memory tests than normal weight individuals. However, this association was attenuated after other cardiovascular risk factors were included in the analyses. Obese individuals did not perform significantly better or worse on memory tasks than normal weight people.

With respect to middle-aged adults, a French study (Cournot et al., 2006) reported an independent association between memory deficits (word list learning) and high BMI in 2,223 healthy men and women. Gunstad and colleagues (2006) also described the relationship between memory performance (word list learning) and obesity in young and middle-aged adults. Obese individuals learned and recognized fewer words than overweight and normal weight individuals. These findings were confirmed by a more recent study conducted by the same research group (Gunstad, Lhotsky, Wendell, Ferrucci, & Zonderman, 2010). That cross-sectional examination of 1,703 participants of the Baltimore Longitudinal Study of Aging showed that obesity indices (BMI, waist circumference, waist–hip ratio) were significantly related to reduced memory performance.

Attention

Several studies have also found reduced attention abilities in overweight/obese people. For example, individuals with attention deficit/hyperactivity disorder (ADHD), who have attentional problems by definition, are at a higher risk of being overweight or obese (Altfas, 2002; Fleming, Levy, & Levitan, 2005; Levy, Fleming, & Klar, 2009). However, research based on cognitive tests provides mixed results regarding this proposed association. For instance, a French study (Cournot et al., 2006) reported an association between higher BMI and lower performance on a selective attention test that was significant in women, but not men. The findings of a Hungarian-Belgian study (Cserjési, Luminet, Poncelet, & Lénárd, 2009) revealed increased depressive symptoms and reduced sustained attention capacity in obese people. More specifically, they reported that obese women performed significantly worse on the d2 attention test than normal weight women, and that sustained attention was not associated with negative emotional status. In contrast, cross-sectional results of the Baltimore Longitudinal Study of Aging published by Gunstad, Lhotsky, and colleagues (2010) showed that participants with higher BMI, waist circumference, and waist–hip ratio exhibited better performance on the Trail Making Test A than persons with lower body composition indices. In another study Gunstad et al. (2007) found no differences in attention performance between healthy overweight/obese individuals and normal weight subjects. When explaining these unexpected results, the authors cited the relatively healthy status of their sample, which was characterized by the absence of medical and psychiatric conditions, including ADHD.

Executive Function

The concept of executive function includes higher-order cognitive abilities that are necessary to engage in goal-directed behavior, to respond in an adaptive manner in novel situations, and for self-control (Miller & Cohen, 2001; Barkley, 2001; Lezak, 2004). These executive control processes are thought to be located in the prefrontal cortex and frontal systems. They are relevant when alternative behaviors must be compared with each other and prioritized on the basis of their consequences. The term *executive function* combines the actions of planning, inhibitory control, strategy development and use, flexible sequencing of actions, maintenance of behavioral set, interrupting ongoing responses, and resistance to interference. Executive control and impulsivity, defined as a tendency toward unplanned actions (Moeller, Barratt, Dougherty, Schmitz, & Swann, 2001), are linked such that elevated impulsivity is associated with poorer executive control.

There is evidence that heightened levels of impulsivity are involved in overweight/obesity and dysregulated eating (Nederkoorn, Smulders,

Havermans, Roefs, & Jansen, 2006). For example, cognitive and motivational aspects of impulsivity, in particular urgency and sensitivity to reward, seem to be associated with eating disorder psychopathology in overweight and obese individuals (Mobbs, Crépin, Thiéry, Golay, & van der Linden, 2010). In overweight individuals with binge eating, level of impulsivity predicted the amount of test meal consumption (Galanti, Gluck, & Geliebter, 2007). Pilot data (Mueller, Fischer, Mitchell, & de Zwaan, unpublished data) suggest high rates of impulse control disorders (ICDs) among morbidly obese individuals that did not significantly differ from those assessed in a psychiatric inpatient sample (Mueller et al., unpublished data). Based on structured clinical interviews, a current ICD rate of 19% was found, primarily pathological skin picking (8%), compulsive buying (6%), and intermittent explosive disorder (5%).

Based on neuropsychological tasks, several studies found that obese individuals are less able to inhibit a response and more often choose an instant reward over a larger delayed reward. Performing the Iowa gambling task, obese adults preferred high immediate gain, but larger future losses, versus lower immediate gain, but smaller future loss (Davis, Levitan, Muglia, Bewell, & Kennedy, 2004; Pignatti et al., 2006). With respect to other decision-making tasks, the findings are inconsistent. For instance, Nederkoorn, Smulders, Havermans, Roefs, and Jansen (2006) did not find compelling differences between obese women and lean controls on the delay discounting task with hypothetical money reward. Potentially, differences in income (not assessed in that study) may have influenced the result. The delay discounting task was also used in a study conducted by Weller, Cook, Avsar, and Cox (2008). Independent of age, income, or IQ, obese female but not male students discounted delays to a greater extent than normal weight women.

Recently, Davis, Patte, Curtis, and Reid (2010) assessed obese women with and without binge eating disorder, and normal weight women on both the Iowa gambling task and the delay discounting task. The two obese groups performed worse on both tasks compared to normal weight controls, but did not differ from each other. Of note, when education level was included into the analyses the group differences no longer reached statistical significance. Using data from Brain Resource International Database, in which persons with significant medical and psychiatric conditions were excluded, Gunstad and colleagues (2007) found reduced executive function (verbal interference, maze errors) in overweight/obese adults relative to normal weight adults. Findings support the association between excess weight and reduced planning and response inhibition. Waldstein and Katzel (2006) examined executive function in healthy middle-aged and older adults using Trail Making Test B and the Stroop Color Word Test. Independent of several confounding factors (e.g., metabolic syndrome), the authors noted interactive relations between central obesity and hypertension with regard to executive function. Recently, the link between reduced executive abilities and adiposity was confirmed in samples of morbidly obese individuals seeking surgical treatment (Cserjési et al., 2009; Boeka & Lokken, 2008; Lokken, Boeka, Yellumahanthi, Wesley, & Clements, 2010). Bariatric surgery candidates exhibited deficits on tasks of problem solving, planning, and mental flexibility in comparison to normative data (Boeka & Lokken, 2008; Lokken et al., 2010; Gunstad et al., in press). With regard to possible influence of emotional status, Cserjési and colleagues (2009) described a mediating role of depression in the relationship between obesity and response inhibition. Published data on executive function in children or adolescents are sparse. However, the few existing publications suggest that similar to adults, obese children and adolescents tend to exhibit deficits in executive functioning (Li, Dai, Jackson, & Zhang, 2008; Lokken, Boeka, Austin, Gunstad, & Harmon, 2009; Verdejo-García et al., 2010).

Conclusion

There is growing evidence that obesity is associated with reduced cognitive abilities, including memory, attention, and executive function. Although many studies provide support for this link, the question whether obesity itself or indirectly (i.e., via metabolic changes) leads to cognitive decline remains unresolved. In addition, it is unknown whether adiposity is a cause or a result of reduced cognitive function. Poor cognitive abilities, elevated levels of impulsivity, and reduced inhibitory control are plausible explanations for overeating, binge eating, or loss of control eating. The impaired ability to delay gratification may negatively affect weight maintenance after successful surgical treatment. Furthermore, it is unclear whether a subgroup of patients who significantly lose weight due to bariatric surgery subsequently develop or increase impulsive behaviors (e.g., compulsive buying, pathological skin picking, exercise dependence) beyond those associated with food, such as overeating, binge eating, or loss of control eating.

Mechanisms for Cognitive Impairment in Obesity

Given the many physiological changes associated with obesity, it appears likely that its adverse neurocognitive effects are the product of a combination of related processes. Work is just beginning to clarify the causal pathways in this complex phenomenon and will likely involve an interaction of established and novel risk factors.

For example, obesity is associated with a number of known risk factors for poor neurocognitive outcome. Obese individuals often exhibit comorbid hypertension and type 2 diabetes; in turn, each of the conditions is associated with pathological changes to the brain and reduced cognitive function

(Raz, Rodrigue, & Acker, 2003; Kumar, Anstey, Cherbuin, Wen, & Sachdev, 2008; Aloia, Arnedt, David, Riggs, & Byrd, 2004; Elias, Elias, Sullivan, Wolf, & D'Agostino, 2003, 2005). Similarly, sleep apnea is common in obese persons and associated with both brain abnormalities and cognitive dysfunction (Canessa et al., 2011). Interestingly, recent work suggests that conditions like hypertension, diabetes, and sleep apnea may interact with each other in complicated ways (Pandey et al., 2011; Reishstein, 2011), raising the possibility of previously unexamined mechanisms for cerebral injury.

Closely related to these conditions are circulating biomarkers that may be important contributors to the cognitive impairment found in obese individuals. One such mechanism involves altered levels of adipokines, which are secreted by adipose tissue and are linked to both neurocognitive dysfunction and structural brain abnormalities (Scharf & Ahima, 2004; Pannacciulli, Le, Chen, Reiman, & Krakoff, 2007; Gunstad, Paul et al., 2008). The pro-inflammatory state associated with increased BMI reflects another potential mechanism, as it is a known contributor to poor neurocognitive outcomes in other populations (Sweat et al., 2008; Bastard et al., 2006; Jefferson et al., 2007; Rosenberg, 2009). Recent work on biomarkers traditionally examined for eating and weight behavior such as leptin and ghrelin has shown an important, though still unexplained, link to cognitive function (see Gunstad, Spitznagel et al., 2008b regarding leptin; Spitznagel et al., 2010 regarding ghrelin). Future work will undoubtedly reveal many additional biomarkers important for these relationships.

Although the exact mechanisms are currently unclear, a growing number of studies demonstrate brain abnormalities on neuroimaging or pathology studies in obese individuals. On structural imaging, obese individuals exhibit global brain atrophy and reductions in both frontal and temporal brain regions (Ward, Carlsson, Trivedi, Sager, & Johnson, 2005; Taki et al., 2008; Gunstad, Paul et al., 2008a; Pannacciulli et al., 2006; Raji et al., 2010; Walther, Birdsill, Glisky, & Ryan, 2010; Jagust, Harvey, Mungas, & Haan, 2005; Gustafson, Lissner, Bengtsson, Bjorkelund, & Skoog, 2004). White matter abnormalities can also be found, including reduced volume, increased white matter hyperintensities, and decreased functionality connectivity measured by diffusion tensor imaging (Gustafson, Steen, & Skoog, 2004; Jagust et al., 2005; Haltia et al., 2007; Stanek et al., 2011). Neurochemical evidence also suggests white matter injury in obese persons, with reduced concentrations of N-acetylaspartate in frontal, parietal, and temporal white matter, as well as reduced concentrations of choline-containing metabolite in frontal white matter (Gazdzinski, Kornak, Weiner, & Meyerhoff, 2008). Finally, pathology studies have found increased expression of Alzheimer's disease–related markers, including tau protein, amyloid precursor protein, and amyloid-β peptide (Mrak, 2009).

In summary, overweight and obesity appear to be most strongly associated with the cognitive domains associated with frontal/subcortical brain function (such as attention, working memory, speeded cognitive processing, and executive function) as well as memory. Behavioral manifestations of these reduced cognitive functions may include increased impulsivity, poor self-monitoring, and behavioral constraint, as well as diminished planning and problem solving (Fuster, 2008). In turn, these behavioral expressions of reduced cognition may impact adherence and outcome in the bariatric surgery patient. For example, reduced ability to plan and problem solve may hinder maintenance of postsurgical lifestyle changes, or impulsivity may lead to difficulty adhering to dietary restrictions. Similarly, these difficulties are also associated with increased risk for mood disturbance (Savitz & Drevets, 2009), which could further worsen outcomes.

Cognitive Effects of Bariatric Surgery

One of our current projects is directly examining the possible cognitive effects of bariatric surgery. We are conducting prospective, comprehensive cognitive assessment in 250 bariatric surgery patients and obese controls at preoperative, 12 weeks postop, 12 months postop, and 24 months postop. As bariatric surgery patients often exhibit alleviation or even resolution of medical conditions associated with cognitive dysfunction (e.g., hypertension, type 2 diabetes), we hoped that the postsurgical weight loss might improve cognitive test performance.

The first paper from this study has just been published and compared cognitive test performance in surgery patients and controls at baseline and 12-week time points (Gunstad et al., in press). Three important findings emerged from this initial comparison. First, cognitive dysfunction was prevalent in bariatric surgery candidates, with many having clinically meaningful impairments on testing (i.e., >1.5 standard deviations below normative values). For example, nearly a quarter of patients had clinically meaningful deficits on measures of learning of new information and recognition memory. This is far more prevalent than would be expected in a nonobese sample.

Next, we compared rates of cognitive decline from baseline to 12 weeks in both surgery and control patients to examine whether bariatric surgery might produce cognitive dysfunction. Many major surgeries have been linked to adverse, acute cognitive impairment (e.g., cardiovascular surgeries), and it was unknown if bariatric surgery patients would show a similar pattern. No such pattern emerged in the sample, indicating that uncomplicated bariatric surgery does not impair cognitive function at 12-week follow-up.

Finally, we examined the possible cognitive improvements and found that bariatric surgery patients exhibited improvement in multiple cognitive domains, including memory, attention, and executive function. When accounting for those abilities that also improved in controls (thus accounting for any possible practice effects), bariatric surgery patients showed consistent improvements in memory function at 12 weeks. At the time of this writing, longitudinal analyses are currently under way to better understand these effects over a longer interval (i.e., 12 months, 24 months), as weight loss is rapid during the first 6 months postoperatively and continues until 24 months, where weight loss often plateaus or starts to regress (O'Brien et al., 2004).

Neuropsychological Assessment of Bariatric Surgery Candidates

On the basis of these and other findings, the coming years will likely produce increased awareness of cognitive impairment in bariatric surgery patients. The American Society for Bariatric Surgery has recently recommended neuropsychological evaluation in bariatric surgery candidates. Importantly, many third-party payers have now agreed to reimburse providers for these services, granting access to a larger number of patients and important data to health professionals. Similar policies in persons undergoing surgery for cardiovascular disease (e.g., coronary artery bypass graft) resulted in rapid gains in knowledge regarding the physiological mechanisms that predict short- and long-term patient outcomes.

The best measures for assessing neuropsychological function in bariatric surgery patients have not yet been empirically established. Below, we suggest an initial approach based on our clinical and research experience in this population, though further work is needed to determine the sensitivity and predictive validity of these and other measures in this population. The selected tests are commonly used instruments that are widely available, and many are known to be sensitive to the cognitive deficits associated with cardiovascular disease and type 2 diabetes—conditions frequently comorbid to obesity.

Neuropsychological testing for bariatric surgery patients would ideally be sensitive to both cognitive impairment during preoperative visits to help tailor interventions and possible postoperative changes in cognitive function due to surgical complications. Each of these approaches is briefly presented below.

Preoperative Evaluations

Prior to surgery, neuropsychological evaluation should test for impairment in all primary cognitive domains, including global cognitive function, as well as multiple aspects of attention, executive function, memory, language, visuospatial, and motor function. See Table 6.1 for a listing of suggested tests. These tests should be considered in addition to traditional

Table 6.1 Proposed Neuropsychological Test Battery for Bariatric Surgery Candidates

Domain	Measures	Cognitive Ability
Effort	Test of memory malingering	Effort during testing
Global cognitive function	Modified Mini Mental State Exam	Estimate of global function
Attention/executive functioning	Digit span	Basic auditory attention
	Letter number sequencing	Working memory
	Trail Making Tests A and B	Psychomotor speed, set shifting
	Stroop Color Word Test	Cognitive inhibition
	Wisconsin Card Sort Test	Hypothesis testing, reasoning
	Iowa gambling task	Response inhibition, decision making
	Tower of Hanoi	Planning
	Continuous Performance Test	Sustained attention
Memory	Auditory Verbal Learning Test	Verbal list learning and memory
	Complex Figure Test Recall	Nonverbal memory
	Logical memory	Verbal story memory
Language Boston Naming Test	Confrontation naming	
	Controlled Oral Word Association Test	Phonemic verbal fluency
	Animal naming	Semantic verbal fluency
Visuospatial	Complex figure test-copy	Complex visuoconstruction
	Hooper Visual Organization Test	Motor-free perceptual organization
Motor	Grooved pegboard	Speeded dexterity
Reading	WRAT-4 Word Reading	Basic reading skills
	WRAT-4 Sentence Comprehension	Basic comprehension
Psychopathology/mood	MMPI-RF	
	Patient Health Questionnaire (PHQ)	

measures of psychopathology and mood that are sensitive to dysfunction in this population. As described above, obesity has been associated with cognitive dysfunction in multiple domains, and a comprehensive evaluation will minimize the risk of overlooking an important cognitive skill that could adversely impact long-term outcomes.

We also encourage clinicians to closely examine each patient's level of executive function and memory prior to surgery. In addition to being frequently impaired in obese individuals, executive function and memory abilities are closely related to adherence to medical regimen and patient outcomes in other populations (Feil et al., 2009; Hayes, Larimer, Adami, & Kaye, 2009). It is easy to imagine that patients with deficits in problem solving or memory could experience difficulties in adhering to the complex postoperative medical regimen and thus be at elevated risk for poor outcomes. For example, our preliminary work shows that bariatric surgery patients with better memory function at baseline lose weight more quickly postoperatively. Though many possible explanations exist, a likely explanation is that such persons more closely adhere to the prescribed regimen and thus have better outcomes. We are examining this possibility at the time of this writing.

Consistent with this, a better understanding of the cognitive profile of obese older adults and adolescents is much needed. Even normal aging is associated with reductions in executive function and memory, and it is likely that the mechanisms responsible for these changes may interact with obesity changes to exacerbate cognitive impairment. As a result, the growing number of older adults seeking bariatric surgery may be at elevated risk for cognitive impairment and thus encounter difficulties adhering to both pre- and postoperative care guidelines. Similarly, recent work shows adolescents presenting for bariatric surgery exhibit cognitive dysfunction (Lokken et al., 2009), and its impacts on treatment outcomes are not fully understood.

A final consideration for preoperative assessment of cognitive function in bariatric surgery candidates is patient reading level. Bariatric surgery patients are frequently given large amounts of text to independently read and understand. Even subtle difficulties in comprehension may promote medical complications, weight regain, or significant emotional distress. For example, one of us heard the story of a patient that was functionally illiterate but was not identified as such until several months postoperatively. This individual was asked to read a large collection of materials prior to this time without detection. Although these cases are likely very rare, determination of a patient's ability to read and comprehend written materials may help optimize short- and long-term outcomes. Similarly, the written materials provided to patients should be routinely examined to ensure that the reading level is appropriate, especially when describing complex concepts or multistep activities.

Table 6.2 Proposed Neuropsychological Test Battery for
Postoperative Bariatric Surgery Patients

Domain	Test
Global cognitive ability	Modified Mini Mental State Exam
Attention	Digit span

Postoperative Evaluations

In addition to a comprehensive evaluation prior to surgery, screening of cognitive function at postoperative visits may also be help to optimize patient outcomes. Bariatric surgery patients are at risk for vitamin deficiencies with known neurological consequences, including low levels of iron, folate, and B12 (Clegg, Colquitt, Sidhu, Royle, & Walker, 2003; Skroubis et al., 2002; Berger, 2004; Choi & Scarborough, 2004; Escalona et al., 2004; Loh et al., 2004). These changes occur in a small number of patients, but are known to emerge up to 20 months postoperatively (Abarbanel, Berginer, Osimani, Solomon, & Cherugi, 1987; Berger, 2004; Thaisetthawatkul et al., 2008). Screening for postoperative changes in cognitive function can be conducted in just a few minutes and could be incorporated into the routine follow-up visits (see Table 6.2). These evaluations could be similar to those for delirium or other inpatient settings and quickly screen global cognitive abilities, attention, executive function, and memory function. Using alternate forms of the measures used during the preoperative assessment is strongly recommended to detect such changes, though studies are needed to determine reliable change indices for this population. As noted above, we found that patients who underwent uncomplicated bariatric surgery did not exhibit significant cognitive changes. However, it appears likely that cognitive dysfunction would be more likely in patients with a more complicated recovery, and early detection could provide many benefits.

Summary and Conclusion

The growing evidence for cognitive impairment in obese individuals has significant implications for persons working with bariatric surgery patients. This population is at elevated risk for problems with memory and executive function—cognitive abilities important for adhering to pre- and postoperative regimens. Comprehensive evaluation of neuropsychological function prior to surgery and regular monitoring after surgery may help to optimize patient outcomes. Additional research is much needed to clearly determine the most sensitive and specific tests in bariatric surgery patients, particularly older adults and other special populations.

References

Abarbanel, J., Berginer, V., Osimani, A., Solomon, H., & Cheruzi, I. (1987). Neurologic complications after gastric restriction surgery for morbid obesity. *Neurology, 37,* 196–200.

Adams, K.F., Schatzkin, A., Harris, T.B., Kipnis, V., Mouw, T., Ballard-Barbash, R. et al. (2006). Overweight, obesity, and mortality in a large prospective cohort of persons 50 to 71 years old. *New England Journal of Medicine, 355,* 763–778.

Aloia, M., Arnedt, J., Davis, J., Riggs, R.L., & Byrd, D. (2004). Neuropsychological sequelae of obstructive sleep apnea-hypopnea syndrome: A critical review. *Journal of the International Neuropsychological Society, 10,* 772–785.

Altfas, J.R. (2002). Prevalence of attention deficit/hyperactivity disorder among adults in obesity treatment. *BMC Psychiatry, 2,* 9.

Barkley, R.A. (2001). The executive functions and self-regulation: An evolutionary neuropsychological perspective. *Neuropsychological Review, 11,* 1–29.

Bastard, J.P., Maachi, M., Lagathu, C., Kim, M.J., Caron, M., Vidal, H. et al. (2006). Recent advances in the relationship between obesity, inflammation, and insulin resistance. *European Cytokine Network, 17,* 4–12.

Berger, J. (2004). The neurological complications of bariatric surgery. *Archives of Neurology, 61,* 1185–1189.

Boeka, A.G., & Lokken, K.L. (2008). Neuropsychological performance of a clinical sample of extremely obese individuals. *Archives of Clinical Neuropsychology, 23,* 467–474.

Canessa, N., Castronovo, V., Cappa, S., Aloia, M., Marelli, S., Falini, A. et al. (2011) Obstructive sleep apnea: Brain structural changes and neurocognitive function before and after treatment. *American Journal of Respiratory and Critical Care Medicine, 183,* 1419–1426.

Clegg, A., Colquitt, J., Sidhu, M., Royle, P., & Walker, A. (2003). Clinical and cost effectiveness of surgery for morbid obesity: A systematic review and economic evaluation. *International Journal of Obesity and Related Metabolic Disorders, 27,* 1167–1177.

Cournot, M., Marquié, J.C., Ansiau, D., Martinaud, C., Fonds, H., Ferrières, J. et al. (2006). Relation between body mass index and cognitive function in healthy middle-aged men and women. *Neurology, 67,* 1208–1214.

Cserjési, R., Luminet, O., Poncelet, A.S., & Lénárd, L. (2009). Altered executive function in obesity. Exploration of the role of affective states on cognitive abilities. *Appetite, 52,* 535–539.

Davis, C., Levitan, R.D., Muglia, P., Bewell, C., & Kennedy, J.L. (2004). Decision-making deficits and overeating: A risk model for obesity. *Obesity Research, 12,* 929–935.

Davis, C., Patte, K., Curtis, C., & Reid, C. (2010). Immediate pleasures and future consequences. A neuropsychological study of binge eating and obesity. *Appetite, 54,* 208–213.

Elias, M.F., Elias, P.K., Sullivan, L.M., Wolf, P.A., & D'Agostino, R.B. (2003). Lower cognitive function in the presence of obesity and hypertension: The Framingham Heart Study. *International Journal of Obesity and Related Metabolic Disorders, 27,* 260–268.

Elias, M.F., Elias, P.K., Sullivan, L.M., Wolf, P.A., & D'Agostino, R.B. (2005). Obesity, diabetes and cognitive deficit: The Framingham Heart Study. *Neurobiology of Aging, 26,* 11–16.

Feil, D.G., Pearman, A., Victor, T., Harwood, D., Weinreb, J., Kahle, K. et al. (2009). The role of cognitive impairment and caregiver support in diabetes management of older outpatients. *International Journal of Psychiatry in Medicine, 39,* 199–214.

Fleming, J.P., Levy, L.D., & Levitan, R.D. (2005). Symptoms of attention deficit hyperactivity disorder in severely obese women. *Eating and Weight Disorders, 10,* 10–13.

Fuster, J.M. (2008). *The prefrontal cortex* (4th ed.). London: Academic Press.

Galanti, K., Gluck, M. E., & Geliebter, A. (2007). Test meal intake in obese binge eaters in relation to impulsivity and compulsivity. *International Journal of Eating Disorders, 40,* 727–732.

Gazdzinski, S., Kornak, J., Weiner, M.W., & Meyerhoff, D.J. (2008). Body mass index and magnetic resonance markers of brain integrity in adults. *Annals of Neurology, 63,* 652–657.

Gunstad, J., Lhotsky, A., Wendell, C.R., Ferrucci, L., & Zonderman, A.B. (2010). Longitudinal examination of obesity and cognitive function: Results from the Baltimore longitudinal study of aging. *Neuroepidemiology, 34,* 222–229.

Gunstad, J., Paul, R., Cohen, R., Spitznagel, M., Tate, D., Grieve, S. et al. (2008). Relationship between body mass index and brain volume in healthy adults. *International Journal of Neuroscience, 118,* 1582–1593.

Gunstad, J., Paul, R.H. Cohen, R.A., Tate, D.F., & Gordon, E. (2006). Obesity is associated with memory deficits in young and middle-aged adults. *Eating and Weight Disorders, 11,* 15–19.

Gunstad, J., Paul, R.H., Cohen, R.A., Tate, D.F., Spitznagel, M.B., & Gordon, E. (2007). Elevated body mass index is associated with executive dysfunction in otherwise healthy adults. *Comprehensive Psychiatry, 48,* 57–61.

Gunstad, J., Spitznagel, M., Keary, T., Glickman, E., Alexander, T., Karrer, J. et al. (2008). Serum leptin levels are associated with cognitive function in older adults. *Brain Research, 1230,* 233–236.

Gunstad, J., Strain, G., Devlin, M., Wing, R., Cohen, R., Paul, R. et al. (In press). Improved memory function 12 weeks after bariatric surgery. *Surgery for Obesity and Related Diseases.*

Gustafson, D., Lissner, L., Bengtsson, C., Bjorkelund, C., & Skoog, I. (2004). A 24-year follow-up of body mass index and cerebral atrophy. *Neurology, 63,* 1876–1881.

Gustafson, D.R., Steen, B., & Skoog, I. (2004b). Body mass index and white matter lesions in elderly women. An 18-year longitudinal study. *International Psychogeriatrics, 16,* 327–336.

Haltia, L.T., Viljanen, A., Parkkola, R., Kemppainen, N., Rinne, J., Nuutila, P. et al. (2007). Brain white matter expansion in human obesity and the recovering effect of dieting. *Journal of Clinical Endocrinology and Metabolism, 92,* 3278–3284.

Hayes, T.L., Larimer, N., Adami, A., & Kaye, J.A. (2009). Medication adherence in healthy elders: Small cognitive changes make a big difference. *Journal of Aging and Health, 21,* 567–580.

Jagust, W., Harvey, D., Mungas, D., & Haan, M. (2005). Central obesity and the aging brain. *Archives of Neurology, 62*, 1545–1548.

Jefferson, A.L., Massaro, J.M., Wolf, P.A., Seshadri, S., Au, R., Vasan, R.S. et al. (2007). Inflammatory biomarkers are associated with total brain volume: The Framingham Heart Study. *Neurology, 68*, 1032–1038.

Kumar, R., Anstey, K.J., Cherbuin, N., Wen, W., & Sachdev, P.S. (2008). Association of type 2 diabetes with depression, brain atrophy, and reduced fine motor speed in a 60- to 64-year-old community sample. *American Journal of Geriatric Psychiatry, 16*, 989–998.

Kuo, H.K., Jones, R.N., Milberg, W.P., Tennstedt, S., Talbot, L., Morris, J.N. et al. (2006). Cognitive function in normal-weight, overweight, and obese older adults: An analysis of the Advanced Cognitive Training for Independent and Vital Elderly cohort. *Journal of the American Geriatrics Society, 54*, 97–103.

Levy, L.D., Fleming, J.P., & Klar, D. (2009). Treatment of refractory obesity in severely obese adults following management of newly diagnosed attention deficit hyperactivity disorder. *International Journal of Obesity, 33*, 326–334.

Lezak, M.D. (2004). *Neuropsychological assessment*. New York: Oxford University Press.

Li, Y., Dai, Q., Jackson, J.C., & Zhang, J. (2008). Overweight is associated with decreased cognitive functioning among school-age children and adolescents. *Obesity, 16*, 1809–1815.

Lokken, K.L., Boeka, A.G., Austin, H.M., Gunstad, J., & Harmon, C.M. (2009). Evidence of executive dysfunction in extremely obese adolescents: A pilot study. *Surgery for Obesity and Related Diseases, 5*, 547–552.

Lokken, K.L., Boeka, A.G., Yellumahanthi, K., Wesley, M., & Clements, R.H. (2010). Cognitive performance of morbidly obese patients seeking bariatric surgery. *American Surgeon, 76*, 55–59.

Miller, E.K., & Cohen, J.D. (2001). An integrative theory of prefrontal cortex function. *Annual Review of Neuroscience, 24*, 167–202.

Moeller, F.G., Barratt, E.S., Dougherty, D.M., Schmitz, J.M., & Swann, A.C. (2001). Psychiatric aspects of impulsivity. *American Journal of Psychiatry, 158*, 1783–1793.

Mobbs, O., Crépin, C., Thiéry, C., Golay, A., & van der Linden, M. (2010). Obesity and the four facets of impulsivity. *Patient Education and Counseling, 79*, 372–377.

Mrak, R.E. (2009). Alzheimer-type neuropathological changes in morbidly obese individuals. *Clinical Neuropathology, 28*, 40–45.

Mueller, A., Rein, K., Kollei, I., Jacobi, A., Rotter, A., Schütz, P. et al. Impulse control disorders in a German psychiatric inpatient sample. Manuscript submitted for publication.

Nederkoorn, C., Smulders, F.T., Havermans, R.C., Roefs, A., & Jansen, A. (2006). Impulsivity in obese women. *Appetite, 47*, 253–256.

O'Brien, P., Dixon, J., & Brown, W. (2004). Obesity is a surgical disease: Overview of obesity and bariatric surgery. *Australian and New Zealand Journal of Surgery, 74*, 200–204.

Ogden, C.L., Yanovski, S.Z., Carroll, M.D., & Flegal, K.M. (2007). The epidemiology of obesity. *Gastroenterology, 132*, 2087–2102.

Pandey, A., Demede, M., Zizi, F., Al Haija'a, O., Nwamaghinna, F., Jean-Louis, G. et al. (2011). Sleep apnea and diabetes: Insights into the emerging epidemic. *Current Diabetes Reports, 11*, 35–40.

Pannacciulli, N., Del Parigi, A., Chen, K., Le, D.S., N.T., Reiman, E.M., & Tataranni, P.A. (2006). Brain abnormalities in human obesity: A voxel-based morphometric study. *NeuroImage, 31*, 1419–1425.

Pannacciulli, N., Le, D.S., Chen, K., Reiman, E.M., & Krakoff, J. (2007). Relationships between plasma leptin concentrations and human brain structure: A voxel-based morphometric study. *Neuroscience Letters, 412*, 248–253.

Pignatti, R., Bertella, L., Albani, G., Mauro, A., Molinari, E., & Semenza, C. (2006). Decision-making in obesity: A study using the gambling task. *Eating and Weight Disorders, 11*, 126–132.

Raji, C.A., Ho. A.J., Parikshak, N.N., Becker, J.T., Lopez, O.L., Kuller, L.H. et al. (2010). Brain structure and obesity. *Human Brain Mapping, 31*, 353–364.

Raz, N., Rodrigue, K.M., & Acker, J.D. (2003). Hypertension and the brain: Vulnerability of the prefrontal regions and executive functions. *Behavioral Neuroscience, 117*, 1169–1180.

Reishstein, J. (2011). Obstructive sleep apnea: A risk factor for cardiovascular disease. *Journal of Cardiovascular Nursing*, 26, 106–116.

Rosenberg, G.A. (2009). Inflammation and white matter damage in vascular cognitive impairment. *Stroke, 40*, S20–S23.

Savitz, J., & Drevets, W.C. (2009). Bipolar and major depressive disorder: Neuroimaging the developmental-degenerative divide. *Neuroscience and Biobehavioral Reviews, 33*, 699–771.

Scharf, M.T., & Ahima, R.S. (2004). Gut peptides and other regulators in obesity. *Seminars in Liver Disease, 24*, 335–347.

Skroubis, G., Sakellaropoulos, G., Pouggouras, K., Mead, N., Nikiforidis, G., & Kalfarentzos, F. (2002). Comparison of nutritional deficiencies after Roux-en-Y gastric bypass and after billopancreatic diversion with Roux-en-Y gastric bypass. *Obesity Surgery, 12*, 551–558.

Spitznagel, M., Benitez, A., Updegraff, J., Potter, V., Alexander, T., Glickman, E. et al. (2010). Serum ghrelin is inversely associated with cognitive function in a sample of non-demented elderly. *Psychiatry and Clinical Neurosciences, 64*, 608–611.

Stanek, K., Grieve, S., Brickman, A., Korgaonkar, M., Paul, R., Cohen, R. et al. (2011). Obesity is associated with reduced white matter integrity in otherwise healthy adults. *Obesity, 19*, 500–504.

Sweat, V., Starr, V. Bruehl, H., Arentoft, A., Tirsi, A., Javier, E. et al. (2008). C-reactive protein is linked to lower cognitive performance in overweight and obese women. *Inflammation, 31*, 198–207.

Taki, Y., Kinomura, S., Sato, K., Inoue, K., Goto, R., Okada, K. et al. (2008). Relationship between body mass index and gray matter volume in 1,428 healthy individuals. *Obesity, 16*, 119–124.

Thaisetthawatkul, P. (2008). Neuromuscular complications of bariatric surgery. *Physical Rehabilitation Clinics of North America, 19*, 111–124.

Verdejo-García, A., Pérez-Expósito, M., Schmidt-Río-Valle, J., Fernández-Serrano, M.J., Cruz, F., Pérez-García, M. et al. (2010). Selective alterations within executive functions in adolescents with excess weight. *Obesity, 18*, 1572–1578.

Waldstein, S.R., & Katzel, L.I. (2006). Interactive relations of central versus total obesity and blood pressure to cognitive function. *International Journal of Obesity, 30,* 201–207.

Walther, K., Birdsill, A.C., Glisky, E.L., & Ryan, L. (2010). Structural brain differences and cognitive functioning related to body mass index in older females. *Human Brain Mapping, 31,* 1052–1064.

Ward, M.A., Carlsson, C.M, Trivedi, M.A., Sager, M.A., & Johnson, S.C. (2005). The effect of body mass index on global brain volume in middle-aged adults: A cross sectional study. *BMC Neurology, 5,* 23.

Weller, R.E., Cook, E.W., Avsar, K.B., & Cox, J.E. (2008). Obese women show greater delay discounting than healthy-weight women, *Appetite, 51,* 563–569.

CHAPTER 7

Psychopharmacology Pre- and Postbariatric Surgery

KRISTINE J. STEFFEN, JAMES L. ROERIG,
and SCOTT G. ENGEL

Introduction

Candidates for bariatric surgery frequently have comorbid medical problems, and therefore often take multiple medications preoperatively. In a managed care sample, the mean number of prescription claims per person was 6.9 prior to bariatric surgery and 4.9 six months after surgery (Hodo, Waller, Martindale, & Fick, 2008). Among nearly 5,000 bariatric surgery candidates studied through the Longitudinal Assessment of Bariatric Surgery (LABS) study (Longitudinal Assessment of Bariatric Surgery Consortium, 2009), 39.9% of patients reported taking an antidepressant medication. In this study, antidepressants were the most commonly used class of drugs, followed by statins (26.6%), beta-blockers (17.9%), and narcotics (16.1%). As comorbidities often improve or resolve following bariatric surgery, patients are frequently able to simplify their medication regimens. Antidepressants have been consistently identified as the exception.

Among a sample of patients studied by Malone and Alger-Mayer (2005), 43% were taking a selective serotonin reuptake inhibitor (SSRI) prior to surgery, and 30.7% were still taking one 24 months postsurgery. Bariatric surgery patient records from a large prescription claims database showed that use of antidiabetic, antihypertensive, and antihyperlipidemic medication decreased by over 50% by 12 months postsurgery. In contrast, antidepressant use decreased by only 9% following bariatric surgery over the same time frame (Segal et al., 2009). Most recently, an analysis of disability and health insurance claims was performed by Crémieux and colleagues (Crémieux, Ledoux, Clerici, Cremieux, & Buessing, 2010). Among over 5,500 patients, who served as their own controls in the study, 37.4% were on a psychotropic medication presurgery. Postsurgery, 32.6 and 39.3% were on a psychotropic medication after 4 months and 3 years, respectively.

Following the high prevalence of obesity, there were over 220,000 bariatric procedures performed in 2008 (ASMBS, 2009). Roux-en-Y gastric bypass (RYGBP), a malabsorptive procedure, accounts for the majority of the bariatric surgeries performed in the United States (BOLD, Surgical Review Corporation). The RYGBP leads to a significantly modified gastrointestinal (GI) tract, involving the exclusion of the duodenum from the alimentary flow and the creation of a small gastric pouch. In addition, RYGBP leads to substantial changes in body weight coupled with potential changes in hepatic function. These alterations have the potential to influence the pharmacokinetic (PK) parameters (absorption, distribution, and elimination) of medications. Changes in the PK profile of selected medications can affect efficacy and tolerability. For example, the potential for altered drug absorption following RYGBP has been discussed in the literature (Miller & Smith, 2006; Padwal, Brocks, & Sharma, 2010; others). This may result in reduced, or in some cases elevated, plasma levels of medications.

The extent and direction of the change in PKs that may occur appear to be dependent upon the characteristics of the medication involved (Padwal et al., 2010). For example, while the absorption of many medications is likely to decrease, for some drugs it may be accelerated or increased. Alcohol, for example, has been associated with higher (Klockhoff, Naslund, & Jones, 2002; Hagedorn, Encarnacion, Brat, & Morton, 2007) and more rapidly achieved (Klockhoff et al., 2002) peak plasma concentrations in post–RYGBP surgery patients relative to controls. Sleeve gastrectomy patients appear to have higher and prolonged breath alcohol levels following surgery (Maluenda et al., 2010). These trials will be discussed further in this chapter.

Given the percentage of patients taking psychotropic medications before and after surgery, changes in the PKs of these drugs are particularly relevant. In addition, there have been recent reports in the literature suggesting that the suicide rate may be heightened in patients who have undergone bariatric surgery (Adams et al., 2007; Tindle et al., 2010). Therefore, it is critical that patients who require antidepressant or other psychotropic medication continue to receive therapeutic doses after surgery. Currently, there are few data available to aid the clinician in determining which drugs are affected following RYGBP, and when dosage adjustments or therapeutic switches are warranted.

The remainder of this chapter will include a review of the extant PK bariatric surgery literature with medications as well as with alcohol, a description of the potential PK changes that may occur following RYGBP, and a discussion of issues of clinical relevance. Finally, the chapter will conclude with suggested areas for future research.

Potential Effects of RYGBP on PK Parameters

Pharmacokinetics can be conceptualized by considering three major processes: absorption, distribution, and elimination. Each of these areas may be impacted by RYGBP, which leads to numerous changes in the anatomy and physiology of the patient. Factors relevant to gastric bypass that may influence each of these PK processes will be subsequently discussed. With adjustable gastric banding, the majority of these issues do not apply.

Absorption

Numerous changes in the GI tract result from RYGBP that have the potential to alter the rate or extent of medication absorption. Three of these alterations appear to have the greatest potential to lead to changes in drug absorption and will be described in greater detail: (1) reduced GI surface area available for medication absorption, (2) decreased gastric acidity, and (3) alterations in gastrointestinal transit time.

The absorptive surface area in the GI tract is significantly reduced following RYGBP. The surgery involves transecting the stomach to form a small proximal gastric pouch of 15–25 ml in capacity (Buchwald, 2005). This pouch is then anastomosed to the jejunum. The resulting Roux limb can be highly variable in length, ranging from 60–250 cm or more, depending upon obesity severity and surgeon preference (Needleman & Happel, 2008). Thus, at minimum, the distal stomach, the entire duodenum, and at least 16% (40 cm) of the proximal jejunum are usually excluded from the alimentary flow (Buchwald, 2005). Consequently, there is a substantial reduction in GI surface area available for drug contact and absorption.

Removing the duodenum from the alimentary flow creates a significant reduction in available surface area for drug absorption. Theoretically, this will lead to a reduction in the bioavailability of medications that depend upon this portion of the intestine for absorption. For drugs that are substrates of the cytochrome P450 3A4/3A5 (CYP3A4/3A5) metabolic enzymes, however, bioavailability could increase in some cases following surgery. This is possible due to the expression of CYP3A4/3A5 in the proximal GI tract, including the duodenum. CYP3A4/3A5 acts as part of the first-pass metabolism before the drug enters the systemic circulation. Elimination of the duodenum may reduce the first-pass metabolism, leaving more drug available for absorption. This issue is further addressed in the discussion of the recent atorvastatin PK study by Skottheim and colleagues (2009). Research will also need to address whether the remaining GI tract will upregulate its absorptive capacity to compensate for the unavailability of the duodenum over time. Intestinal drug transporters may also be involved in PK changes observed following RYGB, and although discussed in the literature (Skottheim et al., 2009), it has not been well studied to date.

The absorption process consists of several steps. Solid dosage forms of medication (e.g., tablets, capsules) must disintegrate to form small particles that subsequently dissolve into solution prior to absorption. The efficiency of these processes is dependent upon GI pH as well as the physiochemical properties of the drug. Achlorhydria, which has been described following RYGBP (Smith et al., 1993; Melissas et al., 2002; Miller & Smith, 2006; Seaman, Bowers, Dixon, & Schindler, 2005), may lead to alterations in drug absorption. Seaman and colleagues have considered the reduction in gastric acid content in an *in vitro* experiment in which they evaluated the influence of increased pH on drug dissolution following RYGBP (Seaman et al., 2005). Several of the drugs tested in the simulated post-RYGBP environment demonstrated impaired dissolution compared to a control model. More recent literature shows that gastric acid is still produced following RYGBP. Thus, the contribution of gastric acidity changes on PK parameters are not clear.

The gastric emptying rate can also affect the rate and extent of medication absorption. There may be differences between patients in how the rate of gastric emptying changes following RYGBP. Akkary and colleagues (2009) suggest that the initial stomal diameter may account for the observation that some patients experience very slow gastric emptying following surgery and others experience accelerated emptying. Horowitz and colleagues (1982) studied 12 patients after gastric bypass however, and found that stomal size did not account for gastric emptying rate. The same group demonstrated that following RYGBP, patients experience slower emptying of solid foods and faster emptying of liquids relative to controls during a test meal. Gastric emptying also appears to change over time following surgery. Research has shown that gastric emptying is slower at 2 months following surgery than at 12 months following surgery (I. Näslund & Beckman, 1987). Other factors also influence gastric emptying rate, which may also exhibit time-dependent changes. For instance, peptide hormones including GLP-1 and PYY3-36, which are altered following gastric bypass, also function to regulate the gastric emptying rate (E. Näslund & Kral, 2005). Type II diabetes mellitus, which is present in approximately one-third of prebariatric surgery patients (Longitudinal Assessment of Bariatric Surgery Consortium, 2009), can result in slowing of the gastric emptying rate and in some cases gastroparesis. This condition generally improves or remits following surgery, which may lead to additional changes in GI transit time. Finally, some surgeons place a ring around the gastric pouch above the anastomosis between the pouch and the intestinal Roux limb (ASMBS, 2008). The goal of this procedure is to prevent dilatation of the gastric stoma and to slow gastric emptying rate and increase satiety (ASMBS, 2008).

Overall, the most significant factor that may affect medication absorption following RYGBP is likely the significant reduction in available GI surface area. Other factors such as gastric acid concentration, gastrointestinal transit time, contact with transporters, and cytochrome P450 enzymes in the gut may also play a role.

Distribution

The volume of distribution of medications is also likely to change following RYGBP. The two major ways in which volume of distribution may change following surgery is through changes in body weight and composition following surgery, and through changes in plasma protein concentrations. Two plasma proteins of relevance to drug binding are albumin and the acute phase protein alpha-1-acid glycoprotein (AAG). A drug that is bound to plasma proteins is retained in plasma, unable to penetrate through membranes, and therefore unable to enter tissues and reach the site(s) of action and produce a pharmacological effect (Dawidowicz, Kobielski, & Pieniadz, 2008). Rather, it is the unbound (free) drug that is active. Therefore, reductions in plasma protein concentrations could increase the free fraction of medications, which would be most significant for highly protein-bound drugs. Typically, RYGBP does not cause significant protein-calorie malnutrition and associated hypoalbuminemia (Ritz et al., 2009; Shuster & Vazquez, 2005), although it does occur in a minority of patients (Faintuch et al., 2004; Bavaresco et al., 2010). AAG decreases in response to weight loss, and has been shown to significantly change between presurgery and 12 months postsurgery (Poitou et al., 2006; Iannelli et al., 2009). In another study changes were observed as early as 3 months postsurgery and were significantly reduced by 6 months after surgery (van Dielen, Buurman, Hadfoune, Nijhuis, & Greve, 2004). AAG is also affected by numerous other variables, including other disease states, demographic variables, psychiatric conditions, and medication (Israili & Dayton, 2001). AAG and, to a lesser degree, albumin may be reduced in patients post-RGYBP. Changes in plasma protein concentration can influence the PK properties of medications. The clinical significance of these changes for the antidepressant drugs may be limited.

Body weight changes dramatically and rapidly following RYGBP, and body composition changes as well, which could impact the volume of distribution of medications (Shargel, Yu, & Wu-Pong, 2005). Following RYGBP, the rate of weight loss is most rapid in the first 12 months. Percent excess weight loss has been reported to be between 51 and 76% across studies at 12 months postsurgery (Tice, Karliner, Walsh, Petersen, & Feldman, 2008), and maximum weight loss typically occurs between 18 and 24 months following surgery (ASMBS, 2008). Numerous studies have examined body composition following bariatric surgery, several of which have been reviewed by Chaston, Dixon, and O'Brien, (2007). It is not clear whether body composition changes will affect PKs of psychotropic medications.

Metabolism

Obesity is associated with nonalcoholic fatty liver disease (NAFLD), which is present in the majority of prebariatric surgery candidates, and 25% of patients have the necroinflammatory and fibrotic condition nonalcoholic steatohepatitis (NASH) (Dixon, 2007). RYGBP typically results in improvement in these conditions over time, but early on in the rapid weight loss phase, visceral free fatty acids are liberated and hepatic fat is depleted, resulting in a potential worsening of inflammation (Dixon, 2007). Some reports have shown alterations in particular cytochrome P450 enzymes in patients with steatosis (Gómez-Lechón, Jover, & Donato 2009; Donato et al., 2006; Fisher et al., 2009), which could alter drug metabolism. Collectively, changes in drug absorption, distribution, and metabolism could impact the PK properties of many medications, including psychotropic drugs.

Bariatric Surgery Pharmacokinetic Literature: Medications

There have been a few reviews and commentaries published on the topic of PK postbariatric surgery (Macgregor & Boggs, 1996; Malone, 2003; Hunteman, 2003; Malone & Alger-Mayer, 2005; Miller & Smith, 2006; Motylev, 2008; Padwal et al., 2010), yet there are few data available concerning this issue. While still limited, more data are available addressing medication absorption following the malabsorptive jejunoileal bypass (JIB) procedure compared with the combination restrictive-malabsorptive RYGBP procedure. The JIB procedure is now of historical significance only, and it is unclear whether data generated following this procedure are informative regarding PK changes following RYGBP.

Drugs investigated after JIB include digoxin (Marcus et al., 1977; Gerson, Lowe, & Lindenbaum, 1980), oral contraceptives (Andersen, Lebech, Sørensen, & Borggaard, 1982; Victor, Odlind, & Kral, 1987), cyclosporine (Knight et al., 1988; Chenhsu, Wu, Katz, & Rayhill, 2003), sulfisoxazole (Garrett, Suverkrup, Eberst, Yost, & O'Leary, 1981), and tacrolimus (Kelley et al., 2005). Although the finding is not consistent, most of these reports show a reduction in medication absorption following JIB. Collectively, these reports also reflect a significant amount of variability among drugs in the effect this surgery has on their PK properties.

Table 7.1 Summary of Data Following RYGBP With Oral Medications

Reference	Drug	Sample Size	Increased or Decreased Bioavailability?
Skottheim et al., 2009	Atorvastatin	12	Patient specific
Wills, Zekman, Bestul, Kuwajerwala, & Decker, 2010	Tamoxifen	3	Decrease
Rogers et al., 2008	Sirolimus, mycophenolate mofetil, tacrolimus	6	Decrease
Magee et al., 2007	Amoxicillin, nitrofurantoin	1	Decrease[a]
Marterre et al., 1996	Cyclosporine A	3	Decrease
Fuller et al., 1986	Haloperidol	1	No change
Prince, 1984	Erythromycin	1 gastric bypass, 6 gastroplasty	Decrease

[a] No plasma level data.

There is a dearth of literature concerning medication PKs following the RYGBP. Existing reports consist of small studies and case reports, as summarized briefly in Table 7.1. Medications studied include sirolimus, tacrolimus, and mycophenolic acid (Rogers et al., 2008), cyclosporine (Marterre, Hariharan, First, & Alexander, 1996), haloperidol (Fuller, Tingle, DeVane, Scott, & Stewart, 1986), erythromycin (Prince, 1984), amoxicillin and nitrofurantoin (Magee, Shih, & Hume, 2007), and atorvastatin (Skottheim et al., 2009). In addition to these oral medications, there have been a few small studies with injectable medications, including amikacin (Blouin et al., 1985), vancomycin (Blouin, Bauer, Miller, Record, & Griffen, 1982), and subcutaneous heparin (Shepherd, Rosborough, & Schwartz, 2003). These studies have generally, although not consistently, shown alterations in PKs following RYGBP, suggesting the need for larger investigations in this area. Published *in vivo* psychotropic data remain at the level of case reports although studies in this area are currently underway.

The largest and the only prospective longitudinal study published in this area to date involved the statin medication atorvastatin (Skottheim et al., 2009). Pharmacokinetic comparisons were performed on 12 patients who were taking atorvastatin (doses varied) before and again 3 to 6 weeks after RYGBP. Considerable variability was observed between patients on the magnitude and direction of change in atorvastatin area under the plasma concentration time curve (AUC) following surgery. In eight of the 12 patients, atorvastatin bioavailability increased following surgery. However, changes in the systemic exposure to atorvastatin following gastric bypass in this study ranged from increases of up to 2.3-fold to decreases of up to 2.9-fold. The investigators of this study observed that the patients with the highest systemic exposure to the drug prior to surgery exhibited reductions in AUC following surgery. The reverse was also true; patients with lower AUCs prior to surgery had an increase in the AUC of atorvastatin following surgery. As the authors point out, atorvastatin is poorly bioavailable (12%), resulting from substantial metabolism through the cytochrome P450 enzymes CYP3A4 and CYP3A5. As a substrate for CYP3A4 and CYP3A5, which are highly expressed in the proximal gut, atorvastatin is subject to presystemic metabolism in the upper bowel as well as in the liver. Thus, removal of proximal gut during the RYGBP could theoretically increase atorvastatin bioavailability through a reduction in first-pass metabolism. Therefore, investigators genotyped study participants for CYP3A5 and ABCB1 (p-glycoprotein). Interestingly, genotype was not associated with the changes observed in systemic exposure following gastric bypass, although the investigators suggest that the study may have been underpowered to identify such correlations. Appropriate interpretation of these data will likely require larger investigations aimed at determining the underlying mechanism(s) responsible for the changes observed.

There has also been an *in vitro* drug dissolution trial conducted that involved psychotropic medications (Seaman et al., 2005). This study included several antidepressants, mood stabilizers, and benzodiazepines. Dissolution of crushed psychotropic preparations was compared in two simulated GI environments. One of these GI environments was designed with a pH of 6.8 to mimic the GI tract post-RYGBP. The other, with a pH of 1.2, was used as a control to resemble the presurgery GI environment. Of the 22 psychotropics evaluated, 12 dissolved differently in the post-RYGBP and control conditions. These data suggest that for several psychotropic drugs, dissolution may be altered post-RYGBP. There are, however, several factors beyond drug dissolution that are important to consider when determining if drug absorption will be altered post-RYGBP. It is probable that additional drugs beyond these 12 would be altered. Several of these potential changes will be described later in this chapter.

Bariatric Surgery Pharmacokinetic Literature: Alcohol

Although limited, extant research also suggests that following bariatric surgery, the PK parameters of alcohol appear to be altered (Klockhoff et al., 2002; Hagedorn et al., 2007) and alcohol sensitivity may be heightened in some patients (Ertelt et al., 2008; Buffington, 2007). Klockhoff and colleagues (2002) performed a cross-sectional blood alcohol concentration (BAC) comparison between 12 post-gastric bypass patients and 12 body mass index (BMI) and age-matched controls. Following a single 0.30 g/kg dose of 95% v/v alcohol, the time to maximum BAC (Tmax) was shorter in the gastric bypass group (10 vs. 30 minutes), the maximum BAC (Cmax) was higher in the gastric bypass group (0.74 versus 0.58 g/L), and the BAC remained higher in the gastric bypass group at 10 and 20 minutes postdose relative to the control group. Hagedorn and colleagues (2007) found similar results in a cross-sectional comparison of 19 post–gastric bypass patients with 17 nonsurgical controls. Consumption of 5 ounces of red wine produced a higher peak breath alcohol level in the gastric bypass group versus controls (0.08% vs. 0.05%) as well as a longer time to reach a breath alcohol level of 0 (108 vs. 72 minutes). Maluenda and colleagues (2010) recently completed a trial in which they provided a dose of wine based upon total body water concentration to 12 patients before and 30 days after sleeve gastrectomy. They found that patients had higher peak breath alcohol levels after sleeve gastrectomy than before surgery (4.0 g/L vs. 1.5 g/L), and alcohol levels were measurable by breathalyzer for a longer period of time following gastrectomy in comparison with the presurgery evaluation (204 vs. 177.4 minutes). The earliest breath measurement reported in this study occurred at 10 minutes postdose, which was the measurement that corresponded with the peak alcohol concentration in both groups. Thus, it is not possible to determine whether patients experienced an earlier peak postsurgery compared to before surgery.

Extending these PK findings, Ertelt and colleagues (2008) reported that in a survey of 70 postbariatric surgery patients, 54.3% experienced changes in their response to alcohol, with 34.3% indicating that they became intoxicated more quickly. Similarly, 84% of postbariatric surgery patients in a survey by Buffington (2007) reported feeling more sensitive to the effects of alcohol than before surgery.

There may be several anatomical and physiological changes produced by surgery that could account for alterations in alcohol absorption or metabolism, some of which include: (1) significant weight loss, which results in relatively higher dosages of alcohol after surgery on a mg/kg basis; (2) accelerated emptying of liquids from the gastric pouch following surgery (Horowitz, Collins, Harding, & Shearman, 1986); and (3) substantially reduced stomach volume, which theoretically results in decreased availability of gastric alcohol dehydrogenase, which is responsible for oxidation of approximately 6–8% of an oral alcohol dosage (Meier & Seitz, 2008). This idea is supported by research from Caballeria and colleagues (1989), who demonstrated that following gastrectomy the areas under the curve (AUCs) following oral and intravenous alcohol administration were similar, whereas the AUC was significantly higher following intravenous dosing than after oral dosing in nongastrectomized patients. One mechanism suggested for this finding is a decrease in gastric oxidation (first-pass effect) of alcohol following gastrectomy, due to a reduction in gastric alcohol dehydrogenase activity in the remnant stomach or a reduction in alcohol contact time with this gastric enzyme (Caballeria et al., 1989). Finally, it is likely that before surgery patients consume alcohol while eating. Following surgery, patients are encouraged to avoid consuming food and beverages simultaneously, which would be expected to increase the speed of alcohol absorption and the effect patients experience. There may be significant implications associated with these changes in alcohol PKs and sensitivity to alcohol, including more rapid or extensive impairment and potential changes in the reinforcing value of alcohol.

Clinical Issues Related to Antidepressant Medications

Many commonly used psychotropic medications are available in delayed or extended release preparations, for example, duloxetine, venlafaxine, bupropion, valproate sodium, and others. Some have advocated for avoiding the use of extended release medications in patients who have undergone RYGBP (Miller & Smith, 2006). Miller and Smith (2006) suggest that the extended release, long absorptive phase products may not remain in the shortened GI tract for a sufficient amount of time to permit adequate absorption. Yet, there are currently no data to inform the appropriateness of the practice of switching from these to immediate release or liquid formulations. Extended release products typically provide reduced dosing frequency requirements, often in combination with improved tolerability. Thus, switching patients off of these in favor of immediate release formulations is not always without consequence. Data are needed to address the issue of whether switching patients from extended to immediate release formulations is necessary.

Future Research Needed

Pharmacokinetic research generally involves administering a dose of the medication of interest and gathering a series of precisely timed plasma samples. These trials are clearly needed with psychotropic medications in patients who have undergone RYGBP. The research in this area is in its infancy, and several questions need to be answered before prescribing guidelines can be established. For instance, it is unclear how well data obtained with one medication in a class will translate to other drugs in the same class. As demonstrated in the research study by Skottheim and colleagues (2009) with atorvastatin, there may also be considerable variety between patients in the effect that RYGBP has on systemic exposure to medications. The mechanism(s) responsible for these variations will need to be addressed. Research should also examine whether the magnitude of the change in PK properties of a medication change temporally following bariatric surgery. Theoretically, more distal segments of the bowel may have the capability to increase their absorptive capacity in the absence of the duodenum. Data evaluating the absorption of extended release medications following RYGBP are also needed. Finally, as surgical procedures continue to evolve, additional data will be needed. Maluenda and colleagues (2010) have demonstrated alterations in alcohol absorption following sleeve gastrectomy. Thus, investigation of medication PK properties following sleeve gastrectomy is also warranted.

Once data are available, the clinical significance of any changes in PK properties associated with various medications should be considered. Until data are available to guide clinical decision making, psychiatric care providers should be vigilant in monitoring patients for potential decreases in psychotropic efficacy as well as problems with tolerability. Obtaining medication plasma levels in cases where the provider suspects a clinically meaningful change in drug concentration should also be considered. Finally, patients should be informed about the potential for altered drug and alcohol absorption following bariatric surgery, and they should be encouraged to speak with a physician about any deterioration in mental health or problems with alcohol use.

References

Adams, T.D., Gress, R.E., Smith, S.C., Halverson, R.C., Simper, S.C., Rosamond, W.D., et al. (2007). Long-term mortality after gastric bypass surgery. *New England Journal of Medicine, 357,* 753–761.

Akkary, E., Sidani, S., Boonsiri, J., Yu, S., Dziura, J., Duffy, A.J., et al. (2009). The paradox of the pouch: Prompt emptying predicts improved weight loss after laparoscopic Roux-Y gastric bypass. *Surgical Endoscopy, 23,* 790–794.

Andersen, A.N., Lebech, P.E., Sørensen, T.I., & Borggaard, B. (1982). Sex hormone levels and intestinal absorption of estradiol and D-norgestrel in women following bypass surgery for morbid obesity. *International Journal of Obesity, 6,* 91–96.

ASMBS. (2008). Retrieved January 29, 2009, from http://www.asbs.org

ASMBS. (2009). American Society of Metabolic and Bariatric Surgery fact sheet. Retrieved September 2010 from www.asmbs.org/.../ASMBS_Metabolic_Bariatric_Surgery_Overview_FINAL_09.pdf

Bavaresco, M., Paganini, S., Lima, T.P., Salgado, W., Jr., Ceneviva, R., Dos Santos, J.E., et al. (2010). Nutritional course of patients submitted to bariatric surgery. *Obesity Surgery, 20,* 716–721.

Blouin, R.A., Bauer, L.A., Miller, D.D., Record, K.E., & Griffen, W.O., Jr. (1982). Vancomycin pharmacokinetics in normal and morbidly obese subjects. *Antimicrobial Agents and Chemotherapy, 21,* 575–580.

Blouin, R.A., Brouwer, K.L., Record, K.E., Griffen, W.O., Jr., Plezia, P.M., & John, W. (1985). Amikacin pharmacokinetics in morbidly obese patients undergoing gastric-bypass surgery. *Clinical Pharmacy, 4,* 70–72.

BOLD (Bariatric Outcomes Longitudinal Database), Surgical Review Corporation. Accessed July 6, 2011. http://www.surgicalreview.org/bold/overview

Buchwald, H. (2005). Consensus conference statement: Bariatric surgery for morbid obesity: Health implications for patients, health professionals, and third-party payers. *Surgery for Obesity and Related Diseases, 1,* 371–381.

Buffington, C.K. (2007). Alcohol use and health risks: Survey results. *Bariatric Times, 4,* 21–23.

Caballeria, J., Frezza, M., Hernandez-Munoz, R., DiPadova, C., Korsten, M.A., Baraona, E. et al. (1989). Gastric origin of the first-pass metabolism of ethanol in humans: Effect of gastrectomy. *Gastroenterology, 97,* 1205–1209.

Chaston, T.B., Dixon, J.B., & O'Brien, P.E. (2007). Changes in fat-free mass during significant weight loss: A systematic review. *International Journal of Obesity, 31,* 743–750.

Chenhsu, R.Y., Wu, Y., Katz, D., & Rayhill, S. (2003). Dose-adjusted cyclosporine C2 in a patient with jejunoileal bypass as compared to seven other liver transplant recipients. *Therapeutic Drug Monitoring, 25,* 665–670.

Crémieux, P., Ledoux, S., Clerici, C., Cremieux, F., & Buessing, M. (2010). The impact of bariatric surgery on comorbidities and medication use among obese patients. *Obesity Surgery, 20,* 861–870.

Dawidowicz, A.L., Kobielski, M., & Pieniadz, J. (2008). Anomalous relationship between free drug fraction and its total concentration in drug-protein systems. II. Binding of different ligands to plasma proteins. *European Journal of Pharmaceutical Sciences, 35,* 136–141.

Dixon, J.B. (2007). Surgical treatment for obesity and its impact on non-alcoholic steatohepatitis. *Clinics in Liver Disease, 11,* 141–154.

Donato, M.T., Lahoz, A., Jiménez, N., Pérez, G., Serralta, A., Mir, J. et al. (2006). Potential impact of steatosis on cytochrome P450 enzymes of human hepatocytes isolated from fatty liver grafts. *Drug Metabolism and Disposition: The Biological Fate of Chemical, 34,* 1556–1562.

Ertelt, T.W., Mitchell, J.E., Lancaster, K., Crosby, R., Steffen, K., & Marino, J. (2008). Alcohol abuse and dependence before and after bariatric surgery: A review of the literature and report of a new data set. *Surgery for Obesity and Related Diseases, 4,* 647–650.

Faintuch, J., Matsuda, M., Cruz, M.E., Silva, M.M., Teivelis, M.P., Garrido, A.B. et al. (2004). Severe protein-calorie malnutrition after bariatric procedures. *Obesity Surgery, 14,* 175–181.

Fisher, C.D., Lickteig, A.J., Augustine, L.M., Ranger-Moore, J., Jackson, J.P., Ferguson, S.S. et al. (2009). Hepatic cytochrome P450 enzyme alterations in humans with progressive stages of nonalcoholic fatty liver disease. *Drug Metabolism and Disposition, 37,* 2087–2094.

Fuller, A.K., Tingle, D., DeVane, C.L., Scott, J.A., & Stewart, R.B. (1986). Haloperidol pharmacokinetics following gastric bypass surgery. *Journal of Clinical Psychopharmacology, 6,* 376–378.

Garrett, E.R., Suverkrup, R.S., Eberst, K., Yost, R.L., & O'Leary, J.P. (1981). Surgically affected sulfisoxazole pharmacokinetics in the morbidly obese. *Biopharmaceutics and Drug Disposition, 2,* 329–365.

Gerson, C.D., Lowe, E.H., & Lindenbaum, J. (1980). Bioavailability of digoxin tablets in patients with gastrointestinal dysfunction. *American Journal of Medicine, 69,* 43–49.

Gómez-Lechón, M.J., Jover, R., & Donato, M.T. (2009). Cytochrome P450 and steatosis. *Current Drug Metabolism, 10,* 692–699.

Hagedorn, J.C., Encarnacion, B., Brat, G.A., & Morton, J.M. (2007). Does gastric bypass alter alcohol metabolism? *Surgery for Obesity and Related Diseases, 3,* 543–548.

Hodo, D.M., Waller, J.L., Martindale, R.G., & Fick, D.M. (2008). Medication use after bariatric surgery in a managed care cohort. *Surgery for Obesity and Related Diseases, 4,* 601–607.

Horowitz, M., Collins, P.J., Harding, P.E., & Shearman, D.J.C. (1986). Gastric emptying after gastric bypass. *International Journal of Obesity, 10,* 117–121.

Horowitz, M., Cook, D.J., Collins, P.J., Harding, P.E., Hooper, M.J. Walsh, J.F. et al. (1982). Measurement of gastric emptying after gastric bypass surgery using radionuclides. *British Journal of Surgery, 69,* 655–657.

Hunteman, L.M. (2003). Potential role of medication therapy management for bariatric surgery patients. *Journal of the American Pharmaceutical Association, 48,* 440–442.

Iannelli, A., Anty, R., Piche, T., Dahman, M., Gual, P., Tran, A. et al. (2009). Impact of laparoscopic Roux-en-Y gastric bypass on metabolic syndrome, inflammation, and insulin resistance in super versus morbidly obese women. *Obesity Surgery, 19,* 577–582.

Israili, Z.H., & Dayton, P.G. (2001). Human alpha-1-glycoprotein and its interactions with drugs. *Drug Metabolism Reviews, 33,* 161–235.

Kelley, M., Jain, A., Kashyap, R., Orloff, M., Abt, P., Wrobble, K. et al. (2005). Change in oral absorption of tacrolimus in a liver transplant recipient after reversal of jejunoileal bypass: Case report. *Transplant Proceedings, 37,* 3165–3167.

Klockhoff, H., Naslund, I., & Jones, A. (2002). Faster absorption of ethanol and higher peak concentration in women after gastric bypass surgery. *British Journal of Clinical Pharmacy, 54,* 587–591.

Knight, G.C., Macris, M.P., Peric, M., Duncan, J.M., Frazier, O.H., & Colley, D.A. (1988). Cyclosporine A pharmacokinetics in a cardiac allograft recipient with a jejuno-ileal bypass. *Transplant Proceedings, 20,* 351–355.

Longitudinal Assessment of Bariatric Surgery (LABS) Consortium. (2009). Perioperative safety in the Longitudinal Assessment of Bariatric Surgery. *New England Journal of Medicine, 361,* 445–454.

Macgregor, A.M.C., & Boggs, L. (1996). Drug distribution in obesity and following bariatric surgery: A literature review. *Obesity Surgery, 6,* 17–27.

Magee, S.R., Shih, G., & Hume, A. (2007). Malabsorption of oral antibiotics in pregnancy after gastric bypass surgery. *Journal of the American Board of Family Medicine, 20,* 310–313.

Malone, M. (2003). Altered drug disposition in obesity and after bariatric surgery. *Nutrition in Clinical Practice, 18,* 131–135.

Malone, M., & Alger-Mayer, S.A. (2005). Medication use patterns after gastric bypass surgery for weight management. *Annals of Pharmacotherapy, 39,* 637–642.

Maluenda, F., Csendes, A., De Aretxabala, X., Poniachik, J., Salvo, K., Delgado, I. et al. (2010). Alcohol absorption modification after a laparoscopic sleeve gastrectomy due to obesity. *Obesity Surgery, 20*, 744–748.

Marcus, F.I., Quinn, E.J., Horton, H., Jacobs, S., Pippin, S., Stafford, M. et al. (1977). The effect of jejunoileal bypass on the pharmacokinetics of digoxin in man. *Circulation, 55*, 537–541.

Marterre, W.F., Hariharan, S., First, M.R., & Alexander, J.W. (1996). Gastric bypass in morbidly obese kidney transplant recipients. *Clinical Transplantation, 10*, 414–419.

Meier, P., & Seitz, H.K. (2008). Age, alcohol, metabolism, and liver disease. *Current Opinion in Clinical Nutrition and Metabolic Care, 11*, 21–26.

Melissas, J., Kampitakis, E., Schoretsanitis, G., Mouzas, J., Kouroumalis, E., & Tsiftsis, D. (2002). Does reduction in gastric acid secretion in bariatric surgery increase diet-induced thermogenesis? *Obesity Surgery, 12*, 399–403.

Miller, A.D., & Smith, K.M. (2006). Medication and nutrient administration considerations after bariatric surgery. *American Journal of Health-System Pharmacy, 63*, 1852–1857.

Motylev, A. (2008). The operating room pharmacist and bariatric surgery. *U.S. Pharmacist, 33*, HS19–HS27.

Näslund, E., & Kral, J.G. (2005). Patient selection and the physiology of gastrointestinal antiobesity operations. *Surgical Clinics of North America, 85*, 725–740.

Näslund, I., & Beckman, K.W. (1987). Gastric emptying rate after gastric bypass and gastroplasty. *Scandanavian Journal of Gastroenterology, 22*, 193–201.

Needleman, B.J., & Happel, L.C. (2008). Bariatric surgery: Choosing the optimal procedure. *Surgical Clinics of North America, 88*, 991–1007.

Padwal, R., Brocks, D., & Sharma, A. (2010). A systematic review of drug absorption following bariatric surgery and its theoretical implications. *Obesity Reviews, 11*, 41–50.

Poitou, C., Coussieu, C., Rouault, C., Coupaye, M., Cancello, R., Bedel, J.F. et al. (2006). Serum amyloid A: A marker of adiposity-induced low-grade inflammation but not of metabolic status. *Obesity, 14*, 309–318.

Prince, R.A. (1984). Influence of bariatric surgery on erythromycin absorption. *Journal of Clinical Pharmacology, 24*, 523–527.

Ritz, P., Becouarn, G., Douay, O., Sallé, A., Topart, P., & Rohmer, V. (2009). Gastric bypass is not associated with protein malnutrition in morbidly obese patients. *Obesity Surgery, 19*, 840–844.

Rogers, C.C., Alloway, R.R., Alexander, J.W., Cardi, M., Trofe, J., & Vinks, A.A. (2008). Pharmacokinetics of mycophenolic acid, tacrolimus and sirolimus after gastric bypass surgery in end-stage renal disease and transplant patients: A pilot study. *Clinical Transplantation, 22*, 281–291.

Seaman, J.S., Bowers, S.P., Dixon, P., & Schindler, L. (2005). Dissolution of common psychiatric medications in a Roux-en-Y gastric bypass model. *Psychosomatics, 46*, 250–253.

Segal, J., Clark, J., Shore, A., Dominici, F., Magnuson, T., Richards, T. et al. (2009). Prompt reduction in use of medications for comorbid conditions after bariatric surgery. *Obesity Surgery, 19*, 1646–1656.

Shargel, L., Yu, A.B., & Wu-Pong, S. (2005). *Applied biopharmaceutics and pharmacokinetics* (5th ed.). New York: McGraw-Hill Professional Publishing.

Shepherd, M.F., Rosborough, T.K., & Schwartz, M.L. (2003). Heparin thromboprophylaxis in gastric bypass surgery. *Obesity Surgery, 13*, 249–253.

Shuster, M.H., & Vazquez, J.A. (2005). Nutritional concerns related to Roux-en-Y gastric bypass: What every clinician needs to know. *Critical Care Nursing Quarterly, 28*, 227–260.

Skottheim, I., Stormark, K., Christensen, H., Jakobsen, G., Hjelmesaeth, J., & Jenssen, T., et al. (2009). Significantly altered systemic exposure to atorvastatin acid following gastric bypass surgery in morbidly obese patients. *Clinical Pharmacology and Therapeutics, 86*, 311–318.

Smith, C.D., Herkes, S.B., Behrns, K.E., Fairbanks, V.F., Kelly, K.A., & Sarr, M.G. (1993). Gastric acid secretion and vitamin B12 absorption after vertical Roux-en-Y gastric bypass for morbid obesity. *Annals of Surgery, 218*, 91–96.

Tice, J.A., Karliner, L., Walsh, J., Petersen, A.J., & Feldman, M.D. (2008). Gastric banding or bypass? A systematic review comparing the two most popular bariatric procedures. *American Journal of Medicine, 121*, 885–893.

van Dielen, F.M.H., Buurman, W.A., Hadfoune, M., Nijhuis, J., & Greve, J.W. (2004). Macrophage inhibitory factor, plasminogen activator inhibitor-1, other acute phase proteins, and inflammatory mediators normalize as a result of weight loss in morbidly obese subjects treated with gastric restrictive surgery. *Journal of Clinical Endocrinology and Metabolism, 89*, 4062–4068.

Victor, A., Odlind, V., & Kral, J.G. (1987). Oral contraceptive absorption and sex hormone binding globulins in obese women: Effects of jejunoileal bypass. *Gastroenterology Clinics of North America, 16*, 483–491.

Wills, S., Zekman, R., Bestul, D., Kuwajerwala, N., & Decker, D. (2010). Tamoxifen malabsorption after Roux-en-Y gastric bypass surgery: Case series and review of the literature. *Pharmacotherapy, 30*, 217.

CHAPTER **8**

Physical Activity Pre- and Postbariatric Surgery

CHRISTIE ZUNKER and WENDY KING

The bariatric team has many responsibilities for ensuring success among their patients, including promoting healthy behaviors. Given the health benefits of physical activity (PA), ideally, all bariatric teams at comprehensive surgical centers would include a fitness specialist to provide PA counseling and support. However, until medical insurance companies provide financial reimbursement for PA counseling, many surgical centers will rely on team members without expertise in fitness to provide PA counseling, or refer patients out of practice. This chapter seeks to help the nonfitness specialist or the nonbariatrician by reviewing (1) the health benefits of and guidelines for PA, (2) PA participation of pre- and postsurgical patients, and (3) elements of effective PA counseling. First some key terms and concepts are reviewed.

Terminology

The term *exercise*, as used here, is defined as specifically planned, structured PA that is usually done in order to improve cardiovascular fitness, gain strength, expend calories, or gain other health benefits. In addition to exercise, PA includes activities from all aspects of life (e.g., recreation, household, transportation, occupation) that involve bodily movement produced by the contraction of skeletal muscles that increases energy expenditure (Caspersen, Powell, & Christenson, 1985). In this chapter, *PA* generally refers to health-enhancing PA (i.e., any form of PA that benefits health and fitness without undue harm or risk) (HEPA Europe, 2005).

One of the key factors to whether PA is health enhancing is the *PA intensity*, or the magnitude of the effort (i.e., exertion) required to perform the PA (Hagströmer, 2007). *Moderate-intensity PA* (MPA) is generally equivalent to a brisk walk and noticeably accelerates the heart rate, while *vigorous-intensity PA* (VPA) causes a substantial increase in heart rate and rapid breathing (Haskell et al., 2007). By default, *low-intensity PA* (LPA) is PA performed at a lower intensity than MPA, but higher than *sedentary activities*, which require almost no physical movement.

Basic methods of assessing PA intensity include using a talk test, based on an individual's ability to talk and sing during PA, and the Borg Rating of Perceived Exertion (RPE) scale, based on an individual's interpretation of how hard he or she feels his or her body is working (DNPAO, 2010). For example, when adults are capable of speaking a few words, but unable to carry on a full conversation or sing, and report working "somewhat hard" on the RPE scale, they are likely achieving MPA. PA intensity can also be defined more precisely by directly measuring physiological responses to PA. For example, MPA can be defined by a heart rate that is 50 to <70% of its maximum value (max HR), which is often predicted with the equation 220 – Age. However, 220 – .5 × Age has been proposed as a more accurate equation to predict max HR in obese individuals (W.C. Miller, Wallace, & Eggert, 1993). Two common methods to determine PA intensity in research settings are to measure individuals' oxygen demand during PA and either (1) divide it by their maximum volume of oxygen uptake (VO_2max) to calculate percentage VO_2max, or (2) divide it by their oxygen demand at rest (which equals 1 metabolic equivalent (MET)) to calculate the PA's MET value. Using these methods, MPA is defined as PA done at 50 to <75% of VO_2max, or 3.0 to 6.0 METs (Haskell et al., 2007).

Table 8.1 shows examples of how some commonly performed PAs are usually categorized. While such tables are useful for getting a general idea about PA intensity, it is important to note that many activities can be performed at various intensities. For example, the same individual can swim at MPA or VPA, depending on effort level. In addition, the PA intensity of individuals performing the same absolute workload (i.e., same activity at the same speed) differs depending on fitness level (Andersen & Jakicic, 2009; K.H. Miller, Ogletree, & Welshimer, 2002), age (Andersen & Jakicic, 2009), and weight status (Hills, Byrne, Wearing, & Armstrong, 2006; Mattsson, Larsson, & Rossner, 1997). Thus, what might be a MPA for a fit, young, normal-weight adult might be a VPA for a sedentary, older, obese adult.

Accurate assessment of PA is needed to determine dose-response relationships between PA and health outcomes, specify which aspects of PA are important for particular health outcomes, and examine the effect of

Table 8.1 Examples of Different Physical Activity (PA) Categorized by Domain and Intensity

Domain	Sedentary	Low	PA Intensity Moderate	Vigorous
Exercise	NA	Yoga Stretching	Low-impact aerobics "Brisk" walking Weight lifting Water aerobics	High-impact aerobics Jogging Jumping rope Swimming laps Cycling class
Leisure time/ recreational	Reading a book Watching TV	Fishing (sitting) Catch Playing musical instrument Darts Billiards	Volleyball Doubles tennis Shooting baskets Bowling Ballroom dancing Golf	Soccer Singles tennis Basketball Racquetball Beach volleyball Hiking uphill
Household	Paying bills Knitting	Dressing Showering Dusting Washing dishes Ironing Watering plants	Vacuuming Sweeping Mopping Mowing with power mower Pruning shrubs Painting	Chopping wood Tilling a garden Mowing with hand mower Shoveling snow
Transportation	Sitting in a car	Driving a car	Walking	Biking
Occupational	Using a computer Sitting at a desk	Bartending Filing Working a cash register	Carrying light loads Packing boxes Custodial work Auto repair	Lifting heavy loads Digging Construction

interventions (Wareham & Rennie, 1998). There are several methods for measuring PA. *PA questionnaires*, or *surveys*, are most frequently used in large studies because the methodology is relatively inexpensive and allows application in large studies. In addition, there is little participant burden and they can be used to measure "habitual" free-living PA (Valanou, Bamia, & Trichopoulou, 2006). However, PA surveys rely on study participants to accurately recall frequency, duration, and intensity of PA (this is called *self-reported PA*). Thus, in general, the reliability and validity of PA by questionnaire is low (Westerterp, 2009). Behavioral observation and physiological markers (e.g., doubly labeled water) can provide very accurate assessment of various aspects of PA (e.g., what specific activities were done, or how many calories were expended), but they are generally not suitable for use in large studies (e.g., due to researcher and participant burden and cost). Therefore, activity monitors such as *pedometers*, which record steps; *step activity monitors*, which record steps per time period; and *accelerometers*, which measure movement intensity as counts per time period, are often the best options for objectively assessing free-living PA in large studies (Troiano, 2007; Ward et al., 2005). Unfortunately, the cost for high-quality activity monitors, burden of retrieving monitors from participants, and required technical expertise to process the data have prohibited their use in many studies (Ward et al., 2005).

Physical Activity and Health

Physical Activity's Role in Weight Gain and Weight Loss

Excess body fat develops from an imbalance of energy intake and expenditure. PA increases energy expenditure directly. In addition, PA enhances metabolic rate via its effect on building or maintaining lean body tissue and stimulating metabolic rate following PA. Regular PA also alters fat distribution by selectively mobilizing central fat, improving the body's ability to burn fat as fuel, and reducing fat cell size (Sallis & Owen, 1999). Thus, PA is an important contributor to weight management.

Research suggests a cyclical relationship between PA and weight, such that insufficient PA produces weight gain (Fogelholm, Kukkonen-Harjula, Nenonen, & Pasanen, 2000; Kahn et al., 1997, Rissanen, Heliövaara, Knekt, Reunanen, & Aromaa, 1991) and weight gain leads to a reduction in PA (Levine et al., 2008; Petersen, Schnohr, & Sørensen, 2004). Conversely, increasing PA improves weight loss in overweight and obese adults. A systematic review of studies examining the role of PA in weight loss (Donnelly et al., 2009) suggests that the combination of diet plus PA results in an additional loss of 2 to 3% of initial weight in a 6-month period compared to weight loss achieved with diet alone. While most studies in this review were limited to overweight or Class 1 obese adults, a recent study of 130 Class 2 (BMI 35 to <40.0 kg/m²) and 3 (BMI ≥ 40 kg/m²) obese adults similarly showed that after 6 months, PA in combination with diet promoted greater weight loss and resulted in greater improvements in waist circumference and hepatic steatosis than diet alone (Goodpaster et al., 2010).

Given what we know about the additive benefit of PA during behaviorally induced weight loss, researchers have hypothesized that PA level contributes to weight loss following bariatric surgery. In 2010, two systematic reviews were published, identifying a total of 17 studies that examined the relationship between PA and postsurgery weight loss (Jacobi, Ciangura, Couet, & Oppert, 2011; Livhits et al., 2010). While 14 of the 17 studies found a positive association between PA and weight loss, authors of both reviews noted a causal relationship has not yet been established since all of the reviewed studies were observational and many were cross-sectional. The authors also noted that more rigorous assessment of PA is needed. With the exception of one study that included pedometer data on a subset of participants (Colles, Dixon, & O'Brien, 2008), all studies relied on self-reported PA, the majority of which utilized self-developed surveys. In addition, most studies tested whether weight loss differed between "physically active" and "nonactive" participants according to an arbitrary minimal threshold of PA. Thus, there is a need for randomized PA studies utilizing more sophisticated PA assessment and analyses to determine whether there is a dose-response relationship between PA and weight loss following surgery.

While the goal of bariatric surgery is to reduce total body mass, and in particular body fat, it also results in loss of lean body mass (e.g., muscle, bone density), especially during the period of rapid weight loss shortly after surgery (Metcalf, Rabkin, Rabkin, Metcalf, & Lehman-Becker, 2005). However, evidence is mounting that just as PA improves body composition during behaviorally induced weight loss by reducing muscle mass loss and increasing fat loss (Chomentowski et al., 2009; Rippe and Hess, 1998), PA also plays a role in improving body composition within the first year after surgery. A study with 100 adults whom had undergone the duodenal switch operation showed that those who self-reported exercising at least 30 min at least three times a week in the first 6 months following surgery lost 8% more of their presurgery fat mass and retained 20% more of their original lean body mass at 6 months postsurgery than those who did not report exercising at least three times a week (Metcalf et al., 2005). Similarly, an analysis of 277 participants in the Longitudinal Assessment of Bariatric Surgery–2 (LABS-2) found that both increasing PA from pre- to 1 year postsurgery and a higher 1-year postsurgery PA level were independently associated with favorable changes in body composition in the first year following bariatric surgery (King, Hsu, Courcoulas, et al., 2011). In addition, a clinical trial of 60 patients who underwent Roux-en-Y gastric bypass found that those who were randomized to exercise twice a week for 24 months had greater fat mass loss compared to those who were rendomized to exercise once a week (Shang & Hasenberg, 2010). Together these studies provide evidence that PA may be important in maintaining or building of fat-free mass during weight loss following surgical intervention.

Physical Activity's Role in Weight Loss Maintenance

While no studies have rigorously examined how PA relates to weight loss maintenance post–bariatric surgery, studies of nonsurgical weight loss have shown that regular PA is an important contributor to long-term weight maintenance (NHLBI, 1998; Rippe & Hess, 1998). For example, a study of 45 previously obese subjects found that 2 years after weight loss from a very low-calorie diet, higher total exercise calories (estimated from the type, frequency, and duration of PA reported) independently predicted less weight regain (Ewbank, Darga, & Lucas, 1995). Insight can also be gained from the National Weight Control Registry (NWCR), which was established to investigate the characteristics and behaviors of individuals who have been successful at long-term weight loss maintenance (Klem, Wing, McGuire, Seagle, & Hill, 1997). Since 1994, adults have been able to enroll in the NWCR after maintaining a weight loss of at least 13.6 kg (30 pounds) for at least one year. Self-report (Catenacci et al., 2008) as well as objective PA data (Catenacci et al., 2011) have shown that NWCR participants engage in high levels of PA (e.g., 41.5 ± 35.1 min/day of sustained moderate to vigorous physical activity (MVPA) as measured by accelerometer; significantly than obese and normal weight controls). This level of PA is similar to what has been shown to be necessary to prevent weight regain after diet and PA-induced weight loss in several prospective studies (Jakicic et al., 1998, 2003, 2008; Weinsier et al., 2000). However, there may be considerable variation in the amount of MVPA required to maintain weight loss. For example, while 25% of NWCR participants averaged at least 57 min/day, 25% averaged less than 19 min/day (Catenacci et al., 2011). Likewise, a study of 89 formerly obese adults found that some participants maintained weight loss with minimal PA by following a low-calorie, low-energy-density dietary pattern (Cox et al., 2007).

Additional Benefits of Physical Activity

In addition to contributing to a healthy weight and body composition, regular PA improves health, independent of weight loss, in the following ways (U.S. Department of Health and Human Services, 2008):

- Improves flexibility, strength, and balance, which reduces stiffness, joint pain, and risk of injury
- Helps build and maintain healthy bones

- Reduces risk of developing cardiovascular disease, stroke, Type 2 diabetes, breast cancer, and colon cancer
- Improves heart health risk factors, like blood pressure, blood cholesterol levels, insulin sensitivity, and C-reactive protein
- Improves immunity
- Reduces feelings of depression and anxiety
- Promotes psychological well-being
- Improves or maintains some aspects of cognitive function
- Enhances quality of sleep
- Delays all-cause mortality

Thus, in addition to promoting weight loss, retention of lean mass, and weight loss maintenance, PA likely plays an important role in the resolution of comorbidities (such as hypertension, hypercholesterolemia, Type 2 diabetes, coronary heart disease, gallbladder disease, and osteoarthritis) following bariatric surgery.

Physical Activity Recommendations

Many government and public health agencies around the world have published PA guidelines. For substantial health benefits the U.S. federal government recommends healthy adults accumulate at least 150 min of aerobic MPA or 75 min of aerobic VPA a week in episodes of at least 10 min, spread throughout the week, plus muscle-strengthening activities for major muscle groups at least 2 days/week (USDHHS, 2008). In addition, the following points are made:

- All adults should avoid inactivity. Some PA is better than none, and adults who participate in any amount of PA gain some health benefits.
- Additional benefits occur with more PA (higher intensity, greater frequency, and longer duration).
- Health benefits of PA occur for all people, including those who have disabilities.
- People with chronic conditions and symptoms should consult their health care providers about the types and amounts of activity appropriate for them.
- The benefits of PA far outweigh the possibility of adverse outcomes.

While there are no PA guidelines specifying the amount of PA needed to maximize weight loss after surgery, experts agree that more PA is required for preventing weight gain or regain than for many other health benefits of PA. For example, the American College of Sports Medicine (ACSM) recommends that obese adults accumulate a least 250 minutes of MPA a week for long-term weight management (Donnelly, Blair, Jakicic, Manore, Rankin, & Smith, 2009), and the International Association for the Study of Obesity (IASO), suggests 60- to 90-minutes of MPA a day (or lesser amounts of VPA) may be required to prevent weight regain among formerly obese individuals (Saris et al., 2003).

How Active Are Patients?

Physical Activity of the Presurgical Patient

Despite the known health benefits of PA, several large public health surveillance systems have shown that the majority of U.S. adults do not meet current federal PA guidelines (Troiano et al., 2008). Sweden (Hagströmer, 2007) and several other countries have reported similar findings. Physical inactivity is even more prevalent in persons who are obese (Guthold, Ono, Strong, Chatterji, & Morabia, 2008). Thus, it should be of no surprise that as a group, bariatric surgery candidates are insufficiently active. However, research studies have demonstrated that there is tremendous variation in the PA level of presurgical patients. For example, a LABS-2 analysis of 756 bariatric surgery candidates with objective PA assessment found that while 20% of participants were "sedentary" (<5,000 steps/day), 20% were "active" (≥10,000 steps/day), and the other 60% were in between (5,000 to <10,000 steps/day) (King, Belle, Eid et al., 2008). Self-reported exercise showed similar variation: 39% reported no exercise while 18% of participants reported exercising, on average, at least 30 min/day. Likewise, a study with accelerometer data from 38 bariatric surgery candidates found that while most participants were inactive or insufficiently active (e.g., over two-thirds did not engage in any bouts of MVPA and only 5% accumulated at least 150 min/week of MVPA), there was a wide range of PA levels (e.g., some averaged less than 10,000 counts/h while others averaged over 20,000 counts/h) (Bond, Jackicic, Vithiananthan et al., 2010).

To date, very few studies have investigated factors associated with the PA level of bariatric surgery candidates. An analysis with 760 LABS-2 participants found that several correlates of higher PA found in the general population (i.e., lower BMI, younger age, Hispanic ethnicity, higher income, being single) were also related to the PA level of bariatric surgery candidates, while other characteristics (i.e., male sex and white race) were not (King, Belle, Chapman et al., 2008). A study that objectively measured sedentary time, LPA, and MVPA in 42 surgery candidates also found lower BMI was associated with less sedentary time and more MVPA (Bond, Unick et al., 2010). However, an analysis comparing 31 sufficiently active bariatric surgery candidates (defined as self-reporting 5 or more days of MPA for at least 30 min/day, or 3 or more days of VPA for at least 20 min/day) to 58 insufficiently active bariatric surgery candidates found no significant differences in age, gender, race, BMI, or number of comorbidities between the groups, although self-reported physical function was significantly higher among those who were sufficiently active (Bond et al., 2006a). Thus, more work is needed to help identify groups that may be in greatest need of PA support prior to surgery.

Physical Activity of the Postsurgical Patient

While studies of self-reported PA have consistently shown that patients are more active following surgery (Jacobi et al., 2010), it is unclear whether these increases are at least partially explained by misperception or a reporting bias, (i.e., knowing that they should be more active, patients may feel more pressure to over-report their PA following surgery). For example, a recent study utilizing both a PA survey and an accelerometer (RT3) in 20 gastric bypass and adjustable gastric banding patients found that while self-reported MVPA significantly increased, on average, from 45 min/wk pre-surgery to 212 min/wk six months post-surgery (P < .005), there was no significant difference in MVPA measured by accelerometer (mean of 186 and 151 min/wk; P > .25) (Bond et al., 2010c). On the contrary, a study of 20 gastric bypass patients found a significant increase in pedometer-measured PA (from a mean of 4621 to 7370 steps/d; P = .003) 3 months post surgery among 11 (55%) participants with adequate pedometer data (Josbeno et al., 2010). Likewise, a study of 129 adjustable gastric banding patients found a significant increase in pedometer-measured PA (from a mean of 6061 to 8716 steps/day; P < .01) 1 year post surgery among 48 (37%) participants with adequate pedometer data (Colles et al., 2008). However, authors of both studies noted selection bias might have affected results since a large percentage of participants were excluded from analysis and change in PA might have differed between those who were versus were not compliant with the pedometer protocol. It is also possible that the pedometers used in these studies (Digi-walker SW-200, and Sportline 330, respectively) were more likely to under-count steps prior to surgery, as the accuracy of these pedometers is worse at slow walking speeds and in those with abnormal gaits (Schneider et al., 2003; Melanson et al., 2004; Cyarto, Myers, & Tudor-Locke, 2004), which are more common with severe obesity (Hills 2006; Mattson, Larsson, & Rossner, 1997).

In addition to reviewing group changes in PA pre to post surgery, it is important to consider the potential variability in change in PA following surgery. A recent analysis of 310 LABS-2 participants found that while several PA parameters (mean steps/day, active minutes/day, and high-cadence minutes/wk) measured with an activity monitor were statistically significantly higher (Ps < .0001) one year post surgery than pre-surgery, a quarter of participants actually became at least 5% less active (King et al., 2011b). Using a cut point of ≥ 200 min/wk of walking and MVPA to define "active," Bond et al. (2009) also described change in PA pre to one year post surgery. Of 199 patients, 68 (34%) went from inactive to active and 9 (5%) went from active to inactive, while the majority were either active (n = 83; 42%) or inactive (n = 39; 20%) at both time points. Together these studies suggest that not only will some patients fail to increase their PA, some will become less active a year following surgery.

Data from the NWCR suggests that postsurgical patients may rely less on exercise for weight maintenance than those who lose weight without surgery. In a case control study of 134 NWCR participants, Klem and colleagues (2000) found that individuals who lost weight through surgical means reported lower amounts of PA than individuals who lost weight through nonsurgical means (Klem et al., 2000). Bond and colleagues (2009a), who performed a similar study with NWCR participants more recently, also found that surgical patients (n = 105) reported expending fewer calories through PA, and specifically calories expended in VPA, compared to non-surgical-matched participants (n = 210), and that a smaller percentage reported expending at least 2,000 kcal/week from PA. Thus, it appears that more encouragement and support to increase PA postsurgery may be needed to help patients maximize weight loss and other health benefits following bariatric surgery (Bueter et al., 2007).

Counseling Patients

It is important that the bariatric team explains that PA, along with surgery, is a tool toward weight loss and prevention of weight regain, as well as improved health. While the bulk of PA counseling may come from one team member, or someone outside of the team, PA counseling that involves several members of the health care team is more effective (Simons-Morton, Calfas, Oldenburg, & Burton, 1998). Thus, all members should encourage patients to be physically active throughout their care. Receiving a clear, strong message from a health care provider goes a long way in assisting patients to increase their PA level (Marcus et al., 2006; McInnis, 2003).

PA counseling should begin with a patient interview (see Table 8.2) to help the health care provider understand the patient's current PA level, abilities, past experiences, feelings toward PA, barriers, and goals. During the interview the health care provider should also educate the patient on the benefits of regular PA, as well as help the patient develop realistic expectations. For example, PA expends energy (i.e., burns calories) and improves one's health, but PA cannot completely reshape one's body or make hanging skin disappear. Responses should be used to formulate an appropriate PA program that suits patients' needs and lifestyle (Andersen & Jakicic, 2009).

Table 8.2 Discussion Points for Initiating Physical Activity (PA) Counseling

---

Motive for PA

What are some of the benefits of PA? (e.g., weight loss, prevention of weight regain, improvement in physical function, pain, mood, energy level, comorbidities, etc.)

PA History

Are there any PAs you have enjoyed doing in the past? What PAs did you do when you were younger?

Current PA Level

What PAs do you currently do? How often? For how long each time?

Ability/Physical Limitations

Are there any PAs you are unable to do? For instance, can you walk around the grocery store, up and down stairs, bend over, carry groceries, etc.? How long can you walk at one time?

Attitude/Preferences

What PAs do you like/dislike now? Do you prefer to do PA alone or with others? Why?

Environment

Where can you be active? Where do you feel comfortable exercising? Do you have alternative places? Identify safe, convenient, and well-maintained facilities for exercise, and home-based resources for exercise that are comfortable for obese persons.

Social Support

Do you have any friends or family members that could help you become more active by providing childcare while you exercise, providing encouragement to meet your PA goals, or becoming your exercise buddy?

Perceived Obstacles and Barriers

What could make it hard for you to dedicate 30–60 min/day to doing planned PA? What ideas do you have for overcoming these barriers?

Physical Responses to PA

What bodily changes do you notice when you walk, go up stairs, and do other activities? Correct misconceptions: Mild discomfort (e.g., muscle soreness, fatigue, and side ache) during PA is normal.

Signs to Stop PA/Seek Medical Help

You should stop what you are doing if you experience extreme breathlessness, nausea, dizziness, chest pressure, or pain. Has this happened in the past?

PA Goal and Plans to Meet Goal

Help the patient make a specific, attainable, and measurable PA goal. Emphasize starting with LPA and MPA that are perceived as pleasant. Suggest self-monitoring techniques such as pedometers and exercise diaries. Discuss exercise prompts (e.g., packing gym bag night before and placing in front seat of car). Emphasize a regular schedule.

Addressing Barriers

It is challenging for all adults to adopt and maintain a regular PA program. Behavioral, psychological, environmental, and physiological factors can affect patients' success in becoming more physically active. Some common barriers to PA are lack of time (constraints due to multiple roles), childcare, support from family and friends, motivation or self-management skills, energy (sometimes caused from insufficient or poor quality sleep), enjoyment, and a safe and convenient environment to be active (Eyler et al., 2003; Sallis & Hovell, 1990). Additional barriers to PA that may be particularly significant among bariatric surgery patients are feelings of embarrassment (i.e., social physique anxiety), reduced aerobic capacity and mobility limitations, and lack of confidence to be active (i.e., low self-efficacy) due to either lack of experience, past negative experiences, fear of increasing musculoskeletal pain, getting injured, or having a cardiac event (Mattsson et al., 1997).

Patients may feel intimidated to enter a fitness facility if they have no experience using equipment or feel that they will solicit undesired attention. They may be interested in attempting a new type of PA, such as water aerobics, but feel deterred due to their body size or shape concerns (e.g., feel uncomfortable changing in a locker room, afraid others will stare), or insecure of their ability to perform exercises as instructed (e.g., fear of not being able to keep pace with others). In addition, they may feel that the fitness instructor is unapproachable (e.g., he or she would not understand their physical limitations or be able to empathize with their situation). Thus, it is important to help patients develop strategies for coping with new PA environments or determine a PA plan that addresses the patients' concerns (e.g., using exercise videos at home instead of attending classes at a fitness facility).

It is also important to evaluate mobility limitations. A LABS-2 analysis examining the walking capacity of 2,458 presurgical patients, ranging in age from 18–78 years, found that 64% reported limitations walking several blocks, 16% reported some walking aid use, and 7% reported inability to walk 200 ft unassisted (King, Engel et al., 2010). While higher BMI and older age were independently related to reduced walking capacity, almost half (48%) of participants with a BMI of <40 kg/m² and more than half (57%) of 18- to 34-year-olds reported limitations walking several blocks. Thus, even young or less obese bariatric candidates may present with significant walking limitations. This study also found that while 28% of study participants did not attempt a 400 m walk test at a self-selected "usual" walking pace due to contraindication (e.g., recent cardiac symptoms) or choice (e.g., fear of pain), among those who attempted the walk, over half (56%) reported physical discomfort, such as joint pain, from walking.

Thus, PA advice must not be limited to "start a walking program." Instead, patients should be presented with many ideas for how they can become more active.

In addition to fearing or feeling pain, some patients may believe that participating in MPA is dangerous to their health. In a qualitative study overweight and obese weight management participants (n = 21; mean BMI = 36.9 kg/m^2) discussed their fears related to exercise, including how fear leads to avoidance. They reported exaggerated physical reactions to PA and interpreted these as negative physiological responses (Wingo et al., in press). For example, participants reported that they may perceive physiological responses to climbing a flight of stairs (e.g., increased body temperature with a faster heart rate, belabored breathing, and perspiration) as dangerous (Wingo et al., in press). Thus, it is important to teach patients that mild discomfort (e.g., muscle soreness, fatigue, and side ache) is a normal side effect of exercising, especially when increasing PA levels. On the other hand, nausea, light-headedness, dizziness, confusion, poor muscle coordination, cold or clammy skin, noticeable change in heart rhythm, and chest pressure or angina are signals to stop an activity and possibly seek medical attention (ACSM, 2006).

Clinicians providing PA counseling should communicate with the bariatric team to determine whether patients should undergo testing before increasing their PA level. The American College of Sports Medicine (ACSM) guidelines for Exercise and Testing Prescription state that "obese patients can begin an exercise program with a gradual increase in PA without undergoing diagnostic tests." However, formal testing is recommended for patients with symptoms of heart disease, hypertension, or history of metabolic, cardiac, or pulmonary disease (ACSM, 2006). Thus, patients experiencing heart-related symptoms should be referred to a cardiologist to minimize the risk of injury, stroke, and heart attack. In addition, patients should be informed of the potential impact of their medications. For example, heart medications, such as beta-blockers and ACE inhibitors, lower resting heart rate, which can decrease exercise capacity. Calcium channel blockers and vasodilators trigger hypotension; therefore, an extended, progressive cool-down session must be emphasized. In addition, although rare, exercise paired with caloric restriction (i.e., fewer calories with decreased carbohydrates and increased protein) may produce an unwanted side effect of the body shifting into a catabolic state (Petering & Webb, 2009). Thus, patients should be forewarned about signs and symptoms (e.g., feeling lethargic, muscle cramps) that would prompt them to seek medical help.

While environmental barriers to PA are not unique to bariatric surgery patients, this population may have more difficulty finding safe, comfortable, and practical places to be active. For instance, they may be too heavy to use recumbent bikes or treadmills (many have maximum weight limits of 350 pounds or less), or they may not be ready to walk on uneven surfaces or up inclines, which can be hard to avoid in the real world. Thus, it is particularly important to help patients think about where they can be active. Fitness centers, for-profit and non-profit gyms, swimming pools, parks, walking paths, and neighborhood sidewalks are possible options. For those without access to such resources, alternatives should be explored. For example, some churches, public libraries, and other community organizations offer low-impact exercise classes for free or nominal fees. There are also several options for exercising in one's home.

Timing

Given the substantial barriers to PA prior to surgery, it may be argued that patients should not be counseled to increase their PA level until after they benefit from surgery-induced weight loss, which has been shown to reduce pain, improve physical function, and influence perception of PA as less labor intensive (Tompkins, Bosch, Chenowith, Tiede, & Swain, 2008), especially because an early failed attempt at adopting a PA routine might discourage a patient from attempting to increase his or her PA later on. However, there are several reasons to begin PA counseling prior to surgery. First and foremost, PA improves health; higher aerobic fitness at time of surgery may help reduce surgical complications, and facilitate healing and postoperative recovery (McCullough et al., 2006). Second, you don't want to miss out on a teachable moment; a study measuring the PA readiness of 87 bariatric surgery candidates found that almost half (46%) of participants reported that they intended to initiate engagement in regular MPA within the next 30 days (Bond et al., 2006b), suggesting that the preoperative period may be a time when many patients are receptive to PA encouragement and advice. Third, many barriers to PA persist after surgery if they are not addressed (Josbeno et al., 2010). Thus, developing healthy behavioral patterns before surgery may help patients overcome barriers after surgery (e.g., scheduling designated time to exercise prior to surgery may decrease the "lack of time" excuse after surgery). Finally, a few studies have shown that presurgery attitudes and behaviors are related to postsurgery PA behavior. For instance, in a study of 42 bariatric surgery patients, perceiving more exercise benefits and having more confidence to exercise prior to surgery predicted more PA 1 year following surgery (Wouters, Larsen, Zijlstra, van Ramshorst, & Geenen, 2010). In a LABS-2 analysis with 310 bariatric surgery patients, higher PA level, less pain, and not having asthma prior to surgery independently predicted more PA 1 year postsurgery (King, Hsu, Wolfe et al., 2011). Thus, intervening before surgery may positively influence postsurgery

PA. Given the pros and cons of trying to help patients increase their PA level prior to surgery, clinicians should initiate PA counseling during the pre-operative period and help patients set realistic PA goals, which can be adapted several times over the first year in conjunction with weight loss and improvement in fitness and function.

While clinicians should do their best to counsel all patients during the preoperative period, it is possible that some patients will not be receptive to implementing new behaviors, such as PA, until they begin to struggle with losing excess weight after surgery (Leahey & Bond, 2008). However, the clinician should not feel that lack of immediate behavior change indicates that PA counseling is ineffective; some patients will require several prompts as they go through a process that leads to behavior change. Thus, it is important to offer PA counseling to patients at several time points both before and after surgery, so that when patients are ready to make a commitment to improving their health through PA, they have the assistance they need.

Physical Activity Goals

A long-term goal for almost all patients should be to meet PA guidelines for health (USDHHS, 2008). Once that goal is met, patients should be encouraged to increase the frequency and duration of PA to meet PA recommendations for weight loss maintenance (Saris et al., 2003). However, patients may need several months to build up to these goals, and it is important to have several intermediate goals along the way.

The American Society for Metabolic and Bariatric Surgery (ASMBS) recommends presurgical patients start with "mild" exercise 20 min/day, three or four times per week (ASMBS, 2008). In particular, they suggest improving aerobic conditioning with walking, swimming, or bike riding, increasing strength with light weights or resistance training with bands or tubing, and improving lung capacity by blowing up balloons. Regardless of a patient's presurgical PA program, ASMBS recommends that patients begin a walking program immediately following surgery, which should be progressively increased to build endurance (ASMBS, 2008).

Type and method of the bariatric surgical procedure may influence initiation and progression of postoperative PA. Patients who undergo laparoscopic gastric bypass surgery or banding have reduced recovery time compared with patients who have open gastric bypass surgery, and thus may be ready for PA sooner (Evans et al., 2004). The University of Chicago Medical Center recommends the following postsurgical PA schedule (University of Chicago Medical Center, 2008). In the hospital, the patient should get up and walk (e.g., starting with a series of 1 to 2 min walks) to improve circulation, which improves the body's ability to heal. In the first 1 to 4 weeks at home after surgery, the patient should "start slow" (e.g., walk around the house and use stairs as tolerated). With surgeon approval,

PA should be increased in weeks 5–6. However, patients with specific complications may not be ready to increase PA yet. Others should start slowly with low-impact PA such as stationary bike riding, treadmill, and housework. Six weeks postsurgery PA should be increased on a regular basis as tolerated with activities such as stair walking, gardening, cycling, tennis, dancing, and walking.

Once patients are past the initial recovery from surgery it is important that they have clear PA goals with specified duration, frequency, intensity, and type. ACSM-certified health fitness specialists suggest that patients work up to a total of 5 h of weekly cardiovascular exercise of light to moderate intensity by approximately 6 months after surgery (Fujioka, Kearney, & Fischer, 2010, personal communication). However, some patients may be able to reach this goal faster, and others slower, depending on their starting fitness level and initiation of PA. A rule of thumb is that patients should be encouraged to achieve a previously set goal for at least one or two weeks before gradually increasing the goal. For patients starting a walking program, Petering and Webb (2009) suggest using a pedometer to establish baseline steps/day during week 1, then increasing the daily number of steps by 250–500 each week until attaining a goal of 10,000 steps/day. Following this scheme it would take a patient who walks 4,000 steps/day at baseline 6 months to achieve 10,000 steps/day by adding 250 steps/day each week, while someone who walks 7,000 steps/day at baseline would achieve this goal in 6 weeks by adding 500 steps/day each week.

While ideally PA should be done in bouts of 10 min or longer (USDHHS, 2008), it may not be appropriate for a deconditioned severely obese adult to go from no PA to 10 min bouts, as such a change might cause an unreasonable level of soreness or fatigue (Mattson et al., 1997). Thus, patients should be advised according to their fitness and ability level. It is better to have a patient successfully complete four 5 min walking sessions per day than to attempt two 10 min sessions and give up after the first one. Accomplishing small goals helps create a sense of confidence and mastery, which may increase the likelihood of continuing to engage in the behavior.

Just as recommendations for duration and frequency of PA must be tailored to a patient's ability, so must intensity. After measuring the exercise tolerance and functional capacity of 109 presurgical patients, McCullough and colleagues determined presurgical patients may need to do LPA so as not to exceed their anaerobic threshold. They proposed that even slow walking speed (i.e., 1–2.5 mph), at least during the initial weeks of training, may serve to improve aerobic capacity and reduce complications with bariatric surgery (McCullough et al., 2006).

While 2.5 mph is often cited as the minimum walking speed at which moderate intensity is achieved (Ainsworth et al., 2000), obese adults may achieve a physiological response representative of MPA at much slower speeds (King, Hames, & Goodpaster, 2010). There is also evidence that when obese adults are allowed to self-select a walking pace consistent with "walking for pleasure," they have a heart rate response representative of the transition between MPA and VPA (Hills et al., 2006; Mattson et al., 1997). Thus, patients should be encouraged to select a walking speed (or exertion level for other activities) that allows them to meet their frequency and duration goals and does not leave them too sore or exhausted to engage in their next scheduled bout of PA.

It may be helpful to counsel patients on how to self-assess PA intensity with their heart rate, especially once they have gained some fitness and are ready to focus on increasing PA intensity. First, patients should be instructed on the percentage of their max HR they should attempt to achieve (e.g., MPA = 50 to <70% of max HR). Then patients should be taught to monitor their heart rate by measuring their radial pulse (on the inside of the wrist) or their carotid pulse (below the neck). An easy approach to calculate beats per minute is to count the number of beats in 6 s and multiply that number by 10.

Components of a Balanced Exercise Program

Physical activities generally fall into at least one of four main categories: aerobic (also known as endurance), strength, balance, and flexibility. Aerobic activities cause increases in breathing and heart rate for an extended period of time. Strength activities work your major muscles against some kind of resistance to increase muscle tissue. Flexibility activities improve your joints' ability to move through a full range of motion. Stability exercises, such as standing on one leg, are done to establish and improve balance, which may be especially important during rapid weight loss, as the patient's center of balance changes.

A beginner exerciser might start by focusing on one category of PA. However, as the patient progresses he or she should be encouraged to do activities from all categories, as they each offer unique benefits (see Table 8.3). For example, after 2 months of walking a patient may be ready for a more comprehensive program including stretching, balance exercises, weight training, and greater-intensity aerobic activity.

Appropriate Activities

It is important to remind patients that there are many ways to increase their PA level, and it may take several tries to find activities that they feel comfortable doing. Finding acceptable activities is key to maximizing compliance. Considerations for determining appropriate activities include range of motion, agility, balance, coordination, aerobic fitness, and personal preference. As the most popular form of exercise among adults, walking is often promoted as a practical and convenient way to meet PA guidelines for health and weight loss. However, those with significant pain

Table 8.3 Types of Physical Activity (PA) That Improve Physical Function

Aerobic/endurance activities make it easier to:	Strength training can help maintain ability to:
• Vacuum • Rake leaves • Push children on swings • Walk up hill	• Get up from a chair • Carry a full laundry basket from the basement to the second floor • Carry smaller children • Lift bags of mulch in the garden
Flexibility, or stretching, exercises make it possible to:	Stability/balance exercises can help with:
• Make the bed • Bend over to tie your shoes • Look over your shoulder as you back the car out of the driveway	• Standing on tiptoe to reach something on the top shelf • Walking up and down the stairs • Walking on an uneven sidewalk without falling

Source: Adapted from the National Institute on Aging's *Exercise and Physical Activity Guide.* From http://www.nia.nih.gov/HealthInformation/Publications/Exercise Guide/01_getready.htm

or physical limitations may do better by starting with chair-based or water-based exercises, which can be done alone or in group settings at gyms and community centers (e.g., in water aerobics or water therapy classes). While some patients are not initially comfortable with the idea of wearing a bathing suit, exercising in the water eliminates most impact and is thereby well tolerated by many patients, even those with knee, hip, or back pain. Exercising in the water also offers a unique, safe environment to improve balance (e.g., falling is safer in a pool than on land). Thus, patients should be encouraged to consider this option. Tai chi or "restorative" yoga classes, which help with both flexibility and balance, may also offer an appropriate level of challenge.

Patients should also be informed of safe and appropriate home exercise programs offered on television (consult your local listings) and exercise DVDs (e.g., low-impact dance videos, chair aerobics, beginner yoga) that can be purchased online or may be available at the public library. In particular, beginner exercisers might like *Walk Away the Pounds*, an in-home walking program created by Leslie Sansone that combines music with a variety of walking styles, or *Sweatin' to the Oldies*, with Richard Simmons, which focuses on having fun while doing a low-impact workout. Exercise DVDs and television shows have several advantages. They are inexpensive, can be used in the privacy of the patient's home, at any time, and are not affected by inclement weather.

An alternative to exercise videos, which still allows patients to exercise in their home at their convenience, is home exercise equipment. While some exercise machines are quite costly or have weight restrictions, portable pedal exercisers are not. Pedal exercisers with adjustable tension are available for around $50, and because they are used while the patient sits in his or her own chair, there is no weight restriction. Pedal exercises can be used to improve both upper body and lower body circulation and strength, as well as improve aerobic capacity. One appeal is that they can be used while patients watch their favorite TV shows, turning a sedentary activity into a PA.

In addition to aerobic PA, light resistance training is recommended to help correct posture, build fat-free mass, and improve balance and coordination. Patients should begin at a lower intensity that permits 15 repetitions per set to reduce musculoskeletal injury. By the last repetition muscles should feel fatigued but not be brought to failure. To ensure safety, patients should be in a supported position during all exercises. Using machines is recommended, but is not always an option due to size limits. Light free weights can also be used but may lead to injury due to the range of free motion if correct form is not used. Thus, patients planning to use free weights should be encouraged to seek instruction from a qualified professional.

There is a growing body of literature supporting the importance of reducing sedentary time, even with LPA, as frequency and duration of movement appear to play a role in health outcomes such as achieving and maintaining a healthy weight (Andersen & Jakicic, 2009). Thus, in addition to encouraging patients to stick with their scheduled PA, patients should be encouraged to increase their incidental PA (e.g., use stairs instead of taking elevators or escalators (if joints allow), park their car farther from their intended destination, carry their groceries in from the car, take a walk during a lunch break, and do their own housework and yard work). Patients should also be encouraged to decrease sedentary behaviors, such as watching TV and using the computer.

Can They Do It?

While there is a great deal of concern about what bariatric surgery patients can do, a recent lifestyle intervention with 130 Class 2 and 3 obese adults reported that participants did not present with any particular physical limitations that precluded them from initiating a PA program at the onset of the weight loss intervention (Goodpaster et al., 2010). Participants were randomized to 12 months of diet and PA or 6 months of diet only followed by 6 months of diet and PA. Once PA was introduced it was gradually increased until participants could do 60 min of MPA, 5 days/week. The 60 daily minutes could be broken down into multiple sessions of at least 10 min each. Participants were also given a pedometer with a step goal of at least 10,000 steps/day and asked to self-monitor PA in a weekly diary. In the first 6 months the initial PA group had significant increases in PA (e.g., mean of 7,048 to 8,475 steps/day; mean of 34 to 71 VPA min/week).

In the second 6 months the delayed PA group had similar increases in PA. While adults willing to engage in an intensive lifestyle intervention may not be representative of bariatric surgery patients, this study supports the idea that unless there are clear clinical indications of why PA should not be increased, severely obese adults who are motivated and have support are able to increase their PA level to be in compliance with weight loss and weight maintenance recommendations.

Exercise Basics

Given that many patients will be new to exercise, the clinician should not assume they know what to do. Going over the following list of dos and don'ts may be surprisingly helpful.

Do

- Start every workout with a warm-up and end every workout with a cool-down.
- Stay hydrated by drinking plenty of water before, during, and after exercise.
- Dress properly with comfortable clothing.
- Wear supportive shoes appropriate for your activity. Good athletic shoes can be costly, but investing in good shoes is an investment in good health.
- Avoid holding the breath during PA.
- See a physician if you develop an injury with radiating or severe pain with swelling or numbness, or that makes moving the affected body part difficult.
- Rest for a few days if experiencing minor pain. Ice, compression and elevation, and heat can all help with the healing process.

Do Not

- Engage in ballistic stretching (i.e., avoid bouncing); instead practice holding each stretch 20–30 s.
- Wear restrictive clothing or rubber suits to increase sweating.
- Do contraindicated movements (e.g., straight-leg situps).
- Exercise immediately after eating.
- Take a hot sauna, shower, or steam bath until 10 min after exercising.
- Ignore an injury.

Keys to Staying Active

Short lapses in PA are common and should be expected; however, a long lapse or relapse should be avoided. When patients "fall off the wagon" it is important to encourage them to do any small activity to get restarted.

Helping patients maintain a positive attitude is crucial to their success. Some keys to staying active are:

- Start slowly and gradually increase duration, frequency, and intensity. This is especially important when returning to PA after an injury. Too much too soon often results in failure and disappointment.
- Set realistic, attainable, and specific goals along with commensurate rewards.
- Try different activities, such as outdoor activities, to avoid boredom and stick with the most enjoyable ones.
- Find a group or exercise buddy to help with accountability.
- Stay well fueled: Keep hydrated and eat enough protein.

Referrals

Depending on the depth of PA support at a bariatric center, the proximity of the bariatric center to the patient's home, and the patient's physical function and motivation, the patient may need professional PA support outside of the bariatric team. Patients experiencing pain associated with PA or physical limitations that make it difficult to increase PA should be referred to a physical therapist. Patients needing additional guidance or encouragement to establish a healthy PA routine should be encouraged to see a certified exercise specialist, such as a personal trainer or lifestyle coach (Andersen & Jakicic, 2009). A certified, experienced trainer can build rapport and help struggling patients build structure, confidence, commitment, and compliance. Exercise professionals most qualified to work with special populations, such as obese, sedentary patients, will usually have an advanced certification from an organization such as the American Council on Exercise (ACE), American College of Sports Medicine (ACSM), or the National Strength and Conditioning Association (NSCA). In addition, they may have college degrees in kinesiology, exercise science, or a related field. Fitness professionals can be found in cardiac rehabilitation programs, health clubs, community recreation centers, or other high-quality fitness facilities (Garber, 2009).

Chapter Summary

Increasing PA from pre- to postsurgery and higher postsurgery PA level are associated with greater weight loss and improved body composition following surgery. In addition, regular PA improves fitness, strength, balance, physical function, and psychological well-being, and reduces the risk of heart disease, colon and breast cancers, osteoporosis, and diabetes. Prior to surgery the majority of bariatric surgery patients are sedentary or insufficiently active. A number of patients report an increase in their PA postsurgery, but many of them do not meet PA guidelines for general health, weight loss, or weight maintenance, and some actually become less active. To help patients maximize weight loss and other health benefits following bariatric surgery, patients need more PA encouragement and support.

All members of the bariatric team should encourage patients to become and remain physically active. The clinician initiating PA counseling should start by interviewing the patient so advice is tailored to the patient's abilities and barriers to PA. While meeting PA recommendations for weight maintenance (e.g., 60–90 min MVPA/day) is an appropriate long-term goal for most patients, health professionals should help patients set realistic, attainable, measurable short-term goals, and gradually increase the amount and intensity of PA over time. PA counseling should also address ways to stay motivated and make PA more enjoyable. Patients experiencing pain associated with PA or physical limitations that make it difficult to increase PA should be referred to a physical therapist. Patients needing additional guidance or encouragement to establish a healthy PA routine should be encouraged to consult a certified exercise specialist, such as a personal trainer or lifestyle coach, with references and experience working with this type of clientele. The overall goal is partnering with bariatric patients to incorporate PA into their lives; it is crucial for health care providers to be a part of this transformation.

Internet Resources

- In the "2008 Physical Activity Guidelines for Americans" the U.S. Department of Health and Human Service describes the types and amounts of PA that offer substantial health benefits by age, health status, and so on, at www.health.gov/paguidelines/.
- The Centers for Disease Control and Prevention's website "Physical Activity for Everyone" offers exercise recommendations and patient educational materials at www.cdc.gov/physicalactivity/everyone/guidelines/index.html.
- Exercise is Medicine, a nonprofit initiative to encourage all health care providers to assess and review PA at every office visit, offers materials for health care providers and patients at www.exerciseismedcine.org.
- The American College of Sports Medicine provides physical activity resources at www.acsm.org.
- The American Heart Association provides healthy lifestyle tips at www.heart.org.

- The American Society of Bariatric Surgery offers information and discussion points on postoperative concerns at http://www.asbs. org/html/pdf/asbs_bspc.pdf.

References

Ainsworth, B.E., Haskell, W.L., Whitt, M.C., Irwin, M.L., Swartz, A.M., Strath, S.J. et al. (2000). Compendium of physical activities: An update of activity codes and MET intensities. *Medicine and Science in Sports and Exercise, 32,* S498–S504.

American College of Sports Medicine (ACSM). (2006). *Guidelines for Exercise Testing and Prescription* (7th ed.). New York: Lippincott Williams & Wilkins.

Andersen, R.E., & Jakicic, J.M. (2009). Interpreting the physical activity guidelines for health and weight management. *Journal of Physical Activity and Health, 6,* 651–656.

ASMBS Public/Professional Education Committee. (2008). Bariatric surgery: Postoperative concerns. Retrieved October 14, 2010, from http://www.asbs. org/html/pdf/asbs_bspc.pdf

Bond, D.S., Evans, R.K., DeMaria, E., Wolfe, L., Meador, J., Kellum, J. et al. (2006a). Physical activity and quality of life improvements before obesity surgery. *American Journal of Health Behavior, 30,* 422–434.

Bond, D.S., Evans, R.K., DeMaria, E.J., Wolfe, L.G., Meador, J.G., Kellum, J.M. et al. (2006b). Physical activity stage of readiness predicts moderate-vigorous physical activity participation among morbidly obese gastric bypass surgery candidates. *Surgery for Obesity and Related Diseases, 2,* 128–132.

Bond, D.S., Jakicic, J.M., Unick, J.L., Vithianathan, S., Pohl, D., Roye, G.D. et al. (2010). Pre- to postoperative physical activity changes in bariatric surgery patients: Self-report vs. objective measures. *Obesity, 18,* 2395–2397 (Epub April 8, 2010).

Bond, D.S., Jakicic, J.M., Vithiananthan, S., Thomas, J.G., Leahey, T.M., Sax, H.C. et al. (2010). Objective quantification of physical activity in bariatric surgery candidates and normal-weight controls. *Surgery for Obesity and Related Diseases, 6,* 72–78.

Bond, D.S., Phelan, S., Leahey, T.M., Hill, J.O., & Wing, R.R. (2009). Weight-loss maintenance in successful weight losers: Surgical vs non-surgical methods. *International Journal of Obesity, 33,* 173–180.

Bond, D.S., Phelan, S., Wolfe, L.G., Evans, R.K., Meador, J.G., Kellum, J.M. et al. (2009). Becoming physically active after bariatric surgery is associated with improved weight loss and health-related quality of life. *Obesity, 17,* 78–83 (Epub November 6, 2008).

Bond, D.S., Unick, J.L., Jakicic, J.M., Vithianathan, S., Pohl, D., Roye, G.D. et al. (2011). Objective assessment of time spent being sedentary in bariatric surgery candidates. *Obesity Surgery, 21,* 811–814.

Bueter, M., Thalheimer, A., Lager, C., Schowalter, M., Illert, B., & Fein, M. (2007). Who benefits from gastric banding? *Obesity Surgery, 17,* 1608–1613.

Caspersen, C.J., Powell, K.E., &, Christenson, G.M. (1985). Physical activity, exercise, and physical fitness: Definitions and distinctions for health-related research. *Public Health Report*, *100*, 126–131.

Catenacci, V.A., Grunwald, G.K., Ingebrigtsen, J.P., Jakicic, J.M., McDermott, M.D., Phelan, S. et al. (2011). Physical activity patterns using accelerometry in the National Weight Control Registry. *Obesity* (Silver Spring), *19*, 1163–1170.

Catenacci, V.A., Ogden, L.G., Stuht, J., Phelan, S. Wing, R.R., Hill, J.O. et al. (2008). Physical activity patterns in the National Weight Control Registry. *Obesity* (Silver Spring), *16*, 153–161.

Chomentowski, P., Dubé, J.J., Amati, F., Stefanovic-Racic, M., Zhu, S., Toledo, F.G.S. et al. (2009). Moderate exercise attenuates the loss of skeletal muscle mass that occurs with intentional caloric restriction-induced weight loss in older, overweight to obese adults. *Journals of Gerontology Series A: Biological Sciences and Medical Sciences*, *64*, 575–580.

Colles, S.L., Dixon, J.B., & O'Brien, P.E. (2008). Hunger control and regular physical activity facilitate weight loss after laparoscopic adjustable gastric banding. *Obesity Surgery*, *18*, 833–840.

Cox, T.L., Malpede, C.Z., Desmond, R., Faulk, L., Myer, R., Henson, S. et al. (2007). Physical activity patterns during weight maintenance following a low-energy dense dietary intervention. *Obesity*, *15*, 1226–1232.

Cyarto, E.V., Myers, A.M., & Tudor-Locke, C. (2004). Pedometer accuracy in nursing home and community-dwelling older adults. *Medicine and Science in Sports and Exercise*, *36*, 205–209.

Division of Nutrition, Physical Activity and Obesity, National Center for Chronic Disease Prevention and Health Promotion (DNPAO). (2010). Measuring physical activity intensity. Retrieved December 3, 2010, from http://www.cdc.gov/physicalactivity/everyone/measuring/index.html

Donnelly, J.E., Blair, S.N. Jakicic, J.M., Manore, M.M., Rankin, J.W., & Smith, B.K. (2009). Appropriate physical activity intervention strategies for weight loss and prevention of weight regain for adults. *Medicine and Science in Sports and Exercise*, *41*, 459–471.

Evans, R.K., Bond, D.S., DeMaria, E.J., Wolfe, L.G., Meador, J.G., & Kellum, J.M. (2004). Initiation and progression of physical activity after laparoscopic and open gastric bypass surgery. *Surgery Innovation*, *11*, 235–239.

Ewbank, P.P., Darga, L.L., & Lucas, C.P. (1995). Physical activity as a predictor of weight maintenance in previously obese subjects. *Obesity Research*, *3*, 257–263.

Eyler, A.A., Matson-Koffman, D., Young, D.R., Wilcox, S., Wilbur, J., Thompson, J.L. et al. (2003). Quantitative study of correlates of physical activity in women from diverse racial/ethnic groups. *American Journal of Preventive Medicine*, *25*, 5–14.

Fogelholm, M., Kukkonen-Harjula, K., Nenonen, A., & Pasanen, M. (2000). Effects of walking training on weight maintenance after a very-low-energy diet in premenopausal obese women: A randomized controlled trial. *Archives of Internal Medicine*, *160*, 2177–2184.

Fujioka, K., Kearney, J., & Fischer, M. (2010, October 4). Exercise and bariatrics (e-mail).

Garber, C.E. (2009, July). Promoting a physically active lifestyle in bariatric patients. *Bariatric Times*. Retrieved December 16, 2010, from http://bariatrictimes. com/category/issue-archives/2009-july/

Goodpaster, B.H., DeLany, J.P., Otto, A.D., Kuller, L., Vockley, J., South-Paul, J.E. et al. (2010). Effects of diet and physical activity interventions on weight loss and cardiometabolic risk factors in severely obese adults: A randomized trial. *Journal of the American Medical Association, 304*, 1795–1802.

Guthold, R., Ono, T., Strong, K.L., Chatterji, S., & Morabia, A. (2008). Worldwide variability in physical inactivity: A 51-country survey. *American Journal of Preventive Medicine, 34*, 486–494.

Hagströmer, M. (2007). Assessment of health-enhancing physical activity at population level. Stockholm: Karolinska Insitute. Retrieved December 21, 2010, from http://publications.ki.se/jspui/bitstream/10616/39827/1/ thesis.pdf

Haskell, W.L., Lee, I.M., Pate, R.R., Powell, K.E., Blair, S.N., Franklin, B.A. et al. (2007). Physical activity and public health: Updated recommendation for adults from the American College of Sports Medicine and the American Heart Association. *Circulation, 116*, 1081–1093 (Epub August 1, 2007).

HEPA Europe. (2005). European Network for the Promotion of Health-Enhancing Physical Activity. Copenhagen, WHO Regional Office for Europe. Retrieved December 21, 2010, from http://www.euro.who.int/__data/assets/pdf_ file/0019/101692/HEPA_leaflet.pdf

Hills, A.P., Byrne, N.M., Wearing, S., & Armstrong, T. (2006). Validation of the intensity of walking for pleasure in obese adults. *Preventive Medicine, 42*, 47–50 (Epub 2005 Dec 1).

Jacobi, D., Ciangura, C., Couet, C., & Oppert, J.M. (2011). Physical activity and weight loss following bariatric surgery. *Obesity Reviews, 12*, 366–377.

Jakicic, J.M., Marcus, B.H., Gallagher, K.I., Napolitano, M., & Lang, W. (2003). Effect of exercise duration and intensity on weight loss in overweight, sedentary women: A randomized trial. *Journal of the American Medical Association, 290*, 1323–1330.

Jakicic, J.M., Marcus, B.H., Lang, W., & Janney, C. (2008). Effect of exercise on 24-month weight loss maintenance in overweight women. *Archives of Internal Medicine, 168*, 1550–1559.

Jakicic, J.M., Polley, B.A., & Wing, R.R. (1998). Accuracy of self-reported exercise and the relationship with weight loss in overweight women. *Medicine and Science in Sports and Exercise, 30*, 634–638.

Josbeno, D.A., Jakicic, J.M., Hergenroeder, A., & Eid, G.M. (2010). Physical activity and physical function changes in obese individuals after gastric bypass surgery. *Surgery for Obesity and Related Diseases, 6*, 361–366 (Epub August 14, 2008).

Kahn, H.S., Tatham, L.M., Rodriguez, C., Calle, E.E., Thun, M.J., & Heath, C.W., Jr. (1997). Stable behaviors associated with adults' 10-year change in body mass index and likelihood of gain at the waist. *American Journal of Public Health, 87*, 747–754.

King, W.C., Belle, S.H., Chapman, W.H., Courcoulas, A.P., Dakin, G.F., Eid, G.M. et al. (2008). Correlates of physical activity level of bariatric surgery candidates. *Obesity, 16*, S246.

King, W.C., Belle, S.H., Eid, G.M., Dakin, G.F., Inabnet, W.B., Mitchell, J.E. et al. (2008). Physical activity levels of patients undergoing bariatric surgery. *Surgery for Obesity and Related Diseases, 4,* 721–728.

King, W.C., Engel, S.G., Elder, K.A., Chapman, W.H., Eid, G.M., & Wolfe, B.M. (in press). Walking capacity of bariatric surgery candidates. *Surgery for Obesity and Related Diseases.*

King, W.C., Hames, K., & Goodpaster, B. (2010). BMI predicts walking speed at which moderate-intensity physical activity is achieved. *Medicine and Science in Sports and Exercise, 42,* S514.

King, W.C., Hsu, J.Y., Courcoulas, A.P., Eid, G.M., Flum, D.R., Karr, T.M. et al. (2011). Association of physical activity with change in weight and percentage body fat following bariatric surgery. *Medicine and Science in Sports and Exercise, 43,* S80.

King, W.C., Hsu, J.Y., Wolfe, B.M., Smith, M.D., Steffen, K.J., Courcoulas, A.P. et al. (2011). Pre- to post-operative changes in physical activity: Report from the Longitudinal Assessment of Bariatric Surgery-2 (LABS-2). *Surgery for Obesity and Related Diseases, 7,* 361.

Klem, M.L., Wing, R.R, Chang, C.C., Lang, W., McGuire, M.T., Sugerman, H.J. et al. (2000). A case-control study of successful maintenance of a substantial weight loss: Individuals who lost weight through surgery versus those who lost weight through non-surgical means. *International Journal of Obesity and Related Metabolic Disorders, 24,* 573–579.

Klem, M.L., Wing, R.R., McGuire, M.T., Seagle, H.M., & Hill, J.O. (1997). A descriptive study of individuals successful at long-term maintenance of substantial weight loss. *American Journal of Clinical Nutrition, 66,* 239–246.

Levine, J.A., McCrady, S.K., Lanningham-Foster, L.M., Kane, P.H., Foster, R.C., & Manohar, C.U. (2008). The role of free-living daily walking in human weight gain and obesity. *Diabetes, 57,* 548–554 (Epub November 14, 2007).

Livhits, M., Mercado, C., Yermilov, I., Parikh, J.A., Dutson, E., Mehran, A. et al. (2010). Exercise following bariatric surgery: A systematic review. *Obesity Surgery, 20,* 657–665.

Marcus, B.H., Williams, D.M., Dubbert, P.M., Sallis, J.F., King, A.C., Yancey, A.K. et al. (2006). Physical activity intervention studies: What we know and what we need to know: A scientific statement from the American Heart Association Council on Nutrition, Physical Activity, and Metabolism (Subcommittee on Physical Activity); Council on Cardiovascular Disease in the Young; and the Interdisciplinary Working Group on Quality of Care and Outcomes Research. *Circulation, 114,* 2739–2752.

Mattsson, E., Larsson, U.E., & Rossner, S. (1997). Is walking for exercise too exhausting for obese women? *International Journal of Obesity, 21,* 380–386.

McCullough, P.A., Gallagher, M.J., deJong, A.T., Sandberg, K.R., Trivax, J.E., Alexander, D. et al. (2006). Cardiorespiratory fitness and short-term complications after bariatric surgery. *Chest, 130,* 517–525.

McInnis, K.J. (2003). Diet, exercise, and the challenge of combating obesity in primary care. *Journal of Cardiovascular Nursing, 18,* 93–100.

Melanson, E.L., Knoll, J.R., Bell, M.L., Donahoo, W.T., Hill, H.O., Nysse, L.J. et al. (2004). Commercially available pedometers: Considerations for accurate step counting. *Preventive Medicine, 39,* 361–368.

Metcalf, B., Rabkin, R.A., Rabkin, J.M., Metcalf, L., & Lehman-Becker, L.B. (2005). Weight loss composition: The effects of exercise following obesity surgery as measured by bioelectrical impedance analysis. *Obesity Surgery, 15*, 183–186.

Miller, K.H., Ogletree, R.J., & Welshimer, K. (2002). Impact of activity behaviors on physical activity identity and self-efficacy. *American Journal of Health Behavior, 26*, 323–330.

Miller, W.C., Wallace, J.P., & Eggert, K.E. (1993). Predicting max HR and the HR-VO2 relationship for exercise prescription in obesity. *Medicine and Science in Sports and Exercise, 25*, 1077–1081.

National Heart Lung and Blood Institute (NHLBI). (1998). Clinical guidelines on the identification, evaluation, and treatment of overweight and obesity in adults—Executive summary. Retrieved December 21, 2010, from http://www. nhlbi.nih.gov/guidelines/obesity/sum_clin.htm

National Institute of Aging. (2009). Exercise guide. Retrieved December 21, 2010, from http://www.nia.nih.gov/HealthInformation/Publications/ExerciseGuide/01_ getready.htm

Petering, R., & Webb, C.W. (2009). Exercise, fluid, and nutrition recommendations for the postgastric bypass exerciser. *Current Sports Medicine Reports, 8*, 92–97.

Petersen, L., Schnohr, P., & Sørensen, T.I. (2004). Longitudinal study of the long-term relation between physical activity and obesity in adults. *International Journal of Obesity and Related Metabolic Disorders, 28*, 105–112.

Rippe, J.M., & Hess, S. (1998). The role of physical activity in the prevention and management of obesity. *Journal of the American Dietetic Association, 98*, S31–S38.

Rissanen, A.M., Heliövaara, M., Knekt, P., Reunanen, A., & Aromaa, A. (1991). Determinants of weight gain and overweight in adult Finns. *European Journal of Clinical Nutrition, 45*, 419–430.

Sallis, J.F., & Hovell, M.F. (1990). Determinants of exercise behavior. *Exercise and Sports Sciences Reviews, 18*, 307–330.

Sallis, J.F., & Owen, N. (1999). *Physical activity and behavioral medicine*. Thousand Oaks, CA: Sage Publications.

Saris, W.H., Blair, S.N., van Baak, M.A., Eaton, S.B., Davies, P.S., Di Pietro, L. et al. (2003). How much physical activity is enough to prevent unhealthy weight gain? Outcome of the IASO 1st Stock Conference and consensus statement. *Obesity Reviews, 4*, 101–114.

Schneider, P.L., Crouter, S.E., Lukajic, O., & Bassett, D.R., Jr. (2003). Accuracy and reliability of 10 pedometers for measuring steps over a 400-m walk. *Medicine and Science in Sports and Exercise, 35*, 1779–1784.

Shang, E., & Hasenberg, T. (2010). Aerobic endurance training improves weight loss, body composition, and co-morbidities in patients after laprascopic Roux-en-Y gastric bypass. *Surgery for Obesity and Related Diseases, 6*, 260–266.

Simons-Morton, D.G., Calfas, K.J, Oldenburg, B., & Burton, N.W. (1998). Effects of interventions in health care settings on physical activity or cardiorespiratory fitness. *American Journal of Preventive Medicine, 15*, 413–430.

Tompkins, J., Bosch, P.R., Chenowith, R., Tiede, J.L., & Swain, J.M. (2008). Changes in functional walking distance and health-related quality of life after gastric bypass surgery. *Physical Therapy, 88*, 928–935.

Troiano, R.P. (2007). Large-scale applications of accelerometers: New frontiers and new questions. *Medicine and Science in Sports and Exercise, 39,* 1501.

Troiano, R.P., Berrigan, D., Dodd, K.W, Masse, L.C., Tilert, T., & McDowell, M. (2008). Physical activity in the United States measured by accelerometer. *Medicine and Science in Sports and Exercise, 40,* 181–188.

University of Chicago Medical Center. (2008). *Physical activity and exercise strategies for bariatric surgery patients.* Chicago: University of Chicago Hospitals Center for the Surgical Treatment of Obesity.

U.S. Department of Health and Human Services (USDHHS). (2008). Physical activity guidelines advisory committee report, 2008. Retrieved November 23, 2010, from http://www.health.gov/paguidelines/report/pdf/committeereport.pdf

Valanou, E.M., Bamia, C., & Trichopoulou, A. (2006). Methodology of physical-activity and energy-expenditure assessment: A review. *Journal of Public Health, 14,* 58–65. DOI: 10.1007/s10389–006–0021–0.

Ward, D.S., Evenson, K.R., Vaughn, A., Rodgers, A.B., & Troiano, R.P. (2005). Accelerometer use in physical activity: Best practices and research recommendations. *Medicine and Science in Sports and Exercise, 37,* S582–S588.

Wareham, N.J., & Rennie, K.L. (1998). The assessment of physical activity in individuals and populations: Why try to be more precise about how physical activity is assessed? *International Journal of Obesity and Related Metabolic Disorders, 22,* S30–S38.

Weinsier, R.L., Hunter, G.R., Zuckerman, P.A., Redden, D.T., Darnell, B.E., Larson, D.E. et al. (2000). Energy expenditure and free-living physical activity in black and white women: Comparison before and after weight loss. *American Journal of Clinical Nutrition, 71,* 1138–1146.

Westerterp, K.R. (2009). Assessment of physical activity: A critical appraisal. *European Journal of Applied Physiology, 105,* 823–828 (Epub February 11, 2009).

Wingo, B.C., Evans, R.R., Ard, J.D., Grimley, D.M., Roy, J., Snyder, S.W. et al. (In press). Fear of physical response to exercise among overweight and obese adults. *Qualitative Research in Exercise and Science.*

Wouters, E.J., Larsen, J.K., Zijlstra, H., van Ramshorst, B., & Geenen, R. (2010). Physical activity after surgery for severe obesity: The role of exercise cognitions. *Obesity Surgery* (Epub ahead of print).

CHAPTER **9**

Nutritional Care of the Bariatric Surgery Patient

SUE CUMMINGS and MARGARET FURTADO

Introduction

The decision to recommend weight loss surgery (WLS) for patients with obesity requires a multidisciplinary team to evaluate the indications for an operation, to define and manage comorbidities, and to provide short- and long-term post-WLS monitoring, support, and education. Although there is a growing body of research in the field, most current recommendations for the medical, nutritional, and psychological care of WLS patients are based on case reports, nonrandomized, small-sample, retrospective studies, and expert opinion. To date, there has been no standardization of care across surgical centers. Recently, major organizations and societies have been working to analyze the existing data and, where evidence is lacking, standardize recommendations based on expert opinion (Aills, Blankenship, Buffington, Furtado, & Parrott, 2008; AACE, 2008). All WLS procedures have nutritional implications, and this chapter will provide guidance for the nutritional evaluation and care of the WLS patient.

The registered dietitian's role within the multidisciplinary team is multifaceted. The dietitian's responsibilities include pre- and postoperative education focusing on evaluation and assessment of nutritional status, screening for clinical issues that require physician follow-up, assisting the patient in making an informed decision about the procedure, and assessing and treating nutritional deficiencies (Cunningham, 2006; Lehman Center Weight Loss Surgery Expert Panel, 2005). Research on the mechanisms of action of weight loss surgery procedures has led to a better understanding of the metabolic influences of each procedure as well as how each of these procedures impacts the weight regulatory system, specifically, hunger, satiety, and the body's weight "set point" (Ashrafian & le Roux, 2009). Given this understanding, weight loss surgeries are now considered metabolic procedures. The nutritional postoperative care of patients is determined by the type of procedure performed, as each has different nutritional implications. Weight loss surgery procedures are categorized into three groups:

1. *Purely restrictive procedures* work specifically and solely by restricting the amount of food that can be eaten at any given time. These procedures include the vertical banded gastroplasty (VBG), which was the most commonly performed procedure in the 1970s and 1980s and has been primarily replaced by the laparoscopic adjustable gastric band (LAGB). The VBG and LAGB procedures do not change food pathway through the digestive tract, and therefore do not have any nutrient malabsorption consequences.

2. *Malabsorptive procedures* include the biliopancreatic diversion (BPD) and the biliopancreatic diversion with the duodenal switch (BPD/DS). These procedures cause excessive malabsorption of both micro- and macronutrients, potentially leading to severe vitamin and mineral deficiencies. Although still performed by some surgeons, the BPD and BPD/DS are not commonly performed today and will not be addressed in detail in this chapter. Patients undergoing these procedures should have lifelong monitoring by health care providers who specialize in the care of BPD and BPD/DS patients, as these procedures pose lifelong metabolic and nutritional risks.

3. *Combination procedures* work through both neural and hormonal pathways, with some malabsorption of micronutrients (vitamins and minerals). The combination procedures do not cause any significant malabsorption of macronutrients (protein, carbohydrates, and fat). The Roux-en-Y gastric bypass (RYGBP) and the sleeve gastrectomy (SG) fall into this category. The RYGBP is the most commonly performed procedure in the United States today. The SG was developed in 2002 as a first-step approach to the BPD/DS. It was thought that the SG, having fewer risks associated with it, would be performed initially and then converted to a BPD/DS after the patient lost some weight, reducing the surgical risks of a more complicated procedure. However the 5-year outcome data

on the SG is very promising, and this procedure is now being performed as a stand-alone one. Because the SG is a newer procedure with limited long-term data, it is not routinely covered by health insurance at this time.

Nutritional Assessment Pre- and Postbariatric Surgery

Since we have limited capacity to predict success or failure of a given procedure in a given patient, the choice of which procedure to perform is often influenced by the local or regional expertise of surgeons and patient preference. However, strong consideration should be given to risk stratification, patient comorbidities, and weight loss expectations. The criteria most commonly used for patient selection are from the 1991 National Institutes of Health (NIH) Consensus Conference on bariatric surgery, which were updated in 2004 (Buchwald, 2005). These indications include a body mass index (BMI) greater than 40 kg/m^2 or a BMI greater than 35 kg/m^2 with an obesity-related comorbid condition (such as type-2 diabetes, sleep apnea, or coronary artery disease) and a failure of nonsurgical weight loss therapies. In December 2010, the Federal Drug Administration (FDA) ruled that BMI criteria for gastric banding may now include a BMI as low as 30 kg/m^2 along with significant comorbidities or 35 kg/m^2 without comorbidities.

Given the advanced knowledge of the mechanisms of how these procedures influence both body weight and comorbidities, there is a strong argument that decisions regarding whether or not WLS is indicated and which procedure to perform should be based on additional criteria that focus on comorbidity versus BMI alone. This argument suggests that the following questions should be a part of the initial assessment regarding the decision to recommend WLS (Dixon, 2009):

- What is the strength of the relationship between the comorbidity and obesity?
  - How serious is the comorbidity?
  - What is the effectiveness of weight loss for the comorbidity?
  - How effective is current therapy for the patient's condition?
  - When does the benefit outweigh the risk?: At a certain BMI or with a certain constellation of comorbidities

Although risk will never be totally eliminated, it is important that we make every attempt to do so through careful and thorough medical, psychological, nutritional, and surgical evaluation and provide additional support as needed. A preoperative preparation period and intense early and late postoperative follow-up should be part of every weight loss surgical patient's global care.

Presurgery Nutrition Assessment

Table 9.1 provides an outline of the components of the nutritional assessment for patients considering weight loss surgery. By synthesizing and classifying client assessment information, the dietitians can then assign *nutrition diagnoses*, formulate a *nutrition prescription*, and identify the *desired goals and outcomes* of nutrition intervention(s) both before and after WLS (Cummings, 2009). Presurgery nutrition education and care includes assisting patients with an understanding of how the procedures work and the influence of each procedure on nutritional status, food choices, and eating behaviors both short- and long-term postsurgery. Once patients make a decision to have weight loss surgery, the process of preparation should begin immediately. Patients should be advised to prepare for surgery by getting themselves in the best physical condition they can. Components of a presurgical nutrition program should include guiding patients toward healthy eating and activity, achieving better control of nutrition-related comorbidities, and losing some weight prior to surgery to reduce the size of the liver, and thereby reducing the risks during the actual procedure by technically making the procedure less difficult to perform laparoscopically.

Improving Presurgical Nutrition Status

Presurgery Nutritional Labs

An individual with obesity does not necessarily have normal levels of vitamins and trace minerals. To the contrary, poor nutritional intake may lead

Table 9.1 Nutrition Assessment Pre-Weight Loss Surgery

- Height and weight, calculate BMI
- Nutrition related comorbidities; medications, and adherence to previous diet recommendation
- Dieting history
- Weight history
- Food intake; supplements (vitamins, minerals, or dietary supplements)
- Cultural, social history affecting weight
- Eating behaviors
  - Meal/snack patterns
  - Eating style
- Physical activity and limitations
- Knowledge of surgeries including weight expectations, impact on current eating behaviors and habits
- Motivation for weight loss and readiness for diet changes
- Nutritional labs; specifically assess for those micronutrients affected by the specific procedure; replete all that are deficient before WLS

to nutritional deficiencies, and a person with obesity may have malnutrition. Because bariatric surgery procedures that alter nutrient absorption (RYGB, GS, BPD, and BPD/DS) can lead to nutritional deficiencies, all patients should be tested preoperatively and deficiencies corrected before surgery (Flancbaum, Belsley, Drake, Colarusso, & Tayler, 2006).

Vitamins and minerals that should be screened pre-WLS and repleted as needed include vitamins B12, D, and folate, iron, and calcium (Flancbaum et al., 2006). Special considerations should be given to vitamin D deficiency, which is common in the U.S. population. The primary source of vitamin D is the sun; sunscreens block the absorption of vitamin D, and many individuals do not get adequate sun exposure throughout the year. Patients with obesity are at higher risk of vitamin D deficiency. Vitamin D repletion often requires a 6- to 8-week therapeutic dose of 50,000 units once a week. Thiamin (vitamin B1) deficiency is not uncommon, especially in African American and Hispanic patients with obesity; patients should be screened and deficiencies repleted prior to surgery. Very often an over-the-counter dosage of 50–100 mg vitamin B complex is sufficient. However, the need for a prescription dose should be determined by a medical practitioner (medical doctor, nurse practitioner, or physician assistant). Folate (folic acid) should be tested and repleted, especially in women of childbearing age. Pregnancy is discouraged until 12–24 months post-WLS, and women who are planning a pregnancy should be screened for folate deficiency prior to conception. Folic acid is required in the very early stages of pregnancy, often before a mother is even aware she is pregnant. Folic acid deficiency can lead to spina bifida in the fetus. Women of childbearing age should be educated about the importance of folate in the early stages of pregnancy. Iron deficiency may be a particular problem for women who are menstruating, and they should be screened and "iron repleted" if deficient prior to surgery. It would be prudent to recommend all women who are menstruating to start a multivitamin with iron prior to surgery. Women who are peri- or postmenopausal should be instructed to have a baseline bone density test. Serum calcium is not indicative of bone status, and patients are at risk for osteoporosis years after WLS if they are not supplementing calcium (see postoperative guidelines) and engaging in weight-bearing activity. Guidelines for the recommended biochemical surveillance of nutritional status after malabsorptive bariatric surgery have been published (AACE, 2008).

Presurgery Nutrition Prescription

After a comprehensive initial nutrition assessment, the dietitian will then prescribe/recommend a nutrition intervention. This intervention may be for several medical nutrition therapy sessions to reinforce the importance of a balanced diet, to assist the patient in structuring his or her meal patterns, or to set presurgery weight or nutrition goals. Depending on the

Table 9.2 Nutrition-Related Laboratory Tests Recommended Before Weight Loss Surgery

Complete blood count with differential
Glucose, HbA1C
Serum lipids
Serum iron, ferritin, and TIBC
Serum calcium, alkaline phosphatase
Serum vitamin B12 (MMA, HCy)
Folate (in women of childbearing age); consider plasma homocysteine
Parathyroid hormone, 25-hydroxyvitamin D
Thiamine
Abbreviations: HbA1C, glycated hemoglobin; TIBC, total iron-binding capacity.

Source: Cummings, S., in C. Nonas & G. Foster (Eds.), *Practical Applications in Managing Obesity: A Clinical Guide,* Chap. 9, Part B, 2009.

patient's nutrition diagnoses, the registered dietitian (RD) may determine that the patient would benefit from a comprehensive nutrition program over the course of several months. In some cases, the RD and surgical team may determine the patient is ready for surgery; however, the insurance provider may require a presurgical nutrition and psychology program.

Presurgery Weight Loss

A weight loss of at least 5% of total body weight before weight loss surgery is associated with decreased operative time, which may potentially decrease surgical risk (Alvarado et al., 2005; Alami et al., 2007). One study involving patients who followed a very low-calorie diet before weight loss surgery had a substantial decrease in liver volume, resulting in a reduction in reported surgical difficulty and a reduction in conversion from a laparoscopic procedure to an open procedure during surgery (Colles, Dixon, Marks, Strauss, & O'Brien, 2006). Most surgical centers require a preoperative weight loss ranging from 5–10% of current weight.

Preoperative Insurance-Mandated Nutrition Programs

There are private insurance carriers who require documentation that patients have participated in a presurgical medical program that includes medical nutrition therapy (MNT) and psychology visits before they will authorize weight loss surgery. The program requirements can range from 3 to 12 months. These requirements can be burdensome to patients both financially and time-wise, and delays before surgery can be an obstacle for patients in the most need of effective obesity treatment. Providers can help patients through this process by (1) establishing cost-effective programs, (2) motivating patients by emphasizing the benefits of presurgical preparation, both physically and psychologically, and (3) using this time to shape patient expectations regarding the early postsurgical challenges and the lifestyle changes required for long-term success. Some nutritional changes patients can begin to initiate prior to surgery include:

- *Eliminating caffeine*: Caffeine is a diuretic, and since adequate hydration post-WLS is a top nutrition priority, patients should not consume a beverage that may potentially contribute to dehydration.
- *Physical activity*: Walking after surgery is essential to decrease the risk of developing life-threatening blood clots. Encourage all patients who are able to take mini-walks throughout the day before surgery to develop strength and stamina.
- *Hydration*: Encourage patients to get in the habit of drinking 48 to 64 ounces of noncalorie, noncarbonated, noncaffeinated beverages each day.
- *Mindful eating*: One of the biggest challenges many patients encounter, especially early postoperative, is how slow they need to eat and drink. Since the new pouch will not grind food or secrete acid or digestive enzymes and their new pouch/stomach is small, restricting the amount of food or liquid they can consume at any given time, patients need to learn to chew food thoroughly, to breathe between bites, and to check in with their body to assess fullness. Teaching patients techniques of mindful eating and encouraging them to start practicing this presurgery will prepare them, if not physically, at least psychologically for the dramatic change in eating style required postsurgery.

Perioperative Care of the Bariatric Patient

While there is no doubt that the surgical procedure is an excellent weight loss tool, it is imperative that ongoing nutritional assessment and follow-up occur at regular intervals to help ensure long-term weight loss success. Nutritional management after bariatric surgery has been determined to be a significant factor in postoperative patients maintaining weight loss. The importance of medical nutrition therapy and nutrition education among bariatric patients, including the perioperative and long-term postoperative periods, cannot be understated. Suggestions regarding important areas of pre- and postoperative nutritional assessment and education have been elucidated in the American Society for Metabolic and Bariatric Surgery (ASMBS) nutritional guidelines for the surgical weight loss patient (Aills et al., 2008).

Hydration The number one nutritional priority post-WLS, regardless of the surgical procedure, is to stay hydrated. Many patients find it difficult to reach the often recommended minimum goal of 48–64 ounces of fluid per day. Patients may report, among the challenges, the feeling of water feeling "heavy" or cite anorexia, which is common among perioperative patients who have undergone the RYGBP or SG. This may result in their forgetting or not wanting to drink. Water has a high solute load, and patients can be instructed to have other nonsugar, noncarbonated fluids available. Other postoperative patients may be afraid to drink too much at one time for fear of stretching their new anatomy or vomiting, which may increase the risk of dehydration. It remains a challenge among many centers to decrease the readmissions in the perioperative period due to dehydration. It is not uncommon for patients to be discharged on their preoperative hypertension medications, including diuretics. If this should happen, patients need to be monitored very closely and medications adjusted accordingly. Patient should be taught signs and symptoms of dehydration—dark urine, dizziness upon standing, and extreme fatigue—and given suggestions for how to increase fluids through solid liquids (e.g., sugar-free ice pops) and include salty liquids such as broth and tomato juice. If a patient is experiencing labored breathing or lack of concentration, he or she needs to go to a hospital emergency room for IV rehydration. Since IV hydration contains a glucose/dextrose solution, administration of 100 mg of thiamin (vitamin B1) should be included in the IV to avoid precipitation of thiamin deficiency.

Dietary Protein Regardless of the bariatric procedure, it is imperative that patients be counseled regarding the importance of proper intake of protein, as well as other macronutrients, in the diet. Although there may be some disparity among surgical centers with regard to the optimal level of protein intake, a large number of surgical programs advise a range between 60 and 80 g of protein per day or 1.0 and 1.5 g/kg ideal body weight (IBW). However, more research is needed to better ascertain protein needs postoperatively. The recommended dietary allowance (RDA) for protein is approximately 50 g of protein per day for normal adults (National Academy of Science, 2004).

In the early postoperative period, many surgical centers advise including liquid protein supplements at least once daily to help ensure adequate protein intake, as well as adding to overall hydration and caloric intake. Patients should not consume a diet exclusively of protein. Experienced bariatric providers have reported that the inclusion of 100 g of carbohydrates daily may decrease muscle loss seen in modified protein fasts up to 40% (Scopinaro et al., 1998).

Protein Supplements Body protein is composed of 9 indispensable (essential, meaning that they must be consumed in the diet) amino acids and 11 dispensable (nonessential) amino acids. It is very important that protein supplements containing all nine indispensable amino acids for optimal protein utilization be recommended, particularly if the supplement is the sole source of dietary protein intake. Modular protein supplements have been divided into four major categories, based on a comprehensive assessment of those available today (Castellanos, Litchford, & Campbell, 2006). Although taste, cost, and availability of protein supplements are all important factors, it is vital that the quality of a protein supplement be deemed the most important variable in order to allow for optimal protein absorption and repletion in the postoperative bariatric patient.

In 1991, an objective measurement of protein supplement quality was created, called the protein digestibility corrected amino acid score (PDCAAS), which compares the indispensable amino acids (IAAs) of a protein versus the dispensable amino acid content. Therefore, the PDCAAS allows even the new bariatric practitioner or non-RD team member to objectively assess the quality of a particular protein supplement. The score is indicative of the ability of the human body to utilize a particular protein source for protein synthesis. A perfect PDCAAS of 100 is found among protein sources, including whey, casein, milk, soy, and egg whites (Castellanos et al., 2006).

Of course, a great deal of education on protein supplements, both pre- and postoperatively, is imperative to help ensure patients are not wasting money on protein supplements that do not allow for adequate protein repletion. Unfortunately, it is "buyer beware" when it comes to the myriad protein supplements available to bariatric patients. Even when the label states a PCAAS of 100, there have been cases where the nutritional analysis of the IAAs reveals a score that is 15 to 40% of that on the label. Overall, the highest-quality protein supplements contain whey protein, due to the high amounts of branched-chain amino acids, vital in periods of physiological stress, such as found in the bariatric surgery perioperative period. Whey concentrates are also of high quality, but unlike whey isolates, they may contain significant amounts of lactose. Since some gastric bypass surgery patients may encounter lactose intolerance issues postoperatively, and this may be a condition many patients already have preoperatively, lactose-free protein products, such as soy, egg white, or whey protein isolates, may be preferable for many bariatric patients.

Dietary Carbohydrates   Although distinct carbohydrate goals after bariatric procedures have not been researched in great detail, it seems prudent to aim for the RDA for carbohydrates (130 g/day) after several months postoperatively. Anecdotally, dietitians may assess carbohydrate intake at particular time points for bariatric patients, such as 70 g of carbohydrate at 3 months postoperatively, 100 g at 6 months postoperatively, and 130 g (RDA) of total carbohydrates by 1 year postoperatively. A great deal of education is needed to help ensure patients are consuming healthy carbohydrate sources, such as fresh fruits, vegetables, and whole grains, versus the processed/refined carbohydrates so prevalent today. See overall dietary goals in the next section for bariatric patients 2 years and beyond.

Dietary Fat   Many bariatric patients may be ingesting very little fat in their diet in the perioperative period, perhaps due to the anorexia usually seen with many procedures, such as RYGBP, GS, and DS, and also intolerance to high-fat foods, such as fried or greasy foods. It's advisable to avoid setting a fat limit/goal for many patients, but rather encouraging lean protein foods that include moderate amounts of fat for absorption of fat-soluble vitamins. Moderate amounts of fat combined with protein and fiber will allow for early satiety, particularly important for patients who experience hunger in the perioperative period, including many gastric banding patients (especially prior to fills/adjustments). Patients having the LAGB will report more hunger than those undergoing the RYGBP and GS, which should be explained to patients presurgery.

Calorie Goals   It is not unusual for bariatric patients to become concerned regarding caloric intake in the perioperative period and beyond, and it is imperative to change the focus from emphasis on caloric intake, which many bariatric patients struggle with prepoperatively, to focus on obtaining adequate amounts of macronutrients, including protein and healthy carbohydrates. Patients should be advised of the great variability of caloric intake postoperatively, and the RD should assess each patient individually, in terms of his or her specific dietary goals. Emphasis should be shifted to adequate nutrition, including proper hydration, protein, carbohydrate intake, and adherence with multivitamin/mineral regimen.

Although some patients may worry they are not consuming sufficient calories in the perioperative period, it is important to recall that they are, in fact, utilizing their fat stores. Since 1 pound of body fat contains approximately 3,500 calories, and their adipose tissue is the primary source of calories, bariatric patients should be reassured that caloric intake is not a concern. Therefore, nutrition recommendations postoperatively should be described as a "nutrition prescription," meaning they have to get in certain nutrition (e.g., hydration, protein, vitamin, and mineral supplements), whether they want to or not, and whether they are hungry or not.

Early Postoperative Nutrition Prescription

1. *Hydration, hydration, hydration* (minimum total of 60 ounces for men; 48–60 for women). Hydration is the first and foremost nutrition priority.
2. *A protein source three to five times a day.* This may be limited initially to 1–3 tablespoons per meal, as the amount is specifically determined by the patient's tolerance and fullness. It is essential to reassure

patients that as the weeks and months go by, they will be able to tolerate increased portion sizes. Adding a liquid protein source (whey protein shake) once a day will help to ensure adequate protein intake. Listening to his or her body through mindful eating is the key to learning when to stop eating. A small amount of fruits and vegetables should be consumed with the protein at least three times a day.

3. *Vitamin and mineral supplements.* Standard supplementation includes a daily multivitamin with a minimum of 100% of DRI for B vitamins, including B1, biotin, B12, and folate; vitamin K, vitamin D, and iron; a sublingual B12; and calcium citrate with vitamin D in divided doses.

Dietary Progression in the Perioperative Period

In terms of diet progression in the perioperative period, there is a great deal of variability as to the number of diet stages and types of food recommended at each stage. However, the common theme in diet progression post–weight loss surgery is that the stages are focused on nutritional needs and the texture of the foods. The use of a clear liquid diet is usually short term (1–2 days), which is then advanced to a full liquid diet (liquids that contain dietary nutrients, specifically protein), starting at day 3 or 4 postoperative and lasting ~10–14 days, at which time patients are advanced to "soft" solid foods (pureed, diced, ground, moist protein sources). Protein supplements are often included within all phases of dietary progression. Food tolerances and the pace and rate of the diet progression vary widely among patients, which is why close and frequent postoperative nutritional support and counseling are recommended. Examples of diet stages are outlined in Tables 9.3 and 9.4. The following bullet points describe some possible nutritional concerns specific to the type of surgery performed:

- *Laparoscopic adjustable gastric band*: Gastric banding is a purely restrictive procedure, meaning there is no malabsorption of micronutrients or macronutrients. Therefore, the goal for protein intake

Table 9.3 Potential Nutrition-Related Complications

Gastric Bypass	Gastric Band	Gastric Sleeve
Dehydration	Dehydration	Dehydration
Vitamin deficiencies	Vitamin deficiencies	Vitamin deficiencies
Dumping syndrome	Protein energy malnutrition	Protein energy malnutrition
Bowel changes	Insufficient weight loss/regain	Nausea/vomiting
Nausea/vomiting	Bowel changes	GERD
Bloating/flatulence	Nausea/vomiting	
	GERD	
	Band erosion/band slipping	

Table 9.4

Diet Stage[b]	Diet	Stages	RYGBP[a]
	Begin	Fluids/Food	Guidelines
Stage I	Postop days 1 and 2	GBP clear liquids Noncarbonated; no calories No sugar; no caffeine	Postop day 1 patients undergo a gastrogaffin swallow test for leak; once tested, begin sips of GBP clear liquids
Stage II	Postop day 3 (discharge diet)	GBP clear liquids • Variety of no sugar liquids or artificially sweetened liquids • High sodium fluids such as broth and boullion • Solid liquids: Sugar-free ice pops Plus GBP full liquids • Less than 25 g sugar per serving in full liquids Protein-rich liquids (limit 25–30 g protein per serving of added powders)	Patients should consume a minimum of 48–64 ounces of total fluids per day; 24–32 ounces or more GBP clear liquids; plus 24–32 ounces of any combination of full liquids: 1% or skim milk mixed with: • Whey or soy protein powder (limit 25–30 g protein per serving) • Lactaid milk or soy milk mix with soy protein powder • Light yogurt, blended • Plain yogurt; Greek yogurt
Begin supplementation: Chewable multivitamin with minerals, 2×/day Chewable or liquid calcium citrate with vitamin D Sublingual 350–500 mg vitamin B12			

Stage III	Postop days 10–14[b]	Increase GBP clear liquids (total liquids 48–64 plus ounces per day) and replace full liquids with soft, moist, diced, ground, or pureed protein sources as tolerated	Protein food choices are encouraged for 3–6 small meals per day; patients may only be able to tolerate a couple of tablespoons at each meal/snack
		Stage III, Week 1: Eggs, ground meats, poultry, soft, moist fish, added gravy, bouillon, light mayo to moisten, cooked beans, hearty bean soups, cottage cheese, low-fat cheese, yogurt	Encourage patients not to drink with meals and to wait ~30 minutes after each meal before resuming fluids
Stage III: Week 2	4 weeks postop	Advance diet as tolerated; if protein foods, add well-cooked, soft vegetables and soft or peeled fruit; always eat protein first	Adequate hydration is essential and a priority for all patients during the rapid weight loss phase
Stage III: Week 3 May switch to pill form supplementation	5 weeks postop	Continue to consume protein with some fruit or vegetable at each meal; some people tolerate salads 1 month postop	Avoid rice, bread, and pasta until patient is comfortably consuming 60 g of protein per day and fruits/vegetables
Stage IV Vitamin and mineral supplementation daily[c]	As hunger increases and more food is tolerated	Healthy solid food diet	Healthy, balanced diet consisting of adequate protein, fruits, vegetables, and whole grains; calorie needs based on height, weight, age

(Continued)

Table 9.4 (Continued)

		Stages	
	Diet		RYGBP[a]
LAGB Diet Stage[b]	Begin	Fluids/Food	Guidelines
Stage I	Postop days 1 and 2	LAGB clear liquids Noncarbonated; no calories No sugar; no caffeine	Postop LAGB day 1, patients may begin sips of water, ice chips, and Crystal Lite™; avoid carbonation
Stage II Begin supplementation: Chewable multivitamin with minerals, 2×/day Chewable or liquid calcium citrate with vitamin D	Postop days 2–3 (discharge diet)	LAGB clear liquids • Variety of no sugar liquids or artificially sweetened liquids Plus LAGB full liquids Less than 25 g sugar per serving, and no more than 3 g fat per serving of protein-rich liquids	Patients should consume a minimum of 48–64 ounces of total fluids per day; 24–32 ounces or more AGB clear liquids; plus 24–32 ounces of any combination of full liquids: 1% or skim milk mixed with: • Whey or soy protein powder (limit 20 g protein per serving) • Lactaid milk or soy milk mix with soy protein powder • Light yogurt, blended • Plain yogurt
Stage III: Week I	Postop day 10–14[b]	Increase LAGB clear liquids (total liquids 48–64 plus ounces per day) and replace full liquids with soft, moist, diced, ground, or pureed protein sources as tolerated	Note: Patients should be reassured that hunger is common and normal after AGB • Protein food (moist, ground) choices are encouraged for 3–6 small meals per day, to help with satiety, since hunger is common within a week or so of LAGB

Stage III: Week 1	Eggs, ground meats, poultry, soft, moist fish, added gravy, bouillon, light mayo to moisten, cooked beans, hearty bean soups, cottage cheese, low-fat cheese, yogurt	• Mindful, slow eating is essential • Encourage patients not to drink with meals and to wait ~30 minutes after each meal before resuming fluids
Stage III: Week 2 4 weeks postop	Advance diet as tolerated; if protein foods well tolerated in Week 1, add well-cooked soft vegetables and soft or peeled fruit	Adequate hydration is essential and a priority for all patients during the rapid weight loss phase Protein at every meal and snack, especially if increased hunger noted prior to initial fill or adjustment; very well-cooked vegetables may also help to increase satiety
Stage III: Week 3 5 weeks postop	Continue to consume protein with some fruit or vegetable at each meal; some people tolerate salads 1 month postop	If patient is tolerating soft, moist, ground, diced, or pureed proteins with small amounts of fruits and vegetables, may add crackers (use with protein) Avoid rice, bread, and pasta
Stage IV Vitamin and mineral supplementation daily As hunger increases and more food is tolerated	Healthy solid food diet	Healthy, balanced diet consisting of adequate protein, fruits, vegetables, and whole grains Calorie needs based on height, weight, age

(Continued)

Table 9.4 (Continued)

	Diet	Stages	RYGBP[a]
LAGB Diet Stage[b]	**Begin**	**Fluids/Food**	**Guidelines**
Post-LAGB fill/adjustment	~6 weeks postop LAGB, and possibly every 6 weeks until satiety reached	Full liquids 2× days postfill; advance to Stage III, Week 1 guidelines above, as tolerated (= 4–5 days), then advance as above	Same as Stage II liquids above × 48 hours (or as otherwise advised by surgeon) Note: When diet advanced to soft solids, special attention to mindful eating and chewing until liquid is key, since more restriction may increase risk for food getting stuck above stoma of band if not properly chewed (e.g., if not chewed until liquid)

Source: Sue Cummings, MS, RD, MGH Weight Center, Boston. With permission.

[a] RYGBP, Roux-en-Y gastric bypass.

[b] There is no standardization of diet stages. There are a wide variety of diet protocols varying from how long patients stay on each stage and what types of fluids/foods are recommended.

[c] Nutritional labs should be drawn 2, 6, and 12 months and yearly indefinitely. Bone density test at baseline and every 2–5 years.

should be based on the patient's individual needs during a rapid weight loss phase. Protein intake of 60–80 g/day, even for patients with higher lean body mass (LBM), may be sufficient. Adequate fluid intake is essential, and patients taking in higher protein amounts should also increase fluid accordingly, as higher protein intakes may increase the risk for dehydration. Since the total amount of calories consumed is restricted, careful consideration to a healthy, well-balanced diet is essential. Tough or dry meats and poultry, if not well chewed, may "get stuck" in the restricted area and should be ground, diced, moist, and chewed thoroughly. Many patients also find that breads and other doughy products might get stuck and are therefore not well tolerated. Because liquids and very soft foods pass through the restricted area easily, patients should be cautioned against consuming high-calorie, soft foods, which include high-calorie beverages, cream-based soups, and ice cream.

- *Roux-en-Y gastric bypass*: The general recommendation for protein is 60–80 g/day; however, in the first weeks post-RYGBP, the majority of patients will not be able to consume that much protein through diet sources without supplementing with at least one protein shake a day. In addition, adequate carbohydrate intake cannot be underestimated in order to allow for protein sparing and fat oxidation. Early postoperation, while patients are gradually increasing their intake, fruits and vegetables should be encouraged, as they provide carbohydrate and fiber. Protein powders that are mixed with milk or adding yogurt to the diet is a convenient way to consume protein and carbohydrate. Vegetarians can use soy milk or yogurt products, and patients who are lactose intolerant can use whey protein isolate powders or lactaid milk products.

- *Sleeve gastrectomy*: Data on the nutritional needs of the patient undergoing gastric sleeve is limited. Nutritional recommendations are based on expert opinion. Most surgical centers that are performing the gastric sleeve use the same diet stages and recommendations as the RYGBP. Since there is no alteration of the food pathway with the gastric sleeve, absorption of vitamins and minerals should not be compromised, with the exception of vitamin B12. Stomach acid is needed to cleave B12 from dietary protein, and the new sleeve may not, at least initially, produce adequate amounts of stomach acid. In addition, secretion of intrinsic factor that is needed to absorb B12 may also be affected by the creation of the sleeve. Currently the standard vitamin and mineral supplementation recommended for the sleeve gastrectomy is the same as for those having the RYGBP. Incidence rates of 67% and higher at 1 month post-GS of gastric esophageal reflux (GERD) have been reported (Weiner et al., 2007). This typically decreases greatly or resolves by 2 years postop. As with any WLS procedure, patients need to be taught how to prepare food so that it is a tolerable texture and to eat mindfully, stopping between bites to breathe and check in on their level of fullness before taking that one or two bites too much.

- *Biliopancreatic diversion (BPD) with duodenal switch (DS)*: Although this procedure, commonly abbreviated DS and referred to as the switch, is not as commonly performed in the United States, when compared to gastric banding and gastric bypass procedures, some surgeons are performing this procedure, so it is important to at least cite some of the issues briefly in this chapter. Although the initial biliopancreatic diversion (BPD) procedure still exists, most U.S. surgeons perform the BPD with duodenal switch (DS) procedure to allow for inclusion of the pylorus, and therefore circumventing issues related to dumping syndrome. Therefore, DS will be discussed exclusively versus the BPD procedure. In terms of protein, the postoperative DS patient is believed to result in the malabsorption of protein at a ~21% rate. Therefore, the daily protein goal should be raised to at least 30% to allow for malabsorption, resulting in an average protein requirement of about 90 g/day (Slater et al., 2004). Of note among BPD or DS patients is the rate of fat malabsorption (approximately 70%), so the diet should be modified accordingly by the RD to the patient's individual needs and tolerances.

Monitoring and Evaluation: What the Psychologist Needs to Know

Short-Term Postoperative Challenges (First 2 Years)

- *Weight loss goals and expectations*: It has been suggested that a gain of 20% of total excess weight loss is to be expected between 2 and 5 years among gastric bypass patients, with the vast majority losing 60–70% of their excess weight at their nadir (usually reached before or by the 2-year period). Most patients have retained at least 50% excess weight loss at the 5-year mark. While these statistics may be disappointing to some patients, it is important to remind them that these numbers far exceed the dismal statistics for nonsurgical weight loss, with 95% of medical weight loss patients regaining weight lost and ending up heavier than their initial weights (Pajecki et al., 2007; Sjöström et al., 2007).

While some bariatric patients insist on weighing themselves daily, and some frequently throughout the day, it is imperative that they be reminded of the emphasis on health and improvement in comorbidities rather than obsessing about the scale. Patients should be taught that body fat is relatively light compared to lean muscle mass and fluid. In the initial rapid weight loss phase the weight changes they are seeing on the scale are "weight changes," not "fat changes," and that since fluid is very heavy and the first few weeks postop they are losing an enormous amount of excess fluid, the number on the scale will decrease rapidly. Once they have lost the excess fluid that all patients with obesity carry, the scale losses will slow. It may be prudent to recommend that during the rapid weight loss phase after WLS that patients do not weigh themselves at home. Emphasizing the changes in clothes size is more indicative of fat loss than the number on the scale. The goal is to lose weight in as healthy a manner as possible, not as fast as possible. The rate and amount of weight loss will vary greatly among patients, and they should be encouraged not to share/compare weight losses. Health care providers should also be very careful about giving patients goals regarding the scale.

Potential factors in weight regain may be attributed to weight-promoting medications (e.g., steroids, psychiatric medications). Patients on these medications should be closely monitored, and although there are no data to suggest that they may be at the lower end of the weight loss curve, there is that potential, and patients should be made aware of this. There is some suggestion that enteric-coated, sustained, or time-released medications may not be well absorbed after bariatric procedures; therefore, monitoring the continued efficacy of these medications or changing to a form that is not time released is recommended (Padwal, Brocks, & Sharma, 2010).

- *Protein status*: There are no data reporting that the "uncomplicated" RYGBP, GS, or LAGB patients are at risk for protein malnutrition. It is not uncommon for both health care professionals and laypersons, especially in today's society, where high-protein diets are popular, to oversubscribe dietary intake of protein through high biological sources such as excessive amounts of animal protein or protein shakes. Excessive amounts of protein intake can lead to metabolic complications including dehydration.
- *Eating behaviors*: In the first 18–24 months post–weight loss, patients report diminished hunger and early satiety. However, as their weight stabilizes, hunger and satiety will increase since the body will no longer be relying on fat stores for daily energy/calorie

needs. Many patients return to unhealthy eating habits, such as skipping meals, consuming higher-calorie, convenient processed foods, and engaging in emotionally triggered eating. Referral to a dietitian for medical nutrition therapy, to assist patients in normalizing eating patterns, planning and preparing meals, learning to purchase healthy convenient foods, resuming a schedule of daily postsurgical vitamin and mineral supplementation, and incorporating a routine exercise schedule, is essential to long-term success. In fact, the same behavioral and nutritional changes that trigger weight regain after weight loss surgery are no different than those that trigger nonsurgical dieters to regain weight (Cummings & Lentendre, 2009; Orth, Madan, Taddeucci, Coday, & Tichansky, 2008). Weight loss surgery influences the biological triggers to obesity; however, it does not change the environment. Patients need to work with this "tool" called surgery by challenging nonhunger environmental triggers to overconsuming calories. Physical activity is highly correlated with weight maintenance and should also be encouraged. Many postbariatric patients have a history of all-or-nothing behaviors, and this doesn't change postsurgery. Cognitive restructuring is an important part of the postsurgical behavioral counseling, as patients need to learn how to recover from a slip or a lapse and to incorporate a healthy lifestyle that includes healthy eating and activity. Patients need to learn that "normal" eating is sometimes undereating and sometimes overeating, but that if they can adopt a healthy lifestyle 80% of the time and have their slip-ups, holidays, and vacations 20% of the time, they will be successful.

- *Post–weight loss surgery dieting*: Since there is strong evidence that the Roux-en-Y gastric bypass procedure impacts the weight regulatory system at multiple levels and "resets the patient's preoperative weight set point," patients need to be warned against embarking on restrictive dieting any time postsurgery (Ashrafian & le Roux, 2009; Stylopoulos, Hoppin, & Kaplan, 2009). Restrictive dieting often means ignoring one's physical hunger and satiety in an effort to lose weight. However, there is a biological basis for excessive weight gain after each dieting attempt. Many patients report that when their restrictive diet ends, they not only gain back what they lost, but most often, they regain more weight. This may be due to the body protecting itself from "starvation," and this survival mechanism is highly overactive in patients with genetic predispositions to obesity. Yo-yo dieting after the RYGBP may cause the body to reset its "new postop set point" to a higher weight range after each restrictive dieting attempt.

One of the major benefits of weight loss surgery is the strong physical signs of hunger and satiety that, at least initially, patients cannot ignore. Many patients over their lifetime, and especially in the early developmental years of their life, have learned to ignore the physical signs of hunger and satiety by having to finish everything on their plate. Food makes them feel better and provides rewards, and they establish relationships with particular foods that go beyond the nutritional value. Therefore, eating becomes more about the external triggers that lead to overeating. Teaching patients to pay attention to hunger and satiety, to eat when their body is physically hungry and to stop when they are comfortably full, is essential to maintaining their weight loss. Teaching mindful eating is an invaluable skill many patients need to learn.

Planning and preparing for meals and snacks is something patients tend to do almost religiously in the first year after surgery, but as time goes on these habits often fade. In the first 2 years after surgery, they are losing weight, people are telling them they look great, they come off of many of their medications, and are able to buy smaller-sized clothes. As time goes on, no one is telling them they look great anymore, since others are used to them at their new size. The daily demands of family, home, and work begin to take over, and they give up the time they may have been dedicating to exercise and healthy eating, and little by little, old habits return. Patients may begin to ignore their body's signs of hunger and fullness, they may stop planning meals, grocery shopping, and exercising, and the environmental influences take over. Every effort should be made to educate, counsel, and support patients in identifying what possible nutritional and behavioral patterns might be contributing to their weight gain. Cognitive restructuring, nutrition counseling, and motivational interviewing are all skills that dietitians incorporate in working with patients, who, since childhood, have developed unhealthy eating behaviors. Now, for the first time in years, their body is speaking to them, is willing to work with them to maintain a healthier body weight, and it is their job to pay attention, and to take responsibility for challenging the everyday environmental influences to eat unhealthy, lead a sedentary lifestyle, and ignore their body.

- *Meal replacements*: There are strong data in favor of the use of meal replacements in helping patients adhere to a structured eating pattern, especially those with very busy, stressful, or hectic schedules (Ditschuneit, Flechtner-Mors, Johnson, & Adler, 1999). Although the emphasis on any healthy meal planning should be primarily on whole foods containing fruits, vegetables, whole grains, and lean proteins, there are times when a preprepared packaged meal may be incorporated into a healthy diet. Since most individuals are getting their nutrition education from advertisements, nutrition claims made on labels and the nonregulated diet industry, psychologists and other health care providers should encourage patients to work with a dietitian to design a meal plan that incorporates convenient, affordable, and healthy foods.

- *Vitamin and mineral supplementation*: Adherence to the standard post-WLS vitamin and mineral supplements is of utmost importance.

  LAGB: 100% daily value MVI/minerals, 1,200 (men and premenopausal women) to 1,500 mg (peri- and postmenopausal women) calcium in divided doses.

  RYGBP: 200% daily value, 1,500–2,000 mg elemental calcium (as calcium citrate, in divided doses) with vitamin D, vitamin B12 (350–500 µg/day or 1,000 µg/month IM), and extra iron for menstruating women or anemic patients (additional 18–27 mg from MVI/minerals).

  Although there have yet to be published guidelines for vitamin/mineral supplementation among gastric sleeve patients, it seems prudent to advise a minimum of 100% daily value (and anecdotally, some surgical centers advise 200% daily value), at least 1500 mg of elemental calcium (as calcium citrate, in divided doses), vitamin B12 supplementation (as per GBP protocol), and perhaps additional iron, as above, for menstruating women or patients with anemia.

  Patients who are unwilling to commit to lifelong daily nutritional supplementation and yearly biochemical surveillance of nutrition laboratory assessment should be discouraged from weight loss surgery. The longer a patient goes out from surgery, the higher his or her risk of vitamin deficiency, and unfortunately, long-term compliance to daily vitamin and mineral supplementation and monitoring tends to decrease. Any provider seeing postoperative weight loss surgery patients should question them about their intake of supplementation and their frequency of nutritional monitoring. Patients should be encouraged to give their primary care physician a list of the nutritional labs that need to be monitored, at the least, yearly. There are published guidelines for the nutritional labs and the frequency by which they should be monitored by weight loss procedure (Mechanick et al., 2008).

Conclusion

The field of bariatric nutrition is a highly specialized area, and providers seeing patients in their practice who have undergone weight loss surgery should be encouraged to know the bariatric nutrition experts in their area for whom they can refer. Given the nature of the multi-billion-dollar-a-year dieting industry, patients and health care providers alike tend to be influenced by diet claims made in the popular media and are misinformed about the metabolic effects of weight loss surgery and the concomitant nutritional risks. Weight loss surgery is not "another diet." The RYGBP and the SG, specifically, are permanent interventions that alter food pathway and the absorption of essential dietary nutrients. Most patients also need education, support, and counseling regarding the daily challenges of living a healthy lifestyle in an unhealthy environment. Patients should be educated presurgery regarding the nutritional consequences of WLS, about weight loss and regain expectations, and how to work with their new anatomy to maintain their newly obtained healthier weight. Health care providers seeing patients' post–weight loss surgery should query them regarding their frequency of postoperative follow-up with bariatric specialists. When indicated, encourage patients to seek yearly follow-up with their surgical center or establish new relationships with bariatric specialists in their area for lifelong monitoring and support.

References

Aills, L., Blankenship, J., Buffington, C., Furtado, M., & Parrott, J. (2008). ASMBS allied health nutritional guidelines for the surgical weight loss patient. *Surgery for Obesity and Related Diseases, 4*, S73–S108.

Alami, R.S., Morton, J.M., Schuster, R., Lie, J., Sanchez, B.R., Peters, A. et al. (2007). Is there a benefit to preoperative weight loss in gastric bypass patients? A prospective randomized trial. *Surgery for Obesity and Related Disease, 3*, 141–145.

Alvarado, R., Alami, R.S., Hsu, G., Safadi, B.Y., Sanchez, B.R., Morton, J.M. et al. (2005). The impact of preoperative weight loss in patients undergoing laparoscopic Roux-en-Y gastric bypass. *Obesity Surgery, 15*, 1282–1286.

American Association of Clinical Endocrinologists (AACE), the Obesity Society (TOS), & American Society of Metabolic and Bariatric Surgery (ASMBS). (2008). Clinical practice guidelines for the perioperative nutritional, metabolic and nonsurgical support of the bariatric surgery patient. *Endocrine Practice, 14*(Suppl 1).

Ashrafian, H., & le Roux, C.W. (2009). Metabolic surgery and gut hormones—A review of bariatric entero-humoral modulation. *Physiological Behaviors, 97*, 620–631.

Buchwald, H. (2005). Consensus conference statement: Bariatric surgery for morbid obesity: Health implications for patients, health professionals, and third-party payers. *Journal of American College of Surgeons, 200,* 593–604.

Castellanos, V., Litchford, M., & Campbell, W. (2006). Modular protein supplements and their application to long-term care. *Nutrition in Clinical Practice, 21,* 485–504.

Colles, S.L., Dixon, J.B., Marks, P., Strauss, B.J., & O'Brien, P.E. (2006). Preoperative weight loss with a very-low-energy diet: Quantitation of changes in liver and abdominal fat by serial imaging. *American Journal of Clinical Nutrition, 84,* 304–311.

Cummings, S. (2009). Surgery part B: practical applications. In C. Nonas & G. Foster (Eds.), *Managing obesity: A clinical guide* (pp. 149–166). Chicago: American Dietetic Association.

Cummings, S., & Lentendre, J. (2009). Weight regain after the RYGBP: Surgery failure or poor patient compliance? *Weight Management Matters, 6*(3).

Cunningham, E. (2006). What is the registered dietitian's role in the preoperative assessment of a client contemplating bariatric surgery? *Journal of the American Dietician Association, 106,* 163.

Ditschuneit, H., Flechtner-Mors, M., Johnson, T., & Adler, G. (1999). Metabolic and weight-loss effects of a long-term dietary intervention in obese patients. *American Journal of Clinical Nutrition, 69,* 198–204.

Dixon, J.B. (2009). Referral for a bariatric surgical consultation: It is time to set a standard of care. *Obesity Surgery, 19,* 641–644.

Flancbaum, L., Belsley, S., Drake, V., Colarusso, T., & Tayler, E. (2006). Preoperative nutritional status of patients undergoing Roux-en-Y gastric bypass for morbid obesity. *Journal of Gastrointestinal Surgery, 10,* 1033–1037.

Lehman Center Weight Loss Surgery Expert Panel. (2005). Commonwealth of Massachusetts Betsy Lehman Center for Patient Safety and Medical Error Reduction Expert Panel on Weight Loss Surgery: Executive report. *Obesity Research, 13,* 205–226.

Mechanick, J.I., Kushner, R.F., Sugerman, H.J., Gonzalez-Campoy, M., Collazo-Clavell, M.L., Guven, S. et al. (2008, July/August). AACE/TOS/ASMBS guidelines: American Association of Clinical Endocrinologists, the Obesity Society, and American Society for Metabolic and Bariatric Surgery medical guidelines for clinical practice for the perioperative nutritional, metabolic and nonsurgical support of the bariatric surgery patient. *Endocrine Practice, 14,* S1–S83.

National Academy of Science, Institute of Medicine, Food and Nutrition Board. (2004). Dietary reference intake. Retrieved from www.nal.usda.gov/fnic.

Orth, W.S., Madan, A.K., Taddeucci, R.J., Coday, M., & Tichansky, D.S. (2008). Support group meeting attendance is associated with better weight loss. *Obesity Surgery, 18,* 391–394.

Padwal, R., Brocks, D., & Sharma, R.A. (2010). A systematic review of drug absorption following bariatric surgery and its theoretical implications. *Obesity Review, 11,* 41–50.

Pajecki, D., Dalcanalle, L., Souza de Oliveira, C.P., Zilberstein, B., Halpern, A., Garrido, A.B. Jr. et al. (2007). Follow-up of Roux-en-Y gastric bypass patients at 5 or more years postoperatively. *Obesity Surgery, 17,* 601–607.

Scopinaro, N., Adami, G.F., Marinari, G.M., Gianetla, E., Treverso, E., Friedman, D. et al. (1998). Biliopancreatic diversion. *World Journal of Surgery, 22,* 936–946.

Sjöström, L., Narbro, K., Sjöström, D., Karason, K., Larsson B., Wedel, H. et al. (2007). Effects of bariatric surgery on mortality in Swedish obese subjects. *New England Journal of Medicine, 357,* 741–752.

Slater, G.H., Ren, C.J., Siegel, N., Williams, T., Barr, D., Wolfe, B. et al. (2004). Serum fat-soluble vitamin deficiency and abnormal calcium metabolism after malabsorptive bariatric surgery. *Journal of Gastrointestinal Surgery, 8,* 48–55.

Stylopoulos, N., Hoppin, A.G., & Kaplan, L.M. (2009). Roux-en-Y gastric bypass enhances energy expenditure and extends lifespan in diet-induced obese rats. *Obesity, 17,* 1839–1847.

Weiner, R.A., Weiner, S., Pomhoff, I., Jacobi, C., Makarewicz, W., & Weigand, G. (2007). Laparoscopic sleeve gastrectomy—Influence of sleeve size and resected gastric volume. *Obesity Surgery, 17,* 1297–1305.

CHAPTER 10

Special Issues in the Assessment and Treatment of Adolescent Bariatric Surgery Patients

ROBYN SYSKO and MICHAEL J. DEVLIN

Use of Bariatric Surgery Among Adolescents

Overweight and obesity* among children and adolescents in the United States have reached epidemic proportions. While some data suggest that the prevalence of overweight among youth has stabilized (Ogden, Carroll, & Flegal, 2008), significant increases in weight among children and adolescents have been documented over the past few decades. Some estimate a 39% increase in obesity in the late twentieth century (Troiano & Flegal, 1998), with the greatest increases in weight occurring at the highest end of the weight continuum (Flegal & Troiano, 2000). Obese youth are at risk for developing significant and debilitating medical complications, including early-onset Type 2 diabetes, hyptertension, hyperlipidemia, polycystic ovarian syndrome, and obstructive sleep apnea (S. Baker et al., 2005; Lee, 2007). Conditions such as Type 2 diabetes, previously considered a disease of adulthood, are now much more common in youth as a result of increasing rates of overweight (Rosenbloom, Joe, Young, & Winter, 1999). Weight status during adolescence can have a significant impact on medical

---

* For children and adolescents, overweight is defined as a body mass index (BMI) (kg/m²) of ≥85th percentile and <95th percentile, and obesity is defined as a BMI ≥ 95th percentile for age and gender (Ogden et al., 2002).

185

complications later in life (Srinivasan, Bao, Wattigney, & Berenson, 1996; Thompson et al., 2007; Yarnell, Patterson, Thomas, & Sweetnam, 2000). As weight and age increase during childhood, so does risk for serious medical complications in adulthood, including coronary heart disease. The strongest prediction of risk for coronary heart disease occurs during adolescence (J.L. Baker, Olsen, & Sorensen, 2007), and excess weight in adolescence exerts a significant negative impact on multiple cardiovascular risk factors (Srinivasan et al., 1996), including risk for mortality (Yarnell et al., 2000). In comparison to healthy youth, obese children and adolescents report significantly impaired health-related quality of life, and indicate quality of life scores similar to those of children and adolescents with cancer (Schwimmer, Burwinkle, & Varni, 2003). These data suggest that the proportion of youth currently classified as overweight or obese represents a public health crisis.

Psychosocial treatments for obesity among children and adolescents, including behavioral and cognitive-behavioral therapies and family interventions, are effective for some (Marcus, Levine, Kalarchian, & Wisniewski, 2003), although these interventions are less beneficial for severely obese youth (Yanovski & Yanovski, 2003). A recent study of family-based behavioral weight control found a 7.58% decrease in percent overweight among severely obese children after 6 months of treatment, but these changes were not sustained at 12- and 18-month assessments (Kalarchian et al., 2009). As achieving changes in weight substantial enough to affect health outcomes is difficult over the long term for significantly overweight adolescents, surgical interventions have become an option for these youth.

Some estimates suggest that younger patients represent only a small fraction of the total number of bariatric surgeries performed in the United States (Tsai, Inge, & Burd, 2007); however, in recent years bariatric procedures among adolescents have increased significantly (Jen et al., 2010; Schilling, Davis, Albanese, Dutta, & Morton, 2008; Tsai et al., 2007). As in adults, most adolescents receiving bariatric surgery undergo gastric bypass (Tsai et al., 2007), which is effective for producing both long-term weight loss and significant improvements in weight-related medical comorbidities with low rates of morbidity and mortality (Buchwald et al., 2004; Garcia, Langford, & Inge, 2003). A meta-analysis of studies of adolescents receiving Roux-en-Y gastric bypass noted significant decreases in weight during the follow-up (1.0 to 6.3 years), with a range of 17.8 to 22.3 body mass index (BMI) units (kg/m^2) lost (Treadwell, Sun, & Schoelles, 2008). However, questions have arisen regarding whether this procedure is preferable for younger patients, with some arguing that laparoscopic adjustable gastric banding (LAGB) should be the standard procedure for adolescents (Garcia et al., 2003).

For adults, the LAGB procedure produces significantly greater reductions in weight and improvements in metabolic syndrome and quality of life in comparison to a nonsurgical intensive therapy (O'Brien et al., 2006), but is less effective for weight loss than gastric bypass (Tice, Karliner, Walsh, Petersen, & Feldman, 2008). The use of LAGB in patients under the age of 18 is not currently approved by the Food and Drug Administration (FDA); however, recent data suggest that the use of this procedure in adolescents has increased dramatically in some parts of the United States (Jen et al., 2010). In comparison to gastric bypass, LAGB offers advantages for adolescents, including the ability to adjust the device for a gradual decline in weight over the long term or reduce the restriction of the band during pregnancy, avoiding unpleasant symptoms associated with gastric bypass (e.g., dumping, diarrhea, nutritional deficiencies), and the possibility of reversing the procedure by removing the LAP-BAND® (Garcia et al., 2003). As in studies of gastric bypass, initial reports of adolescents receiving LAGB have observed outcomes similar to those of adults (Dillard et al., 2007; Holterman et al., 2007). However, notable variability in weight loss has been observed for adolescents undergoing LAGB. For example, in a comparison of adult and adolescents receiving LAGB from the same bariatric surgery center, Dillard and colleagues (2007) reported substantial heterogeneity in the percent of excess weight lost postsurgery. After 3 years, percent excess weight loss in adults ranged between 5% and 115%, and among adolescents, between 4% and 64% (Dillard et al., 2007). A recent randomized controlled study of LAGB found an average decrease in weight of 76.28 pounds over the 2 years following surgery, which was an excess weight loss of 78.8%, significantly greater than a group of adolescents participating in a supervised lifestyle intervention (O'Brien et al., 2010).

Psychosocial Assessment of Adolescent Bariatric Surgery Candidates

Elevated rates of psychopathology are documented in studies of severely obese adult and adolescent patients in bariatric surgery programs. Approximately half of all adult patients present with a current or past DSM-IV Axis I disorder (Guisado, Vaz, Lopez-Ibor, & Rubio, 2001; Kalarchian et al., 2007; Sarwer et al., 2004) or impaired health-related quality of life (Fabricatore, Wadden, Sarwer, & Faith, 2005), with some programs reporting rates of lifetime psychiatric diagnoses as high as 70% (Glinski, Wetzler, & Goodman, 2001; Mühlhans, Horbach, & de Zwaan, 2009). Although the data are still limited for adolescents, the extant studies have identified similarly high rates of psychopathology, including depression, eating problems, stigmatization, and social isolation (Kim et al., 2008; Zeller, Roehrig, Modi Daniels, & Inge, 2006). In particular, Zeller and colleagues (2006) and Kim and colleagues (2008) found 30 and 16%, respectively, of adolescent bariatric surgery candidates scored in the clinical range on the Beck Depression Inventory (total ≥ 17), and Kim and colleagues (2008) observed a significant percentage of adolescents with binge eating episodes (48%).

The involvement of a mental health professional on multidisciplinary teams is suggested by best practice guidelines for pediatric and adolescent bariatric surgery for the purpose of evaluating adolescents presurgery (Pratt et al., 2009). However, limited empirical information is available to suggest how to conduct such psychiatric evaluations. Psychologists and psychiatrists in our clinic have completed psychosocial assessments with more than 150 adolescents presenting at the Center for Adolescent Bariatric Surgery (CABS) program at the Morgan Stanley Children's Hospital of New York Presbyterian. In the sections that follow, we present a proposal for conducting clinical interviews with adolescent candidates and their parent(s), highlight issues of particular concern for adolescents receiving the LAP-BAND, and present some data from 125 adolescents, with complete data from this interview. In addition, the appendix of this chapter provides a template for this psychosocial assessment in this age group.

As illustrated in greater detail by the appendix, the interview begins by obtaining basic demographics from the adolescent (date of birth, ethnicity). Information relevant to weight loss surgery is collected next, which includes an assessment of the adolescent's knowledge of the surgical procedure and the pre- and postsurgery nutritional recommendations of the program, behaviors that suggest the adolescent is motivated to make lifestyle changes, support for lifestyle changes and the surgery, barriers to lifestyle change, and weight loss goals and anticipated challenges following surgery. As part of a weight and eating history, adolescents are asked about impairments related to weight, the ways in which weight has affected their self-esteem and other important aspects of their life (e.g., peer relationships), any previous formal weight loss attempts, their current eating pattern and exercise routine, and the amount of time spent in sedentary activity. Eating disordered symptoms, including binge eating, night eating, and compensatory behaviors, are assessed in all adolescents, and can subsequently be used to generate a DSM-IV diagnosis, if applicable. Other current and past psychiatric symptoms and treatment are assessed in the next section, including symptoms of attention deficit/hyperactivity disorder, oppositional defiant disorder, and conduct disorder, followed by a school and social history. Family functioning and a mental status examination are the final two components of the interview with the adolescent.

During the presurgery evaluations, at least one parent is interviewed by the clinician to evaluate: (1) the adolescent's developmental and medical history; (2) the family psychiatric and medical history, including family members who are overweight and obese; (3) the parent's motivation for his or her child to receive bariatric surgery; and (4) the adolescent's report regarding previous weight loss attempts and psychiatric status. This portion of the interview is a useful means of evaluating the consistency of the reports from the parent and adolescent. Further, adolescents are often at least partially dependent on parents for assistance with recommendations for diet and exercise. In particular, parents may be involved with the purchasing of food, meal planning, support for physical activity (e.g., purchasing a gym membership), and scheduling and attending pre- and postsurgery clinic appointments. Thus, eliciting descriptions of how parents are currently involved in these areas and plans for continued support postsurgery are particularly informative when a clinician evaluates the likelihood that an adolescent will have the necessary assistance to be successful in losing weight following bariatric surgery. Parent reports may also be valuable in identifying particular challenges their adolescent will face after weight loss surgery.

An important component of this interview for adolescents preparing for LAGB is to ask about the dietary changes that are attempted presurgery (e.g., eliminating caloric beverages, eating breakfast), what portions of the adolescent's diet still need to be changed, and what changes will need to occur postsurgery (e.g., drinking liquids before meals for adolescents receiving the LAP-BAND). As LAGB is more limited in the degree to which it alters the gastrointestinal anatomy in comparison to other bariatric procedures, lifestyle changes may be of particular importance. Among adults, some factors related to diet and exercise can influence weight loss following the insertion of the LAP-BAND (Colles, Dixon, & O'Brien, 2008). Although the assessment of eating disordered behaviors is important for all weight loss surgeries, self-induced vomiting is of particular concern with LAGB, as this can produce complications related to the LAP-BAND.

Using the aforementioned psychosocial interview, a number of the candidates in the CABS program report clinically significant symptoms. Among our sample of 125 adolescents, 16.8% (n = 21) endorsed current binge eating, 9.6% (n = 12) reported current night eating, 32.8% (n = 41) were receiving current psychiatric treatment, and 2.4% (n = 3) described current nonsuicidal self-injurious behaviors. Past significant suicidal ideation was reported by 19.2% (n = 24) of the adolescents, but use of alcohol and drugs was much less common, with 8.8% (n = 11) of the adolescents reporting regular alcohol consumption and 4% (n = 5) endorsing past problems with illicit substances. In addition, some adolescents enrolled in the CABS program have academic difficulties, and a subset have chosen to be home schooled due to weight-related problems. Social services had been involved with 17.6% (n = 22) of the families evaluated as part of the CABS program. Of course, these data may underestimate the actual prevalence of these problems, as mental health evaluations are conducted as part of the presurgery screening process. It is possible that adolescents and parents chose not to disclose information that they feel may interfere with being approved to receive surgery. However, one recent study suggests that unlike adults (e.g., Fabricatore, Sarwer, Wadden, Combs, & Krasucki, 2007), impression management for psychiatric symptoms, in particular depressed mood, may be less of an issue among adolescents (Ratcliff, Reiter-Purtill, Inge, & Zeller, 2011).

Best practice guidelines suggest the use of specific assessments of quality of life, depression, and eating disturbances for this population (Pratt et al., 2009), and our clinic also employs paper-and-pencil measures to measure these and other constructs relevant for adolescent bariatric surgery candidates.

We recently analyzed the combined information from our presurgery psychiatric evaluation (described above) and several self-report questionnaires measuring the domains suggested by Pratt and colleagues (2009), including the Beck Depression Inventory (Beck, Ward, Mendelson, Mock, & Erbaugh, 1961), Eating Disorders Examination–Questionnaire (Fairburn & Beglin, 1994) or Questionnaire on Eating and Weight Patterns–Revised (Spitzer, Yanovski, & Marcus, 1993), and the Pediatric Quality of Life Inventory (Varni, Seid, & Rode, 1999). The study examined whether subgroups of adolescents could be found among our sample of 125 candidates presenting for bariatric surgery (Sysko, Zakarin, Devlin, Bush, & Walsh, 2011). Using latent class analysis, we identified three distinct clinically relevant subgroups of adolescents, including a group exhibiting high levels of both eating disordered and other forms of psychopathology, a second group with intermediate nonspecific psychopathology, and a final group with fewer overall problems. Further, while a number of self-report assessments were used in this study, the results supported the recommendations of Pratt and colleagues (2009) that clinicians assessing adolescent bariatric surgery candidates should pay particular attention to measures of eating behavior. Binge eating or night eating behaviors could indicate a higher risk of individual or familial psychopathology, whereas adolescents who deny eating disturbances appear to be at lower risk for psychiatric symptoms (Sysko et al., 2011).

Clinicians could also consider administering other self-report assessments of self-esteem, body image, weight-related teasing, or weight bias. We recently examined the psychometric properties and clinical correlates of the Weight Bias Internalization Scale (WBIS) (Durso & Latner, 2008) in a subset of 65 adolescents enrolled in the CABS program (Roberto et al., in press). The WBIS measures attributions about one's self or the internalization of weight bias, rather than just the presence of antifat attitudes, as this construct may have an important effect on negative psychological outcomes among overweight or obese individuals. We found the WBIS to have excellent psychometric properties among adolescent bariatric surgery candidates, and it was significantly correlated with levels of self-reported psychopathology. In addition, our study suggests that the WBIS could be a helpful measure for the assessment of internalized weight bias in this population, and could potentially identify adolescents who may benefit from information on coping with weight stigma to bolster weight loss efforts (Roberto et al., in press).

Although psychiatric symptoms, in particular depressed mood and eating pathology, are frequently observed among bariatric surgery candidates (Kim et al., 2008; Zeller et al., 2006), only limited data are available to evaluate the postoperative psychosocial outcomes of adolescents. In the first prospective longitudinal study of adolescents, Zeller, Modi, Noll, Long, and Inge (2009) found significant improvements in depressive symptoms and health-related quality of life following a Roux-en-Y gastric bypass. Additional research is needed to evaluate psychosocial functioning of youth postsurgery, and to determine whether presurgery psychopathology affects weight loss outcomes.

Treatment of Adolescent Bariatric Surgery Candidates

Psychological treatment is not a usual part of the clinical management of individuals seeking bariatric surgery, which may be related to the absence of data suggesting any impact of psychological factors on surgical outcomes (Kalarchian & Marcus, 2003). However, options for treatment, and in particular cognitive-behavioral interventions, have been presented for adults receiving weight loss surgery. Kalarchian and Marcus (2003) suggested that in the preoperative phase, a cognitive-behavioral therapist could offer services such as treating individuals with "severe, uncontrolled psychiatric symptomology" (p. 115), conducting a decisional balance to weigh the pros and cons of bariatric surgery, or providing referrals to address other problems (e.g., marital therapy). Postoperatively, Kalarchian and Marcus (2003) described a possible role for the cognitive-behavioral therapist in increasing compliance with medical and lifestyle recommendations of the surgical team, intervening for any "problematic eating behavior, vomiting, or insufficient weight loss" (p. 116), and treating any emergent psychiatric disorders. Although the aforementioned options are intended for the treatment of adults, similar types of pre- and postsurgery cognitive-behavioral interventions could be considered for adolescents.

In adapting treatment for the particular needs of overweight adolescents, several factors must be considered. First, cognitive-behavioral interventions must take into account that the adolescent brain is not fully mature. Classic developmental psychological studies have demonstrated that the capacity for abstract thinking develops largely during adolescence

(Piaget & Inhelder, 2000), and more recent neurobiological research suggests that differential development of bottom-up limbic systems and top-down control systems may account for suboptimal and at times risky decision-making during adolescence (Casey, Jones, & Hare, 2008). Second, although body image–related issues are prominent in adults undergoing bariatric surgery, adolescents in the midst of puberty-related changes are often particularly sensitive to these issues and may have particular treatment needs in this regard that differ from those of adults. Finally, like body image–related issues, obesity-related stigma, while certainly not limited to adolescents, may manifest differently in an adolescent-specific environment such as high school. In our clinical experience, schools are highly variable in the degree to which individuals of varying body size and shape are accepted or stigmatized. In addition, adolescents making the transition from high school to college may find that their eating environment, as well as the degree of supervision of their eating by parents, is radically altered. Fortunately, adolescent-specific adaptations of CBT for a variety of disorders, including eating disorders, are available (Evans et al., 2005; Kendall, 2006). Cognitive-behavioral interventions for adolescents undergoing bariatric surgery may draw from these approaches, incorporating features of pre- and postoperative interventions mentioned above for adults undergoing bariatric surgery.

While there are few empirical data to guide specific recommendations about the pre- and postoperative treatment of adolescents, the literature for adult patients and our clinical experience with the CABS program highlights some psychiatric symptoms that are also relevant for younger patients. The emergence of eating disorders characterized by symptoms such as overconcern with shape and weight, overly rapid weight loss, extreme fear of weight regain, uncontrolled eating, and purging in individuals who have undergone bariatric surgery has been noted in case reports and one case series (Segal, Kinoshita Kussunoki, & Larino, 2004). While this phenomenon has not yet been characterized specifically in adolescents undergoing bariatric surgery, it is likely that the vulnerability of adolescents to this complication is equal to or greater than that of adults, as adolescence and early adulthood are the periods of greatest risk for the development of eating disorders. Some data indicate that suicide occurs more frequently among adults receiving bariatric surgery than other severely obese individuals (Adams et al., 2007; Tindle et al., 2010), which could be related to elevated rates of psychiatric disorders or the effect of surgery on an individual's life in the surgical population (Marcus, Kalarchian, & Courcoulas, 2009). Given the rates of past significant suicidal ideation (19.2%) or past suicide attempts (7.3%) in the CABS sample, the possibility of suicidality should also be monitored closely in a younger group of bariatric surgery patients. Although drug and alcohol use has not been significant in the CABS program, adolescence may be a developmental stage where this could be an important behavior to monitor following weight loss surgery, as these substances are accessible to youth in multiple contexts, including the college environment. In addition to the possibility of misuse, the consumption of alcohol in particular has implications for weight regain due to the caloric density of alcoholic beverages. Most adults do not appear to alter their consumption of alcohol after bariatric surgery, but a small number increase their drinking (Ertelt et al., 2008), which further highlights the need for ongoing monitoring for younger patients to identify any problems and intervene as needed. Clinicians should also be aware that changes in relationship status and sexual activity resulting from weight loss postsurgery can lead to planned and unplanned pregnancies among an adolescent population. A notable subgroup of individuals enrolled in the CABS program have become pregnant in the months and years following the insertion of the LAP-BAND, which can result in complications in the year postsurgery due to an increased frequency of vomiting.

Conclusion

In summary, bariatric surgery has become more common among youth in recent years, and the extant data suggest positive outcomes for weight, at least over the short term. At this time, only limited data are available to evaluate the psychosocial outcomes of adolescents undergoing weight loss surgery. Although depressive symptoms and eating disturbances are common among youth enrolled in bariatric surgery programs, it is unclear whether these symptoms have an effect on weight loss. As additional research is conducted, it will be important to evaluate the relationship between preoperative psychosocial status and postoperative outcome to inform patient selection criteria, improve patient care, and foster healthy development among adolescent patients.

References

Adams, T.D., Gress, R.E., Smith, S.C., Halverson, C., Simper, S.C., Rosamond, W.D. et al. (2007). Long-term mortality after gastric bypass surgery. *New England Journal of Medicine, 357*, 753–761.

Baker, J.L., Olsen, L.W., & Sorensen, T.I.A. (2007). Childhood body-mass index and the risk of coronary heart disease in adulthood. *New England Journal of Medicine, 357*, 2329–2337.

Baker, S., Barlow, S., Cochran, W., Fuchs, G., Klish, W., Krebs, N. et al. (2005). Overweight children and adolescents: A clinical report of the North American Society for Pediatric Gastroenterology, Hepatology, and Nutrition. *Journal of Pediatric Gastroenterology and Nutrition, 40*, 533–543.

Beck, A.T., Ward, C.H., Mendelson, M., Mock, J., & Erbaugh, J. (1961). An inventory for measuring depression. *Archives of General Psychiatry, 4*, 561–571.

Buchwald, H., Avidor, Y., Braunwald, E., Jensen, M.D., Pories, W., Fahrbach, K. et al. (2004). Bariatric surgery: A systematic review and meta-analysis. *JAMA, 292*, 1724–1737.

Casey, B.J., Jones, R.M., & Hare, T.A. (2008). The adolescent brain. *Annals of the New York Academy of Sciences, 1124*, 111–126.

Colles, S.L., Dixon, J.B., & O'Brien, P.E. (2008). Hunger control and regular physical activity facilitate weight loss after laparoscopic adjustable gastric banding. *Obesity Surgery, 18*, 833–840.

Dillard, B.E., 3rd, Gorodner, V., Galvani, C., Holterman, M., Browne, A., Gallo, A. et al. (2007). Initial experience with the adjustable gastric band in morbidly obese US adolescents and recommendations for further investigation. *Journal of Pediatric Gastroenterology and Nutrition, 45*, 240–246.

Durso, L., & Latner, J. (2008). Understanding self-directed stigma: Development of the weight bias internalization scale. *Obesity, 16*, S80–S86.

Ertelt, T.W., Mitchell, J.E., Lancaster, K., Crosby, R.D., Steffen, K.J., & Marino, J.M. (2008). Alcohol abuse and dependence before and after bariatric surgery: A review of the literature and report of a new data set. *Surgery for Obesity and Related Diseases, 4*, 647–650.

Evans, D.L., Foa, E.B., Gur, R.E., Hendin, H., O'Brien, C.P., Seligman, M.E.P. et al. (Eds.). (2005). *Treating and preventing adolescent mental health disorders: What we know and what we don't know, a research agenda for improving the mental health of our youth.* New York: Oxford University Press.

Fabricatore, A.N., Sarwer, D.B., Wadden, T.A., Combs, C.J., & Krasucki, J.L. (2007). Impression management or real change? Reports of depressive symptoms before and after the preoperative psychological evaluation for bariatric surgery. *Obesity Surgery, 17*, 1213–1219.

Fabricatore, A.N., Wadden, T.A., Sarwer, D.B., & Faith, M.S. (2005). Health-related quality of life and symptoms of depression in extremely obese persons seeking bariatric surgery, *Obesity Surgery, 15*, 304–309.

Fairburn, C.G., & Beglin, S.J. (1994). Assessment of eating disorders: Interview or self-report questionnaire? *International Journal of Eating Disorders, 16*, 363–370.

Flegal, K.M., & Troiano, R.P. (2000). Changes in the distribution of body mass index of adults and children in the US population. *International Journal of Obesity, 24*, 807–818.

Garcia, V.F., Langford, L., & Inge, T.H. (2003). Application of laparoscopy for bariatric surgery in adolescents. *Current Opinion in Pediatrics, 15*, 248–255.

Glinski, J., Wetzler, S., & Goodman, E. (2001). The psychology of gastric bypass surgery. *Obesity Surgery, 11*, 581–588.

Guisado, J.A., Vaz, F.J., Lopez-Ibor, J.J., Jr., & Rubio, M.A. (2001). Eating behavior in morbidly obese patients undergoing gastric surgery: Differences between obese people with and without psychiatric disorders. *Obesity Surgery, 11*, 576–580.

Holterman, A.X., Browne, A., Dillard, B.E., Tussing, L., Gorodner, V., Stahl, C. et al. (2007). Short-term outcome in the first 10 morbidly obese adolescent patients in the FDA-approved trial for laparoscopic adjustable gastric banding. *Journal of Pediatric Gastroenterology and Nutrition, 45*, 465–473.

Jen, H.C., Rickard, D.G., Shew, S.B., Maggard, M.A., Slusser, W.M., Dutson, E.P. et al. (2010). Trends and outcomes of adolescent bariatric surgery in California, 2005–2007. *Pediatrics, 126*, e746–e753.

Kalarchian, M.A., Levine, M.D., Arslanian, S.A., Ewing, L.J., Houck, P.R., Cheng, Y. et al. (2009). Family-based treatment of severe pediatric obesity: A randomized, controlled trial. *Pediatrics, 124*, 1060–1068.

Kalarchian, M.A., & Marcus, M.D. (2003). Management of the bariatric surgery patient: Is there a role for the cognitive behavior therapist? *Cognitive and Behavioral Practice, 10*, 112–119.

Kalarchian, M.A., Marcus, M.D., Levine, M.D., Courcoulas, A.P., Pilkonis, P.A., Ringham, R.M. et al. (2007). Psychiatric disorders among bariatric surgery candidates: Relationship to obesity and functional health status. *American Journal of Psychiatry, 164*, 328–334.

Kendall, P.C. (Ed.). (2006). *Child and adolescent therapy: Cognitive-behavioral procedures* (3rd ed.). New York: Guilford Press.

Kim, R.J., Langer, J.M., Baker, A.W., Filter, D.E., Williams, N.N., & Sarwer, D.B. (2008). Psychosocial status in adolescents undergoing bariatric surgery. *Obesity Surgery, 18*, 27–33.

Lee, W.W.R. (2007). An overview of pediatric obesity. *Pediatric Diabetes, 8*, 76–87.

Marcus, M.D., Kalarchian, M.A., & Courcoulas, A.P. (2009). Psychiatric evaluation and follow-up of bariatric surgery patients. *American Journal of Psychiatry, 166*, 285–291.

Marcus, M.D., Levine, M.D., Kalarchian, M.A., & Wisniewski, L. (2003). Cognitive behavioral interventions in the management of severe pediatric obesity. *Cognitive and Behavioral Practice, 10*, 147–156.

Mühlhans, B., Horbach, T., & de Zwaan M. (2009). Psychiatric disorders in bariatric surgery candidates: A review of the literature and results of a German prebariatric surgery sample. *General Hospital Psychiatry, 31*, 414–421.

O'Brien, P.E., Dixon, J.B., Laurie, C., Skinner, S., Proietto, J., McNeil, J. et al. (2006). Treatment of mild to moderate obesity with laparoscopic adjustable gastric banding or an intensive medical program: A randomized trial. *Annals of Internal Medicine, 144*, 625–633.

O'Brien, P.E., Sawyer, S.M., Laurie, C., Brown, W.A., Skinner, S., Veit, F. et al. (2010). Laparoscopic adjustable gastric banding in severely obese adolescents: A randomized trial. *JAMA, 303*, 519–526.

Ogden, C.L., Carroll, M.D., & Flegal, K.M. (2008). High body mass index for age among US children and adolescents, 2003–2006. *JAMA, 299*, 2401–2405.

Ogden, C.L., Kuczmarski, R.J., Flegal, K.M., Mei, Z., Guo, S., Wei, R. et al. (2002). Centers for Disease Control and Prevention 2000 growth charts for the United States: Improvements to the 1977 National Center for Health Statistics version. *Pediatrics, 109*, 45–60.

Piaget, J., & Inhelder, B. (2000). *The psychology of the child.* New York: Basic Books.

Pratt, J.S.A., Lenders, C.M., Dionne, E.A., Hoppin, A.G., Hsu, G.L., Inge, T.H. et al. (2009). Best practice updates for pediatric/adolescent weight loss surgery. *Obesity, 17*, 901–910.

Ratcliff, M.B., Reiter-Purtill, J., Inge, T.H., & Zeller, M.H. (2011). Changes in depressive symptoms among adolescent bariatric candidates from preoperative psychological evaluation to immediately before surgery. *Surgery for Obesity and Related Diseases, 7,* 50–54.

Roberto, C.A., Sysko, R., Bush, J., Pearl, R., Puhl, R.M., Schvey, N.A. et al. (in press). Clinical correlates of the Weight Bias Internalization Scale in a sample of obese adolescents seeking bariatric surgery. *Obesity.*

Rosenbloom, A.L., Joe, J.R., Young, R.S., & Winter, W.E. (1999). Emerging epidemic of type 2 diabetes in youth. *Diabetes Care, 22,* 345–354.

Sarwer D.B., Cohn, N.I., Gibbons, L.M., Magee, L., Crerand, C.E., Raper, S.E. et al. (2004). Psychiatric diagnoses and psychiatric treatment among bariatric surgery candidates. *Obesity Surgery, 14,* 1148–1156.

Schilling, P.L., Davis, M.M., Albanese, C.T., Dutta, S., & Morton, J. (2008). National trends in adolescent bariatric surgical procedures and implications for surgical centers of excellence. *Journal of the American College of Surgeons, 206,* 1–12.

Schwimmer, J.B., Burwinkle, T.M., & Varni, J.W. (2003). Health-related quality of life of severely obese children and adolescents. *JAMA, 289,* 1813–1819.

Segal, A., Kinoshita Kussunoki, D., & Larino, M.A. (2004). Post-surgical refusal to eat: Anorexia nervosa, bulimia nervosa, or a new eating disorder? A case series. *Obesity Surgery, 14,* 353–360.

Spitzer, R.L., Yanovski, S.Z., & Marcus, M.D. (1993). *The Questionnaire on Eating and Weight Patterns–Revised (QEWP-R).* New York: New York State Psychiatric Institute.

Srinivasan, S.R., Bao, W., Wattigney, W.A., & Berenson, G.S. (1996). Adolescent overweight is associated with adult overweight and related multiple cardiovascular risk factors: The Bogalusa Heart Study. *Metabolism, 45,* 235–240.

Sysko, R., Zakarin, E.B., Devlin, M.J., Bush, J., & Walsh, B.T. (2011). A latent class analysis of psychiatric symptoms among 125 adolescents in a bariatric surgery program. *International Journal of Pediatric Obesity. 6,* 289–297.

Thompson, D.R., Obarzanek, E., Franko, D.L., Barton, B.A., Morrison, J., Biro, F.M. et al. (2007). Childhood overweight and cardiovascular disease risk factors: The National Heart, Lung, and Blood Institute Growth and Health Study. *Journal of Pediatrics, 150,* 18–25.

Tice, J.A., Karliner, L., Walsh, J., Petersen, A.J., & Feldman, M.D. (2008). Gastric banding or bypass? A systematic review comparing the two most popular bariatric procedures. *American Journal of Medicine, 121,* 885–893.

Tindle, H.A., Omalu, B., Courcoulas, A., Marcus, M., Hammers, J., & Kuller, L.H. (2010). Risk of suicide after long-term follow-up from bariatric surgery. *American Journal of Medicine, 123,* 1036–1042.

Treadwell, J.R., Sun, F., & Schoelles, K. (2008). Systematic review and meta-analysis of bariatric surgery for pediatric obesity. *Annals of Surgery, 248,* 763–776.

Troiano, R.P., & Flegal, K.M. (1998). Overweight children and adolescents: Description, epidemiology, and demographics. *Pediatrics, 101,* 497–504.

Tsai, W.S., Inge, T.H., & Burd, R.S. (2007). Bariatric surgery in adolescents: Recent national trends in use and in-hospital outcome. *Archives of Pediatric and Adolescent Medicine, 161,* 217–221.

Varni, J.W., Seid, M., & Rode, C.A. (1999). The PedsQL: Measurement model for the Pediatric Quality of Life Inventory. *Medical Care, 37*, 126–139.

Yanovski, J.A., & Yanovski, S.Z. (2003). Treatment of pediatric and adolescent obesity, *JAMA, 289*, 1851–1853.

Yarnell, J.W.G., Patterson, C.C., Thomas, H.F., & Sweetnam, P.M. (2000). Comparison of weight in middle age, weight at 18 years, and weight change between, in predicting subsequent 14 year mortality and coronary events: Caerphilly prospective study. *Journal of Epidemiology and Community Health, 54*, 344–348.

Zeller, M.H., Modi, A.C., Noll, J.G., Long, J.D., & Inge, T.H. (2009). Psychosocial functioning improves following adolescent bariatric surgery. *Obesity, 17*, 985–990.

Zeller, M.H., Roehrig, H.R., Modi, A.C., Daniels, S.R., & Inge, T.H. (2006). Health-related quality of life and depressive symptoms in adolescents with extreme obesity presenting for bariatric surgery. *Pediatrics, 117*, 1155–1161.

CHAPTER 11

Body Image and Body Contouring in Bariatric Surgery Patients

KRISTINE J. STEFFEN, JAMES E. MITCHELL,
and TRISHA M. KARR

Introduction

Bariatric surgery is currently the most efficacious and durable weight loss intervention available for those with severe obesity. Accordingly, over 200,000 bariatric procedures are performed annually (ASMBS, 2009). The most commonly performed weight loss surgery in the United States is the Roux-en-Y gastric bypass (RYGB), which accounts for the majority of bariatric surgeries (BOLD, Surgical Review Corporation). The RYGB typically results in the loss of approximately 50–75% of excess body weight, often by approximately 12 months after surgery (Tice, Karliner, Walsh, Petersen, & Feldman, 2008). Patients usually reach their weight nadir by 18–24 months post-RYGB (Mechanick et al., 2008). While this rapid and massive weight loss leads to the resolution of many obesity-related comorbid conditions, it also frequently leaves patients with large amounts of hanging, residual skin.

Consequently, statistics from the American Society of Plastic Surgery (ASPS, 2009) indicate that in 2008, approximately 58,669 contouring procedures were performed following massive weight loss. According to one survey of approximately 800 patients who underwent body contouring, roughly 11% received plastic surgery (Gusenoff, Messing, O'Malley, & Langstein, 2008).

This redundant skin can be aesthetically displeasing to patients, potentially leaving patients disappointed in the cosmetic outcome of their gastric bypass. Hanging skin can occur on any body region, but is often most pronounced on the abdomen, back, upper arms, breasts, inner and outer thighs, and buttocks (Borud & Warren, 2007; Zuelzer & Baugh, 2007). Skin can also hang on the face and neck regions, causing the appearance of premature aging (Zuelzer & Baugh, 2007). Truncal skin is among the most problematic skin issues patients can develop post–bariatric surgery, often extending circumferentially around the body (Borud & Warren, 2007). Some patients develop a large abdominal pannus, which can overhang the genitalia. Beyond appearance-related issues, hanging, redundant skin after massive weight loss can lead to problems fitting into clothes, exercising, and result in reduced self-esteem (Warner et al., 2009). Excess skin can also result in medical complications such as skin irritation, infection, and ulceration, limitations on physical functioning, musculoskeletal strain and postural problems, difficulty with urine elimination, and impairments in sexual functioning (Zuelzer & Baugh, 2007).

Ultimately, these issues can significantly interfere with patients' lifestyles and diminish their quality of life. It has been suggested that there may be differences in the amount of skin laxity observed following massive weight loss that is achieved through diet and exercise as opposed to weight loss surgery (Sanger & David, 2006). There is also significant interpatient variability in the degree to which hanging skin is problematic following bariatric surgery. Data on this topic have been relatively scarce, but clinicians are increasingly becoming aware of problems with redundant skin and are educating patients on the importance of planning for future contouring procedures. However, data from a recent survey of surgeons showed that only approximately 54% educate their patients on the risk of hanging redundant skin following bariatric surgery (Warner et al., 2009). This group of surgeons also reported that approximately two-thirds of their prebariatric surgery candidates routinely ask about the need for subsequent body contouring procedures. Despite increased awareness of the problems with excess skin following massive weight loss and the obvious medical and psychological detriments that can result from it, most insurance providers continue to view this is as an elective "cosmetic" procedure (Mitchell et al., 2008; Warner et al., 2009; Zuelzer & Baugh, 2007). For patients who do not receive insurance coverage for contouring, the costs associated with these procedures can be prohibitive. For example, average 2009 surgeon/physician fees associated with some common post–bariatric surgery contouring procedures were as follows: mastopexy, $4,185; lower body lift, $7,141; thigh lift, $4,329; abdominoplasty, $4,936; and upper arm lift, $3,568 (ASPS, 2009).

Patients Who Will Require Contouring

While all patients should be educated on the potential need for contouring surgery following bariatric surgery, it is difficult to predict which patients will subsequently require it. Although the amount of hanging loose skin individuals will experience after surgery varies, certain groups of patients may be at particular risk for having problems. For example, McGohan (2007) lists the following factors as potential determinants of skin elasticity, and therefore the degree to which patients will experience redundant skin following bariatric surgery: (1) the severity of the patient's obesity, (2) the amount of weight the patient lost, (3) the number of weight losses and regains the patient has experienced, (4) age, (5) smoking and sun tanning history, and (6) genetic makeup.

Gusenoff and colleagues (2008) performed a survey to identify which subgroups of patients may be most likely to desire plastic surgery following gastric bypass. They mailed surveys to over 2,500 post–gastric bypass patients who had undergone surgery between 1992 and 2006 performed by one of two surgeons at a university-affiliated community hospital. Of the 926 patients who responded to the survey, 817 were women and 109 were men. The mean age of the respondents was 46.5 ± 9.7 years, and mean time since surgery was 2.3 ± 1.7 years. Among this cohort, the body mass index had changed by a mean of 20 ± 7.3 kg/m^2 following surgery. The median income was \$40,000–\$49,000 annually. The majority of survey respondents were married (54.5%), whereas the remainder were single (27.1%), divorced (12.2%), or other (separated, engaged, or with a significant other; 6.2%). The majority of respondents (84.5%) who had not already had a plastic surgery procedure desired body contouring (N = 685/926). Only 15.5% of patients who had not undergone plastic surgery indicated a lack of desire to undergo contouring in the future. Desire for plastic surgery among patients who had undergone gastric bypass was inversely related to age, years since gastric bypass, and having undergone open versus laparoscopic gastric bypass. Interest in contouring procedures was twice as likely among women than men, and among divorced than married individuals. In a stepwise multiple regression analysis, only age, years since gastric bypass, and divorced status related significantly to desire for body contouring. Other associations (i.e., gender, pre–gastric bypass body mass index) with desire for plastic surgery were not significant in this analysis. In conclusion, the authors suggested that the subpopulation of patients with the greatest desire for surgery are young, female, divorced patients who underwent laparoscopic gastric bypass, and that this subpopulation of patients should interact with plastic surgeons early in order to help facilitate timely attainment of contouring surgery.

Although few other data are available on this issue, there is additional literature that addresses this topic. Surgeon members of the American Society for Metabolic and Bariatric Surgery (ASMBS) who responded to a survey on the topic of body contouring indicated that they believed the factors that contributed most to whether or not a patient would decide to undergo contouring are self-image, insurance coverage, economic status, and amount of weight lost (Warner et al., 2009). These surgeons thought that comorbidities, race, and social support played a minor role in whether or not a patient would seek body contouring following massive weight loss. Zuelzer and Baugh (2007) noted other factors that have been observed as negative prognostic indicators for developing skin laxity following bariatric surgery: fair complexion, history of sun tanning, and smoking. Furthermore, Kenkel (2006) suggests that factors influencing tissue laxity most include age, genetics, and amount of weight loss. Thus, the literature contains inconsistent information regarding prognostic indicators of hanging redundant skin following bariatric surgery. Determining precisely which patients are at greatest risk for these sequelae will require a prospective research study that will allow longitudinal assessment of patient data.

Patient Education Regarding Contouring

Increased attention in recent years has been paid to the importance of body contouring following bariatric surgery. For example, a supplement to the journal of *Plastic and Reconstructive Surgery* was published in 2006 involving a panel of plastic surgeons discussing the issue of contouring surgery following massive weight loss (Kenkel, 2006). Most recently, a survey sent to surgeons who were members of the ASMBS highlights the need for more consistent patient counseling by surgeons on the potential necessity of plastic surgery following gastric bypass (Warner et al., 2009). This study involved a survey that was electronically mailed to 500 surgeons and was completed by 188. The majority (56%) of surgeons who responded to this survey had been in practice for 11 years or more, did not complete a postresidency bariatric surgery fellowship (55%), and approximately a third were in solo practice (35%). Fifty percent of respondents performed more than 125 procedures annually. Almost all of the surgeons (94%) worked as part of a multidisciplinary team of clinicians who managed patients pre- and postoperatively. This cohort of surgeons almost unanimously believed that patients are satisfied with the results of their bariatric procedure more than 50% of the time, and 55% of surgeons thought that patients are satisfied with the outcome of bariatric surgery more than 90% of the time. Specific to body contouring, 64% of surgeons stated that pre–bariatric surgery candidates always or almost always ask them about contouring procedures before their weight loss surgery, 33% reported that patients rarely ask, and 3% said that patients never ask about plastic surgery. Surgeon respondents indicated that they counseled patients on the potential aesthetic and functional consequences of bariatric surgery routinely (54%), most of the time (28%), rarely (16%), and never (1%). Over half of the surgeons indicated that they show photographs of typical postsurgery appearance to patients who intend to undergo bariatric surgery. Most (69%) of the surgeons who responded to this survey indicated that they had access to plastic surgeons in their area who were capable of performing contouring for postbariatric surgery patients. While only 7% of the surgeons indicated that they always referred their patients to a plastic surgeon, another 60% referred patients most of the time. The vast majority of this surgeon sample (85%) believed that insurance should cover contouring procedures following massive weight loss. Most of the surgeons (90%) did not, however, believe the success of the bariatric surgery is dependent upon subsequent contouring operations. Many of the surgeons surveyed indicated that patients are not well informed regarding the multiple steps often required in body contouring surgery. Slightly more than half (51%) of these surgeons reported that their patients who had undergone contouring were typically happier and more self-confident, had better self-image, and reported a more favorable perception of their weight loss surgery than those who had not undergone plastic surgery. While these results seem to indicate that many surgeons are counseling patients on this issue, as discussed by the investigators, the surgeons who responded to this survey may be those who are most concerned about body contouring. Over 60% of the surveys sent were not returned, which makes it difficult to interpret the representativeness of these findings.

Timing of Body Contouring and Patient Assessment

As described by McGohan (2007), it is recommended that patients wait to undergo contouring surgery until their weight has stabilized following bariatric surgery. Weight stability can be described by a 3- to 6-month period of time with no major weight changes, and this generally occurs 12–18 months after weight loss surgery (McGohan, 2007). Some patients will desire additional weight loss after this plateau, however, and should delay contouring until they have achieved their expected weight loss nadir (Zuelzer & Baugh, 2007).

There are potential consequences associated with having plastic surgery prematurely following gastric bypass. For example, hormone changes and variability in nutritional status within the first year following surgery can compromise surgical wound healing, and additional redundant skin will result from further weight loss (McGohan, 2007). As discussed by

204 • Kristine J. Steffen, James E. Mitchell, and Trisha M. Karr

Warner and colleagues (2009), bariatric and plastic surgeons must work together to provide optimal patient care following gastric bypass surgery. Typically, patients first visit a plastic surgeon 15–18 months after the bariatric surgery, when approximately 100 pounds or more has been lost and weight loss has stabilized (Zuelzer & Baugh, 2007). Patients should be at approximately an ideal body weight at the time of body contouring surgery (Kenkel, 2006). In addition to ensuring that patients have reached an appropriate and stable body weight prior to undergoing plastic surgery, patients should also be psychologically stable at the time of contouring (Kenkel, 2006).

Kenkel (2006) has suggested several issues that should be addressed prior to body contouring surgery to ensure that patients will have the most optimal outcome possible. Medical stability should be assessed through specific laboratory testing and history and physical examination, in tandem with an anesthesiology consultation. Eating behavior problems identified during the prebariatric surgery psychological consult, particularly compulsive eating, should be adequately treated prior to body contouring surgery. Smoking cessation should occur in advance of contouring surgery to promote adequate wound healing. Given the potential for blood loss due to the amount of excised skin, plans for blood transfusions should be addressed during contouring procedures. Patients should be free of skin infections on the tissue to be removed.

Outcomes of Body Contouring Surgery

Surgical complications arising during or following body contouring procedures can occur. It has been suggested that following massive weight loss and the resolution of many comorbid conditions, patients undergoing body contouring should be at approximately the same surgical risk as the general population (Zuelzer & Baugh, 2007). Higher wound complication rates in patients who have undergone massive weight loss than in the general population were observed at one surgical center (Sanger & David, 2006). In another study, body contouring outcomes were compared between a group of patients who lost greater than 50 pounds through diet and exercise (N = 29) and a group of patients who had undergone gastric bypass surgery (N = 429) (Gusenoff, Coon, & Rubin, 2009). For comparison between the two groups, patients were matched into pairs based upon type of contouring surgery performed, as well as demographic variables such as age, gender, and body mass index. When matched, the two groups had similar rates of complications, including wound dehiscence, seroma, cellulitis, necrosis, and hematoma. Therefore, the findings of this study do not support differences in risk associated with contouring based upon method of weight loss.

Body contouring surgery is generally successful in removing much of the excess skin patients wish to have excised. Yet, patient perceptions on the successfulness of contouring surgery may be varied. Surgeons indicate that the outcome of body contouring surgery is generally positive for most, but a minority of patients express concerns regarding the scarring they experience following contouring (Warner et al., 2009). A survey of post–bariatric surgery patients by Mitchell and colleagues (2008) echoes the variability observed among patients' satisfaction with contoured regions. Among the sample analyzed by Mitchell and colleagues (2008), some patients found the contoured sites attractive, while others found them unattractive. A German study also showed that there is often discrepancy between the patients' perceptions and the surgeons' evaluations of contouring outcomes (Rhomberg & Piza-Katzer, 2002).

In regard to patient quality of life, the outcomes of body contouring procedures are also inconsistent. Song et al. (2006) assessed various factors of quality of life among postbariatric surgery patients who had previously received body contouring surgery. After bariatric surgery, significant improvements were shown for quality of life on the Health-Related Quality of Life (HRQOL) survey; however, similar results were not found after contouring. This assessment included various factors such as physical, sexual, and work functioning. In contrast, improvements in quality of life were found after contouring surgery on the Post–Bariatric Surgery Quality of Life (PBSQOL) survey. This instrument included elements specific to bariatric surgery patients, such as feelings of attractiveness, public embarrassment about loose skin, and ease of exercise. These conflicting results suggest that the pattern of improvement in quality of life following body contouring procedures may differ across the specific categories of functioning examined. It is important, state Zuelzer and Baugh (2007), that during body contouring counseling patients are informed that they will be exchanging their excess tissue for scars. Some investigators have suggested showing patients pictures of typical outcomes following contouring (Rhomberg & Piza-Katzer, 2002). Further, these authors suggest informing patients that their scars will fade over the first year following contouring, but they will always remain visible, and in many cases unattractive. In one study with a mean of a 14-month follow-up most patients appeared to be successful in avoiding significant weight gain or loss following body contouring surgery (Shermak, Bluebond-Langner, & Chang, 2008). One small cross-sectional study that used the Body Uneasiness Test to evaluate body image attitudes found that patients who had undergone contouring following a biliopancreatic diversion (BPD) procedure had lower body uneasiness concerns than a group of post-BPD patients who were seeking contouring surgery (Pecori, Serra-Cervetti, Marinari, Migliori, & Adami, 2007). Both bariatric and plastic surgeons should be open with patients about scarring and other potential negative outcomes of contouring. By providing thorough presurgical education, patients are likely to have more realistic expectations about contouring outcomes.

Future Research and Conclusion

Additional research is needed in the area of contouring surgery following weight loss to more accurately identify patients at risk. It is difficult to quantitatively study hanging skin–related issues at the present time. To perform a well-designed, prospective study that would follow patients longitudinally, an objective method for measuring the quantity and locations of redundant skin needs to be identified. Most of the currently available technology that is suitable for research appears to be unable to accurately isolate and quantify redundant loose skin. The impact of skin laxity following bariatric surgery should also be investigated in relation to mood and quality of life, and the impact body contouring has on these variables should also be examined. Variables that affect skin turgor following weight loss should be prospectively examined so that modifiable risk factors can be addressed and patient education can be targeted toward those patients at highest risk. The literature suggests that clinicians are increasingly aware of the importance of discussing issues with hanging skin with their patients, along with the potential need for subsequent contouring surgery. Perhaps most eloquently articulated by Zuelzer and Baugh (2007, p. II), "Bariatric surgery for weight loss and plastic surgery to correct the excess skin defects should not be seen as two distinct entities, rather they should be seen as two stages of comprehensive surgical care for this patient population." Clinicians and researchers invested in the care of bariatric surgery patients will need to strive to convey this message to insurance providers, with the goal of helping more patients attain the body contouring surgery they need following weight loss surgery.

References

ASMBS. (2009). American Society for Metabolic and Bariatric Surgery fact sheet. Retrieved September 2010 from http://www.asmbs.org/.../ASMBS_Metabolic_Bariatric_Surgery_Overview_FINAL_09.pdf

ASPS (American Society of Plastic Surgeons). (2009). Plastic surgery procedural statistics. Retrieved November 2010 from http://www.plasticsurgery.org/Media/Statistics.html

BOLD (Bariatric Outcomes Longitudinal Database), Surgical Review Corporation. Accessed July 6, 2011. http://www.surgicalreview.org/bold/overview

Borud, L. J., & Warren, A. G. (2007). Modified vertical abdominoplasty in the massive weight loss patient. *Plastic and Reconstructive Surgery, 119,* 1911–1921.

Gusenoff, J. A., Coon, D., & Rubin, J. P. (2009). Implications of weight loss method in body contouring outcomes. *Plastic and Reconstructive Surgery*, *123*, 373–376.

Gusenoff, J. A., Messing, S., O'Malley, W., & Langstein, H. N. (2008). Patterns of plastic surgical use after gastric bypass: Who can afford it and who will return for more. *Plastic and Reconstructive Surgery*, *122*, 951–958.

Kenkel, J.M. (Ed). (2006). Body contouring surgery after massive weight-loss supplement. *Plastic and Reconstructive Surgery*, 117(Supp.), 3S–86S.

McGohan, L.D. (2007). Body contouring following major weight loss. *Journal of Continuing Education in Nursing*, 38: 103–104.

Mechanick, J., Kushner, R. F., Sugerman, H. J., Gonzalez-Campoy, J. M., Collazo-Clavell, M. L., Guven, S. et al. (2008). American Association of Clinical Endocrinologists, the Obesity Society, and American Society for Metabolic and Bariatric Surgery medical guidelines for clinical practice for the perioperative nutritional, metabolic, and nonsurgical support of the bariatric surgery patient. *Surgery for Obesity and Related Diseases*, *4*, S109–S184.

Mitchell, J. E., Crosby, R. D., Ertelt, T. W., Marino, J. M., Sarwer, D. B., Thompson, J. K. et al. (2008). The desire for body contouring surgery after bariatric surgery. *Obesity Surgery*, *18*, 1308–1312.

Pecori, L., Serra-Cervetti, G.G., Marinari, G. M., Migliori, F., & Adami, G. F. (2007). Attitudes of morbidly obese patients to weight loss and body image following bariatric surgery and body contouring. *Obesity Surgery*, *17*, 68–73.

Rhomberg, M., & Piza-Katzer, H. (2002). Plastic reconstructive operations after weight loss through gastric banding. *Chirurg*, *73*, 918–923.

Sanger, C., & David, L. R. (2006). Impact of significant weight loss on outcome of body-contouring surgery. *Annals of Plastic Surgery*, *56*, 9–13.

Shermak, M. A., Bluebond-Langner, R., & Chang, D. (2008). Maintenance of weight loss after body contouring surgery for massive weight loss. *Plastic and Reconstructive Surgery*, *121*, 2114–2119.

Song, A. Y., Rubin, J. P., Thomas, V., Dudas, J. R., Marra, K. G., & Fernstrom, M. H. (2006). Body image and quality of life in post massive weight loss body contouring patients. *Obesity*, *14*, 1626–1636.

Tice, J. A., Karliner, L., Walsh, J., Petersen, A. J., & Feldman, M. D. (2008). Gastric banding or bypass? A systematic review comparing the two most popular bariatric procedures. *American Journal of Medicine*, *121*, 885–893.

Warner, J. P., Stacey, D. H., Sillah, N. M., Gould, J. C., Garren, M. J., & Gutowski, K. A. (2009). National bariatric surgery and massive weight loss body contouring survey. *Plastic and Reconstructive Surgery*, *124*, 926–933.

Zuelzer, H. B., & Baugh, N. G. (2007). Bariatric and body-contouring surgery: A continuum of care for excess and lax skin. *Plastic Surgical Nursing*, *27*, 3–14.

CHAPTER 12

Section 1: Preoperative
Lifestyle Intervention

MELISSA A. KALARCHIAN and MARSHA D. MARCUS

The acceptance and popularity of bariatric surgery have grown due to increases in the prevalence of obesity, advances in surgical techniques, and mounting evidence of the benefits of surgery. In light of the sharp increase in the number of bariatric surgeries performed each year, efforts to optimize patient outcomes will have a direct public health impact (Herron & Bloomberg, 2006; Kelly et al., 2005). We have argued that although bariatric surgery is an undeniably powerful intervention, patients would benefit from lifestyle interventions to promote compliance to the behavioral changes required consequent to surgery (Kalarchian & Marcus, 2003). This chapter will describe the rationale for and content of a preoperative lifestyle intervention developed specifically for bariatric surgery patients. There is compelling evidence to suggest that modest preoperative weight loss in the context of a comprehensive lifestyle intervention will minimize complications after operation and promote self-regulation of eating and activity behaviors needed for long-term weight loss (Kalarchian & Marcus, 2009, 2010).

Preparing Patients for Bariatric Surgery

In clinical practice, bariatric surgery programs vary in their approaches to preparing patients for surgery. Published clinical reports are sparse, but do suggest that preoperative lifestyle interventions are well received by patients. For example, response to a 6-week presurgery program including psychoeducation, a liquid diet, exercise, and behavioral modification techniques included high satisfaction and perceived usefulness (Brandenburg & Kotlowski, 2005). Evidence also suggests that preoperative weight loss is safe and achievable (Dolfing, Wolffenbuttel, ten Hoor-Aukema, & Schweitzer, 2005).

In the United States, insurance carriers frequently require patients to document participation in a "medically supervised diet" before approving patients for bariatric surgery. Available data suggest that this type of insurance requirement is not reliably associated with preoperative weight loss (Ochner, Puma, Raevuori, Teixeira, & Geliebter, 2010). Additionally, clinical reports suggest that an insurance-mandated preoperative diet does not reduce complications or improve weight loss after operation (Jamal et al., 2006; Ochner et al., 2010). Moreover, such programs may increase dropout among individuals who are mandated to participate (Jamal et al., 2006). Thus, there is a need for well-designed, hypothesis-driven, prospective studies to inform efforts to prepare patients for weight loss surgery.

Benefits of Preoperative Weight Loss

Severity of obesity and obesity-related comorbidities have been associated with adverse outcomes after bariatric surgery (Ballantyne et al., 2004; Jamal et al., 2005; Livingston & Ko, 2002), and there is also evidence to suggest that preoperative weight loss carries benefits. Preoperative weight loss makes surgery technically easier to perform with reduced liver volume (Colles, Dixon, Marks, Strauss, & O'Brien, 2006) and fewer perioperative complications (Alvarado et al., 2005; Becouarn, Topart, & Ritz, 2010; Liu, Sabnis, & Chand, 2005; Liu, Sabnis, Forsyth, & Chand, 2005; Riess, Baker, Lambert, Mathiason, & Kothari, 2008). Thus, there is growing clinical consensus that patients should be advised to lose weight immediately prior to operation to reduce risks and complications (Lehman Center Weight Loss Surgery Expert Panel, 2005; Tarnoff, Kaplan, & Shikora, 2008).

There also is some evidence that preoperative weight loss carries benefits for patients after operation. A recent meta-analysis (Livhits et al., 2009) concluded that weight loss before bariatric surgery is associated with greater weight loss postoperatively (when lower-quality studies are excluded) and might help to identify patients who will have better compliance after surgery. However, this review was limited due to the heterogeneity of available studies on this topic.

There has been just one published prospective randomized trial to evaluate whether preoperative weight loss results in better outcomes after bariatric surgery (Alami et al., 2007). Patients undergoing laparoscopic gastric bypass (GBP) (N = 100) were randomized to a group with a 10% preoperative weight loss requirement or to a group that had no weight loss requirement. Preoperative weight loss was associated with significantly decreased operative time and greater weight loss at 3 months after operation. However, by 6 months after operation, the groups had similar resolution of comorbidities and percent excess weight loss, calling into question whether preoperative weight loss carries longer-term benefits.

Although numerous studies have documented the short-term benefits of presurgery weight loss, the impact on longer-term outcomes remains unclear, and many questions remain unanswered (Kalarchian & Marcus, 2009). Should patients be encouraged or required to lose weight? And if so, how much weight? With what dietary intervention? Over what period of time? Do the potential benefits of preparative weight loss vary depending on initial BMI, patient demographics, surgical technique, or other factors? In particular, we have been interested in whether a preoperative weight loss in the context of a 6-month comprehensive lifestyle intervention emphasizing behavioral self-management will optimize short- and longer-term outcomes after operation.

Lifestyle Interventions

Lifestyle interventions focus on systematic utilization of behavioral strategies to help individuals lose weight (Wadden, Crerand, & Brock, 2005). Specifically, goals are to reduce overall calorie intake and increase energy expenditure. Goals are tailored to the individual and broken down into small steps. Motivational interviewing techniques may be used to enhance motivation and reduce ambivalence about behavior change (Miller & Rollnick, 2002). Relapse prevention techniques (Marlatt & Gordon, 1985) are used to help patients anticipate challenges and maintain behavior changes over time.

There has been a vast amount of research on behavioral weight management. A comprehensive program including diet, exercise, and behavior modification techniques induces loss of approximately 10% of initial weight in 4 to 6 months (Wadden, Butryn, & Byrne, 2004). Weight losses of this magnitude have been associated with significant short-term improvements in obesity-related health parameters such as a reduction in the incidence of diabetes in persons at high risk (Knowler et al., 2002). Lifestyle intervention has also been associated with short-term improvements in cardiovascular risk among severely overweight individuals (Goodpaster et al., 2010). However, strictly behavioral approaches have not led to the large, sustained weight loss needed to achieve long-term health benefits for severely obese patients.

Integrating Lifestyle Intervention With Surgery

Despite the limitations in the effectiveness of behavioral interventions alone, long-term behavioral self-management is needed to sustain the benefits of surgery (Kalarchian & Marcus, 2003). Thus there is a need to integrate lifestyle approaches into the multidisciplinary care of patients before and after bariatric surgery. This is compatible with the view of obesity as a chronic health condition requiring ongoing management.

Bond and colleagues (2004) make three major recommendations for a multidisciplinary, health behavior treatment that combines surgical and nonsurgical techniques. First, bariatric surgery should be framed as having the potential to grant patients "a new lease on life" in which permanent weight loss depends on taking personal responsibility for one's health. Second, theory-driven behavioral change interventions to promote increases in new healthy behaviors and decreases in unhealthy behaviors should be implemented before and after surgery, with appreciation that patients may progress through different stages. Third, behavior change interventions and surgery should be viewed as two facets of a comprehensive, multidisciplinary treatment approach to a chronic and refractory disorder. Our approach is consistent with these recommendations in that patients are encouraged to self-manage behavior change prior to operation, with surgery as a "tool" to aid them in sustaining the changes necessary for longer-term weight control.

We have adapted a behavioral weight management program specifically for bariatric surgery patients. As shown in Figure 12.1.1, the intervention targets eating behavior, physical activity, and psychoeducation about surgery. The intervention helps patients achieve a modest preoperative weight loss and better preparation for surgery. After operation, the intervention is expected to be associated with better compliance with recommendations from their health care team, fewer complications and behavior-related eating problems, and lower health care utilization (e.g., fewer trips to the emergency room for severe and persistent vomiting). Ultimately, we anticipate that preoperative lifestyle intervention will lead to better long-term weight loss.

Preoperative Lifestyle Intervention

Our manualized preoperative lifestyle intervention consists of 24 weekly contacts delivered over a 6-month period. Half of the contacts are delivered in face-to-face sessions lasting 1 hour each, and half are delivered by briefer telephone calls of 20 minutes' duration. Specifically, patients are seen once a week for 8 weeks, and once a month for the next 4 months, with phone calls on weeks when they are not seen face-to-face. Interventionists

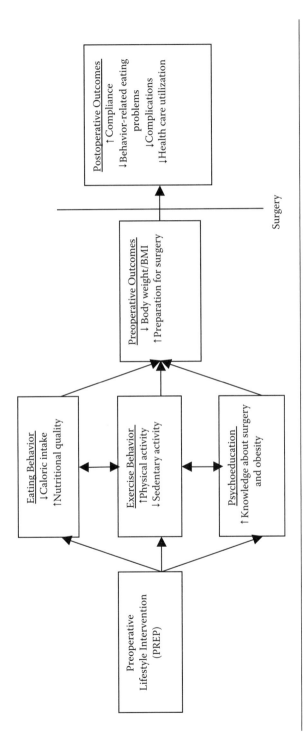

Figure 12.1.1 Model of treatment.

typically are master's-level clinicians with training in the theory and practice of cognitive-behavior therapy. They are provided with specialized training in the treatment of obesity and the behavioral aspects of weight loss surgery.

Each session begins with a private weigh-in and review of self-monitoring records (approximately 15 minutes). Diaries are reviewed with a focus on homework from the previous week and are collected by the interventionist who provides personalized, written feedback for the next session. This is followed by a didactic presentation and discussion with the clinician (approximately 30 minutes). Each session concludes with setting goals and planning homework for the next session (approximately 15 minutes). Participants receive a manual including session-by-session handouts and worksheets to reinforce the program content.

Adaptations to a standard behavioral weight management approach are based on our clinical and research experience in bariatric surgery (Kalarchian, Beagle, & Courcoulas, 2007), including focus groups for patient feedback. Some of these surgery-specific elements are highlighted in Table 12.1.1.

Psychoeducation

All participants in the program receive didactic information on obesity and weight management in general as well as bariatric surgery in particular. Patients are provided with procedure-specific information and given a list of other recommended sources for accurate information about bariatric surgery, such as books and trusted websites. Clinicians also assist patients in setting realistic expectations regarding pre- and postoperative weight loss.

Bariatric surgery is conceptualized as a tool to limit solid food intake at each sitting. Patients are educated that inadequate weight loss and weight regain are possible after surgery, especially if they are prone to certain eating patterns such as nibbling throughout the day or drinking high-calorie liquids. Patients are informed that eventually they will be able to consume a diet with a fairly wide range of healthy foods, with the exception of frequent intolerance to red meats and soft white breads.

Participants also receive information about a range of psychosocial issues relevant to bariatric surgery. Patients are encouraged to consider the impact of weight loss surgery on family, friends, and coworkers. As many report a history of abuse or trauma, patients are advised that if excess body weight has served as a buffer against unwanted sexual advances, then postoperative changes in weight and body image may create unexpected stress. Additional topics include binge eating and depression, found to be relatively common among candidates for weight loss surgery (Kalarchian, Marcus et al., 2007).

Table 12.1.1 Surgery-Specific Adaptations to Behavioral Weight Management

Basics of Behavioral Weight Management	Examples of Surgery-Specific Adaptations
Psychoeducation with information about obesity, energy balance, and weight loss	• Explain benefits of preoperative weight loss • Discuss what to expect after operation • Recommend sources for accurate information about bariatric surgery
Reduced-calorie, nutritionally balanced eating plan	• Limit eating episodes to 3–5 per day • Start a daily multivitamin to initiate pattern of compliance with supplements • Reduce or eliminate alcohol, caffeine, and soda • Begin to implement postoperative guidelines for eating
Regular physical activity	• Careful consideration of physical limitations • Introduce 10-minute bouts of physical activity daily • Set expectation that activity will become easier after postoperative weight loss and is key to weight maintenance
Stress management and social support	• Discuss impact of surgery on partner and family • Plan for telling friends and coworkers about bariatric surgery • Facilitate communication with health care team • Extra focus on mental health, especially depression
Self-monitoring, goal setting, reinforcement, stimulus control, and other behavior change techniques	• Target behavior changes that confer both pre- and postoperative benefits • Practice mindfulness to slow pace of eating to prevent postoperative complications • Prioritize multiple behavior changes such as mandatory preoperative smoking cessation and weight loss

Eating Plan

Patients are provided with a calorie counting guide and placed on a balanced 1,200- to 1,400-calorie diet, with individual modifications for patients with Type 2 diabetes. Patients are instructed to eat three meals and one to two snacks per day. Because multivitamin supplementation reduces the chance of developing postoperative nutritional deficiencies (Gasteyger, Suter, Gaillard, & Giusti, 2008), patients are directed to start taking a daily multivitamin and educated about the importance of compliance with supplements. Patients are advised as to how the eating plan can be adapted after surgery under the supervision of their surgical treatment team, and the need for lifelong medical follow-up is stressed. Clinicians repeatedly emphasize that long-term weight loss by any method requires sustained changes in eating and caloric intake.

Behavioral Change Techniques

Self-monitoring records form the foundation for efforts to initiate healthy behavior change prior to surgery. Patients are trained to record food and beverage intake daily, and self-monitoring is reviewed at each session. Additional behavior change techniques include goal setting, with an emphasis on goals that are specific, measurable, and realistic; shaping as a tool to change behaviors gradually; reinforcement, with most emphasis on self-reinforcement and techniques for obtaining social reinforcement; and stimulus control, which is used to change cues for eating and inactivity in the environment (Wadden et al., 2004). Patients also keep a weekly weight graph. The overall approach is to increase healthy behaviors and decrease unhealthy ones in order to facilitate preoperative weight loss of 1 to 2 pounds per week.

Eating Behaviors

The preoperative lifestyle intervention targets specific eating behaviors that can interfere with weight loss after bariatric surgery. It has been well established that recurrent loss of control eating after operation is associated with poorer outcomes (Niego, Kofman, Weiss, & Geliebter, 2007). For example, among 361 GBP patients, postoperative loss of control was associated with less weight loss at 12 months and 24 months postsurgery (White, Kalarchian, Masheb, Marcus, & Grilo, 2007). Because binge eating is relatively common among candidates for bariatric surgery (Niego et al., 2007), patients are taught a variety of empirically supported techniques to address loss of control before or after operation. Some of these include establishing a regular pattern of eating three meals and one to two snacks, identifying high-risk situations, and developing alternatives to overeating (Fairburn, Marcus, & Wilson, 1993). Additionally, episodes of uncontrolled overeating are often marked by eating very rapidly, eating until feeling uncomfortably full, and eating large amounts when not hungry. Because all of these behaviors can cause vomiting and other complications after operation, patients practice eating slowly, chewing well, and stopping as soon as they feel full prior to operation.

Review of self-monitoring records can also reveal other potentially problematic eating behaviors. For example, a pattern of frequent consumption of food throughout the day (sometimes called grazing or nibbling) can make it possible for patients to consume a large number of calories despite a reduced gastric capacity after operation (Saunders, 2004). Additionally, because bariatric surgery does not limit the intake of softer foods and liquids, regular consumption of items like ice cream and soda can interfere with postoperative weight control. Moreover, high-carbohydrate foods can cause dumping syndrome for patients undergoing procedures associated with malabsorption, such as GBP. Thus, patients work with clinicians to set step-wise goals for decreasing eating behaviors that may interfere with postoperative weight loss. They are discouraged from eating while watching television, in front of the computer, in restaurants, or other settings in which they may be likely to overeat.

Physical Activity Behaviors

The role of physical activity in long-term weight maintenance is emphasized throughout the program. Patients are told that physical activity will become easier after surgery, but that it is crucial to establish an activity habit beforehand. Accordingly, clinicians work with patients to introduce 10-minute bouts of activity into their day prior to operation (Jakicic, Wing, Butler, & Robertson, 1995). Many patients choose walking and are encouraged to identify a "walking buddy." Patients who have difficulty walking may identify an alternate exercise like swimming or riding a stationary bicycle. In addition, patients are encouraged to increase lifestyle activities like getting off the bus one stop early (depending on presurgery mobility). Patients typically self-monitor minutes of activity, but can also use step counts from pedometers or accelerometers, or measure distance traveled. Patients are also assisted in tracking and reducing time spent watching television and excessive time at the computer.

Finally, sometimes it is necessary to help candidates for weight loss surgery prioritize multiple health behavior changes. For example, cessation is mandatory for patients who smoke. Thus some participants aim to quit smoking and lose weight during the 6 months prior to operation.

Summary

We have described the rationale for and content of a preoperative lifestyle intervention designed to help patients achieve a modest weight loss and better preparation for surgery. In order to facilitate engagement among candidates for bariatric surgery—many of whom have physical limitations on their mobility or travel a significant distance to seek care—the intervention is delivered through a combination of face-to-face and telephone counseling sessions. The 6-month period corresponds to the minimum duration of physician-supervised dieting that many insurance companies require prior to approval for surgery in the United States. Furthermore, this duration provides sufficient time to monitor and address specific eating habits such as loss of control over eating, overconsumption of high-calorie liquids, and frequent snacking that can lead to complications and poor weight control after bariatric surgery. Patients are also assisted in establishing a daily exercise habit.

Providing bariatric surgery patients with information and support for preoperative weight loss may reduce risks, improve compliance, and optimize postoperative outcomes. However, much work remains to be done to establish the effects of diet, physical activity, and behavior change for the growing group of patients undergoing weight loss surgery, as well as to determine the most effective ways to combine surgical and nonsurgical interventions.

References

Alami, R.S., Morton, J.M., Schuster, R., Lie, J., Sanchez, B.R., Peters, A. et al. (2007). Is there a benefit to preoperative weight loss in gastric bypass patients? A prospective randomized trial. *Surgery for Obesity and Related Diseases, 3,* 141–145; discussion, 45–46.

Alvarado, R., Alami, R.S., Hsu, G., Safadi, B.Y., Sanchez, B.R., Morton, J.M. et al. (2005). The impact of preoperative weight loss in patients undergoing laparoscopic Roux-en-Y gastric bypass. *Obesity Surgery, 15,* 1282–1286.

Ballantyne, G.H., Svahn, J., Capella, R.F., Capella, J.F., Schmidt, H.J., Wasielewski, A. et al. (2004). Predictors of prolonged hospital stay following open and laparoscopic gastric bypass for morbid obesity: Body mass index, length of surgery, sleep apnea, asthma, and the metabolic syndrome. *Obesity Surgery, 14,* 1042–1050.

Becouarn, G., Topart, P., & Ritz, P. (2010). Weight loss prior to bariatric surgery is not a prerequisite of excess weight loss outcomes in obese patients. *Obesity Surgery, 20,* 574–577.

Bond, D.S., Evans, R.K., DeMaria, E.J., Meador, J.G., Warren, B.J., Shannon, K.A. et al. (2004). A conceptual application of health behavior theory in the design and implementation of a successful surgical weight loss program. *Obesity Surgery, 14,* 849–856.

Brandenburg, D., & Kotlowski, R. (2005). Practice makes perfect? Patient response to a prebariatric surgery behavior modification program. *Obesity Surgery, 15,* 125–132.

Colles, S.L., Dixon, J.B., Marks, P., Strauss, B.J., & O'Brien, P.E. (2006). Preoperative weight loss with a very-low-energy diet: Quantitation of changes in liver and abdominal fat by serial imaging. *American Journal of Clinical Nutrition, 84,* 304–311.

Dolfing, J.G., Wolffenbuttel, B.H., ten Hoor-Aukema, N.M., & Schweitzer, D.H. (2005). Daily high doses of fluoxetine for weight loss and improvement in lifestyle before bariatric surgery. *Obesity Surgery, 15,* 1185–1191.

Fairburn, C.G., Marcus, M.D., & Wilson, G.T. (1993). Cognitive-behavioral therapy for binge eating and bulimia nervosa: A comprehensive treatment manual. In C. G. Fairburn & G. T. Wilson (Eds.), *Binge eating: Nature, assessment and treatment* (pp. 361–404). New York, Guilford Press.

Gasteyger, C., Suter, M., Gaillard, R.C., & Giusti, V. (2008). Nutritional deficiencies after Roux-en-Y gastric bypass for morbid obesity often cannot be prevented by standard multivitamin supplementation. *American Journal of Clinical Nutrition, 87,* 1128–1133.

Goodpaster, B.H., Delany, J.P., Otto, A.D., Kuller, L., Vockley, J., South-Paul, J.E. et al. (2010). Effects of diet and physical activity interventions on weight loss and cardiometabolic risk factors in severely obese adults: A randomized trial. *JAMA: The Journal of the American Medical Association, 304,* 1795–802.

Herron, D.M., & Bloomberg, R. (2006). Complications of bariatric surgery. *Minerva Chirurgica, 61,* 125–139.

Jakicic, J.M., Wing, R.R., Butler, B.A., & Robertson, R.J. (1995). Prescribing exercise in multiple short bouts versus one continuous bout: Effects on adherence, cardiorespiratory fitness, and weight loss in overweight women. *International Journal of Obesity and Related Metabolic Disorders, 19,* 893–901.

Jamal, M.K., DeMaria, E.J., Johnson, J.M., Carmody, B.J., Wolfe, L.G., Kellum, J.M. et al. (2005). Impact of major co-morbidities on mortality and complications after gastric bypass. *Surgery for Obesity and Related Diseases, 1,* 511–516.

Jamal, M.K., DeMaria, E.J., Johnson, J.M., Carmody, B.J., Wolfe, L.G., Kellum, J.M. et al. (2006). Insurance-mandated preoperative dietary counseling does not improve outcome and increases dropout rates in patients considering gastric bypass surgery for morbid obesity. *Surgery for Obesity and Related Diseases, 2,* 122–127.

Kalarchian, M., Beagle, N., & Courcoulas, A. (2007). Behavioral weight control following bariatric surgery. *Bariatric Nursing and Surgical Patient Care, 2,* 189–192.

Kalarchian, M.A., & Marcus, M.D. (2003). Management of the bariatric surgery patient: Is there a role for the cognitive behavioral therapist? *Cognitive and Behavioral Practice, 10,* 112–119.

Kalarchian, M.A., & Marcus, M.D. (2009). Preoperative weight loss in bariatric surgery. *Obesity Surgery, 19,* 539.

Kalarchian, M.A., & Marcus, M.D. (2010). Preoperative weight loss in the context of a comprehensive lifestyle intervention. *Obesity Surgery, 20,* 131.

Kalarchian, M.A., Marcus, M.D., Levine, M.D., Courcoulas, A.P., Pilkonis, P.A., Ringham, R.M. et al. (2007). Psychiatric disorders among bariatric surgery candidates: Relationship to obesity and functional health status. *American Journal of Psychiatry, 164,* 328–34; quiz, 74.

Kelly, J., Tarnoff, M., Shikora, S., Thayer, B., Jones, D.B., Forse, R.A. et al. (2005). Best practice recommendations for surgical care in weight loss surgery. *Obesity Research, 13,* 227–233.

Knowler, W.C., Barrett-Connor, E., Fowler, S.E., Hamman, R.F., Lachin, J.M., Walker, E.A. et al. (2002). Reduction in the incidence of type 2 diabetes with lifestyle intervention or metformin. *New England Journal of Medicine, 346,* 393–403.

Lehman Center Weight Loss Surgery Expert Panel. (2005). Commonwealth of Massachusetts Betsy Lehman Center for Patient Safety and Medical Error Reduction Expert Panel on Weight Loss Surgery: Executive report. *Obesity Research, 13,* 205–226.

Liu, R., Sabnis, A., & Chand, B. (2005). Acute preoperative weight loss: Does it improve ease of laparoscopic bypass? *Surgery for Obesity and Related Diseases, 1,* 292–293.

Liu, R.C., Sabnis, A.A., Forsyth, C., & Chand, B. (2005). The effects of acute preoperative weight loss on laparoscopic Roux-en-Y gastric bypass. *Obesity Surgery, 15,* 1396–1402.

Livhits, M., Mercado, C., Yermilov, I., Parikh, J.A., Dutson, E., Mehran, A. et al. (2009). Does weight loss immediately before bariatric surgery improve outcomes: A systematic review. *Surgery for Obesity and Related Diseases, 5,* 713–721.

Livingston, E.H. and Ko, C.Y. (2002). Assessing the relative contribution of individual risk factors on surgical outcome for gastric bypass surgery: A baseline probability analysis. *Journal of Surgical Research, 105,* 48–52.

Marlatt, G.A., & Gordon, J.R. (1985). *Relapse prevention: Maintenance strategies in the treatment of addictive behaviors.* New York: Guilford Press.

Miller, W., & Rollnick, S. (2002). *Motivational interviewing: Preparing people for change.* New York: Guilford Press.

Niego, S.H., Kofman, M.D., Weiss, J.J., & Geliebter, A. (2007). Binge eating in the bariatric surgery population: A review of the literature. *International Journal of Eating Disorders, 40,* 349–359.

Ochner, C.N., Puma, L.M., Raevuori, A., Teixeira, J., & Geliebter, A. (2010). Effectiveness of a prebariatric surgery insurance-required weight loss regimen and relation to postsurgical weight loss. *Obesity (Silver Spring), 18,* 287–292.

Riess, K.P., Baker, M.T., Lambert, P.J., Mathiason, M.A., & Kothari, S.N. (2008). Effect of preoperative weight loss on laparoscopic gastric bypass outcomes. *Surgery for Obesity and Related Diseases, 4,* 704–708.

Saunders, R. (2004). "Grazing": A high-risk behavior. *Obesity Surgery, 14,* 98–102.

Tarnoff, M., Kaplan, L.M., & Shikora, S. (2008). An evidenced-based assessment of preoperative weight loss in bariatric surgery. *Obesity Surgery, 18,* 1059–1061.

Wadden, T.A., Butryn, M.L., & Byrne, K.J. (2004). Efficacy of lifestyle modification for long-term weight control. *Obesity Research, 12* (Suppl): 151S–162S.

Wadden, T.A., Crerand, C.E., & Brock, J. (2005). Behavioral treatment of obesity. *Psychiatric Clinics of North America, 28,* 151–170, ix.

White, M.A., Kalarchian, M.A., Masheb, R.M., Marcus, M.D., & Grilo, C.M. (2007). The prognostic significance of loss of control over eating on bariatric surgery outcomes. Paper presented at the Eating Disorders Research Society 13th Annual Meeting, Pittsburgh, PA.

Section 2: Group Preparation for Bariatric Surgery

EVA CONCEIÇÃO and PAULO MACHADO

Introduction and Treatment Context

Bariatric surgery is the treatment of choice for morbid obesity. However, individual patients' outcomes are not uniform (Hsu et al., 1998), and the literature on psychological predictors for bariatric surgery success is far from conclusive (Hsu et al., 1998; van Hout, Verschure, & van Heck, 2005; Bocchieri-Ricciardi et al., 2006; van Hout, Hagendoren, Verschure, & Van Heck, 2009; Sallet et al., 2007).

Although the research is not clear about the impact of presurgery eating disordered patterns on treatment outcomes (Mitchell et al., 2001; Saunders, 2001; Bocchieri, Meana, & Fisher, 2002; Niego, Kofman, Weiss, & Geliebter, 2007), weight regain after surgery seems to be associated with dysfunctional eating patterns and failure to comply with nutritional guidelines and prescriptions (Poole et al., 2005). In fact, eating patterns change dramatically after surgery, with new maladaptive eating problems emerging at post-surgery (Bocchieri et al., 2002), and postoperative but not preoperative loss of control over eating seems to be of better predictive value for weight outcomes (Burgmer et al., 2005; White et al., 2010).

Nonetheless, bariatric surgery necessitates an informed decision-making process, and it is important that patients understand the requirements and specificities of the treatment, taking responsibility for outcomes and taking an active role in the process (Dziurowicz-Kozlowska, Wierzbicki, Lisik, Wasiak, & Kosieradzki, 2006). Patients must be aware of the difficulties they will encounter and the adaptations that will be required in their daily life, as well as the fact that they will have to maintain these changes.

Our group has been developing a presurgery intervention aimed at preparing patients for the surgical treatment for morbid obesity, supporting them in making an informed decision, and teaching them skills that will help them cope with postsurgery demands. A cognitive-behavioral therapy (CBT) approach is used in this psychoeducational program, and the main goals are: (1) to inform about the different surgical procedures, (2) to inform about lifestyle changes that will be required by the treatment, (3) to actively involve patients in the treatment process, (4) to increase the participants' sense of responsibility for the treatment outcome, (5) to increase motivation for aftercare treatment involvement, and (6) to prepare participants for the recovery period.

This program is not designed for weight loss, improving self-esteem, or treating psychopathologic symptoms. We believe these aspects should be addressed postsurgically for those patients who need such interventions. For the purpose of this chapter, we will share our views on the guidelines and main objectives in preparing patients for bariatric surgery, as well as discuss particular concerns in dealing with this population. We assume that there is a big variability of effective strategies in addressing particular therapeutic objectives, and for this reason we will not go into much detail regarding the activites/tasks.

All participants in this program had already been cleared for surgery and have completed a psychiatric evaluation. Although screened for severe psychiatric disorders (e.g., psychotic, severe depression), some patients still present mild psychiatric symptoms (e.g., depression, anxiety). The program is open to any participant who is able to make an informed decision to participate.

The Structure of the Program

The program utilizes a group format to allow discussion and the sharing of experiences and knowledge, but it is also probably suitable for individual interventions. Sessions include small groups (N = 5 to 6) to ensure that all participants will be involved in the group activities. Therapists provide a relaxed and supporting environment, attempting to address participants' questions and doubts as many of the participants have not been well informed about the surgery.

Before entering the group, participants are interviewed by a therapist in order to obtain their history and gather personal information that might not be disclosed in a group. At the end of the first session, a small introductory packet of program materials is given to each patient, which includes general information on the structure of the program, obesity, weight and BMI, exercise, and regular weigh-ins. Participants are also asked to keep a food diary that should be turned in at the following session. This usually gives the therapist valuable information on individual eating patterns.

After the initial individual session, participants enroll in the group sessions. Each session lasts 90 minutes and is divided in two parts: (1) a brief individual assessment of weight, and discussion among the participants about changes in weight and difficulties they have encountered between sessions (30 minutes), and (2) the group session focused on a different topic each month (1 hour).

Description of the Sessions

Eating Behavior

The goal of this session is to educate participants about healthy eating habits, strategies to control their eating patterns, and how to reduce behaviors that increase daily caloric intake (such as grazing and skipping meals). We highlight strategies that will help the participant to be able to comply successfully with the postsurgery nutritional plan. We address the presurgery period as a practice time for the healthy eating style required postsurgically, and participants are encouraged to identify their own maladaptive eating behaviors and to start improving their eating patterns.

Relate Weight Loss and Regain With Energy Intake-Expenditure Balance　General information on weight and weight loss is provided. Although body weight can be influenced by several factors (e.g., genetic, biological, social, psychological), ultimately body weight is the result of the dynamic balance between energy intake and energy expenditure (Grilo, Brownell, & Stunkard, 1993). This means that in order to lose weight, the amount of energy spent has to be greater than the energy intake. Thus, weight loss can be achieved by either decreasing caloric intake or increasing activity. This session's focus is on the intake side of the equation, i.e., encouraging participants to change eating behaviors to reduce caloric intake.

Identification of Overeating　Overweight is a result of several factors, but usually it includes overeating. We address the most common forms of overeating: (1) objective and subjective binge eating: the presence of loss of control over eating; (2) grazing: eating in an unplanned and repetitive way throughout the day; and (3) food choices and eating patterns: caloric food choices and having few but large meals during the day. Participants are asked to think about a list of questions that prompt them to understand their own eating problems, such as what are their most difficult situations, foods, days, eating plans.

In our experience, it is common for participants initially to indicate that they never overeat. When this happens, we focus on the other side of the energy balance, expending energy. However, we remind participants that surgery will change eating habits and that they should be prepared to identify unhealthy eating behaviors if they emerge after surgery.

Based on their food diaries we ask participants to identity problematic eating behaviors out of a list that includes several examples: (1) when they eat (e.g., "I only have one meal (dinner) a day"), (2) how much they eat (e.g., "I usually have a second helping"), (3) what they eat ("I drink caloric drinks very often"), and (4) how they eat (e.g., "I always eat in a hurry and very rapidly").

Strategies for Reducing Daily Caloric Intake   After identifying the most common eating problems we discuss a list of general strategies to help participants improve their eating style. Practical tips are given on how to eat slower, how to eat an appropriate number of times per day, how to avoid grazing or nibbling, how to successfully finish a meal, how to better enjoy the meal, and how to control food availability.

It is also very important for participants to learn to eat in response to physical hunger, not in response to other situations, such as emotional distress or boredom, and that meals should be terminated in response to satiation. However, very frequently, obese people report that they eat for reasons other than hunger, and that they stop eating when they feel physical discomfort. Learning to identify physical hunger is thus an important skill.

Physical Exercise: Promoting an Active Lifestyle

The aim of this session is to educate participants about different ways of exercising, particularly focusing on the distinction between physical activity (being active in daily life) and physical exercise (structured physical activities such as attending the gym and participating in team sports).

Education About the Importance of Physical Activity After Surgery   In our experience, misconceptions about physical exercise are common. Some participants have tried to exercise in the past without experiencing a positive impact on weight; others think that only strenuous exercise can be helpful. Generally a sense of low self-efficacy about exercising and low motivational levels regarding physical activity tends to promote a sedentary life (Biddle & Fox, 1998; Larsen et al., 2006). Participants should be conscious that physical exercise should not been seen as a way to compensate for the amount of food eaten but part of an active and healthy lifestyle. Exercising and keeping an active lifestyle is crucial for surgery outcomes in terms of losing weight and maintaining the weight loss (Metcalf, Rabkin, Rabkin, Metcalf, & Lehman-Becker, 2005).

Distinguish Between Physical Activity and Physical Exercise   Having an active lifestyle doesn't always imply structured physical exercise. In fact, simply being active will result in a higher caloric expenditure. For a sedentary person this should be the first step: to be active in daily routines. On the other hand, physical exercise involves more intensive aerobic exercising and improves cardiovascular functioning. This type of activity is crucial for maintaining weight loss and promoting increased colonic expenditure.

Identify Strategies to Increase Physical Activity   Participants are encouraged to estimate their own activity level by calculating the number of hours that they spend being inactive and being active. Strategies to increase each participant's activity level are discussed, and barriers to physical activity are identified. Participants are asked to consider what, where, and when they wish to exercise, as well as with whom, and how frequently it is viable to do it. Since it is important to keep active throughout the years, and not only while they are losing weight, they should also consider and prepare for barriers in the future, such as changes in weather, jobs, or family structure.

Obesity Surgery: Education About Surgical Procedures and Postsurgery Changes

Preparation for surgery includes understanding each step involved in the treatment, from the recovery days to the long-term commitment to a new lifestyle. After surgery, it is common for patients to blame the type of surgery for poor outcomes instead of realizing that they might be engaging in maladaptive eating patterns, so it is important to acknowledge the different surgical procedures, their specifities, outcomes, and possible complications.

Education About Different Surgical Procedures   Relying on gastric models and images, each surgical procedure is explained. Participants are informed about the implications for recovery time, the likely amount of weight loss, the requirements after each surgical procedure, as well as common problems associated with eating.

Tips for Presurgery and Preparation for Postsurgery   Patients are encouraged to consider practical issues in the days immediately pre- and postsurgery. It is also important to think about activities and duties they will not be able to perform during recovery time. Many participants are not aware that they will have to interrupt their daily routine. Also, they should be made aware of the number of expected recovery days at the hospital, and the physical discomfort associated with surgery.

Common Problems After Surgery: Maladaptive Behaviors Versus Healthy Behaviors   Problems may emerge after surgery due to maladaptive eating. It is important for patients to be aware of potential problems with spontaneous vomiting, food intolerance, dumping, and plugging. Usually, we label these as alarm signs from their body, indicating that they are not eating properly. Patients might need to eat slower, to have special attention with some kind of foods, to take more time to eat, and to avoid long periods of time without eating. They should know that it is normal for these problems to occur after surgery, particularly when they try new foods, but it is not normal if they keep reoccurring.

It is also important to discuss maladaptive eating behaviors that might increase caloric intake, such as drinking high-calorie beverages, eating food that easily passes through the gastric band (postbanding), or persistently eating until they feel physical discomfort.

Inform Participants About Cosmetic Surgery After Bariatric Surgery   Many questions usually arise regarding loose skin after surgery, and women usually report feeling very dissatisfied with sagging breasts. These issues should be discussed and participants should be informed that the best time to undergo cosmetic surgery is when they reach a stable weight. Given that weight tends to continue to change until at least 2 years after surgery, participants are cautioned about aesthetic surgery before that time, which means that they will have to deal with the extra loose skin for a significant period of time (Mitchell et al., 2008; Sarwer et al., 2008).

Emotions, Stress, and Eating

Obese people often report eating or overeating in emotional situations. This occurs most frequently with intense emotional states, but also when feeling bored, relaxed, or happy, and in pleasant social situations with friends. In this session we focus on coping with these emotional situations, explaining the vicious cycle that maintains the behavior, and exploring alternative coping strategies that do not include food and eating. Patients need to identify their own reasons for overeating. They frequently mention that eating is the only way to calm them. Some believe that food is a way to fill a sense of emptiness; others might say that food is their only company. One of the aims of this session is to challenge these preconceived notions about the role of food. Without denying the reinforcing and pleasant role of food in our daily lives, we help participants to understand that eating might have become the default response to stressful or emotional events. Giving this framework, we discuss alternative ways to cope with emotionally charged situations.

Education About Emotional Stress   We start with a brief explanation about the dynamic relationship between thoughts, feelings, and behaviors. The main point is to help participants understand that what they think about a particular situation influences the way they feel and behave in response to that situation, and that this cycle tends to be perpetuated and reinforced. Thus, emotions (e.g., stress, happiness, boredom) are related to what we think about situations, and usually trigger a certain behavior such as eating. Changing one of these three components will change the way one reacts to emotions.

Identify Emotional Situations Related to Eating   Based on the food diaries and on their own experience, participants are asked to identify emotions associated with eating, and to understand the role they have assigned to food and eating. They are encouraged to question their eating habits; for example: Do I eat when: (1) I have nothing to do? (2) Instead of shouting and getting irritated with someone? (3) When I am sad or feel lonely?

Promoting Realistic Goals and Expectations About Surgery Outcomes
In order to keep patients motivated throughout the postsurgical period it is important for them to set realistic goals, not only regarding expected weight loss, but also related to changes in daily routine and life in general (van Hout, Verschure, & van Heck, 2005). For example, a patient might remember a period of his or her life when his or her weight was in the normal range, but he or she was also younger, had a different job, and different social and family responsibilities. Others might assume they will become a totally different person after losing weight, believing that life will be much better. Some even think that the surgery is the magical solution that will work by itself. These expectations need to become realistic (what targets are possible to achieve) and real (how these targets will impact their real life).

Education About the Importance of Realistic Expectations   Knowing what to expect is the best way to avoid frustration in the process of change. It helps one to assess the changing process and to understand if additional help is needed to obtain successful outcomes.

Different changes will occur. Some will be, indeed, directly related to the weight loss, such as mobility and feeling more energetic. Some will require additional effort and planning, such as regular eating, different food selection, and more exercise. The rate of weight loss is an important issue and can be stressful, as patients do not lose weight at the same rate in the postsurgical period. After the initial drastic weight loss patients tend to feel anxious about losing less weight each month, and want to maintain their weight loss rate. It is crucial to individually discuss how long it is expected to take for them to achieve their target body weight, and that weight loss is an individual process.

Identifying Individual Meanings for Success and Failure   It is very important for participants to understand what the meaning of success for them is, and what they expect in order to consider the surgery worthwhile. We encourage them to think and make a list of their own indicators of success.

Self-Concept and Self-Care
With weight loss, patients will generally feel better about their own bodies, and excited by other people's compliments. Continuous reinforcement by others and significant changes in appearance due to weight loss put a great

deal of attention on body image, and sometimes shifts the attention away from other important aspects of self-worth. It is important for bariatric surgery patients to realize that they can start feeling better about other aspects of their self-image, as they should understand that better self-esteem doesn't only involve losing weight. Very often, they can start feeling better about themselves regardless of their weight loss.

Understanding the Main Aspects to Incorporate the Individual Self-Worth System   We first present the concept of self-worth and discuss examples using other people. We include significant others, persons that they admire or that they dislike, including public figures, as well as people they idealize. This shows that, very often, the way they evaluate themselves is significantly different from how they evaluate other people, and that weight is almost never mentioned when evaluating others.

Based on a worksheet we ask the participants to indicate the slices on a pie graph corresponding to the aspects of their life that they use for self-evaluation. The variability and size of the slices are discussed.

Education About Body Image and Self-Concept   Despite efforts to expand self-worth, body image plays an important role in the self-concept of the obese patient (Bocchieri et al., 2002), as it is a result of multiple factors including developmental issues, past experiences, the present environment, and even the season of the year.

Education About Body Checking and "Feeling Fat"   The concepts of body checking and weight avoidance are discussed during this activity as dysfunctional mechanisms of weight control. Since these behaviors usually focus the attention on unsatisfactory body parts, they increase preoccupation and anxiety about weight and body image, generally leading to feelings of low self-esteem. Moreover, avoiding weighing will perpetuate these concerns by lack of confrontation with one's body image and weight. Ultimately, these behaviors relate to "feeling fat" that result mostly from these intensive concerns with body weight and body image, and least from "being fat." To illustrate these concepts, and with the support of a worksheet, participants are encouraged to make a list of things or situations that make them "feel fat" and "feel good" about their appearance.

Promoting an Adequate Social Support System

In this session we invite significant others to participate. Often we find out that others have not supported the decision to undergo surgery, and are not knowledgeable of the details of the procedure. Nonetheless, these individuals influence the changing process, and can facilitate adaptation to a healthier lifestyle or hinder the process if not supportive.

It is not always easy to find a significant other is available to participate in the session, nor is it possible to have all of them present. Nonetheless, participants are expected to identify the people that might help in the surgery process, as well as who might create challenging situations.

Address the Possible Impact of Surgery on Others　During the recovery period, significant others might need to be responsible for some tasks that the participant will not be able to complete, and it is very important that they are prepared in advance for this. Moreover, some patients find that they need to restructure their daily routine in order to accommodate their new eating pattern and exercise activities, which might impact the family routines as well. Participants are invited to consider the impact of these changes on significant others' lives.

Significant Others' Remaining Doubts Regarding Surgery　It is important for significant others to be aware of the importance of undergoing surgery, and to address their own beliefs (at times based on unreliable information), and to emphasize the importance of their role in a successful outcome.

Conclusion

Given the variability in the individual trajectories and outcomes and the extreme change in eating patterns with surgery (Bocchieri et al., 2002, Larsen et al., 2004; Mitchell et al., 2001) it seems that postoperative behaviors are the strongest predictors of treatment outcome (Burgmer et al., 2005; White et al., 2010). However, bariatric surgery requires an important commitment to a lifetime change that should go through an informed decision making process, in which preparation is crucial. Nonetheless continuous and long-term monitoring is imperative, and systematic follow-up should be highlighted in the treatment process to continuously detection of problems and prevention of weight regain.

References

Biddle, S.J., & Fox, K.R. (1998). Motivation for physical activity and weight management. *International Journal of Obesity Related Metabolic Disorders*, 22, S39–S47.

Bocchieri, L.E., Meana, M., & Fisher, B.L. (2002). A review of psychosocial outcomes of surgery for morbid obesity. *Journal of Psychosomatic Research*, 52, 155–165.

Bocchieri-Ricciardi, L.E., Chen, E.Y., Munoz, D., Fischer, S., Dymek-Valentine, M., Alverdy, J.C. et al. (2006). Pre-surgery binge eating status: Effect on eating behavior and weight outcome after gastric bypass. *Obesity Surgery*, 16, 1198–1204.

Burgmer, R., Grigutsch, K., Zipfel, S., Wolf, A.M., de Zwaan, M., Husemann, B. et al. (2005). The influence of eating behavior and eating pathology on weight loss after gastric restriction operations. *Obesity Surgery, 15*, 684–691.

Dziurowicz-Kozlowska, A.H., Wierzbicki, Z., Lisik, W., Wasiak, D., & Kosieradzki, M. (2006). The objective of psychological evaluation in the process of qualifying candidates for bariatric surgery. *Obesity Surgery, 16*, 196–202.

Grilo, C., Brownell, K., & Stunkard, A. (1993). The metabolic and psychological importance of exercise in weight control. In A. Stunkard & T. Wadden (Eds.), *Obesity: Theory and therapy* (2nd ed., (pp. 253–273)). New York: Raven Press.

Hsu, L.K.G., Benotti, P.N., Dwyer, J., Roberts, S.B., Saltzman, E., Shikora, S. et al. (1998). Nonsurgical factors that influence the outcome of bariatric surgery: A review. *Psychosomatic Medicine, 60*, 338–346.

Larsen, J.K., Geenen, R., van Ramshorst, B., Brand, N., Hox, J.J., Stroebe, W. et al. (2006). Binge eating and exercise behavior after surgery for severe obesity: A structural equation model. *International Journal of Eating Disorders, 39*, 369–375.

Metcalf, B., Rabkin, R.A., Rabkin, J.M., Metcalf, L.J., & Lehman-Becker, L.B. (2005). Weight loss composition: The effects of exercise following obesity surgery as measured by bioelectrical impedance analysis. *Obesity Surgery, 15*, 183–186.

Mitchell, J.E., Crosby, R.D., Ertelt, T.W., Marino, J.M., Sarwer, D.B., Thompson, J.K. et al. (2008). The desire for body contouring surgery after bariatric surgery. *Obesity Surgery, 18*, 1308–1312.

Mitchell, J.E., Lancaster, K.L., Burgard, M.A., Howell, L.M., Krahn, D.D., Crosby, R.D. et al. (2001). Long-term follow-up of patients' status after gastric bypass. *Obesity Surgery, 11*, 464–468.

Niego, S.H., Kofman, M.D., Weiss, J.J., & Geliebter, A. (2007). Binge eating in the bariatric surgery population: A review of the literature. *International Journal of Eating Disorders, 40*, 349–359.

Poole, N.A., Atar, A.A., Kuhanendran, D., Bidlake, L., Fiennes, A., McCluskey, S. et al. (2005). Compliance with surgical after-care following bariatric surgery for morbid obesity: A retrospective study. *Obesity Surgery, 15*, 261–265.

Sallet, P.C., Sallet, J.A., Dixon, J.B., Collis, E., Pisani, C.E., Levy, A. et al. (2007). Eating behavior as a prognostic factor for weight loss after gastric bypass. *Obesity Surgery, 17*, 445–451.

Sarwer, D.B., Wadden, T.A., Moore, R.H., Baker, A.W., Gibbons, L.M., Raper, S.E. et al. (2008). Preoperative eating behavior, postoperative dietary adherence and weight loss following gastric bypass surgery. *Surgery for Obesity and Related Diseases, 4*, 640–646.

Saunders, R. (2001). Compulsive eating and gastric bypass surgery: What does hunger have to do with it? *Obesity Surgery, 11*, 757–761.

van Hout, G.C.M., Hagendoren, C.A.J.M., Verschure, S.K.M., & Van Heck, G.L. (2009). Psychosocial predictors of success after vertical banded gastroplasty. *Obesity Surgery, 19*, 701–707.

van Hout, G.C.M., Verschure, S.K.M., & van Heck, G.L. (2005). Psychosocial predictors of success following bariatric surgery. *Obesity Surgery, 15*, 552–560.

White, M.A., Kalarchian, M.A., Masheb, R.M., Marcus, M.D., & Grilo, C.M. (2010). Loss of control over eating predicts outcomes in bariatric surgery patients: A prospective, 24-month follow-up study. *Journal of Clinical Psychiatry, 71*, 175–184.

Section 3: Next Step—A Bariatric Psychological Aftercare Program

KIM T. LAHAISE and JAMES E. MITCHELL

For those who struggle with obesity, bariatric surgery has been shown to facilitate significant weight loss, increase physical mobility, decrease negative effects of health-related conditions, and decrease risk of premature death. Significant weight loss is often associated with improved mood, self-esteem, self-confidence, assertiveness, and interpersonal relationships, as well as increased socialization and employability (van Gemert, Severigns, Greve, Groenman, & Soeters, 1998). While bariatric surgery has been shown to be one of the most effective therapies for obesity, with the lowest rate of recidivism (Pomerantz & Peters, 1987), it is an extremely intense and complex process to go through, and individuals may need help, support, and guidance to adapt to the changes they encounter, particularly after the 18- to 24-month "honeymoon" phase of weight loss after gastric bypass procedures.

Eating problems can pose one of the most significant challenges to the bariatric patient. Binge eating behavior is common among individuals who are morbidly obese and may recur after surgery, at times referred to as loss of control eating, since it is usually impossible to eat a large amount of food. Binge eating is also associated with weight regain (Hsu et al., 1998).

Although presurgical psychoeducation and support are integral parts of most bariatric programs, postsurgical psychological support appears to be critically important as well. Bariatric patients may struggle in adjusting to the posthoneymoon phase when their appetite returns, weight starts to creep up, or it becomes more difficult to continue engaging in healthy lifestyle behaviors. The notion that one's obesity or disordered eating patterns may be caused by, or at least are related to, current or chronic psychological conflicts and psychosocial issues, and not just a genetic predisposition (Kinzl, Trefalt, Fiala, & Biebl, 2002), can be disheartening. Because of this, individuals may be primed to accept psychological interventions in this postsurgical phase.

There are varying opinions about the effectiveness of postsurgical support versus structured psychotherapeutic interventions. It has been shown that attendance at support group meetings is associated with a higher percent decrease in BMI (Orth, Madan, Taddeucci, Coday, & Tichansky, 2008;

Elakkary, Elhorr, Aziz, Gazayerli, & Silva, 2006). Although no differences in weight loss were found in those who attended a structured support group versus those who did not, Rabner and Greenstein (1993) found that those who attended the groups were better informed about nutritional issues, made wiser food choices, and were more physically active. Van Hout, Verschure, and van Heck (2005) showed that psychological support after surgery increases patient's compliance and success with weight loss goals. Saunders (2004) employed a structured cognitive-behavioral program targeting binge eating symptoms and found that this was helpful in increasing awareness of problematic eating patterns and developing more adaptive coping skills. Stewart, Olbrisch, and Bean (2010) utilized an 8-week pilot group therapy program, combining cognitive-behavioral and motivation enhancement interventions, to help individuals struggling with weight regain. Significant behavioral changes, enhanced motivation and confidence, and weight loss were found in those who attended the group series. Finally, Leahey, Bond, Irwin, Crowther, and Wing (2009) showed that more individuals attended a postsurgical behavioral intervention group than those who were referred presurgery. Identifying a "teachable moment" was viewed as crucial, as those who already had the surgery were more willing to attend the first session, attended more total sessions, and were more likely to complete the program.

At the Sanford Center of Excellence Bariatric Program in Fargo, North Dakota, we have been running an aftercare treatment group called Next Step for almost 3 years. We continue to learn a great deal from each group and are continually modifying our program in order to meet our patients' needs. Individuals are referred to the group via their health care provider, usually a bariatric surgeon or nurse practitioner, primary care physician, or dietitian. Group members must be at least 3 months postsurgery in order to ensure ample recovery time from their surgery. A majority of these individuals have undergone the Roux-en-Y gastric bypass, while a handful have undergone a lap band procedure. Thus far, we have been unable to separate out the groups according to type of surgery or number of months postsurgery due to relatively small group numbers. As mentioned in previous studies (Kinzl et al., 2002), a majority of individuals may express interest and ask for postsurgical psychological treatment after their surgery, but follow-through with this is at times limited. In our case, about 50% of those referred to Next Step actually enlist in a group and attend the majority of sessions.

Most individuals are referred to Next Step to address significant eating or mood problems following surgery, as well as difficulty adapting to the many lifestyle changes. Many struggle with the return of previous problematic eating behaviors, such as binge eating or excessive sweet eating, or the fear that these patterns will return. Because cognitive-behavior therapy has been shown to be efficacious in addressing binge eating disorder, as well as treating various mood and stress management issues, Next Step is largely based on a cognitive-behavioral model. Actual goals of each group vary and are as patient specific as possible. Although initial goals for bariatric surgery include significant weight loss, decrease in medical risk factors, and improved quality of life, ongoing weight loss is not guaranteed in the group, and in some cases, patients are challenged to reassess their goals for further weight loss as they may be unrealistic. In group, we highlight the need to keep expectations realistic and help maintain a strong motivation for change over time.

Next Step consists of 1-hour group sessions over the course of 12 consecutive weeks. We include both a psychologist and a licensed registered dietitian to facilitate each group. To have a dietitian present at each group has been invaluable as nutrition questions can be immediately addressed in any session and members receive the most up-to-date information from a specialist.

Each group session in Next Step is divided into three periods. The first is a brief check-in, giving members time to briefly discuss any significant events, accomplishments, or hardships over the past week. Occasionally, this portion can take up a great deal of time, so there is a definite need to be time conscious. The second period is psychoeducational in nature, in which either the psychologist or the dietitian presents information regarding the topic of the day. Discussions can get lively during this period and will often take the majority of the hour. The final period is to provide homework assignments and reminders to consider one's personal goals for the week and begin planning how to work on them.

At the initial session, a manual is provided to each group member. Several components of our manual were adapted from Dr. James Mitchell and Dr. Lorraine Swan-Kremeier's Binge Eating Disorder Program. The first chapter includes the dates of each group and proposed topics for each session. It also includes an introduction to the group process and a review of bariatric postsurgical issues. We found that it appears to work best to provide one chapter at a time, so that members can focus and give ample attention to the topic at hand. A new chapter is then provided each week, and that topic is reviewed at the next session. Chapters are purposely kept brief and usually average between 8 and 12 typed pages. While there is a proposed agenda for each session, the schedule is flexible and additional topics can be added or switched around in order to accommodate members' needs.

The first Next Step session begins with introductions of the facilitators and group members. There is a brief review of general housekeeping issues, such as start and stop times, location of restrooms, expected attendance (at least 80% of groups), and general expectations of group members (i.e., arrive on time, bring manual each week, read chapter ahead of time, complete weekly assignments, and participate in group discussions). An integral part of the group therapy process is defined as learning from other group members, supporting each other, and providing open and honest feedback to each other. At the first and last sessions, individual weights are recorded and documented in the medical chart. A brief group note is also documented by the psychologist in the medical chart each week.

At the beginning of the first session and again at the final group, members are asked to complete five assessments that cover topics such as eating behaviors, binge eating, quality of life, mood, and lifestyle behaviors. Group members may complete these over the course of the first week and return them at the second session. At the last session, a brief six-item evaluation form rating the effectiveness of group topics, perceived expertise of the facilitators, and success of the program is also included. Members are also asked to provide suggestions for improving the group in the future. Due to difficulties collecting assessments after the last group, members are now expected to complete these in session.

During the first session, the rationale for utilizing the cognitive-behavioral framework and theoretical background is provided. We also discuss the importance of focusing on present-day issues related to one's bariatric surgery and identifying factors that continue to trigger negative or unwanted thoughts, feelings, or behaviors. Motivational enhancement techniques are also utilized throughout various group sessions. A number of general issues are initially reviewed, including anatomical changes that can lead to problems after eating, such as plugging and dumping, and expected patterns of weight loss. Special focus is given to problematic eating behaviors, such as binge eating, vomiting, grazing, night eating, sweet eating, and chewing and spitting. The risk for developing new eating disordered behaviors is discussed, such as difficulties that arise when those with a history of previous binge eating turn to grazing after surgery. The issue of control is dealt with frequently, especially as it pertains to eating patterns.

A large portion of each group focuses on eating behaviors, as many express difficulty with their eating patterns and report thinking a great deal about food. We often hear disappointment in members' voices as they talk about their wish that they would not have to think about food after surgery. Particular attention is given to specific problem behaviors prior to surgery and how individuals can be especially prone to returning to these same behaviors postsurgery. At the end of the first session, a goal sheet is provided for members to complete prior to Session 2. Each member is asked to identify at least one to three SMART goals (i.e., specific, measureable, action oriented, realistic, and time limited) for the next 12 weeks. Group members are also asked to consider their definition of success following bariatric surgery. Members are encouraged to seek out small, consistent changes in their quality of life, eating behaviors, ability to work, self-esteem, and relationships. Members are also asked to complete a motivational enhancement activity regarding reasons for and against changing unhealthy eating habits.

Sessions 2 and 3 focus on cognitive-behavioral skills to assist in identifying triggers to problem behaviors and how to change them. A cognitive-behavioral framework focusing on cues (e.g., social, situational, emotional, cognitive, physiological, or nutritional), responses (either thoughts, feelings, or behaviors), and positive or negative consequences is discussed in detail. Strategies to rearrange or change these cues, responses, or consequences are then discussed. Several examples are provided and members are asked to reveal their own personal experiences. Immediate thoughts, feelings, and behaviors are discussed, as well as any positive or negative consequences that may arise from eating an unplanned snack. Members are often surprised at how much the environment alone can cue them to eat or engage in other unhealthy behaviors. Being aware of these cues is the first step in being able to eventually change one's habits. Changing one's response to these triggers can involve avoiding a situation altogether, utilizing delay tactics, engaging in alternative, more adaptive behaviors, restricting exposure to these cues, or utilizing other stimulus control measures to increase the likelihood of engaging in preferred behaviors. The importance of self-reinforcement and how to provide mental or material rewards is also discussed in this session. Individuals also have time in session to identify their personal rewards that they can then utilize throughout group treatment. Handouts are given outlining each aspect of the cognitive-behavioral model, and members are challenged to consider how they can intervene in their automatic patterns.

Session 3 focuses on behavioral chains and how to use these as a coping skill to help identify and address any problematic behaviors. Examples of binge eating, uncontrolled eating, difficulty taking vitamins, or difficulty adhering to an exercise program are typically reviewed. Group members are reminded that binge eating is associated with more weight regain and should be taken as an important red flag in one's recovery process (Kalarchian et al., 2002; Mitchell et al., 2001). Several members have expressed surprise that they can have more control over their thoughts, feelings, and actions than they realized. Handouts to construct plans to deal with high-risk foods and situations are also provided in this session.

After a brief review of the week and progress update with treatment goals, the dietitian provides the majority of the information in Session 4. She reviews the most up-to-date vitamin and mineral recommendations and discusses why each one is critical for long-term health. She also problem solves with the group about ways to ensure that vitamins are taken in the most effective combination, typically at least four times throughout the day. In every group, there are usually people who are struggling with their vitamin regimen and may not be taking any at all. The dietitian also focuses on healthy eating recommendations regarding necessary protein intake, portion control, timing of meals, and liquid intake. Because members may be 6 months or 6 years postsurgery, there is significant variability in their meal plans and what they can tolerate. Members who are further out from their surgery often provide invaluable information regarding the progression of eating habits and how and when eating-related symptoms improve over time. Finally, the importance of using food logs to ensure adequate protein intake, establish a pattern of routine meals and snacks, and increase accountability of appropriate food intake is highlighted. It is recommended that members complete at least two or three food logs in the following week in order to see how close their ideal and actual eating habits match up.

The focus for Session 5 is on how to utilize the cognitive-behavioral model when dealing with possible mood or anxiety changes following bariatric surgery. It has been shown that distress about one's obesity may be a positive predictor of surgical outcome, whereas the level of severity of psychological problems is predictive of less positive results (Vallis & Ross, 1993). Initial discussion focuses on the importance of enhancing pleasant moods to help reduce problematic behaviors, how and why tracking daily moods can be helpful, and identifying specific strategies to improve mood. Goal setting, planning ahead, and setting up behavioral contracts to increase pleasant activities are also addressed. The discussion then moves to how we perceive events in our life and how thoughts and feelings affect one's behavior, in both positive and negative ways. Various examples of automatic thoughts and cognitive distortions are provided, such as polarized thinking, catastrophizing, personalization, and overgeneralizing. Instructions are given regarding how to complete an automatic thought record. Basic steps outlining how to identify specific cues to a problematic situation, evaluating thoughts that provide evidence for and against the automatic thought, reframing one's thinking, and noticing the effects of revised thought patterns are reviewed. Members are also asked to identify their typical coping skills and how they can utilize their cognitive skills in daily life.

At the end of Session 5, members are asked to write a "Dear Me" letter to briefly review with the group at next session. The general idea is to write about how their life has changed since bariatric surgery. Members can choose to focus on any aspect of their surgery, recovery process, satisfaction level, lifestyle changes, health condition, or how they feel in their new or different body. Typically, members report benefiting from this activity, as it may highlight changes that they have made, but may not have given themselves credit for, and it helps them to focus on positive aspects of their postsurgical behaviors.

Session 6 focuses on the importance of exercise and increased activity level. Members are informed about the Bariatric Exercise Coaching Program that is offered through the Cardiac Rehabilitation Department in our health system. At least 50% of group members report ongoing struggles with maintaining a consistent exercise routine. Occasionally, a member will discuss how much he or she dislikes exercise, but for the most part, members indicate that they like, or at least don't mind, exercise and want to make it a regular part of their daily regimen. Time is spent identifying possible obstacles that get in the way of maintaining a consistent exercise program. For many, body image issues ("I'm still too big to go to the gym and work out comfortably") are part of the reason for not engaging in exercise more often. Benefits of exercise are reviewed, as well as basic strategies to start increasing general activity level.

In Session 7, the focus switches to body image issues. The definition of body image and focusing on a more holistic view of how their bodies work for them and move in space is highlighted. Various factors that influence body image, such as one's home environment while growing up, others' views of weight and shape, teasing, societal pressures, eating and other health habits, and one's own view of their weight, shape, and appearance are all discussed. Group members are asked to answer questions in the manual pertaining to how they view their body, how recent weight changes may have impacted this, and the importance of physical appearance in their life prior to their surgery compared to now. We discuss how to determine a healthy weight and what factors enter into this equation. Often group members will return to a predetermined weight goal set before surgery, and even though they may be just a few pounds away from this, they cannot accept their current body image until the scale matches up with their ideal goal weight. Cognitive strategies are utilized to challenge and help change one's distorted thoughts about their body image. Finally, all members engage in a perceptual activity in which they estimate actual versus ideal waist circumference size. The vast majority of members tend to overestimate their actual size. These data are used when discussing how misperceptions can occur when focusing on one's weight, size, or appearance.

Session 8 focuses on relationship issues and difficulties following bariatric surgery. Although some members deny concerns about this, many notice at least subtle changes with family, friends, or coworkers. Having to deal with a jealous partner due to weight loss or a disapproving partner because they now are more assertive may be a new experience for these individuals. Issues regarding outright sabotage by loved ones in maintaining healthy eating habits can also occur. "Intimate saboteurs"

(Andrews, 1997) may try to hamper, hurt, or subvert an individual's goal of achieving a healthy body weight. Andrews goes on to say that although a bariatric patient has chosen change, if family or friends are disturbed or threatened by it, they may resist the change, as it will disrupt their position of power or attachment in the relationship. On the other hand, if family or friends experience the change as positive and adjust to it, relationships can be greatly enhanced. Regarding marital relationships, research has shown that if a marriage is solid prior to surgery, couples are likely to weather any changes related to the surgery. However, in those relationships that are dysfunctional, there may be difficulty adapting to a patient's positive changes after surgery, and this could ultimately lead to the demise of the partnership (Stunkard, Stinett, Jordan, & Smoller, 1986).

There is a primary focus in Session 8 on teaching assertiveness skills and on how members may utilize these skills differently before and after surgery. Many reveal increased confidence levels following significant weight loss and feel more able to be assertive with their loved ones, at work, or in social situations. However, the aftermath of doing this can take one by surprise, as the situation may still not work out like they had hoped; they don't get what they asked for, or in some cases, they say the situation only worsens now that they have asserted themselves. Attention is paid to getting one's opinion across in a tactful, respectful manner, while not guaranteeing a positive outcome.

Like relationship difficulties, self-esteem issues can be extremely challenging to address in an hour-long group. In Session 9, group members are reminded that this will only be an introduction to self-esteem, and they are encouraged to continue reading about self-esteem outside of group. Members rate their self-esteem both before surgery and at the present time. Rarely does anyone report a lower self-esteem following surgery, and usually it is a person who is struggling with ongoing medical complications postsurgery. There is a brief discussion of what factors may lead to low self-esteem, signs of low self-esteem, and characteristics found in people with high self-esteem. A self-concept inventory is provided for members to complete at home. Initially, both positive and negative comments are elicited regarding one's physical appearance, relationships, personality characteristics, performance at work, school, or home, intellect, romance, and friends. After completing this step, members are asked to go through the inventory again and attempt to elaborate on their strengths and neutralize any negatives. An example list of positive affirmations is provided.

Session 10 focuses on stress management. Again, although this is a topic to which one could devote hours, we have only 1 hour to review basic tenets of stress management, to discuss how stress affects one physically, mentally, emotionally, and behaviorally, and to review differences between major and minor stresses. Brief psychoeducation is provided regarding managing stress via active problem solving or active coping. A five-step approach to problem solving is reviewed that includes identifying the problem, establishing goals, brainstorming possible solutions, identifying and trying out a plan, and reviewing outcomes. Principles of self-acceptance are discussed.

The final two sessions are focused on reviewing previous topics, providing additional information based on members' requests, and addressing relapse prevention strategies. Members are asked to identify what has been most helpful thus far in group and to provide examples of how they are actively using their skills at home and work. Planning ahead is a primary skill that is reviewed several times throughout the group series. To avoid a possible lapse or full-blown relapse, planning skills appear to be essential in maintaining healthy lifestyle behaviors. The group discusses how to reduce or avoid stressful and high-risk situations. Typical fears of gaining back too much weight are reviewed in detail, as well as how to utilize the skills learned in each session. There are usually concerns raised about not being able to attend a weekly group anymore and not having someone to be accountable to. Several groups have elected to stay connected outside of sessions, and this appears to be going well. Some groups provide each other with their phone numbers or e-mails, although this is not endorsed one way or the other by the group facilitators.

Summary

Although we would prefer to have 8–10 group members, we are typically averaging about 4–6 members by the end of 12 sessions. Several times, members have asked for longer sessions, but because sessions are billed through a person's insurance company and most only pay for a 60-minute group therapy session, we adhere to this timeframe. Feedback from the group has been extremely positive thus far. The primary finding has been a decrease in binge eating behavior over the course of treatment. Because binge eating is related to future weight regain, this appears to be a significant finding and one that remains important to our members.

References

Andrews, G. (1997). Intimate saboteurs. *Obesity Surgery, 7,* 445–448.

Elakkary, E., Elhorr, A., Aziz, F., Gazayerli, M.M., & Silva, Y.J. (2006). Do support groups play a role in weight loss after laparoscopic adjustable gastric banding? *Obesity Surgery, 16,* 331–334.

Hsu, L.K.G., Benotti, P.N., Dwyer, J., Roberts, S.B., Saltzman, E., Shikora, S. et al. (1998). Nonsurgical factors that influence the outcome of bariatric surgery: A review. *Psychosomatic Medicine, 60,* 338–346.

Kalarchian, M.A., Marcus, M.D., Wilson, G.T., Labouvie, E.W., Brolin, R.E., & LaMarca, L.B. (2002). Binge eating among gastric bypass patients at long-term follow-up. *Obesity Surgery, 12*, 270–275.

Kinzl, J.F., Trefalt, E., Fiala, M., & Biebl, W. (2002). Psychotherapeutic treatment of morbidly obese patients after gastric banding. *Obesity Surgery, 12*, 292–294.

Leahey, T.M., Bond, D.S., Irwin, S.R., Crowther, J.H., & Wing, R.R. (2009). When is the best time to deliver behavioral intervention to bariatric surgery patients: Before or after surgery? *Surgery for Obesity and Related Diseases, 5*, 99–102.

Mitchell, J.E., Lancaster, K.L., Burgard, M.A., Howell, L.M., Krahn, D.D., Crosby, R.D. et al. (2001). Long-term follow-up of patients' status after gastric bypass. *Obesity Surgery, 11*, 464–468.

Orth, W.S., Madan, A.K., Taddeucci, R.J., Coday, M., & Tichansky, D.S. (2008). Support group meeting attendance is associated with better weight loss. *Obesity Surgery, 18*, 391–394.

Pomerantz, M.A., & Peters, J. (1987, August). Gastroplasty: Pre- and postoperative counseling for the morbidly obese patient. *Medical Aspects of Human Sexuality, 21*, 89–95.

Rabner, J.G., & Greenstein, R.J. (1993). Antiobesity surgery: Is a structured support group desirable? Preliminary. *Obesity Surgery, 3*, 381–390.

Saunders, R. (2004). "Grazing": A high-risk behavior. *Obesity Surgery, 14*, 98–102.

Stewart, K.E., Olbrisch, M.E., & Bean, M.K. (2010). Back on track: Confronting post-surgical weight gain. *Bariatric Nursing and Surgical Patient Care, 5*, 179–185.

Stunkard, A.J., Stinett, J.L., Jordan, W., & Smoller, A.B. (1986). Psychological and social aspects of the surgical treatment of obesity. *American Journal of Psychiatry, 143*, 417–429.

Vallis, T.M., & Ross, M.A. (1993). The role of psychological factors in bariatric surgery for morbid obesity: Identification of psychological predictors of success. *Obesity Surgery, 3*, 346–359.

van Gemert, W.G., Severeijns, R.M., Greve, J.W.M., Groenman, N., & Soeters, P.B. (1998). Psychological functioning of morbidly obese patients after surgical treatment. *International Journal of Obesity, 22*, 393–398.

van Hout, G.C.M., Verschure, S.K.M., & van Heck, G.L. (2005). Psychosocial predictors of success following bariatric surgery. *Obesity Surgery, 15*, 552–560.

Section 4: The BaSE Program—A Videoconferencing-Based Aftercare

MARTIN TEUFEL, BERNHARD HAIN, NICOLE RIEBER,
WOLFGANG HERZOG, STEPHAN ZIPFEL, and BEATE WILD

The BaSE program consists of a 1-year manualized psychoeducational treatment after bariatric surgery. The content of the group sessions covers topics that are relevant for concerned patients. To break new ground, reach patients in rural regions, and reinforce compliance, a videoconferencing-based approach has been implemented. In this chapter, details of the intervention are described (Hain et al., 2010).

Setting, Intensity, and Duration of the Program

Over the past years, bariatric surgery has been recommended as the most effective therapy available for severely obese patients. However, to ensure long-term success after surgery, patients have to make the appropriate lifestyle changes to sustain their weight loss. For some bariatric patients, weight loss maintenance and adherence to their objectives are major problems. It has been found that patterns of disturbed eating behavior reappear after a 6-month period postsurgery and persist if no specific intervention occurs. Postoperative loss of control eating significantly predicts poorer postsurgical weight loss and psychosocial outcomes. These findings signal a need for clinical attention (Livhits et al., 2011; Papalazarou et al., 2010; Rieber et al., 2010; White, Kalarchian, Masheb, Marcus, & Grilo, 2010; van Hout & van Heck, 2009; Burgmer et al., 2005).

In the BaSE study, a 1-year group program, including face-to-face and videoconferencing-based sessions, is investigated. The structured psycho-educational aftercare is conducted in groups of up to six participants. The intervention program targets the promotion of and compliance with the required lifestyle changes.

During the year of treatment, participants receive 14 group sessions of psychoeducation (see Table 12.4.1).

The first five meetings take place biweekly and the following meetings occur at 4-week intervals (see Figure 12.4.1).

Table 12.4.1 BaSE Manual and Session Topics

Setting	Session	Topic	Aims
Group Sessions (Face-to-Face)	1	Nutrition/food intake after surgery	• Establishment of new eating behavior • Self-monitoring
	2	Living with the new anatomic condition/nutrition	• Coping strategies • Introduction of healthy nutrition
	3	Stress recognition and management	• Stress and emotional eating • Presentation of a relaxation technique • Self-monitoring
	4	Exercise and physical activity	• Theoretical basics of a health-promoting exercise routine • Nordic walking unit
	5	Introduction of videoconferencing	• Telemedicine strategies • Communication by videoconferencing and implications for the group • Operation/control of the videoconferencing systems
Videoconferencing-Based Group Sessions	6	Self-care	Mindfulness: • Pleasant activities • Conscious and structured food intake
	7	Body image	• Development of a positive body image • Perfectionism and body changes after surgery
	8	Social dimensions and conflicts	• Recognition and handling of difficult social situations
	9	Self-care	• Mindfulness, wants, and needs • Sleep hygiene • Television and computer use

Table 12.4.1 (Continued) BaSE Manual and Session Topics

Setting	Session	Topic	Aims
	10	Stress and social conflicts	• Stress management • Coping strategies, acceptance
	11	Relaxation	• Training of the relaxation techniques • Stress management
Group Sessions (Face-to-Face)	12	Exercise and physical activity	• Maintenance of activity in daily life • Nordic walking unit
	13	Nutrition/food intake and relapse prevention	• Feedback of success • Individual strengths and risks • Steps to maintaining weight
	14	Outlook	• Feedback of success • Individual strengths • Perspectives for the next year

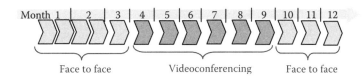

Figure 12.4.1 Time course and setting of the BaSE program.

The aim of the more intensive initial phase is the strengthening of the group coherence, which appears to have a positive effect in weight loss programs (Giel et al., 2008). The intervention begins with five face-to-face group meetings (six patients, 90 minutes), followed by six videoconference sessions in small groups (three patients, 50 minutes), and followed by another three face-to-face group sessions. Sessions are structured according to the topics that have been demonstrated to be important for post-surgery patients: information, postoperative nutrition, coping with stress, relaxation, body image, physical activity, and self-care. These topics are introduced in the face-to-face sessions and are later revisited in the video-conference sessions wherein the patients have an opportunity to discuss their experience.

The use of a telemedical intervention strategy allows patients to avoid extensive travel to specialized centers. Additionally, this approach of

Table 12.4.2 Rules and Agreements Needed to Start a Videoconferencing-Based Group Session

	Requirements
Initiation of the conference	• Everyone has to be ready on time
	• Log-in of patients and building up of the conference
General rules	• Participants speak slowly
	• Interruptions are avoided as much as possible
	• Active listening techniques are used
Session structure	A general structure of the group session is implemented:
	• Patients report status quo (physical and mental health) and current weight
	• Current topics, problems, and needs of the patients are discussed
	• Educational topics corresponding to Table 12.4.1 are addressed
Welcome and the "virtual handshake"	• Expert welcomes the patients
	• Patients get space to greet each other
	• The previously established feeling of alliance is reinforced
Farewell	• The next group meeting date and topic are anticipated
	• Expert and patients say good-bye

interactive communication helps to improve the acceptance of the treatment program in areas with poor medical infrastructure (Marziali, 2009; Teufel, Giel, & Zipfel, 2009). The goal of using new media technology is to increase compliance with the program and to facilitate the integration of necessary lifestyle changes into daily life (Elkins et al., 2005). The necessary rules and agreements needed to conduct a videoconferencing-based group session are summarized in Table 12.4.2.

Structure of Group Sessions

Every meeting consists of three parts:

1. Exchange of currently important information
2. Group work: Educational topic corresponding to Table 12.4.1
3. Homework assignments

Self-monitoring is implemented to facilitate an in-depth analysis of relevant topics. Patients exchange their experiences and discuss their individual problems. Formulations and coping strategies are discussed. The patients are taught structured diary work: Food diaries and scheduled group discussions about problems associated with eating behavior are introduced to support patients in reporting early risk-associated eating behaviors such as loss of control eating, night eating, snacking, and grazing. This also assists them to find behavioral alternatives.

Patients enter their weight on a weekly basis on a therapeutic Web home page. For feedback, an automatic response graph illustrates the course of their body weight. This serves as a basis for subsequent group sessions. Previous studies showed that weight monitoring has a positive influence on weight loss and particularly on long-term weight maintenance. Telephone contacts are offered for crisis situations (Algazi, 2000; Wild et al., 2011).

The Next Steps: Assignments

During the course of the group meetings, a significant amount of time is allotted to address any perceived changes related to weight loss in the patient's everyday life. It is recommended that alternative behaviors that are discussed during the group sessions will be practiced between the meetings. The results and any difficulties encountered are discussed at the following meeting.

Interdiscipline Approach

Using various modules of treatment, psychotherapists/psychiatrists, nutritionists, physiotherapists, and surgeons work together in the aftercare program. Within the scope of the educational component of the program patients are allowed to request specific personal information and receive the relevant expert answers (Marcus & Elkins, 2004).

Topics of the Aftercare Manual

The main objectives of the aftercare program are to assist the patient to perceive and understand physical changes, to strengthen his or her awareness of related psychological processes, to improve his or her self-efficacy, and to reinforce adherence to relevant lifestyle changes after surgery (Wing, Tate, Gorin, Raynor, & Fava, 2006).

The manual is based on the assumption that long-term weight reduction and weight maintenance can be best achieved if modifications in the areas of nutrition/food, activity/exercise, stress, and social interactions are carried out mindfully and conscientiously. Apart from the aforementioned, lifestyle changes should be anchored in mindful improvement of self-perception and strengthened self-control (Elakkary, Elhorr, Aziz, Gazayerli, & Silva, 2006; Kinzl, Trefalt, Fiala, & Biebl, 2002; Leahey, Crowther, & Irwin, 2008).

It is highly recommended that patients are prepared for the relevant group discussion topics. Equally important is assisting the patients in developing an increased awareness of their behavior, as well as in regularly monitoring their goals with regard to weight and physical activity.

Postsurgical Information

Ongoing clarification of relevant information regarding changes in physiology, anatomy, and body perception may contribute to a greater success rate by providing the patients with a sense of safety and predictability. During treatment, the need for information is constantly monitored.

Nutrition and Changes in Food Composition and Eating Habits

The BaSE program was designed primarily for patients after restrictive bariatric procedures. The reduced stomach volume forces the patient to change his or her eating habits. Patients are taught to eat more mindfully and in a more controlled manner. Risks and side effects of the surgery can be reduced by a concomitant adaptation of food composition and eating behavior. The patient is provided with the necessary support to assist him or her in adapting to the necessary modifications in eating behavior, beginning with the first meeting. Comprehensive nutritional counseling is offered and based in part on the individual food diaries. Due to the new and unfamiliar anatomical condition, it is important that a structured eating routine can be established, together with changes in the amount of food consumed. Moreover, information regarding side effects such as feelings of nausea, eructating, or vomiting is provided. Patients are taught to handle and prevent these symptoms. Patients also receive information about a healthy, well-balanced diet. The respective strategies of the individual patient are discussed in the group sessions, and possible difficulties are anticipated. Questions concerning the adaptation of both eating behavior and nutrition are reviewed on a regular basis. If necessary, insufficient weight loss or an increase in weight after the initial weight loss is addressed. These can result from a persistent loss of control that complicates practicing a mindful and structured intake of food.

Persistent patterns of disturbed eating behavior are addressed individually (e.g., sweet eating, night eating, grazing, picking, or snacking) (Faria, de Oliveira Kelly, Lins, & Faria, 2010; Heber et al., 2010; de Zwaan et al., 2010; Saunders, 2004).

Exercise and Physical Activity

Regular and adequate physical activity supports weight loss maintenance, can reduce automatic food intake, and has a positive effect on self-esteem and mood. However, due to joint problems and reduced pulmonary capacity, most patients have reduced their physical activity for several years prior to the surgery. Therefore, it is advisable to discuss and promote realistic goals regarding physical activity. Many patients need structured support over an extended period of time to enable them to maintain their actual activity goals. Because obese patients regularly suffer from disorders of the locomotor system, Nordic walking is recommended. This skill can be acquired with approximately 2 hours of practice. In order to ensure a timely feeling of progress for the patient and to prevent frustration, it is advisable to begin with easy, manageable tasks. Various types of exercise are addressed, tailored to individual preferences and limitations: for example, Nordic walking, bike riding, or swimming. Motivational work is undertaken to encourage the patient to walk more and drive less (Wouters, Larsen, Zijlstra, van Ramshorst, & Geenen, 2010).

Psychosocial Skills

Stress Management   Obesity and associated comorbidities (e.g., osteoarthritis, cardiovascular, pulmonary, and endocrinological diseases) severely affect quality of life. Studies indicate that as a result, patients with severe obesity experience increased stress. Frequently, the only option to the patient perceived as a means to cope with stress and alleviate negative emotional states was the controlled or uncontrolled intake of food.

Social stigmatization and experiences of rejection can increase the risk to develop depressive symptoms or social phobia. In the BaSE program patients learn to recognize the relationship between emotion and eating behavior. Stress management strategies are taught. Special attention is given to the training and use of an imaginative relaxation technique.

Self-Care and Social Conflicts   Within the scope of the intervention patients are motivated to increase their level of self-care. Patients are motivated to experiment with strategies other than food intake for self-reinforcement and self-reward. Problems with social interactions, ways of dealing with annoyance, envy, and disappointment are discussed with the help of individual examples. These coping methods are dealt with and reflected in the group through critical feedback. Alternative behavioral strategies and more adaptive cognitive patterns are introduced (Guerdjikova et al., 2007).

Body Image   After surgery, patients experience a major change in their appearance, triggered by the dramatic weight loss in a very short period of time, and must adapt accordingly. Also, a positive body image can have a positive effect on the maintenance of weight loss. The patients discuss body image issues and reflect their present concerns about their bodies.

Special emphasis is placed on the positive postsurgery results in order to assist the patients in developing a healthier body image. Patients are taught to consciously perceive changes in their bodies in order to improve self-acceptance. Keeping a diary about body image can be helpful. After cosmetic questions regarding successful weight reduction have been discussed, questions about aesthetic surgery usually emerge (Mitchell et al., 2008).

Relapse Prevention

Relapse prevention is the final topic of the program. Positive reinforcement of the patients' achievements is important. It is reflected once more that during the program critical topics have been discussed. Individual coping strategies are recapitulated. Thereof, relapse prevention strategies are developed for possible future crises. Moreover, individual perspectives are developed for the next year.

References

Algazi, L.P. (2000). Transactions in a support group meeting: A case study. *Obesity Surgery, 10*, 186–191.

Burgmer, R., Grigutsch, K., Zipfel, S., Wolf, A.M., de Zwaan, M., Husemann, B. et al. (2005). The influence of eating behavior and eating pathology on weight loss after gastric restriction operations. *Obesity Surgery, 15*, 684–691.

de Zwaan, M., Hilbert, A., Swan-Kremeier, L., Simonich, H., Lancaster, K., Howell, L.M. et al. (2010). Comprehensive interview assessment of eating behavior 18–35 months after gastric bypass surgery for morbid obesity. *Surgery for Obesity and Related Diseases, 6*, 79–85.

Elakkary, E., Elhorr, A., Aziz, F., Gazayerli, M., & Silva, Y. (2006). Do support groups play a role in weight loss after laparoscopic adjustable gastric banding? *Obesity Surgery, 16*, 331–334.

Elkins, G., Whitfield, P., Marcus, J., Symmonds, R., Rodriguez, J., & Cook, T. (2005). Noncompliance with behavioral recommendations following bariatric surgery. *Obesity Surgery, 15*, 546–551.

Faria, S.L., de Oliveira Kelly, E., Lins, R.D., & Faria, O.P. (2010). Nutritional management of weight regain after bariatric surgery. *Obesity Surgery, 20*, 135–139.

Giel, K.E., Binkele, M., Becker, S., Stübler, P., Zipfel, S., & Enck, P. (2008). Weight reduction and maintenance in a specialized outpatient health care center. *Obesity Research and Clinical Practice, 2*, 143–150.

Guerdjikova, A.I., West-Smith, L., McElroy, S.L., Sonnanstine, T., Stanford, K., & Keck, P.E., Jr. (2007). Emotional eating and emotional eating alternatives in subjects undergoing bariatric surgery. *Obesity Surgery, 17*, 1091–1096.

Hain, B., Hünnemeyer, K., Rieber, N., Wild, B., Sauer, H., Königsrainer, A. et al. (2010). Psychoedukative Behandlung nach Adipositaschirurgie. *Adipositas, 4*, 125–130.

Heber, D., Greenway, F.L., Kaplan, L.M., Livingston, E., Salvador, J., & Still, C. (2010). Endocrine and nutritional management of the post-bariatric surgery patient: An Endocrine Society Clinical Practice Guideline. *Journal of Clinical Endocrinology and Metabolism*, *95*, 4823–4843.

Kinzl, J.F., Trefalt, E., Fiala, M., & Biebl, W. (2002). Psychotherapeutic treatment of morbidly obese patients after gastric banding. *Obesity Surgery*, *12*, 292–294.

Leahey, T.M., Crowther, J.H., & Irwin, S.R. (2008). A cognitive-behavioral mindfulness group therapy intervention for the treatment of binge eating in bariatric surgery patients. *Cognitive and Behavioral Practice*, *15*, 364–375.

Livhits, M., Mercado, C., Yermilov, I., Parikh, J.A., Dutson, E., Mehran, A. et al. (2011). Is social support associated with greater weight loss after bariatric surgery? A systematic review. *Obesity Reviews,12*, 142–148.

Marcus, J.D., & Elkins, G.R. (2004). Development of a model for a structured support group for patients following bariatric surgery. *Obesity Surgery*, *14*, 103–106.

Marziali, E. (2009). E-health program for patients with chronic disease. *Telemedicine Journal of E Health*, *15*, 176–181.

Mitchell, J.E., Crosby, R.D., Ertelt, T.W., Marino, J.M., Sarwer, D.B., Thompson, J.K. et al. (2008). The desire for body contouring surgery after bariatric surgery. *Obesity Surgery*, *18*, 1308–1312.

Papalazarou, A., Yannakoulia, M., Kavouras, S.A., Komesidou, V., Dimitriadis, G., Papakonstantinou, A. et al. (2010). Lifestyle intervention favorably affects weight loss and maintenance following obesity surgery. *Obesity*, *18*, 1348–1353.

Rieber, N., Hilbert, A., Teufel, M., Giel, K.E., Warschburger, P., & Zipfel, S. (2010). Weight loss maintenance. *Adipositas*, *4*, 115–124.

Saunders, R. (2004). "Grazing": A high-risk behavior. *Obesity Surgery*, *14*, 98–102.

Teufel, M., Giel, K.E., & Zipfel, S. (2009). Telemedizin und Psychotherapie—Empathie durch das ferne Cyberspace? *Psychotherapie, Psychosomatik und Medizinische Psychologie 59*, 289–290.

van Hout, G., & van Heck, G. (2009). Bariatric psychology, psychological aspects of weight loss surgery. *Obesity Facts*, *2*, 10–15.

White, M.A., Kalarchian, M.A., Masheb, R.M., Marcus, M.D., & Grilo, C.M. (2010). Loss of control over eating predicts outcomes in bariatric surgery patients: A prospective, 24-month follow-up study. *Journal of Clinical Psychiatry*, *71*, 175–184.

Wild, B., Herzog, W., Wesche, D., Niehoff, D., Muller, B., & Hain, B. (2011). Development of a group therapy to enhance treatment motivation and decision making in severely obese patients with a comorbid mental disorder. *Obesity Surgery, 21*, 588–594.

Wing, R.R., Tate, D.F., Gorin, A.A., Raynor, H.A., & Fava, J.L. (2006). A self-regulation program for maintenance of weight loss. *New England Journal of Medicine*, *355*, 1563–1571.

Wouters, E.J., Larsen, J.K., Zijlstra, H., van Ramshorst, B., & Geenen, R. (2010, September 14). Physical activity after surgery for severe obesity: The role of exercise cognitions. *Obesity Surgery*. [Epub ahead of print].

Section 5: Postsurgery Psychotherapy

RONNA SAUNDERS

Introduction

Bariatric surgery may appear to members of the lay community to be a radical approach for dealing with morbid obesity, but to the patient who chooses this option, it is usually a last, desperate attempt to achieve a better quality of life. Surgery is generally successful in producing weight loss in the morbidly obese but appears to be less successful in altering some eating behaviors or psychiatric problems, while creating its own set of issues. Despite the overall positive weight loss outcome, many patients regain a portion of their weight in the long term, while some fail to lose significant weight or regain a majority of weight they have lost (Kalarchian et al., 2002).

In a comprehensive study where patients were interviewed about their eating behavior 18–35 months postsurgery, it was found that a subgroup experienced subjective binge eating episodes as well as used self-induced vomiting to control weight (deZwann et al., 2010). In addition, studies have shown that bariatric surgery patients have a high prevalence of psychiatric comorbidities as well as disturbed eating patterns, and these factors may persist and interfere with the success of the surgical intervention (Marcus et al., 2009). While much has recently been written about the need for presurgical psychological evaluation, and research has been conducted in an effort to identify predictors for surgical outcome, there is no consistent evidence that psychosocial variables are predictive of postsurgery weight loss, or of changes in mental health status (Herpertz et al., 2004). Other studies, however, have found that presurgical binge eating patterns may in fact be predictive of poor weight loss postsurgery (deZwann et al., 2010).

Little has been written about psychological interventions in the postoperative period. Improvements in psychological well-being are likely postoperatively as a result of weight loss, but there is a subset of patients whose improvement is transient. Treatment directed toward this group, focused on eating patterns and emotional adjustment to surgery as well as on other psychological issues, can be an important component of a bariatric surgery program.

Rationale for Postsurgery Psychotherapy

It is much easier to measure biological markers such as weight, blood pressure, and serum glucose than to assess emotional adjustment in someone

who has undergone a significant surgical procedure that requires alteration of many facets of daily life. There is a drastic reduction in the amount
of food that can be eaten, and patients need to learn to eat slowly, chew
their food well, and stop when full. After some procedures, such as gastric bypass, restriction of foods high in fats or sugars is also necessary.
When patients are not compliant, food may become "stuck," resulting in
vomiting, and "dumping" may occur after food intake of certain foods,
resulting in sweating, nausea, diarrhea, and vomiting. Many patients find
it difficult to adhere to these dietary restrictions. Some develop patterns
to "work around" these restrictions by consuming high-calorie liquids or
eating small amounts of food throughout the day, sometimes referred to
as grazing (Saunders, 2004a; Colles, 2008). Some continue eating problematic foods in spite of the negative consequences.

While there have been reports of the development of clinically significant
eating disorders following surgery, this does not appear to be a common
occurrence. Anorexia nervosa has developed in some patients who severely
limit their intake out of fear of regaining weight. Bulimia nervosa has also
been reported in patients who engage in self-induced vomiting to promote
weight loss. A new eating disorder category, postsurgical eating avoidance disorder, has even been proposed (Segal et al., 2004). More typically,
patients present with eating problems that do not fulfill formal diagnostic
criteria for an eating disorder yet are associated with distress and impairment and can still be a barrier to adequate weight loss. These patients may
exhibit restriction, vomiting, excessive exercise, body image dissatisfaction,
and preoccupation with food and weight. They also report loss of control
eating behavior but are no longer able to ingest large amounts of food. Some
develop grazing or engage in chewing and spitting of food. These patterns,
like binge eating, can be accompanied by a sense of loss of control.

Patients who evidence problematic eating patterns prior to surgery may
find that these patterns resurface following surgery. In a review of the literature, it appeared that maladaptive eating patterns tend to reemerge 18–24
months postsurgery after the initial weight loss or the "honeymoon" stage
has passed (Niego, Kofman, Weiss, & Geliebeter, 2007), but such patterns
can begin appearing as early as 6 months after surgery when patients are
able to begin to eat more normally (Saunders, 2001). Understanding what
factors contribute to these maladaptive eating patterns and how to address
them is important in order for patients to be successful over the long term.

The effects of surgery on overall emotional status also must be considered. There has been interest in the impact of presurgical depression on
surgical outcome, and on emotional status following surgery. Generally
the data suggest that depression is improved following weight loss, but
the distinction between a true mood disorder and a more situational
depression reactive to weight issues must be made. In any event, for some,

improvement in mood may only be temporary. Many patients report feelings of loss as their relationship to food changes. Other problems that may emerge include "transfer addictions" (alcohol, shopping, gambling) since food is no longer available to mediate feelings, although the data on this topic are quite limited. Expectations around body image may also have been unrealistic, as some patients may not have the body they anticipated due to loose, hanging skin. All of these factors, in addition to the psychosocial adjustments necessitated by the surgery (e.g., changes in relationships, lifestyle changes), point to the need for careful monitoring and provision of psychotherapy for many patients following surgery (Kinzl et al., 2002).

Treatment Approach

Cognitive-behavioral therapy (CBT) has been shown to be effective in treating many patients with eating disorders (Wifley et al., 2002). Since bariatric patients share many of the same characteristics and issues as more traditional eating disordered patients, it is an appropriate treatment model, and can be utilized on individuals or in a group setting. This involves the use of cognitive and behavioral techniques focusing on normalizing eating as well as challenging dysfunctional thinking and developing nonfood coping mechanisms. Techniques used include making the pattern of behavior clear to the patient through the use of eating diaries, as well as teaching patients to differentiate between hunger and the urge to eat, helping them connect to body signals, to identify cues for eating, and to employ specific strategies to resist urges to eat, as well as to develop other nurturing alternative activities. Elements of interpersonal therapy (IPT) can also be included. The focus of IPT is on relational factors associated with the onset and maintenance of disordered eating. The therapy suggests that there is often a relationship between negative mood, low self-esteem, traumatic life events, interpersonal functioning, and eating behavior. Patients are taught to clarify emotional states, enhance interpersonal communication, and test their own perceptions. While initial sessions are highly structured, later sessions can be more insight oriented. The focus of treatment is therefore on structuring eating, regulating emotion, developing realistic goals and expectations, grieving the loss of the prior relationship to food, enhancing interpersonal effectiveness, and developing healthy coping mechanisms and nurturing activities.

The Compulsive Eater's Program for Bariatric Surgery Patients (CEP-B) was adapted from a treatment program designed by this author for those with compulsive eating who had not had bariatric surgery (Saunders, 2004b). Special modifications were developed to address specific issues related to the surgery. Initial group sessions are psychoeducational in nature and highly structured, but as the program progresses there is a shift to a somewhat more insight-oriented focus, as patients are learning to manage their eating and are therefore more able to access and express feelings. Initially, patients are taught about the cycle of compulsive eating and the need to address thoughts and feelings as well as behaviors. They are given a manual that includes brief chapters for each topic to be discussed. Handouts and experiential exercises are used throughout. Group can be a very powerful agent of change and provides the opportunity to share experiences with others who understand, to receive support, to learn and practice new skills, to receive feedback, and to provide support to others, all in a safe, nonjudgmental setting.

Description of CEP-B

Patients are told about the groups during their initial evaluation and encouraged to attend if they have had a history of problematic behaviors. The presurgical evaluation provides an excellent opportunity to prepare and motivate patients for group. Detailed information regarding eating patterns is collected, in addition to assessing for other psychiatric disorders or psychosocial problems. A questionnaire was designed to help surgeons and their staff identify those with emotional eating and other possible candidates for group. Patients are seen individually prior to group for screening to ensure that they are appropriate for group. At that time, they are given an overview of the group and instructions for keeping a food diary. The diaries are extensive, and address not only what was eaten, but when and where, with notations for hunger versus urge to eat, satisfaction level (to help patients get in touch with body signals), and thoughts, feelings, and situations before, during, and after eating.

The group of six to eight patients is semistructured, time limited (12–16 weeks), and closed. Sessions are held weekly and are 90 minutes in duration. There is also a monthly aftercare group. Initial groups were composed of bariatric surgery patients who had been identified prior to surgery as having compulsive eating, including those who did not meet strict DSM criteria for an eating disorder, as part of a research study (Saunders, 2001). Later groups included any patients who wanted additional help and recognized that they needed more than a support group was designed to offer.

During the first group session patients are given a manual containing short chapters corresponding to each group topic (see Table 12.5.1 for overview).

Supplemental handouts as well as experiential exercises and homework are also used. An initial handout, the "Compulsive Eating Cycle" (Figure 12.5.1), illustrates the general focus of the group sessions and is tied to the phases of treatment. The group initially focuses on behavioral

Table 12.5.1 Stages of Treatment

I. Alter chronic eating habits
- Establish self-monitoring procedures
- Develop strategies and alternatives to out-of-control eating
- Implement psychoeducational materials

II. Identify and challenge attitudes
- Identify dysfunctional thoughts
- Employ cognitive restructuring techniques
- Develop problem-solving skills
- Identify feelings

III. Deal with emotional changes following surgery
- Body image
- Relationships
- Other life issues

IV. Relapse prevention
- Identify high-risk situations
- Develop relapse plan

V. Aftercare
- Monthly group sessions
- Individual sessions as needed
- Insight-oriented group

management of symptoms, since the initial goal of treatment is to interrupt this cycle of maladaptive eating patterns. Although bariatric surgery drastically alters eating and former patterns may be temporarily suppressed, patients need to be aware that these patterns can resurface and that other maladaptive behaviors, such as grazing, can easily develop. Patterns are made conscious by self-monitoring eating via diaries, learning to identify urges versus hunger, and practicing specific behavioral strategies to interrupt such urges. These interventions involve specific distraction techniques at the time of the urge. There is a focus on identifying cues or triggers and developing non-food-related coping skills. Each session also includes a review of accomplishments.

The group then moves on to identifying specific thoughts. Negative cognitions are challenged, employing cognitive restructuring techniques. Bariatric surgery patients often have low self-esteem, as well as symptoms of anxiety and depression. Many have had past traumatic events in their lives and often have experienced discrimination. Of particular importance is challenging the all-or-nothing dichotomous thinking that has been a part of the diet mentality for most of these patients. Other distortions, such as "should" statements or overgeneralizations, are also addressed. Patients are taught to reframe this negative thinking.

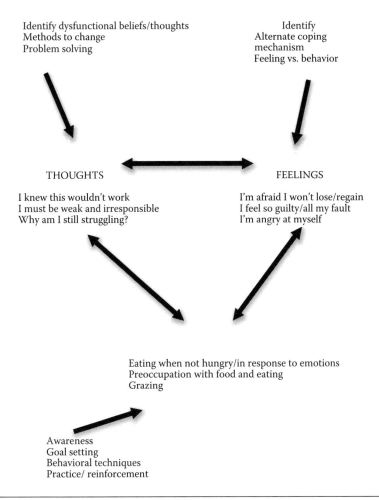

Identify dysfunctional beliefs/thoughts
Methods to change
Problem solving

Identify
Alternate coping
mechanism
Feeling vs. behavior

THOUGHTS

FEELINGS

I knew this wouldn't work
I must be weak and irresponsible
Why am I still struggling?

I'm afraid I won't lose/regain
I feel so guilty/all my fault
I'm angry at myself

Eating when not hungry/in response to emotions
Preoccupation with food and eating
Grazing

Awareness
Goal setting
Behavioral techniques
Practice/ reinforcement

Figure 12.5.1 The compulsive eating cycle.

Topics such as fears of regaining weight, expectations, and body image are discussed.

Later, the focus shifts to deal with emotional adjustment following surgery—interpersonal factors such as self-esteem, relational issues, and where appropriate, past trauma, as well as continuing discussion of body image. A major focus is on affect recognition and modulation—identification of feelings and needs with the development of new skills such as assertiveness and self-nurturing. Since patients have been learning to deal with urges and are no longer "numbing" feelings with food, these emotional factors are now more accessible, and patients need to learn that they can accept and manage such strong feelings.

The monthly aftercare group meets for a 6-month follow-up and is part of the regular program. This group is less structured, and patients are encouraged to bring up issues of current concern. Topics from the structured program are often revisited in more detail. Behavioral goals continue to be set with accomplishments noted. Discussion continues regarding expectations, life changes, self-nurturing, self-esteem, and body image. Some patients want to continue after the 6 months, so an additional ongoing group was added, open to anyone who has completed the regular program. Patients may stay in the ongoing group as long as needed and may return at a later date if they need additional support. Some group members begin or continue with individual therapy to discuss issues specific to them or things they prefer not to discuss in the group context (e.g., sexual abuse, intimacy, and other issues of a more personal nature).

Other Concerns

In designing and developing an effective treatment program, several issues need to be considered:

1. Identification of high-risk patients. The presurgical psychological evaluation provides an excellent opportunity to identify such patients as well as to motivate them to seek additional help pre- or postsurgery. At this point in their process, however, patients are so eager to have surgery that they do not focus on possible postoperative problems. It is therefore important to educate surgeons and clinical staff to gain their support since they can also be very helpful in identifying appropriate patients at follow-up appointments.

2. Optimal time for patients to be involved. Ideally, high-risk patients would be involved in a treatment program prior to surgery to help them begin to normalize their eating pattern. Some patients choose this option, usually involving individual sessions, or are required to do so by their surgeons based on recommendations from the initial evaluation. Most patients, however, fail to follow through unless it is mandatory. Many patients falsely think that surgery will resolve their eating problems. Once they begin to eat a more normal diet after surgery, however, problems may start to develop. The 4- to 6-month postoperative period is therefore a good time to reeducate patients about the group and to encourage them to attend.

3. Definition of a binge eating episode. Since patients are no longer able to eat large amounts following surgery, the definition of a

binge eating episode needs to be modified, focusing on feelings of loss of control rather than on amount eaten. Grazing is a way to circumvent dietary restrictions, and may become the new form of binge eating.

4. Definition of purging. Spontaneous vomiting often occurs when postbariatric patients have eaten too much, too quickly, or eaten inappropriate foods, in order to relieve discomfort. However, self-induced vomiting has also been reported as a means of losing weight, out of a fear of regaining or to avoid the consequences of compulsive eating behaviors.

5. How to measure results. There is a need for long-term follow-up to assess behavioral changes and psychological adjustment, in addition to weight loss. An evaluation form is given to patients at the end of group.

6. "Cross addictions." Some patients report the development of other compulsive behaviors (excess alcohol intake, problematic shopping, sexual promiscuity) when they are no longer able to use food as a coping mechanism. While eating is not considered an addiction, there is little empirical evidence at this time that surgery increases the risk of other addictive behaviors (Sarwer et al., 2008); patients still need to be made aware of this possibility, especially regarding alcohol consumption, if there is a history of alcoholism in the family. Alternative coping skills need to be emphasized throughout the treatment process (Sarwer et al., 2008).

7. CBT versus psychodynamic psychotherapy. While there are specific topics for each group session, there should be flexibility to meet the needs of the specific group. While many time-limited groups remain structured and focused on a cognitive-behavioral "here and now" focus, keeping the distinction between CBT and a psychodynamic group clear, the shift to more insight-oriented therapy in some groups came as a result of feedback from group members. Unlike more traditional psychotherapy groups, the focus continues to be related to the surgery and always retains elements of CBT. This has to be carefully negotiated and may not be appropriate for all groups. Some patients elect individual therapy at this time, but elements of CBT continue in these sessions, and there is always need for some focus on eating patterns and surgery-related issues.

Conclusions

While we have not been able to predict who will have difficulty postoperatively, it appears that high-risk patients are generally underidentified.

Although research has not been conducted to determine what interventions are helpful, there are several potential factors to consider that may put patients at higher risk. Presurgical eating behaviors such as binge eating, grazing, and night eating may be risk factors, as well as a history of alcoholism in the family, a history of trauma and abuse, and lack of support.

A postsurgery treatment program can be of utility with the structured part of the program, with weekly CBT group sessions, viewed as Phase I of treatment. The tasks during this phase include a focus on stabilizing eating, developing specific nonfood coping skills, learning to challenge dysfunctional thoughts, and experiencing and dealing with feelings. Phase II is the aftercare group for 6 months with the task of keeping patients focused and providing continued support. Some patients can then go on to Phase III, consisting of individual therapy or a more insight-oriented psychotherapy group.

Ideally, patients would be seen weekly for individual sessions as they participate in the structured group, allowing them more opportunity to discuss concerns more specific to them and review their eating diaries. If a portion of therapy were mandatory and included in the cost of the surgery, more patients will be willing to participate.

Adjustment to bariatric surgery is a complex process and psychotherapy postsurgery is also seen as a process, using a CBT approach as a treatment model. Although CBT-structured group programs are successful with those who have binge eating, and certainly seem to be so for bariatric surgery patients, this approach in the bariatric population is just being developed, and much follow-up is needed to assess long-term results. CBT-focused individual therapy has also been successful with those who have binge eating, but again, long-term follow-up is needed.

References

Colles, S.L., Dixon, J.B., & O'Brien, P.E. (2008). Grazing and loss of control related to eating: Two high-risk factors following bariatric surgery. *Obesity, 16*, 615–622.

deZwann, M.D., Hilbert, A., Swan-Kremeler, L., Simonich, H., Lancaster, K., Howell, L.M., et al. (2010). Comprehensive interview assessment of eating behavior 18–35 months after gastric bypass surgery for morbid obesity. *Surgery for Obesity and Related Diseases, 6*, 79–85.

Herpertz, S., Kielmann, R., Wolf, A.M., Hebebrand, J., & Senf, W. (2004). Do psychosocial variables predict weight loss or mental health after obesity surgery? A systematic review. *Obesity Research, 12*, 1554–1569.

Kalarchian, M.A., Marcus, M.D., Wilson, G.T., Labouvie, E.W., Brolin, R.E., & LaMarca, L.B. (2002). Binge eating among gastric bypass patients at long-term follow-up. *Obesity Surgery, 12*, 270–275.

Kinzl, J.F., Trefaalt, E., Fiala, M., & Biebl, W. (2002). Psychotherapeutic treatment of morbidly obese patients after gastric banding. *Obesity Surgery, 12,* 292–294.

Marcus, M.D., Kalarchianm M.A., & Courcoulas, A.P. (2009). Psychiatric evaluation and follow-up of bariatric surgery patients. *American Journal of Psychiatry, 166,* 285–291.

Niego, S.H., Kofman, M.D., Weiss, J.J., & Geliebeter, A. (2007). Binge eating in the bariatric surgery popuation: A review of the literature. *International Journal of Eating Disorders, 40,* 349–359.

Sarwer, D.B., Fabricataore, A.N., Jones-Corneille, L.R., Allison, K.C., Faulconbridge, L.N., & Wadden, T.A. (2008). Psycholocial issues following bariatric surgery. *Primary Psychiatry, 15,* 50–55.

Saunders, R. (2001). Compulsive eating and gastric bypass surgery: What does hunger have to do with it? *Obesity Surgery, 11,* 757–61.

Saunders, R. (2004a). "Grazing": A high risk behavior. *Obesity Surgery, 14,* 98–102.

Saunders, R. (2004b). Post-surgery group therapy for gastric bypass patients. *Obesity Surgery, 14,* 1128–1131.

Segal, A., Kussunoki, D.K., & Laarino, M.A. (2004). Post-surgical refusal to eat: Anorexia nervosa, bulimia nervousa or a new eating disorder? *Obesity Surgery, 14,* 353–360.

Wilfley, D.E., Welch, R.R., & Stein, R.I. (2002). A randomized comparison of group cognitive behavioral therapy and group interpersonal psychotherapy for the treatment of overweight individuals with binge eating disorders. *Archives of General Psychiatry, 59,* 713–721.

Section 6: Bariatric Aftercare

JOHANN F. KINZL

Introduction

Because long-term studies have shown more conservative treatments to be ineffective in the treatment of morbid obesity, surgical treatment is seen as the "treatment of choice" for most such patients. The medical usefulness of bariatric surgery has been established by many studies. Such surgery employs various surgical procedures, particularly adjustable laparoscopic gastric banding, sleeve resection, and Roux-en-Y gastric bypass. All three methods are restrictive procedures, aimed at reducing food quantities; gastric bypass also has a malabsorptive effect.

Surgical treatment of obesity is not the solution, but it is a very important precondition for successful management of morbid obesity. However, treatment of morbidly obese patients must be multidisciplinary both pre- and postoperatively: medical, nutritional, surgical, and psychological.

Since improved quality of life and enhanced psychosocial functioning are important goals of bariatric surgery, success following bariatric surgery should include not only weight loss and improvement in comorbid conditions such as diabetes mellitus and high blood pressure, but also improvements in eating behavior, psychosocial variables, and quality of life (van Hout & van Heck, 2009). Despite the finding that bariatric surgery is the favored option for treatment of severe obesity, some patients have difficulties maintaining weight loss over time (Karlsson, Taft, Ryden, Sjöstöm, & Sullivan, 2007).

Bariatric Aftercare Program: The "Model Innsbruck"

Detailed nutrition information is given preoperatively and during the patient's hospital stay in the form of personal instruction and a written brochure. Education is an important key to helping patients achieve optimal health and better quality of life following weight loss surgery. Any educational regimen must include information on diet, vitamin and mineral supplementation, and lifestyle changes as well as expected weight loss and improvements in comorbid conditions (Andris, 2005).

The most important aspects of preoperative psychological evaluation in our center in Innsbruck include gathering sociodemographic data, information on eating behavior, and eating disorders. We do assess the extent of physical activity, previous weight loss attempts, reasons for failure to lose weight, adverse childhood experiences, lifetime or current mental disorder, personality disorder, addiction, and prior pharmacologic or psychotherapeutic treatments.

Furthermore, the preoperative psychological evaluation should:

- Analyze the patient's motivation and likelihood of adherence to the therapeutic program in the long-term
- Assess the social and family context
- Assess the patient's adaptability to new demands (e.g., eating attitude, the ability to tolerate stress)
- Confront unrealistic expectations concerning weight loss
- Clarify the importance of accompanying psychiatric or psychotherapeutic treatment in patients with a comorbid mental disorder
- Provide information on possible negative consequences, for example, the patient needs to be aware of the consequences of surgery, such as hanging, redundant skin

Depression and adjustment disorders are the most common psychiatric disorders seen in morbidly obese bariatric surgery candidates. Some patients can become more depressed postoperatively. Depressed patients are encouraged to receive pharmacologic treatment. Attempts should be made to place the patient on weight-neutral medications, avoiding medication such as tricyclic antidepressants or mirtazapine, which are known to cause weight gain (Sarwer et al., 2004).

The psychological contradictions that are applied in Innsbruck for bariatric surgery candidates are nonstabilized psychotic disorder; severe depressive syndrome and suicidality; severe personality disorder, particularly borderline personality disorder; alcoholism and drug dependence; and an eating disorder.

Regular psychological checkups are offered to all patients at least once a year. However, less than half of the patients are still being followed 1 year postoperatively, with a further decrease over subsequent years.

Regular contacts with the psychologist are used to assess only new eating behaviors that develop as well as degrees of weight loss, the consequences of weight loss for social relationships, the patient's adaptability to deal with the new demands of changes in his or her social role, the patient's psychological condition and quality of life, and the question as to whether or not weight loss corresponds with the patient's expectations.

Some studies have suggested that participation in bariatric support groups can make aftercare easier and more efficient for both patients and surgeons (Funnell, Anderson, & Ahroni, 2005; Algazi, 2000; Marcus & Elkins, 2004; Shen et al., 2004). At the time of the psychological evaluation, patients are informed about the various kinds of psychological support offered before and after bariatric surgery. The following psychological and psychotherapeutic options are offered at our center in Innsbruck (Kinzl, Trefalt, Fiala, & Biebl, 2002):

1. *Psychological support group* ("obesity club"): The club meets once a month and is open to individuals preoperatively as well as after bariatric surgery. The aim of the group is to provide a forum for the exchange of information among individuals planning to undergo bariatric surgery and those who have already had surgery.
2. *Large group psychotherapy*: This is a group meeting once a month. It consists of 20 to 30 postoperative individuals. This group promotes the exchange of information among its members (e.g., problems in modifying eating behavior, coping strategies for solving everyday conflicts) as well as discussion of problems with medical and ancillary specialists, such as prevention of malnutrition through consultations with dieticians, as well as the possibilities of plastic surgery for body contouring.
3. *Small group psychotherapy*: These closed groups of six to eight participants meet twice a month for a minimum of 6 months. Special psychological and psychosocial problems are discussed, such as adapting to new eating behavior, acquiring coping strategies for a more constructive means of solving conflicts, and problems adjusting to the new life situations.
4. *Individual psychotherapy*: About 15% of the patients receive regular outpatient psychotherapeutic treatment.

Some specific psychological topics have proved to be of particular importance. These include changes in self-esteem. In most cases, weight loss causes an increase in the patient's self-esteem. However, some of the patients' partners react with jealousy and disapproval. The improved self-esteem and psychological functioning make it possible for the postoperative patient to be more assertive, which can cause interpersonal problems. Other issues include problems in adopting new eating behaviors and the risk for developing a new eating disordered behavior. The consequences of problematic eating behavior (e.g., eating too much or too quickly) can result in various complaints, and result in vomiting. Patients also should be instructed to initiate regular physical exercise to support weight loss and encourage body contouring.

As in other chronic diseases, the aim of therapeutic interventions must be to help patients discover and develop their inherent capacity to be responsible for their own lives (e.g., empowerment) (Funnell et al., 2005). The role of the patient is to be a well-informed active partner and collaborator in his or her own care. Health professionals have to accept that patients have the right to manage their weight loss course in the way that is best suited to the context and culture of their lives (Funnell et al., 2005). Intervention strategies must be personalized and take into account the limits and possibilities of the obese individual.

The majority of bariatric surgery patients show psychological and inter-personal improvement after surgery, which often is directly related to weight (e.g., Herpertz et al., 2003; Kinzl et al., 2001; van Gemert, Severeijns, Greve, Groenman, & Soeters, 1998; Dymek, Le Grange, Neven, & Alverdy, 2001; deZwaan et al., 2002). Nevertheless, some patients are disappointed that their lives do not dramatically improve (Waters et al., 1991). Some authors emphasize that patients with a personality disorder may frequently have more difficulty adapting to the demands of needing to control their eating behavior (Guisado & Vaz, 2003; Kinzl et al., 2006). This does not mean that severely obese patients with mental disorders should be excluded from bariatric therapy. However, patients with psychiatric disorders need more intensive postoperative care, particularly more psychotherapeutic or psychiatric care.

Despite these observations, in reality acceptance of regular psychotherapeutic contact following bariatric surgery is rather low. This is probably caused by multiple reasons:

- Many patients, especially males, are not willing to accept such treatment, because accepting such support is seen as a sign of weakness, regardless of whether or not they need support.
- About 20% of patients are in psychiatric or psychotherapeutic treatment at the time of preoperative evaluation. These patients often stay with their prior therapist.
- A majority of obese patients enjoy sufficient support from family members, relatives or friends, and those who have had bariatric surgery themselves. This group of patients has no essential problems in adapting to new demands postoperatively, and such patients do not need any psychological support.

Conclusions

Pre- and postoperative therapeutic patient education programs, involving a multidisciplinary approach based on patient-centered education, may be useful in increasing long-term patient compliance, which is often poor (Ziegler et al., 2009).

Some patients fail to adapt to the new demands postoperatively (Hsu et al., 1996; Kalarchian et al., 2002; Mitchell et al., 2004; Larsen et al., 2004; Kinzl et al., 2007). Therefore, a special aim of the multidisciplinary program must be to identify those patients who need specific interventions.

The therapy plan should be tailored to fit the patient's priorities, goals, resources, limits, and lifestyle. To manage bariatric surgery successfully, patients must be able to set goals that are both effective and fitting for their values and lifestyle, while taking into account multiple physiological and personal psychosocial factors (Funnell et al., 2005).

Especially patients with low psychosocial support and patients with mental disorders frequently encounter more difficulties adapting to the strict demands of controlled eating imposed on them by the surgical operation. To achieve the aims of bariatric surgery such as sufficient weight loss and improved quality of life, well-coordinated bariatric aftercare by professionals of a multidisciplinary team is a necessity.

References

Algazi, L.P. (2000). Transactions in a support group meeting: A case study. *Obesity Surgery, 10*, 186–191.

Andris, D.A. (2005). Surgical treatment for obesity: Ensuring success. *Journal of Wound and Ostomy Continence for Nurses, 32*, 393–401.

deZwaan, M., Lancaster, K.L., Mitchell, J.E., Howell, L.M., Monson, N., Roerig, J.L. et al. (2002). Health-related quality of life in morbidly obese patients: Effects of gastric bypass surgery. *Obesity Surgery, 12*, 773–780.

Dymek, M.P., Le Grange, D., Neven, K., & Alverdy, J. (2001). Quality of life and psychosocial adjustment in patients after Roux-en-Y gastric bypass: A brief report. *Obesity Surgery, 11*, 32–39.

Funnell, M.M. (1991). Patient empowerment. *Critical Care Nursing Quarterly, 27*, 201–204.

Funnell, M.M., Anderson, R.M., & Ahroni, J.H. (2005). Empowerment and self-management after weight loss surgery. *Obesity Surgery, 15*, 417–422.

Guisado, J.A., & Vaz, F.J. (2003). Personality profiles of the morbidly obese after vertical banded gastroplasty. *Obesity Surgery, 13*, 394–398.

Herpertz, S., Kielmann, R., Wolf, A.M., Langkafel, M., Senf, W., & Hebebrand, J. (2003). Does obesity surgery improve psychosocial functioning? A systematic review. *International Journal of Obesity and Related Metabolic Disorders, 27*, 1300–1314.

Hsu, L.K., Betancourt, S., & Sullivan, S.P. (1996). Eating disturbances before and after vertical banded gastroplasty: A pilot study. *International Journal of Eating Disorders, 19*, 23–34.

Kalarchian, M.A., Marcus, M.D., Wilson, G.T., Labouvie, E.W., Brolin, R.E., & LaMarca, L.B. (2002). Binge eating among gastric bypass patients at long-term follow-up. *Obesity Surgery, 12*, 270–275.

Karlsson, J., Taft, C., Ryden, A., Sjöstöm, L., & Sullivan, M. (2007). Ten-year trends in health-related quality of life after surgical and conventional treatment for severe obesity: The SOS intervention study. *International Journal of Obesity, 31*, 1248–1261.

Kinzl, J.F. (2007). Psychosocial consequences of weight loss after bariatric surgery in morbidly obese patients. *Minerva Psichiatrica, 48*, 403–409.

Kinzl, J.F., Schrattenecker, M., Traweger, C., Mattesich, M., Fiala, M., & Biebl, W. (2006). Psychosocial predictors of weight loss after bariatric surgery. *Obesity Surgery, 16*, 1609–1614.

Kinzl, J.F., Trefalt, E., Fiala, M., & Biebl, W. (2002). Psychotherapeutic treatment of morbidly obese patients after gastric banding. *Obesity Surgery, 12*, 292–294.

Kinzl, J.F., Trefalt, E., Fiala, M., Hotter, A., Biebl, W., & Aigner, F. (2001). Partnership, sexuality, and sexual disorders in morbidly obese women: Consequences of weight loss after gatric banding. *Obesity Surgery, 11*, 455–458.

Larsen, J.K., van Ramhorst, B., Geenen, R., Brand, N., de Wit, P., Stroebe, W., & van Doornen, L.J. (2004). Binge eating and its relationship to outcome after laparoscopic adjustable gastric banding. *Obesity Surgery, 14*, 1111–1117.

Marcus, J.D., & Elkins, G.R. (2004). Development of a model for a structured support group for patients following bariatric surgery. *Obesity Surgery, 14*, 103–106.

Mitchell, J.E., Lancaster, K.L., Burgard, M.A., Howell, L.M., Krahn, D.D., Crosby, R.D. et al. (2001). Long-term follow-up of patients' status after gastric bypass. *Obesity Surgery, 11*, 464–468.

Sarwer, D.B., Cohn, N.I., Gibbons, L.M., Magee, L., Crerand, C.E., Raper, S.E. et al. (2004). Psychiatric diagnoses and psychiatric treatment among bariatric surgery candidates. *Obesity Surgery, 14*, 1148–1156.

Saunders, R. (2004). "Grazing": A high-risk behavior. *Obesity Surgery, 14*, 98–102.

Shen, R., Dugay, G., Rajaram, K., Cabrera, I., Siegel, N., & Ren, C.J. (2004). Impact of patient follow-up on weight loss after bariatric surgery. *Obesity Surgery, 14*, 514–519.

van Gemert, W.G., Severeijns, R.M., Greve, J.W., Groenman, N., & Soeters, P.B. (1998). Psychological functioning of morbidly obese patients after surgical treatment. *International Journal of Obesity and Related Metabolic Disorders, 22*, 393–398.

van Hout, G., & van Heck, G. (2009). Bariatric psychology, psychological aspects of weight loss surgery. *Obesity Facts, 2*, 10–15.

Waters, G.S., Pories, W.J., Swanson, M.S., Meelheim, H.D., Flickinger, E.G., & May, H.J. (1991). Long-term studies of mental health after the Greenville gastric bypass operation for morbid obesity. *American Journal of Surgery, 161*, 154–158.

Ziegler, O., Sirveaux, M.A., Bronaud, L., Reibel, N., Quilliot, D. (2009). Medical follow-up after bariatric surgery: Nutritional and drug issues. General recommendations for the prevention and treatment of nutritional deficiencies. *Diabetes Metabolism, 35*, 544–557.

Index